God Has Spoken

Volume I:

SEEING CHRIST IN THE OLD TESTAMENT

Part One

God Has Spoken

Vol. I:

Seeing Christ in the Old Testament
Part One (Genesis to Song of Songs)

STEPHEN KAUNG

CHRISTIAN FELLOWSHIP PUBLISHERS, INC.
NEW YORK

GOD HAS SPOKEN, VOLUME I:
SEEING CHRIST IN THE OLD TESTAMENT,
PART ONE (GENESIS TO SONG OF SONGS)

ISBN 13: 978-0-935008-94-4
ISBN 10: 0-935008-94-2

Available from the Publishers at:
11515 Allecingie Parkway
Richmond, Virginia 23235
www.c-f-p.com

Printed in the United States of America

FOREWORD

"The word of God is living and operative" (Hebrews 4:12a). It is "living" and not just letter because it gives life. The Scriptures are "operative" because they contain not only theological ideas to be pondered but also spiritual realities to be experienced. For "every scripture is divinely inspired [God-breathed], and profitable for teaching, for conviction, for correction, for instruction in righteousness; that the man of God may be complete, fully fitted to every good work" (II Timothy 3:16-17).

"Ye search the scriptures," said the Lord Jesus Christ, "for ye think that in them ye have life eternal, and they it is which bear witness concerning me; and ye will not come to me that ye might have life" (John 5:39-40). It behooves us, therefore, to diligently read the Bible and meditate on it.

To encourage God's people to study God's word, brother Stephen Kaung delivered a series of messages on the sixty-six books of the Bible. Commencing in 1983, each Lord's day the survey of one book was shared from the New Testament; and a similar sharing from the Old Testament commenced in 1986. Each message is merely a panoramic view of each book of the Bible; a tasting of the sweetness of God's word. The aim is to provide the saints with some basic understanding in their search of God's word. These being spoken messages, no acknowledgement of the names of the many commentaries consulted is indicated.

This survey of the Holy Bible will be published as Volume I and Volume II under the overall title of *God Has Spoken*: with Volume I bearing the subtitle, *Seeing Christ in the Old Testament,* and consisting of two physical volumes—Part One (Genesis to Song of Songs) and Part Two (Isaiah to Malachi); and Volume II bearing the subtitle, *Seeing Christ in the New Testament.* May God use these volumes to increase our love for His word.

CONTENTS — VOLUME I: PART ONE

Unless otherwise indicated,
Scripture quotations are from the
New Translation by J. N. Darby

INTRODUCTION

Hebrews 1:1-2a—God having spoken in many parts and in many ways formerly to the fathers in the prophets, at the end of these days has spoken to us in the person of the Son.

John 5:39-40—Ye search the scriptures, for ye think that in them ye have life eternal, and they it is which bear witness concerning me; and ye will not come to me that ye might have life.

Luke 24:25-27—And he said to them, O senseless and slow of heart to believe in all that the prophets have spoken! Ought not the Christ to have suffered these things and to enter into his glory? And having begun from Moses and from all the prophets, he interpreted to them in all the scriptures the things concerning himself.

Luke 24:44-45—And he said to them, These are the words which I spoke to you while I was yet with you, that all that is written concerning me in the law of Moses and prophets and psalms must be fulfilled. Then he opened their understanding to understand the scriptures.

Let us pray:

Dear heavenly Father, how we praise and thank Thee that Thou hast given us Thy precious word. We just ask Thee, Lord, at this moment, as we open Thy word in Thy presence that Thy Holy Spirit will quicken our understanding that we may understand what Thou art speaking. We pray, Lord, that Thy word may truly be life and spirit to us; and it is all for Thy glory. We ask in the precious name of our Lord Jesus. Amen.

"God having spoken in many parts and in many ways formerly to the fathers in the prophets, at the end of these days has spoken to us in the person of the Son" (Hebrews 1:1-2a).

This verse and a half joins the Old and New Testaments together. In the Old Testament it is this: God having spoken formerly. In the New Testament it is this: God has spoken at the end of the days. In one, God has spoken to our fathers; in the other, God has spoken to us. In one, God has spoken through the prophets; but now, God has spoken in His beloved Son. Formerly, God has spoken in many ways and in many parts, but today what He has spoken to us in the Son is full and complete.

We do thank God that He is One who speaks. What if God does not speak? We know God is a mystery, and if He does not reveal himself, nobody will ever know Him in any way. And speaking is the plainest, the most direct, and the easiest way to reveal oneself. If we keep our mouth shut, nobody will know who we are. That is the reason why it is said in Proverbs, which is a collection of wise sayings: "A fool who keeps his silence is reckoned as wise" (see 17:28), because once you open your mouth you are found out. Whatever is in your mind, whatever is going on within you, your speech reveals yourself in a most direct, easily recognizable way.

We remember what our Lord Jesus once said: "For of the abundance of the heart the mouth speaks. The good man out of the good treasure brings forth good things; and the wicked man out of the wicked treasure brings forth wicked things. For by thy words thou shalt be justified, and by thy words thou shalt be condemned" (Matthew 12:34b-35, 37).

If only Peter had kept his mouth shut during the time when our Lord Jesus was being judged, they would never have recognized him as one of the followers of Jesus. But unfortunately, he was very talkative; and consequently, the people recognized that he was a Galilean because his speech betrayed who he was.

Thank God, our God is One who speaks; He always speaks. He has been speaking ever since the creation of man, and through His speaking He reveals himself. Nobody can say today that God has not spoken and that therefore he has no way to know God, because He *has* spoken. He has spoken in the past; and He is speaking in the present. He is always speaking and revealing himself to us. There is no excuse for anyone to say that God has not spoken and that therefore he cannot know Him. Our attitude should be like Samuel's: "Speak, Lord, for thy servant heareth" (see I Samuel 3:9). "He that has an ear, let him hear what the Spirit says to the churches" (see Revelation 2:7). We need to have our hearts and ears opened to hear what God is saying.

THE PURITY OF GOD'S WORD

The speaking of God is pure. He does not utter idle words nor utter anything carelessly. His words are crystal clear and pure. "The words of Jehovah are pure words, silver tried in the furnace of earth, purified seven times" (Psalm 12:6).

"Thy word is exceeding pure, and thy servant loveth it" (Psalm 119:140).

The word of God is most pure; that is to say, there is nothing wasted nor is there any idle word: every word is weighed, full of value, clear and refined. We can therefore trust in His word. It is pure, not only in the sense that there are no idle or useless words but also in the sense that His word is single, concentrated, on target—like having a single eye, a single mind, a single heart about something. That, too, is what is meant by God's word being pure. It means that no matter what He is speaking, no matter when He is speaking, no matter what subjects He may be talking about, there is always one single theme behind all His speaking—and that signifies purity. In other words, God has spoken in the past to our fathers and He has spoken to us today in the Son, but when we put all the speakings of God together, we see that He only speaks of one thing—or, to be more accurate, He only speaks of one Person. God speaks out of His heart, and we can discern the heart of God today through what He has been speaking about.

If you go to a home where there is a new baby, the moment you step into the house you will see that all the talk of the parents is being centered upon the baby because that is what is in the heart of the parents. The same thing is true with our God. In His heart there is only one Person on whom He is centered, and that is His beloved Son, the Lord Jesus. And because this is the very heart of God, that is the reason why, whenever He speaks, He can talk about nothing else but His beloved Son. His Son is the sole subject that He talks about. Yes, He may touch upon many things, but all these things are related to His Son. Otherwise, He will not speak; He has nothing to talk about. This is very important to our understanding of the word of God; because if we know what God is speaking about, then the whole Bible is opened up to us.

Oftentimes, we try to find in the Bible this thing or that thing. Some may find in the Bible the law, the commandments. Other people may seek to discover various promises in the Scriptures. Others may search for prophecies in the Bible, while still others may look for some methods or ways. People study the Scriptures in many different ways, attempting to find many different things. Some people even try to uncover astronomy or geology, most certainly zoology, in the Bible. You can find all of that in Genesis. Yes, we can uncover almost everything in the Bible; for God does indeed talk about all the things which we can think about. Yet, if we do not know what He is really talking about, we shall miss the entire matter that is on God's heart.

In the days of our Lord Jesus the Pharisees had searched the Scriptures; they knew them and memorized them. I think they knew the Scriptures far better than we do. Let us suppose, for a moment, that we were living in the days when our Lord Jesus was born and Herod had gathered us together and inquired of us: "Where will the king of the Jews be born?" Do you think we would be able to answer right away through the minor prophet Micah that this King would be born in Bethlehem? Probably we would say, "Wait a minute, let's go back and consult our concordance and try to find out." Not these Pharisees. They had thoroughly studied the Scriptures, which to them were the Old Testament writings. And they knew them so much by heart that they could answer immediately: "It is in Micah. Christ is to be born in Bethlehem." Yet neither they nor Herod went afterwards to see the King that was born.

GOD SPEAKS TO MAN

Whenever we open the Bible, let us remember, first of all, that whenever God opens His mouth and speaks He has but one theme, one subject, in His mind, and that is, His beloved Son. Yet to whom does He speak? In the olden days, He spoke to our fathers, and now He speaks to us. In other words, He speaks to man. Man was created in the image of God. No creature is created in God's image except man—not even the angels. The Bible never says God created the angels in His image—only man. And this is because God has something very special reserved for His Son *in* man. Let us be very careful here. I did not say God has something very special reserved *for* man. (We sometimes think so.) God has something very special reserved for *His Son* in man. God created man in His own image. Out of all the creatures man is very specially created, because God's will is that His beloved Son may have a life companion: a people, a nation, a priesthood, a city, a bride.

In Genesis 2 there is a particular typology brought into view. When God looked at Adam whom He had created, He said, "It is not good for man to be alone; let us make for him a counterpart, a help-mate." And this, in a sense, is a hint that tells us that when God looked at His beloved Son, He said: "It is not good for My Son to be alone. I want to give Him man. I want to give Him some creature that is created in Our image, that can be united with My beloved Son, that can be His partner, His life companion."

It is because of this that God created man, and when He speaks, it is to man about His Son. There is nothing else He can talk about or will talk about.

Why does God talk to us about His Son? Is it that we may have some information about His Son? Certainly not. The reason He speaks to us about His Son is that we may be drawn to His Son, that we may be transformed, and united with His Son. God's speaking to man is not for *information*; it is for *transformation*. It is not primarily for our intellectual knowledge or fact collection; it is for a life-transforming process in us so that we may be conformed to the image of His beloved Son and become His counterpart—become part of Him, part of His body of which He is the Head. That is the reason God speaks and why we have the Bible.

"Every scripture is divinely inspired, and profitable for teaching, for conviction, for correction, for instruction in righteousness; that the man of God may be complete, fully fitted to every good work" (II Timothy 3:16-17).

This passage declares that the Bible is divinely inspired. It is God-breathed; it is the speaking of God and it is profitable. The Bible teaches us, convicts us, corrects us and instructs us in order that the man of God may be complete, fully fitted for all the good works of God so that we may truly be life companions of our Lord Jesus. Hence, this is the purpose behind everything which God speaks.

It is true that when we read the Old and New Testaments there are differences between them. Yet, even though there are differences, both are organically one, because whether it is the Old Testament or the New, it is God speaking. We do not find two different persons speaking. The same Person—

God—speaks. Whether it is the Old or New Testament, what He speaks forth is the same theme: it is Christ; it is His beloved Son. So there is an organic unity between both Testaments.

GOD SPOKE IN PART

Nevertheless, there are certain differences. In the days of the Old Testament, God spoke to our fathers. The speaking was done in many ways and in many parts. At that time God also spoke through the prophets who were the holy men of God. They spoke under the power of the Holy Spirit but they were human beings—limited, weak—so God could not speak through them in fullness or completeness. God could only speak through them in many small parts; that is to say, in fragments and pieces—here a little, there a little. God spoke through the prophets, and they all spoke the word of God, yet it was accomplished piecemeal, so to speak. We therefore need to put all the pieces together in order to see more fully.

THE PROMISE OF THE MESSIAH

For instance, when God in His word speaks of Christ, the Messiah who is to come, such utterances are scattered all through the Old Testament. In Genesis 3:15, immediately after the narration on the fall of man, we learn of God promising man that the seed of the woman would come and crush the head of the serpent—that is, the devil. We find in Genesis 22:18 that God spoke to Abraham and told him that all the nations would be blessed by his seed—"seed" singular, not "seeds" plural—and we know from the New Testament book of Galatians that the seed spoken of in Genesis is Christ. In II Samuel 7 we read that God spoke to David and told him that one day his son, the son of David, would sit upon the throne of David and that his kingdom would know no end. Then, in Isaiah 9:6 we are told that this One who is coming is the Son of God: "For unto us a child is born, unto us a son is given." And in Daniel 7:13-14 this Son of God is also likened to a Son of Man, because in the vision spoken of there, Daniel saw one like the Son of Man who comes to receive all the dominions and the powers from the hand of the Ancient of Days. Furthermore, in the last book of the Old Testament, in Malachi 3:1, we learn that the one who is coming is the Angel of the covenant. Now I have pointed out here only a small portion to show that all these words of God are presented to us in fragments, here a little and there a little; but when we put them all together, we can begin to discern the entire picture.

COVENANTS OF GOD

God is a covenant-making God. He likes to sign contracts. He likes to bind himself under legal frameworks. God does not need to do that since He is the Amen, the faithful One: whatever He says, that is it. He does not need to bind himself by means of a legal contract; yet, for the sake of encouraging our faith God loves to do these things. If we go through the Bible, we shall find Him making covenant after covenant. They are all presented to us as fragments, as pieces, as tiny portions—given here a little and there a little.

God made a covenant with Adam which granted him the dominion over the fowls of the air, the beasts of the field and the fish of the sea; but Adam also had some duties to perform. He had to obey God and not eat the forbidden fruit. He had to guard the garden and till it. Yet Adam failed in his duties; therefore, that Adamic Covenant was abolished. Today, we—as Adam's descendants—do not have dominion over the fowls of the air. We do not have dominion over the beasts of the field. We cannot tell a lion, "Come here. I want you." On the contrary, the lion roars out to man: "I want you!" We have lost such dominion.

We are also told in Genesis, chapter 9, that God made a covenant with Noah, and thank God, that covenant still stands. It is a covenant with mankind and all creatures. The four seasons still continue to this day; and whenever there is an outpouring of rain, we find the rainbow there—a divine sign that betokens to man that in judgment there is mercy. This is the Noahic Covenant, and that covenant still stands.

Later on, God made another covenant, this one with Abraham (see Genesis 15-22). His seed would be as the stars of heaven and as the sand of the seashore. Abraham's seed would eventuate into many nations and all the nations would be blessed by that one seed. It is an Abrahamic Covenant.

When we come to Exodus, we learn that God made a covenant of law with the children of Israel (see chapters 19-20). From Deuteronomy 29, we discover that God made still another covenant with a new generation of the Israelite children who came out of Egypt that they might enter the Promised Land. It is called the Moabic Covenant which God had commanded Moses to make in the land of Moab with the Israelites of that new generation. And, finally, we find in Jeremiah 31 the New Covenant.

GOD'S WORD IS ONE

As we have seen, in Old Testament times God spoke through His prophets in many parts, in many ways. We have to put these parts together in order to see the whole picture. God spoke to the fathers, He has also spoken to us. In the time of Genesis He spoke through biographies, mainly the biographies of eight persons. In the time of Exodus He spoke to us through history. By means of Leviticus He spoke to us through ceremonies and rituals, and by means of Deuteronomy He spoke to us through commandments. Of course, in the prophetic books like Isaiah, Daniel and so forth, God spoke to us through prophecies. He likewise spoke to us in types, in typology, in parables, sometimes in plain words and sometimes in riddles. God spoke through the prophets in many, many different ways during the Old Testament times; nevertheless, it was always God who was speaking.

In the time of the New Testament it is different. God speaks to us in His Son, and it being His Son, there is no limit, there is no restraint. When the Son speaks, it is the Father who speaks, and whatever the Son speaks, it is full, complete, final. When we put the Old and New Testaments together, we realize it is always God speaking.

We are more familiar with the New than with the Old Testament. I do not know if there is any exception—myself included. Sometimes, we neglect the Old Testament because we do not see the value of it as compared with what we see in the New Testament. Some people think that the Old Testament is a thing of the past. There are some dispensationalists and ultra-dispensationalists in Christianity who consider that not only the Old Testament has nothing to do with them, even the Gospels and the book of Acts have nothing to do with them. In their view, all which has anything to do with them are the epistles of Paul. But if we take that kind of attitude, how much we will have missed and how much error we will have made, since God's word is one. We cannot dismiss part of God's word and expect to understand what He is speaking; we must hear all that He says. The whole counsel of God is what we need to know.

The Jewish people have the Old Testament but they do not believe in the New Testament. Because of that, today, they still remain in suspended animation. They are still waiting for the Messiah to come. In this connection, I remember the following story:

"Once there were people who were going around visiting homes, selling the Bible or portions of the New Testament. One day a person came to a house while the husband was away and somehow persuaded the wife to buy a copy of the Gospel of Luke. In the evening when the husband came back and discovered that his wife had spent money to buy a Gospel of Luke, he was very angry: 'Without my permission you spent the money!'

"So the wife said, 'Well, I work, too, and I have my part. Why can't I do it?'

"In anger the husband tore the Gospel of Luke into two and gave one part to the wife and kept the other part, saying: 'All right, you will have part of it and I will have part of it!'

"The next day he went to work, and at lunch time he had nothing to do. He found his part of the Gospel of Luke in his pocket, so he took it out and read it. His part began with the Lord's parable about the prodigal son returning home and the father receiving him, and so forth. It really interested him, and so he wondered what had happened in the parable before this part.

"Meanwhile the wife was at home reading the first part of Luke's Gospel. When she reached the point in her reading about the prodigal son having said, 'I will go back home,' she mused within herself: 'I wonder what happened after he returned home?'

"Both of them wanted very much to know either what happened before or what happened afterward; but of course, to save face, neither one would open up. In the evening when having a meal together, they both wanted to ask something of the other, but neither one dared to say anything. Finally, the husband could not stand it anymore and said, 'Now what about that prodigal son?'"

We cannot ignore part of God's word and expect to understand what He is speaking.

There is the incident in the New Testament when the resurrected Lord Jesus spoke to the two men who were walking from Jerusalem to Emmaus. They were sad because the One whom they believed in had been crucified. Some women were reported to have said that He was resurrected, but they did not believe. Joining these two men the Lord Jesus said to them: "O you senseless and foolish men, slow of heart, don't you know what the Scriptures say? Don't you know what Moses in the law and what the prophets have said concerning Christ, that He must suffer and then enter into glory?" So He began to open up to them Moses and the prophets and revealed to them all things

11

concerning himself. And when these two men heard about that, their hearts were greatly warmed (see Luke 24:13-32).

That same night—probably towards midnight—the Lord Jesus suddenly appeared to the disciples who were gathered together in a room. They, too, did not believe; so the Lord began to open their understanding and to reveal to them all which was said in Moses, the prophets, and the Psalms concerning himself. In other words, the Old Testament speaks of Christ and prepares the way of Christ. If we correctly understand the Old Testament, that will lead us to Christ because in the New Testament book of Galatians it says that the law is like a tutor leading us to Christ. In another New Testament book— Hebrews—it says that the law is the representation, type or shadow of the reality to come that prepares the way for the One to come. And when that One comes, then we know everything. The Old Testament is therefore of tremendous value to us.

The New Testament can be likened to word whereas the Old Testament can be likened to picture. When we are little children, we begin to learn words by looking at pictures. If a word reads "cow" a picture of a cow can be most helpful for a child's understanding. If we give a child a word without a picture, it is abstract. A word actually is an identification, but without an impression, there is nothing by which to identify it. In order to obtain real understanding we need a picture. When we see a picture and then read the word, that word becomes very meaningful and there is an impression left with us; we know what the word really means. It is no longer an abstract thought; rather, it becomes for us a concrete substance. Hence, we often say that the Old Testament is like a picture. God is continually drawing pictures therein, and that is the way He teaches us. He draws the picture first, and then in the New Testament He begins to tell us what the relevant word is. Therefore, when we read the word and refer to the picture, that makes the word so much richer and much more meaningful.

Oftentimes we know the New Testament—that is to say,

we know the words; but because we do not know the Old Testament, the impression is not that deep and not that rich. We cannot see the whole picture. We can only think a little about it because the riches of the word are not there. So it is my desire that we may not only be a people of the New Testament but also be a people of the Old Testament. In other words, we should be people of God's word entirely—period!

THREE DIVISIONS OF THE OLD TESTAMENT

The Old Testament can be divided into three parts. I will not trouble you with how the Jewish rabbis have divided the Old Testament because it is somewhat complicated; rather we shall look at the Old Testament according to the way our Lord Jesus himself has divided it. We read in Luke 24 that beginning with the Law of Moses and the Prophets and the Psalms, Jesus interpreted to the disciples all things therein which concerned himself. So our Lord Jesus divided the Old Testament into three parts—the Law of Moses, the Prophets, the Psalms. And I personally think this is the easiest and also the best way to divide the Old Testament.

The Law

The first division is the Law of Moses, which consists of the first five books of our Old Testament that together are referred to in Greek as the Pentateuch (*penta* = five). Hence, though the Pentateuch is a five-volume work, the Law of Moses is nonetheless viewed as but one lengthy book. And the Law of Moses reveals Christ to us.

In John 1 we learn that the Lord Jesus one day found Philip, and Philip went to find Nathaniel and said to him: "The One that Moses and the prophets wrote about, we have found Him. He is Jesus, the son of Joseph of Nazareth" (see v. 45). Moses wrote about Christ; the prophets also wrote about Christ; and

Philip found Him in the prophets and the law of Moses. And now, he said, "We have found that Person. And He is Jesus."

THE PROPHETS

The second division is the Prophets, and they include two groups. One is what we call historical books and the other is what we call prophetic books. For instance, Joshua, Judges, Samuel, Kings, Chronicles, Ezra, Nehemiah, and Esther are historical books. But these historical books are classified under the prophets. Then there are the prophetic books that appear from Isaiah to Malachi.

Why is it that the historical books and the prophetic books are all classified under the prophets? There is a very good reason for it. What is prophecy? We often think of prophecy as foretelling the mind of God, and that it certainly is; but prophecy is more than *fore*telling the mind of God. Prophecy is also *forth*telling His mind. Foretelling refers to the future and that is what we usually think of as prophecy— we prophesy something that is going to happen in the distant future. But actually, prophecy not only predicts the future, it also tells forth the mind of God concerning a current situation. Prophecy is the speaking forth of the mind of God. He speaks His mind to His people touching their conscience. Therefore, the historical books in the Bible are prophecies and not mere histories. If we read these historical books in the Bible as only histories, we shall miss the whole theme of God. Yes, they do give us history, but God is not interested in simply giving us some historical records. The reason these histories are given is because through them God wants to show His mind to us. He wants to tell us something. He wants to touch our conscience. Above all else, He wants us to see Christ. It is thus more than just history; it is also prophecy. Therefore, these historical narratives possess the same sentiment as do the prophetic books. When we read the prophetic books, of course, we are looking for something specific: What is it that God is trying to say to us? In just the same way, we need to approach these historical books with the same aim in view: What is it God is trying to say to us? They, too, are considered as prophetic works.

THE PSALMS

The third and final Old Testament section is the Psalms, and this portion includes not only the one hundred and fifty Psalms but also Job, Proverbs, Ecclesiastes and Song of Songs. These all are considered to be psalms because here we find the heartbeat of God's people, reflecting or revealing as they do the heartbeat of the Messiah.

Hence, as we read the Old Testament we find that it is divided into these three parts, and interestingly enough, the New Testament is divided in the same way. There are the four Gospels and the book of Acts, which we call history. We also have the Epistles or the Letters, and finally we have the book of Revelation. The Law of Moses—the Pentateuch—lays the foundation, just as the Gospels and Acts do. The prophets build on that foundation, and that is what the Epistles are. And then the Psalms crown the whole superstructure, and this is what Revelation represents. The Law reveals the purpose of God, and this is fulfilled in the Gospels and Acts. The purpose of God is Christ and His church—that is to say, Christ with His people. Then, the prophets explain and develop this purpose of God, and that is what the Epistles do. They explain Christ and His church to us. And, finally, the Psalms crown everything, and that is the same with the book of Revelation.

We want to look to the Lord that by His Spirit, as He reveals Christ to us, He will transform us and draw us into His Son. This is but an introduction to the Old Testament aspect of God having spoken.

Let us pray:

> *Dear heavenly Father, we do praise and thank Thee that*
> *Thou art the God who speaks. What if Thou shouldst keep*
> *quiet? Then we would be totally lost. But we do praise and*
> *thank Thee that Thou dost speak, and Thou art speaking*
> *even today through Thy word by Thy Spirit. So we ask Thee,*
> *O Lord, that Thou wilt give us a hearing heart and a pierced*
> *ear that we may hear what the Spirit says to the church, that*
> *we may respond to Thee. Speak, Lord, Thy servant heareth.*
> *May this be our attitude as we approach Thy word. We ask*
> *in the name of our Lord Jesus. Amen.*

GENESIS

THE WILL OF GOD

Genesis 1:1—In the beginning God created the heavens and the earth.

Genesis 1:26-27—And God said, Let us make man in our image, after our likeness; and let them have dominion over the fish of the sea, and over the fowl of the heavens, and over the cattle, and over the whole earth, and over every creeping thing that creepeth on the earth. And God created Man in his image, in the image of God created he him; male and female created he them.

Let us pray:

Dear heavenly Father, we do thank Thee for giving us Thy beloved Son, our Lord Jesus Christ, and we do thank Thee for giving us Thy precious word. We thank Thee for giving us Thy Holy Spirit, that through Thy Holy Spirit we may understand Thy word and see Thy Son, our Lord Jesus. Oh, our Father, how we praise and thank Thee because this is Thy will that we shall see Thy beloved Son, and not only see Him but be transformed and be conformed to His image. Oh Father, we do thank Thee for all Thy mercy and grace, Thy purpose, Thy plan. We do worship Thee. We ask Thee to open Thy word to us that it may be life and spirit to us; and to Thee be the glory. In the name of our Lord Jesus. Amen.

The first book in the Bible is Genesis, although according to the antiquity of the books of the Bible, Genesis may not be the first one written. The book of Job was written before

Genesis because Job was probably written during the age of the patriarchs. And we know Genesis was written during the Mosaic Age. Even so, it is most appropriate that Genesis is listed at the very beginning of the Bible. This is because the title of the book is derived from a Hebrew word that serves as the first word in the Hebrew Bible. Therefore, we call this book *Genesis* which in Greek means "origin." This is a book of origins, a book of beginnings. Immediately, you can discern—through the very title of this book—the scope and the limit of the book.

Genesis is the seed plot for the entire Bible. Here, the germ of every truth and every subject to be found in the Bible has been planted, and these seeds will be developed throughout the whole content of the Bible. However, it deals only with the beginnings, except, of course, the beginning of God, because God is the beginning. It tells us of the beginning of creation, the Sabbath, man, life, sin, redemption, family, nation, and race. It tells us the beginning of everything; but remember, it is just the beginning. It does not deal with the end, the final result, because it is a book of beginnings. All these beginnings will be developed throughout all the pages of the Bible until we come to the book of Revelation. Then, we shall see the end, the result, the final outcome.

The book of Genesis is one volume of the five-volume work called the Pentateuch. It gives us primitive history as well as the history of the patriarchs. The primitive history narrates the creation to the fall of man, continues from the fall of man to the flood, and from the flood to the tower of Babel. After that, the rest of Genesis gives us the history of the later patriarchs—the story of Abraham, Isaac, Jacob, and Joseph.

Both Jewish and Christian traditions agree that the Pentateuch was written by Moses. The Talmud tells us that Moses wrote the entire Pentateuch except for the last eight verses, which were written by Joshua. I think this is self-evident because the last eight verses tell of the death of Moses.

How did Moses compile this book of Genesis (and, for that

matter, the four other parts of the Pentateuch)? He compiled this book under the power of the Holy Spirit—a man moved by the Holy Spirit of God (see II Peter 1:21b). It was partly by direct revelation from God. How can we say this? Because Moses gave the story of creation and nobody was there to tell him about it. So, evidently, he received the story of creation through direct revelation from God. Then part of it was probably the result of oral traditions, because we know the early patriarchs, the early fathers, had lived very long lives—even for hundreds and hundreds of years. Therefore, they were able to pass on what had transpired in their lifetimes to the other generations and on and on. So, probably, Moses was able to compose this book on the basis of oral traditions he had collected from among the people.

Moses was the most fitting instrument to write Genesis because he was a very learned man. He had acquired all the learning of Egypt (see Acts 7:22), the greatest nation in the world at that time, whose civilization was at its peak. He was also one who was greatly disciplined by God. He knew the discipline of the Lord during two periods of forty years each. On the one hand, there was great learning; on the other hand, there was deep discipline. By the combination of these two factors a suitable vessel was available to God for His use in giving us this tremendous book of Genesis. Most likely Moses wrote Genesis around the year 1500 B.C. What he wrote covered a period of roughly two thousand years—from the story of creation to the death of Joseph.

There are many ways to approach this book. It can be approached, for example, historically, prophetically, dispensationally, typologically, or spiritually. Though there are many different approaches, what I would like to do is to approach this book biographically.

Before we delve into Genesis, it will probably be helpful for us to have a general idea of what each of the five books of Moses, the Pentateuch, is centrally about. Let me put it very simply:

> Genesis tells us of the *will* of God.
> Exodus tells us of the *works* of God.
> Leviticus tells us of the *ways* of God.
> Numbers tells us of the *walk* of God.
> Deuteronomy tells us of the *word* of God.

As intimated earlier, Genesis is a book of beginnings or origins, and whenever we think of beginnings or origins, immediately such is associated with purpose and will. Our God is the God of beginnings. Indeed, He *is* the beginning. He is also the God of purpose, possessing the supreme will in the universe. God is not like man. Sometimes we do things without thinking or by accident, but God is never like that. His is the supreme will. Whatever He does, He has already had His mind made up. Once God's purpose is decided, He will lay down a plan and work accordingly until it is accomplished. This is our God.

Whatever God does He does according to the good pleasure of His will. In Ephesians 1:5 Paul wrote: "According to the good pleasure of His will ..." There is His will, and His will is not influenced by anybody; rather, it is according to His good pleasure. That is the way which pleases Him. That is the way He likes it to be; and hence, He decides that it shall be that way. Everything is done according to the good pleasure of His will, and out of the good pleasure of His will, He begins everything. He begins to lay out everything, until finally, everything gathered together is to be summed up in His will. So it is important for us to see what God's will and purpose are at the very beginning. If we do not know what His will is, we will not be able to understand what He is doing. But if we know what His will is, that will explain everything. So we must know His will. That is what the book of Genesis is about—the will of God.

Yet, what is the supreme, ultimate, all-inclusive will of God? I think it is evident. The will of God is nothing but His beloved Son. Of course, it is in relation to mankind. That is true. But what is in God's mind is His beloved Son. He sees a Man, a perfect Man, a Man of His own heart, and He is working to establish the life and character of that Man in many men. He reveals that Man, His beloved Son, to mankind in order that by His Spirit He may work that one Man into many men until they are conformed to this one Man so that the Son may lead many sons into glory. God is looking for *the* man, a universal man, a man patterned after the perfect Man. And *the* one perfect Man, in a sense, becomes corporate for the purpose of embracing many, many men with Him. Such is the will of God.

That expression, "one and many," can be found in Romans 5. There is the one and there are the many, but the many come from that one. And the many will return to that one, be joined together to that one, and that becomes the one new Man (see vv. 15, 17, 19). This is the will of God, and it is for this reason that Genesis is a book of biographies. God is not interested in methods; God is not interested in theories; He is not interested in theology, either—He is interested in man. Therefore, the first book of the Bible records the biographies of eight different persons: Adam, Abel, Enoch, Noah, Abraham, Isaac, Jacob and Joseph. Of course, there are many other persons mentioned in Genesis, but the names of these other persons are merely mentioned and then disappear into oblivion. Indeed, there is recorded in this first book of the Bible the personal histories of only those men whose lives are intertwined and intimately related with *the* Man—that is to say, with the Man of God's heart, His beloved Son.

What is history? History, it has been said, is "his story." Whose story? Of course, we who are Christians know it is *His* story; for us, there can be nobody else: it is our Lord Jesus. History is His story. Therefore, in both the primitive history and the patriarchal history of Genesis, it is but the history or the story of our Lord Jesus. We can see Him in all these lives. God has so worked the life of our Lord Jesus into these lives, as it were, that when we gather these eight people together, we see Christ. In each one of these lives there is a glimpse or small view of Christ which can be seen, and when they are all added together we have a full picture of His story. And this, it seems to me, is what the book of Genesis is all about. With this approach to the book in view, let us therefore consider in turn the life of each one of these eight men.

ADAM

Adam means "red earth." God used the red earth to form the body of a man. But even though he was formed of red earth, he was created in God's image. In the whole creation of all the created beings, man is the only one that is created in God's image. Not even the angels were created in God's image, only man. Think of that! God breathed the breath of life into the nostrils of this form, which was formed with red earth, and man became a living soul. Hence, there is something in man that corresponds and responds to God. Man is made for God in a special way. That is the reason why St. Augustine once declared: "My soul can never enter into rest until it rests in Thee, O God."

Man is uniquely made—in the image of God. He is made in such a way that without God he is empty, unfulfilled, incomplete. Not unlike a vessel made for containing something, man is created to contain God's life.

Now God gave this created man dominion over the fowls of the air, the beasts of the field, and the fishes of the sea. And why? That he might rule the whole earth on behalf of God. When man was created, he was created perfect. He had a spirit, a soul, and a body. He had five complete senses: all the members of his body were complete. Moreover, he had all the faculties of his soul alive—he was a living soul: for he could think, feel, decide, choose. Furthermore, man had a spirit that could commune with God, know God, even possess God, and be fully possessed by God. In short, when man was created he was created perfect; and yet, he needed to be perfected. How do we know that?

After God created that man, He put him in the *garden of Eden*. The phrase garden of Eden signifies "a garden of pleasure," for *Eden* means "pleasure." God wanted man to enjoy His created things and to guard, till, and have dominion over His created things. This, however, was conditional on one thing: man needed to be perfected. So God placed man before two trees, the tree of life and the tree of the knowledge of good and evil. It was as if God had said: "You are created perfect, but if you want to enjoy everything that I have created and exercise dominion over all things on My behalf as My governor, then you will need to eat the fruit of the tree of life. You need My life. It is only after you possess My life and My life possesses you that you shall be able to enjoy everything that I have made and rule over all things that I have created. But, there is also before you the tree of the knowledge of good and evil. If you eat of that tree, it is true that your soul-life will be greatly developed. You will gain a knowledge of good and evil outside of Me, outside of true life, you doing so simply by reasoning and rationalizing. Indeed, you will be able to distinguish good and evil, yet not by life but by reasoning things out. You *will* have that power, but in so doing you will be declaring your independence of Me because you desire to make a god of yourself, and the result shall be spiritual death, for you will not be able to enjoy the things I have created nor be able to rule over the created things."

Unfortunately, our forebears, Adam and Eve, partook of the tree of the knowledge of good and evil instead of the tree of life. In other words, they had rather be independent than depend upon God; they had rather be on their own than be in union with God in life. And we know the result: sin entered the world and also death, the wages of sin (see Romans 5:12, 6:23a).

But thank God, He gave man a second chance. One day we see One who bore our sins in His body on the tree in order that being dead to sins we are made alive unto righteousness (see I Peter 2:24). Our forebears missed out on the tree of life, but thank God, by our Lord Jesus Christ having been crucified on Calvary's cross, that cross becomes none other than a tree of life. Nobody will nail a robber on a cross that is smoothed, painted, or gold-plated. They will simply cut down a tree and hang him there. So when our Lord Jesus was crucified on the tree, the Bible says that out of that tree there comes forth life to us. When we believe in the Lord Jesus, thank God, we in reality have eaten of the Tree of Life. God's life is thus now in us, and if we allow that life to rule over us, then we will be able to have dominion as well as enjoyment. Otherwise, without the life of God, there is no enjoyment and no dominion. Every enjoyment in this world carries with it its sorrow; but when we enjoy everything that is in the life of God, it is real enjoyment and there is also dominion.

ABEL

Abel means "breath" or "vanity." Why did Adam and Eve give this child the name of Abel? When they had their firstborn, Cain, they said they had acquired a man from Jehovah, since *Cain* means "acquisition." They thought that in Cain they had the promised seed of the woman (see Genesis 3:15), but what a letdown he was. So when Abel was born, in essence they called that son "a breath"—"vanity."

Actually, there is but one breath between us and death, and everything under the earth is vanity. The Preacher has told us that. Solomon declared: "Vanity of vanities; all is vanity. Everything under the sun is vanity" (see Ecclesiastes 1:3; 12:8). How true it is; and because Abel realized that he was but a breath that separated him from death, he sacrificed a better sacrifice—a lamb—than that of his brother Cain. Abel recognized that man under sin could not enjoy anything because, everything being vanity, all results in vanity and death. Therefore, acknowledging his sin, Abel trusted in the atoning blood of the Lamb; and because he offered up a better sacrifice, Abel, unlike his unbelieving brother, was accepted by God.

All of this is true with us today. We need to see that there is only one breath between us and death. Life is so short, so uncertain, so quick; and even when we have that breath, everything is vain—vanity of vanities. Should that not stir up our hearts to acknowledge our sins, to humble ourselves before God, to accept His prepared Lamb? "Behold the Lamb of God who takes away the sin of the world" (John 1:29). And if we do, we are accepted by God in the Beloved; yet not because we are better than anybody else, but because of the better sacrifice —even the Lamb of God.

Enoch

Enoch means "discipline" or "devoted." When he was sixty-five years old Enoch begat a child, Methuselah, and evidently something unusual happened at that moment. A revelation was given to him that upon the death of this child something tremendously disastrous, a catastrophe, would happen to this world. And because of this revelation, by faith, Enoch began to walk with God and did so for three hundred years.

Do you like to walk with God? Probably, you like God to walk with you. To walk with God requires much discipline. Unless you are fully devoted to Him, you will not be able to walk with Him for a day, let alone three hundred years. But Enoch walked with God three hundred years: steadily walking, walking and walking until he found himself in heaven—"until he was not" (see Genesis 5:22, 24). God had taken him. By faith Enoch was taken up to heaven by God; but before he was taken, he demonstrated the evidence to prove that he had pleased God (see Hebrews 11:5a, 5c).

We do thank God that Methuselah lived nine hundred and sixty-nine years, as far as can be known the longest life ever lived upon this earth. In China, according to legend, the one who lived longest was Peng Zu. He lived eight hundred years, but even with that, Methuselah lived a hundred and sixty-nine years longer! And why? It was the mercy of God, who was patient with mankind because we know that with the death of Methuselah came the flood.

Here was the man Enoch, who walked with God three hundred years accepting the discipline of the Lord and devoting himself totally to God. And because of that constant devotion he was raptured, he was taken: heaven was his reward. If we walk with God and are willing to suffer with Him, we shall be glorified with Him (see Romans 8:17b).

Noah

Noah means "repose" because when he was born his father Lemech said, "Through this son we will have rest from our works, from the toil of our hands, because the earth is cursed by God" (see Genesis 5:29).

The most prominent event in Noah's life was the building of the ark—Noah's ark. Because of the ark, he and his family were hidden in it. When the flood came, when the judgment of this world came, they were preserved. After the flood was over, Noah came out upon a new earth, and he became the heir of the righteousness according to God.

I think the picture that is before us is of Noah and his family in the ark, and it simply means this: abiding in Christ. The Ark represents Christ, and we need to abide in Him. If we abide in Christ, then, when the world is condemned and judged, we will not be judged; instead, we shall be the heirs of righteousness. We shall inherit the coming kingdom which is ruled by righteousness. How important it is that we learn to abide in Christ!

The Lord Jesus said, "I am the vine, ye are the branches. Abide in me and I in you. In this is my Father glorified, that ye bear much fruit" (John 15:5a, 4a, 8a).

To abide simply means to make our home in Christ. Let us not visit Christ just once a day or once a month or once a week on Sunday, but let us make Him our home. Let us stay there. And if we stay in Him, we will not be condemned with the world that is under judgment. On the contrary, we shall inherit righteousness, even the kingdom of righteousness.

ABRAHAM

Abraham means "the father of a multitude." We find that throughout Abraham's life he had built a number of altars. Nobody will build an altar for himself. An altar is a symbol of spiritual life because it is built in order to worship God, to call upon the name of the Lord. So we see in Abraham a spiritual life, a life with God. God called him out of Ur of Chaldea to Canaan. To be more accurate, God called Abraham to himself, and by faith he obeyed God (see Hebrews 11:8). So we see in this man a spiritual life.

What is spiritual life? It is none other than a life with God. We do not measure spiritual life by how much we know, even of the Bible. We measure spiritual life by how much we experience God, how much God has us as His friend. That is spiritual life.

In the Old Testament you find the altar; in the New Testament you find the cross. This is because the Old Testament altar represents the New Testament cross. In Hebrews 13, when the writer there says, "We have an altar ...," he is not referring to the altar in the temple in Jerusalem where they offered burnt offerings. He has reference to the cross that stands outside the gate of Jerusalem where Christ was crucified. The cross and Christ are inseparable, and because of this you learn that the cross has become the symbol or emblem of Christians. You cannot have a Christ without a cross. A crossless Christ is no Christ at all. Such a Christ cannot save us. In the same way, how can a Christian be truly a Christian, experientially, if there is no mark of the cross in his life, if there are no wounds? (I am speaking here of our experience, not of our position.) Such lack means he has never been dealt with. It means he remains as he was before—a man of the flesh, a carnal man. Even though that person has the life of Christ in him, he is nonetheless a carnal man. That person needs the cross to deal with him in order to make him a spiritual man, one who is living a spiritual life.

In Abraham's lifetime he built four altars. He built the first altar at Shechem. It is the altar of revelation because there God appeared to him and said, "Unto thy seed I will give the land." Then Abraham built a second altar in between Ai and Bethel and called upon the name of the Lord there. It is the altar of separation, for he had put Ai behind him and now had Bethel before him. *Ai* means "a heap of ruins." The world is just that: a heap of ruins; therefore, Abraham left it behind. He marched forward, facing himself towards Bethel, meaning "the house of God." The house of God shall be his home. It is thus the altar of separation. Abraham built a third altar at *Hebron*, which means "communion." After separating himself from Lot, he was in constant communion with God at Hebron. Finally, he built an altar on *Mount Moriah* where he offered to God his son Isaac. It is the altar of worship.

Let us understand that it is the cross which gives us revelation. Without the cross there can be no revelation. It is also the cross that separates us from the world and unto the church. Moreover, it is the cross which enables us to have that unceasing fellowship with God, and it is likewise the cross that stirs up our worship unto God. How we need the cross to be the emblem of our Christian life! It is not something to be hung on our neck, but is something which is to be wrought into our very life.

ISAAC

Isaac means "laughter." He was the son of Abraham, and he

inherited everything from his father; but Isaac the son increased what he had inherited. Isaac's life was continually related to the digging of wells. He was always engaged in this activity. Now naturally speaking, it is quite true that because he was a farmer, a cattle raiser, he needed water. But speaking spiritually, there is a spiritual meaning to it. Water in the Scriptures speaks of the living water of life, the Spirit of life. God's life, the Spirit of life, is living—ever flowing, ever bubbling, ever refreshing, never ceasing.

Isaac repeatedly dug wells, and of course a well is to contain the water. Therefore, *well* in the Scriptures speaks of "the capacity," or "the measure of containing the life of God." We all have the life of God in us. In John 4 we read how the Lord had said to the Samaritan woman: "If you drink of the water that I shall give to you, it will become a fountain within you. It will spring up without ceasing."

Thank God, we have that fountain within us, but we need to dig wells to contain or keep that ever-flowing fountain of water. A well is something we have to dig. The more wells we dig, the more water we will have. How we need to have the Holy Spirit working in our lives—digging and digging and digging in us— thus removing the dirt and the dust from our lives. We have much rubbish in us and all this rubbish of ourselves needs to be dug out, to be emptied—our opinion, feeling, thought, concern, interest, influence, right. We are full of self, and in a sense all this rubbish within us stops the flow of water. The water is certainly there, for it is a living fountain, a flowing river; but it is stopped up. So, we need to dig, dig, and dig some more. And as the Holy Spirit begins to work in our lives and we cooperate with Him and let Him dig, the outcome will be that the more He digs in us the less we become, but the more filled we are with the living water, even with the Holy Spirit. That is life, abundant life, and that will bring forth laughter. Not only will you and I enjoy having a laugh at all of this but God shall laugh, too. He is made happy.

JACOB

Jacob means "twister, supplanter, heel-holder." Yet, God changed his name into Israel, meaning "a prince of God." God worked in Jacob's life through many dealings. Jacob dealt with others and others dealt with him; moreover, God was dealing with him all the time and he was dealing with God all the time. Jacob was the person who wrestled with the angel of God and prevailed. Yet he prevailed by being defeated, for ever afterwards he walked with a limp. Isn't that a picture of what we are? How we deal with other people and other people deal with us! How we deal with God and God deals with us! Oftentimes we discover we are so strong that we even prevail over the angel of God, but by prevailing over him we are crippled. We at last see God face to face and we are transformed.

Therefore, throughout Jacob's life he was always raising pillars. He raised one pillar after another, and we know that pillar in the Scriptures stands for testimony. What is our testimony? Is it not the result of the Spirit's dealing, of God's dealing in our lives? If we do not allow God to deal with our life, we have no testimony. The more we allow Him to deal with our life, the more testimony we have to offer this world, because we are not to testify of what we are; we are to testify of what He is in us. The testimony of Jesus is entrusted to us today (cf. Revelation 1:9; 6:9; 12:11, 17; 19:10).

JOSEPH

Joseph means "He will add." In Joseph's life there was much suffering. He suffered not because he was bad but because he had vision and was good. He feared God. And he did not have to wait until he finished suffering to receive a crown or experience the throne. For during the time of his suffering the throne was there. For instance, in his home he suffered from his brothers, yet he was above it all. In the house of Potiphar he suffered as a slave, nevertheless, he was in charge. In the tower he suffered as a prisoner, but he was put in full charge of the prison. Finally, after he had suffered enough and had matured through his sufferings, he was qualified to sit next to Pharaoh—throne life.

The life we receive from our Lord Jesus is not only abundant life, it is also throne life. In other words, wherever we are, whatever circumstances we may be in, let us remember that we are not supposed to be under these circumstances, we are to be above them. It is not because we are strong in will; rather, it is because we have God's throne life within us: assuming charge, having dominion, and experiencing enjoyment.

In each of these eight persons we can see a portion of Christ:

> In Adam we see the tree of life.
> In Abel we see the better sacrifice.
> In Enoch we see heaven.
> In Noah we see the ark.
> In Abraham we see the altar.
> In Isaac we see the water, the well.
> In Jacob we see the pillar.
> In Joseph we see the throne.

Christ is the tree of life. He is the better sacrifice. He is heaven. What is heaven? Christ. Where Christ is, there is heaven. If we are with Christ, we are in heaven. Heaven can be nothing better than the very presence of Christ. Some people may want to walk on the golden street, but the golden street may be too hard to walk upon. However, if it is Christ, thank God, that is perfect. Christ is the Ark—our place of abode. He is the altar, the cross of Jesus Christ. He is the water of the well. He is the testimony of that pillar, and He is our throne. Christ is everything. God is working Christ, the Man of His own heart, into these men and many others, and every man is able to absorb, as it were, something of Christ. That becomes the main thing in each of their lives; or to put it another way, that is the meaning of their very life. Without Christ there is no meaning to one's life. But if we have Christ in us, and a little of Christ is being inwrought and constituted in us, then that gives meaning to our life, and that is eternal. It shall never pass away.

God is still working all this out today with you and me. The biographies do not stop at the end of the Patriarchal Age. They continue on and on and on. God is still working in man and what He works in man is nothing less than the working of His Man into us until we can be joined back to Him as the bride to the Bridegroom, as the body to the Head. Then we see the one new Man, the universal man, the will and purpose of God having been accomplished. Of course, in Genesis, we only see the beginning. God is still working. Thank God for that.

Let us pray:

> *Dear heavenly Father, we do thank Thee for Thy perfect will, that Thou dost desire that Thy Son, the Man, shall be wrought in many men and women, that we may become that one universal man—that one new Man to satisfy Thy heart. Oh, our Father, we do pray that our eyes may be opened that we may see Thy great purpose, Thy grand plan. We thank Thee that we are privileged to be part of that plan and of that purpose; and Father, we ask that Thou wilt enable us to lay down ourselves, to let go of ourselves, and let Thee work and let Christ be formed in us. Oh, our Father, Thou art satisfied only with one Man, Thy beloved Son. So we pray that Thou wilt be satisfied with Him in us. It is all of grace and mercy. And to Thee be the glory. In Thy precious name. Amen.*

EXODUS

THE WORKS OF GOD

Exodus 3:2-10—And the Angel of Jehovah appeared to him in a flame of fire out of the midst of a thorn-bush: and he looked, and behold, the thorn-bush burned with fire, and the thorn-bush was not being consumed. And Moses said, Let me now turn aside and see this great sight, why the thorn-bush is not burnt. And Jehovah saw that he turned aside to see, and God called to him out of the midst of the thorn-bush and said, Moses, Moses! And he said, Here am I. And he said, Draw not nigh hither: loose thy sandals from off thy feet, for the place whereon thou standest is holy ground. And he said, I am the God of thy father, the God of Abraham, the God of Isaac, and the God of Jacob. And Moses hid his face; for he was afraid to look at God.

And Jehovah said, I have seen assuredly the affliction of my people who are in Egypt, and their cry have I heard on account of their taskmasters; for I know their sorrows. And I am come down to deliver them out of the hand of the Egyptians, and to bring them up out of that land unto a good and spacious land, unto a land flowing with milk and honey, unto the place of the Canaanites, and the Hittites, and the Amorites, and the Perizzites, and the Hivites, and the Jebusites. And now behold, the cry of the children of Israel is come unto me; and I have also seen the oppression with which the Egyptians oppress them. And now come, and I will send thee unto Pharaoh, that thou mayest bring forth my people the children of Israel out of Egypt.

Exodus 15:13-18—Thou by thy mercy hast led forth the people that thou hast redeemed;
Thou hast guided them by thy strength unto the abode of thy holiness.

The peoples heard it, they were afraid:
A thrill seized the inhabitants of Philistia.
Then the princes of Edom were amazed;
The mighty men of Moab, trembling hath seized them;
All the inhabitants of Canaan melted away.
Fear and dread fall upon them;
By the greatness of thine arm they are still as a stone;
Till thy people pass over, Jehovah,
Till the people pass over that thou hast purchased.
Thou shalt bring them in, and plant them in the mountain of
thine inheritance,
The place that thou, Jehovah, hast made thy dwelling,
The Sanctuary, Lord, that thy hands have prepared.
Jehovah shall reign for ever and ever!

Exodus 19:1-6—In the third month after the departure of the
children of Israel out of the land of Egypt, the same day came
they into the wilderness of Sinai: they departed from Rephidim,
and came into the wilderness of Sinai, and encamped in the wil-
derness; and Israel encamped there before the mountain. And
Moses went up to God, and Jehovah called to him out of the
mountain, saying, Thus shalt thou say to the house of Jacob,
and tell the children of Israel: Ye have seen what I have done to
the Egyptians, and how I have borne you on eagles' wings and
brought you to myself. And now, if ye will hearken to my voice
indeed and keep my covenant, then shall ye be my own posses-
sion out of all the peoples—for all the earth is mine—and ye
shall be to me a kingdom of priests, and a holy nation. These
are the words which thou shalt speak to the children of Israel.

Exodus 40:34-35—And the cloud covered the tent of meeting,
and the glory of Jehovah filled the tabernacle. And Moses could
not enter into the tent of meeting, for the cloud abode on it, and
the glory of Jehovah filled the tabernacle.

Let us pray:

Dear heavenly Father, we do commit Thy word into Thy

hands and ask Thee to break it, to bless it, and to give it to us. We ask in Thy precious name. Amen.

Exodus is volume two of Moses' Pentateuch. In Genesis we see the will of God, how His will is centered upon man, the man of His own heart, that corporate man, Christ and His church. Exodus tells us of the *works* of God. What God has promised by His word, He is to accomplish by His own work. Exodus follows upon Genesis very closely in time. By reading the end of Genesis we learn of Joseph's death when he was one hundred and ten years old. His body was embalmed and placed in a coffin in Egypt. Then, at the beginning of Exodus we learn this: "And these are the names of the sons of Israel who had come into Egypt ... And Joseph died, and all his brethren, and all that generation." So we readily see the connection between Genesis and Exodus. Indeed, Exodus is the continuation of the historical narrative which began in Genesis.

The word *Exodus* means "the way out, departure." In this book we see how the children of Israel, who had become slaves, were delivered out of Egypt; and God led them on until they arrived at Mount Sinai. And this history, recorded in the word of God, is definitely for our admonition.

"For as many things as have been written before [in the Old Testament Scriptures] have been written for our instruction, that through endurance and through encouragement of the scriptures we might have hope" (Romans 15:4).

"Now all these things happened to them as types and have been written for our admonition, upon whom the ends of the ages are come" (I Corinthians 10:11).

Let us bear in mind that we are not merely studying history. It is history, yes, but this history is recorded in the Bible, in the word of God, for it serves as a type for us today. In the deliverance of the children of Israel out of Egypt we can see how God delivered us out of sin, death, Satan, and the world. So it should be viewed as something personal to us. We should not approach the book of Exodus as just history, but we should see in that history our personal story; and that is the purpose of this book.

Exodus can be roughly divided into three parts. The first part is Chapters 1-5. On the one hand, there is bondage; on the other hand, we see the Redeemer. The second part is Chapters 6-18. This is the story of deliverance, and it tells us of redemption. The third part is Chapters 19-40. Here, we have revelation, and actually, through the revelation we see the redeemed people.

BONDAGE

We recall from Genesis that Jacob had gone with his family to Egypt to be preserved from the famine, and at that time Joseph was the prime minister there. God blessed the children of Israel during that period in Egypt, and hence they had a very good time there. The first part of Exodus gives us the story of the children of Israel in Egypt. After Joseph, his brethren, and that entire generation had died, a new king came on the throne. The Jewish historian, Josephus, tells us that it was a new dynasty, and the new ruler did not know about Joseph or what Joseph had done for Egypt.

We must take note here of something most interesting. During the sojourning of Abraham, Isaac and Jacob in the Promised Land, God had indeed blessed them there; yet so far as population is concerned, after all those years of sojourning, when they entered Egypt there were only seventy-five persons. Even though they had lived in peace and prosperity, the population was nonetheless very limited—only seventy-five people could be counted. After they entered Egypt, however, God began to multiply them enormously. During those years when the children of Israel were in Egypt, especially when they were under persecution and oppression, the number grew so much that when they came out of Egypt, the men numbered six hundred thousand besides children, women, and a mixed multitude who came out with them. Probably, it amounted to between two and two and a half million people. So we see how the Lord works, and we know that the promises of the Lord are true. Even during such great persecution God greatly multiplied the people—they growing from a large family into a veritable nation.

However, as the children of Israel multiplied in Egypt under the blessing of God, the new Pharaoh grew alarmed. He saw that they were becoming stronger and stronger; so he began to adopt measures to oppress them. He forced them into hard labor to build cities, canals, and things like that. Even so, the people continued to multiply. Then Pharaoh ordered that all the male children who were to be born thereafter must be thrown into the Nile River. It was a genocidal attempt to terminate that race of the children of Israel, but it did not succeed: the people continued to multiply. The children of Israel were under great oppression, and they cried out to God because of their affliction. Unknown to them, God was preparing a savior in the person of Moses.

THE REDEEMER

Moses was born into a family of Levites who, out of the fear of God, kept that child for three months. When they could not hide him anymore, they put the child in an ark or basket they had made, and placed it in the Nile River. The daughter of Pharaoh came to bathe, and when she saw the basket, she asked her maid to bring it to her. When the basket was opened, the baby cried, and it touched the heart of this woman. She adopted Moses as her son and took him into the palace. Josephus, the Jewish historian, tells us that the name of Pharaoh's daughter was Thermuthis, and the king who was reigning when Moses was raised was Rameses IV.

When Moses was very little his mother nursed him for a short period and, during that time, somehow, the mother was able to share God and His purpose with this little child. As he grew up in the palace he acquired all the learning of Egypt (see Acts 7:22); he was mighty in words and in deeds. But when he was forty years old, it came into his heart to go out and visit his brethren; so he went out. He saw an Egyptian beating a Hebrew, and so Moses—because he was mighty in deed—beat that Egyptian to death and buried him in the sand. The next day when he again went out he saw two Hebrews who were quarreling with each other. He tried to use his eloquence to bring peace between them, but he was rejected by those of his own people. The news spread, so Moses fled for his life. He had failed in his first attempt, but God had allowed him to fail because he was doing it in his own strength.

For the next forty years Moses was in the wilderness shepherding some sheep. There he unlearned all he had learned in Egypt and now learned directly from God. When he was eighty years old, he thought it was the end of his life, since in Psalm 90 it was said that "the life span of a person is seventy years old and if he is strong he may live to be eighty years old."

Hence Moses had given up every hope of being used by God in delivering His people; but when he was at his life's end, God had His beginning. God apprehended him and revealed himself to him in a burning bush. The thorn bush was burning, but it was not consumed because God was there. He thereafter called Moses and sent him to Egypt to deliver His people.

We do see here an analogy of God's love for us today. Before we knew the Lord Jesus we were in this world under the control and the domination of the prince of this world. The prince of this world is the god of this age, the adversary, Satan. All who are born into this world are under the tyranny of this world's god, the prince of this world, Satan. And like Pharaoh, he is so cruel; he puts us all into hard labor. Life is very hard, and we have to work hard in order to make a living. Satan works us so hard; he takes away all our time so that we have no strength to think of spiritual things, no strength to even think of our soul. That is the trick of the enemy. He causes us to be so occupied with mere living, which is hard living, that we are not able to even think of God or of our soul. Not only that, his purpose behind it all is to put us to death. He knows that he himself is destined for hell and he wants company. Now let us remember that God has not created hell for man; hell was made for Satan; but Satan tries to entice as many people as possible to be with him.

The Bible says we were dead in sins and transgressions (see Ephesians 2:1). That was our condition. We were helpless and hopeless; but without our knowledge God was preparing our Savior. And in the fullness of time, He sent His Son into this world, born of woman, born under the Law, that He might deliver us out from the curse of the Law so that we might receive sonship (see Galatians 4:4-5; 3:13). So we do thank God that He has prepared the Savior for us: Christ has come into this world.

We know our Lord Jesus is greater than Moses. Moses was the savior of the children of Israel, but our Lord Jesus is the Savior of the world. Moses failed once in his life, but in the life of our Lord Jesus, He never fails. Our Lord Jesus once died for us, and the eternal redemption is accomplished. How we thank God for our Lord Jesus Christ, the Savior!

DELIVERANCE

The second part of Exodus gives us the deliverance (Exodus 6-18). God sent Moses to Egypt to deliver His people. He went to Pharaoh and declared: "God said: 'Let My people go that they may serve Me'" (see Exodus 5:1). But, of course, Pharaoh would not think of letting the people go. God had to use plague upon plague (altogether ten of them) in order to force Pharaoh to let His people go. Through these ten plagues God destroyed not only Egypt but the gods of Egypt as well. Every plague had something to do with the deities—the idols—that the Egyptians worshiped. Therefore, God not only destroyed Egypt, He also destroyed their gods. But Pharaoh would not give in until finally the last plague came upon the Egyptians—the slaying of the firstborn. On that night the angel of God passed through the whole land of Egypt and slew all the firstborn there: the firstborn of Pharaoh, of the Egyptian people, of the slaves, and all the firstborn of their cattle and their flocks. But God prepared a way for the children of Israel, and this was the Paschal or Passover lamb. God told the children of Israel that every family must prepare a lamb on the tenth of the first month. It was to be a spotless lamb, and they were to keep it for four days. On the fourteenth, between the two evenings, every family was to gather in the house and kill the lamb. Its blood was to be put on the lintel and doorposts and the whole family was to roast the lamb and eat the meat. When the angel passed through the entire land that night and whenever he saw blood on the door, he passed over. But if there was no blood on the door he would go in and slay the firstborn. This is Passover. The children of Israel, in obeying God's word, were preserved by that blood.

The children of Israel were also to eat the meat of the lamb. Why? It was because they were to be ready to march out of Egypt, and the meat thus gave them strength for the journey. And they ate it in a hurry because God was ready to bring them out. Here, again, we find an analogy between their deliverance and our deliverance. We are delivered, not by corruptible silver or gold, but we are redeemed by the blood of the Lamb, without spot and without blemish, even the blood of Christ, the Lamb of God (see I Peter 1:18,19 and John 1:29). It is only by the blood of the Lamb that we too are passed over, that we too are redeemed. All other methods are of no avail. There is but one way if destruction and death are to pass over us—it is by the blood of the Lamb. Thank God, the blood of the Lamb was shed two thousand years ago when our Lord Jesus was crucified on Calvary's cross. It has already been shed, but have we applied that blood upon our hearts? Even when the children of Israel killed the Paschal lamb, if they forgot to put the blood on the doorpost, then the angel would still have gone in and slain the firstborn.

REDEMPTION

The redemption of our Lord Jesus is sufficient for all the world. His blood is more than sufficient for the remission of the sins of the whole world. Then why is it that some people's sins are forgiven and others are not? It is not because of the insufficiency of the blood of the Lord Jesus; it is because some people have applied that blood upon their heart but other people have refused to do so. Have we sprinkled the blood upon the conscience of our heart? Only the blood of our Lord Jesus is able to cleanse our conscience of our sins. Only His blood satisfies the righteousness of God. Only His blood shuts the mouth of the accuser, Satan. How precious is the blood of our Lord Jesus! We are saved. Our sins are forgiven by His blood.

However, that is not all. It is the will of God in redemption that we not only have the blood of the Lord Jesus, we also have the meat—that is, His flesh. The Lord Jesus said, "He that eats my flesh and drinks my blood has life eternal, and I will raise him up at the last day" (John 6:54).

Not only has the blood of the Lord Jesus washed us, cleansed us, satisfied God's demand, and shut Satan's mouth; but also the life of the Lord Jesus, represented by the Lamb's meat, is now in us. By faith we have received and have taken in the Lord Jesus. He is now our life, He is now our strength, and by His life we are able to walk out of the world and walk into heaven. So let us remember that we have the life of the Lord Jesus in us. It is only by that life of His that we are able to go through this world until, finally, we make it to heaven.

Now when Moses was trying to get the people out of Egypt, Pharaoh would not let them go. Whenever pressure was put on Pharaoh, he tried to bargain and to negotiate. Again and again, whenever a plague came and Pharaoh could not stand it anymore, he would say: "I am wrong. Take the plague away and I will let you go." But when the plague was lifted, he still would not let them go. Then another plague came which brought him under pressure again, and so he would say this time: "All right, if you want to serve God, serve Him here. Don't go, but serve Him here."

But Moses replied: "No, we cannot keep the feast of the Lord here in Egypt because we might sacrifice things which are an abomination to the Egyptians, and we will be stoned. We cannot serve God here; we have to go three days' journey in order to keep the feast of Jehovah."

Then Pharaoh said, "All right, if you must go, don't go too far away. Just be close by."

"No," Moses replied, "we have to go three days' journey."

The next thing Pharaoh asked was: "Who is going?"

Moses said, "The men, the women, the old and the young, our daughters, our sons, our flocks, and our herds—all will go."

"No, no, no; if you men want to serve God, you go, but leave the family here."

Moses replied, "No, it cannot be done."

Then Pharaoh said, "All right, you go with your sons and with your daughters, but leave the herds and the flocks here."

Moses said, "Not a hoof can remain. Everything must go."

Finally, on that night of the Passover, Pharaoh said, "All right, you go. Go quickly!" So they all went.

Is that not a lesson for us today? Why does God save us in the first place? He does not save us just that we may be free. Yes, we are free, but God does not save us merely that we may be free to live the way we want to live. No. Once we served Satan and the world, and Satan tries to hold on to us; but God says, "Let My people go that they may serve Me."

We must realize that no one in bondage can serve God. He needs free people, and only when we are set free are we able to serve Him. The purpose of life is to serve and worship

God. How can we serve if we are not free? How can we serve if we are in the world, still in Egypt? There is no way to serve because the Egyptians will interfere with our service. They will say, "No, not that way. This is the better way to do it." Unfortunately, Christianity today is in the world trying to serve God according to the world. No wonder all these worldly things, all these worldly methods and the ingenuity of man have dominated the service of Christianity. We cannot serve God in the world. We have to be separated.

Yet who, exactly, is going to serve God? Let us see that God's salvation is household salvation. In other words, the Paschal lamb is one lamb for each house. If those in that household are too few, they can have some other people with them to make up that household, for it was to be a lamb per house. That is the salvation of God. His salvation is therefore for the men, the women, the old, the young, the parents, and the sons and the daughters; not only that, but even the herds and the flocks were to be included. In the redemption of God He has redeemed us completely—the whole house with all that God has blessed us with. It is God's will that not only the men and the women serve Him but our children are to serve Him, too. And we are to serve Him with all the blessings and all the things with which He has blessed us. They are rightfully His, and we need to present all our families and possessions to God and let Him be served. That is the way we keep the feast of the Lord.

After the Passover and the children of Israel were delivered from death, immediately, they started the journey out of Egypt. God took them through the Red Sea. Actually, one can go to Canaan by land, but God did not lead them that way. That was the way of the Philistines. Instead, God led them through the Red Sea because He said that if the Israelites went by land and met opposition, they might repent and want to go back. Therefore, God led them by way of the Red Sea so that they could not go back. Pharaoh and his army chased them to the Red Sea, but God opened it up, and the children of Israel went through on dry ground. After they went through, the waters came back and all the chariots and men of Pharaoh were drowned. Only then were the children of Israel finally out of Egypt.

The same is true with us. The Red Sea is a type of baptism. Some people say, "I believe in the Lord Jesus but I do not need to be baptized. The water does not cleanse me from my sins. It is the blood that cleanses me. Isn't that enough? Why should I be baptized?"

It is true, the waters of baptism never cleanse us from our sin, but baptism marks a separation. By baptism we are now separated forever from the world. Before they went through the Red Sea the children of Israel had been serving Pharaoh because they belonged to him; but God delivered them and led them through the Red Sea. I Corinthians 10:1-2 tells us how the children of Israel went through the Red Sea under the cloud, with the waters standing up on both sides; and thus they were baptized unto Moses—a type of Christ.

What is baptism? Once we belonged to Pharaoh, to Satan, to the kingdom of darkness; but through baptism we no longer belong to that kingdom; indeed, we are removed from that kingdom. God has delivered us from the power of darkness and has translated us into the kingdom of the Son of His love (see Colossians 1:13). So, by baptism we are baptized unto Christ. By baptism we declare that we belong to Christ and no longer to the world (Egypt) nor to Satan (Pharaoh). We do not even belong to ourselves—we belong totally to Christ. That is a declaration and a testimony of our separation. And with that declaration we are separated from the world forever and now belong to Christ. Hence, baptism is very important; for when we are baptized, it registers something in our spiritual life. It gives us strength to stand on the ground of separation which declares that we belong to no one but to Christ and Him alone. That is baptism.

After the Israelites went through the Red Sea they sang a song of victory. In the inspired words of this song of victory God revealed for the first time to the children of Israel the purpose of deliverance. Why did God deliver them out? It is true: God had heard their cry and was touched by their affliction. He wanted to deliver them. But why? The song gives the reason: "Thou by thy mercy hast led forth the people that thou hast redeemed; thou hast guided them by thy strength unto the abode of thy holiness ... Thou shalt bring them in, and plant them in the mountain of thine inheritance, the place that thou, Jehovah, hast made thy dwelling, the Sanctuary, Lord, that thy hands have prepared. Jehovah shall reign for ever and ever!" (Exodus 15:13, 17-18)

In other words, the purpose of deliverance is not just *out*; it is also *in*. God delivered them out in order to bring them in—out of Egypt and into Canaan; out of bondage and into a land flowing with milk and honey; out of the fiery furnace and into a dwelling place. God wants to deliver the people to himself and make them His dwelling place. He wants to dwell among His people, and He wants to be King over them. And that is the purpose of redemption.

REVELATION

Now we come to the last part and this is revelation (Exodus 19-40). The children of Israel were delivered, and God brought them as "on eagles' wings" into the Sinai. It took them three months to get there, and during those three months the way God dealt with them was all of grace. By grace God delivered them out of Egypt; by grace He opened the Red Sea; by grace He showered down manna to be their food; by grace He caused water to flow out of the rock; and by grace He led them to Mount Sinai. There, God began to announce His purpose. He said, "Now I have brought you to myself. If you hearken to My voice and keep My covenant then I will make you My people, the people of My possession out of all the nations ... And I will make you a nation of priests, a holy nation" (see Exodus 19:4-6).

This reveals God's purpose for redeeming us today. It is not that we may merely come out, that we may simply be saved from sin, that we may only come out of the world, that we may just be free. No, God saved us in order that He may bring us in. He wants to bring us into a Promised Land. Thank God, our Promised Land is Christ. He has delivered us out of the world and is putting us in Christ so that we may know all the riches that are in Christ. God's purpose is that in knowing the riches of Christ we may have in us the same character as His character in order that we may become a dwelling place for God. God can dwell among us, He can reign over us, and we can be a nation of priests serving Him. That is God's purpose.

Thank God, we have come out. But have we entered *in* experientially? Do we know the fullness that is in Christ? The more we know the riches of Christ the more we are transformed and conformed to His image, and only in that way is God able to dwell among us. God cannot dwell in a foreign environment. He can only dwell in a place that is agreeable and corresponds to Him, a place that is one with Him. That is the reason why we have to be transformed. And transformation simply means we have to come out of ourselves and enter more and more into Christ. As Christ is gradually formed in us, then the building of God will begin to come into being, and He will be able to dwell in our midst and be served by us. We are to be a kingdom of priests. That is God's purpose.

God revealed His mind and purpose to His people, and in order to facilitate this purpose of His, He gave them two things. He gave them the Law (see Exodus 20-24) and the tabernacle (see Exodus 25-40). With these two things—the Law and the tabernacle—God was going to fulfill His purpose among His people.

THE LAW

The gist of the Law is the Ten Commandments. God gave the children of Israel two tablets of stone. On the first tablet there were four commandments engraved thereon by the finger of God (see Exodus 31:18), and on the second tablet there were six commandments. The first tablet's contents speak of man's relationship with God. We are created by Him and there is a duty, responsibility, and relationship we are to have towards our Creator, Maker, and God. Accordingly, the first four commandments regulate our relationship with Him:

> Aside from Him, you shall have no other God.
> You shall not make any images nor worship them.
> You shall not name the name of the Lord in vain.
> You shall keep the Sabbath.

All of this is in relation to God.

The six commandments on the second tablet are for regulating the relationship between man and man. We are created by God as fellow men. Therefore, how should we deal with one another? We are to honor our parents, we are not to murder, and so on. Life basically consists of relationships and the Law regulates these relationships. If the children of Israel were to keep the Law, they could live and become God's people because they would be taking upon themselves His character. In a sense, God's Law reveals His character. Our God is just. Our God is holy. He is unique. He is love. The Law reveals the character of God. So if the Israelites would keep these commandments, then they could become God's people. But when God gave them the commandments, how did they react? Again and again and again—three times—they said, "All which God has told us we will do." Isn't that good? No, it is bad, because they did not truly know themselves. They were presumptuous. They thought they were able to keep the Law of God, but they could not do it.

Why, then, did God give the Law to them? We have to go to the New Testament to learn the reason. In Romans 7 Paul wrote that the Law is good. The commandments are holy, just and right. There is nothing wrong with them. If we keep them we live and we become God's people. The wrong is with us; for in us, that is, in our flesh, there is no good (see v. 18); but, the children of Israel did not know their flesh. It took them forty years in the wilderness to find out what their flesh was like;

but thank God, He gave them the Law. The Law is something *added* to God's promise made to Abraham (see Galatians 3:18-19); and it is not opposite to that promise. God has His promise, but the Law is not opposite to His promise. On the contrary, the Scripture has shut up everybody under sin so that the Law as our tutor may lead us to Christ (see Galatians 3:22-23). In other words, if we discern the right and beneficial way of applying the Law to ourselves, nothing could be better than that.

Why, then, is the Law? The Law is that which is added to God's promise on account of our transgressions so that we may know our sins and may be shut up unto Christ. If the Law can serve *that* purpose, would that not be wonderful? Unfortunately, the children of Israel did not realize that. They thought they could keep the commandments of the Law, but when Moses was on the mountain receiving the Ten Commandments, and even before the tablets of the Law had reached their hands, they had already broken the Law: they worshiped the golden calf. Let us recall that during the first three months of their coming out of Egypt and traveling over to Mount Sinai they were under grace; but during the time from chapter 20 onward, God gave them the Law—that is to say, they were under the Law. However, from the time of chapter 34 forward, we find they had already broken the Law; therefore, through the mediatorship of Moses, God continued His covenant with the Israelites but accompanied it with grace.

THE TABERNACLE

On the one hand, God gave them the Law by which to reveal His holiness. On the other hand, God commanded them to build Him a tabernacle. We do not have time to go into the details of the tabernacle, but thank God for the tabernacle. As a matter of fact, probably all we remember is the Law that Moses received on Mount Sinai; but actually, the discussion of the Law here is only a few chapters in length (Exodus 20-24). On the other hand, from chapter 25 onward to the end of Exodus, it is the tabernacle that is in view. In other words, the tabernacle represents God's purpose. In short, we may say that the Law is the means to lead us into the tabernacle.

The tabernacle primarily speaks of Christ. Do we not read in the New Testament: "The Word became flesh, and tabernacled among us ... full of grace and truth" (John 1:14 mg)? When our Lord Jesus was on earth, He was the Tabernacle of God, full of grace and truth. The tabernacle of old was full of beauty and glory. And everything in it spoke of the Lord Jesus. The brazen altar where the sacrifices were offered speaks of the Lord Jesus as our sacrifice. Through His blood our sins are forgiven. Our Lord Jesus is also the brazen laver where we are washed day by day. We are not only washed once, we are likewise washed day by day so that we may be fit to serve Him. He is our light, our life and our worship—as represented by the candlestick of gold, the golden table of shewbread and the golden altar of incense. He is also the ark and the mercy seat. Everything in the tabernacle speaks of the Lord Jesus—what He is and what He has done for us.

God has provided a way for us to be unto himself. It is through all the finished work of Christ that we are able to approach the throne of grace. In the New Testament, in the book of Hebrews, it is said that, today, we have boldness to enter into the holiest of all, to enter into the very presence of God by the blood of the Lord Jesus, by that new and living way which Jesus has opened up for us through the veil, that is, through His flesh. And we have our great High Priest living and interceding for us (see Hebrews 10:19-21). Therefore, let us go in.

In other words, God is calling us to draw near to Him. We who were once dead in sins and transgressions are now redeemed, and we are called to draw near to God to worship Him, serve Him, and be the house of God for Him to dwell in by His Spirit. And this is redemption. Hence, the whole book of Exodus tells us of redemption and what redemption is. Moreover, we have a wonderful Redeemer. And because of that, the work of redemption is complete; and thank God, we are the redeemed. Accordingly, let the redeemed of the Lord praise His name!

Let us pray:

> *Dear heavenly Father, we do praise and thank Thee for Thy great love towards us. Thou hast sent Thy beloved Son, our Lord Jesus, to this world to be our Redeemer and what a wonderful Redeemer He is. Oh, how comprehensive, how complete, how perfect is His work of redemption! We do praise and thank Thee that we today by faith and by Thy grace are now the redeemed of the Lord; and as the redeemed of the Lord, we say, Lord, we do not want to go out free. We want to serve Thee in Thy house forever and forever. And may Thy name be glorified. We ask in the name of our Lord Jesus. Amen.*

LEVITICUS

THE WAYS OF GOD

Leviticus 1:1-2—And Jehovah called to Moses and spoke to him out of the tent of meeting, saying, Speak unto the children of Israel and say unto them, When any man of you presenteth an offering to Jehovah, ye shall present your offering of the cattle, of the herd and of the flock.

Leviticus 19:1-2—And Jehovah spoke to Moses, saying, Speak unto all the assembly of the children of Israel, and say unto them, Holy shall ye be, for I Jehovah your God am holy.

Leviticus 23:1-2—And Jehovah spoke to Moses, saying, Speak unto the children of Israel, and say unto them, Concerning the set feasts of Jehovah, which ye shall proclaim as holy convocations—these are my set feasts.

Leviticus 27:1-2—And Jehovah spoke to Moses, saying, Speak unto the children of Israel and say unto them, When any one devoteth anything by a vow, the persons shall be for Jehovah according to thy valuation.

Let us pray:

Dear heavenly Father, we are in Thy presence, and we do ask Thy Holy Spirit to open Thy word to us that we may not only understand but we may be led into Thy truth. In the name of our Lord Jesus. Amen.

We are now in volume three of the Pentateuch, the books of Moses. In Genesis we see the will of God which revolves around man—the Man Jesus Christ and the corporate Man: the Christ. In Exodus we see the work of God which is redemption. The book of Leviticus speaks of the ways of God—worship.

In the Hebrew Bible the title for this third book of Moses was taken from the first word of this book in Hebrew: Leviticus—and which in English translates as: *And He called*. God spoke out of the tent of meeting or tabernacle to His people and He called them to come, to worship, and to serve Him. This book of Leviticus is a book of Law, but it is the Law which governs worship. Sometimes it is called the handbook of the priests because the priests are those who were ordained to worship and serve.

The word *Leviticus* is derived from Levi, the priestly tribe of the Israelites. They were set apart to serve God in the tabernacle and later on in the temple. All in all, therefore, the book of Leviticus is concerned with this matter of worship and service, but of course, spiritually speaking, there is no way to separate these two activities.

We learn from the New Testament, in Romans 12:1: "Present your bodies a living sacrifice, holy, acceptable to God, which is your reasonable service" (AV). In some other versions it reads: "which is your spiritual worship," because worship and service are the two sides of one thing. When we speak of worship, we are thinking more of the inward reality—the spirit; and when we speak of service, probably we are thinking more concerning outward activities. Yet what will be the outward activity if there is not that inward spirit? If we have that inward spirit it will surely result in outward activities. We worship and we serve. As we serve, we worship; and as we worship, we serve. These are actually one and the same thing. I Peter 2 tells us we are as "living stones" being built up together "a spiritual house, a holy priesthood." Today, every believer, every child of God, is a priest. And that is our calling, our vocation: to come to worship God and to serve Him.

As stated earlier, Leviticus is volume three of the five-volume Pentateuch. It is a continuation of Exodus because by the time of the end of Exodus the tabernacle or tent of meeting had been set up and the glory of God had filled that place. So that at the time of the beginning of Leviticus, we see that God has taken possession of that tabernacle, in that His glory has come, He has entered His dwelling place, and now at the beginning of Leviticus He speaks out of the tabernacle and calls to His people.

Time-wise, Leviticus does not cover much time. By the first day of the first month of the second year, which was after the children of Israel came out of Egypt, they had set up the tabernacle. And we learn from the book of Numbers, in chapter 1, that on the first day of the second month of the second year, God numbered His people. And thus all which is recorded in Leviticus actually takes place in between these two events. Hence, Leviticus covers only about one month of time, but spiritually, it covers a great deal.

Let us contrast these two books of Exodus and Leviticus. Exodus begins with sinners because the children of Israel were in bondage; but Leviticus starts with saints. These people have already been delivered and they are here at the tabernacle to hear what God has to say to them. In Exodus it is redemption that is in view; in Leviticus, though, it is worship. In Exodus it is righteousness, but in Leviticus it is holiness. In Exodus we see deliverance, whereas in Leviticus we see dedication. In Exodus there is union between God and His people, but in Leviticus there is communion. In Exodus we see God as love; in Leviticus we see Him as light. In Exodus we have God coming to man, whereas in Leviticus we have man approaching God. In Exodus we learn how God speaks out of Mount Sinai and gives the moral law governing His people's relationship with Him and with one another; in Leviticus, however, we learn how God speaks out of the tabernacle and gives His people the laws governing worship. So actually, Leviticus is a continuation and an advance upon the book of Exodus: God's people are called to worship.

True, Leviticus is a book of laws governing worship; but of course, we know that the Old Testament books are full of types and shadows; and the reality is found in the New Testament. The children of Israel were called to serve and to worship, but that was in a physical way. We today are called to serve and to worship in spirit and in truth.

Let us recall how in John 4 it states that the Father is seeking for true worshipers, those who shall worship Him in spirit and in truth. It is no longer a matter of place—where, nor is it any longer a matter of time—when. It is no longer in Jerusalem nor on Mount Gerizim as the place of worship; it is now a matter of spirit and truth. This is only possible because Christ has come and accomplished everything for us, enabling us to be true worshipers of the Father. Then why should we study Leviticus, since we are not any longer to offer up sheep, goats and cattle to God? It is because, even though the form is now different, the spiritual principle is the same. Therefore, we can learn much from the book of Leviticus because this book is given to us for our admonition, to teach us how to worship God in spirit and in truth.

OFFERINGS

This book begins with offerings (Leviticus 1—6:7), and there are five of them. Then there are the laws of the offerings (Leviticus 6:8—7). These offerings are found at the very beginning of this book. This is because, God being a righteous and holy God, we know that whoever is to approach Him has to approach Him through these offerings. In other words, there is no way for us to draw near to God on our own ground. God is holy and we are sinful. God is righteous and we are defiled. There is therefore no way for us to approach God on our ground. If we do, we will be smitten to death immediately. The only way in which people can draw near to God is through offerings like these. For all these different kinds of offerings are but pictures and types of the various aspects of Christ—what Christ is and what He does for us. It is only on the ground of Christ that we are able to come near to God to worship and serve Him. Hence

Christ is the way to God, and there is no other way. If we want to worship and serve God, we have to come *through* Christ, *in* Christ, *with* Christ, and *by* Christ. It is all of Christ. He is the offering by which we are able to come before God and worship.

The burnt offering speaks of our Lord Jesus, who offered himself spotless to God by the eternal Spirit in order to purify our conscience from dead works, that we may worship the living God (see Hebrews 9:14). A burnt offering is a whole offering, one that is totally burned and completely offered to God. It is a voluntary love offering. Our Lord Jesus, because of His love of the Father and His love for us, voluntarily gave himself up to be that burnt offering to God for us. And the spirit lying behind that burnt offering is found in Philippians 2. There we are told that our Lord Jesus, who, though being equal with God did not consider this as something to be grasped at and held onto, emptied himself to take the form of a slave. And being in the fashion of a man, He further humbled himself and died on the cross for us as a burnt offering for God. The thought of burnt offering has more to do with the idea of acceptance than of atonement. Leviticus 1 does in fact touch upon atonement or the covering of sin; but, basically, a burnt offering has more to do with the matter of acceptance—namely, that we may be accepted by God in the Beloved (see Ephesians 1:6). We are accepted in the Beloved, and to be accepted simply means we are taken into God's favor. We are being put in a position of grace and favor, accepted by God, and it is all because of the Lord Jesus. He is our burnt offering.

The second offering is the oblation or meal offering. It speaks of the life of our Lord Jesus on earth. He is the grain of wheat that falls into the ground and dies (see John 12:24). He is ground into fine powder. Every area of His life is holy, pure, fine, sinless; and yet, like a meal offering, He is made into a cake and baked. In other words, our Lord Jesus has gone through the suffering of the cross so that He may be food to God and food to us.

In a meal offering there are always the elements of frankincense, salt and oil. Frankincense simply means "frank incense." The fragrance is open and frank; it is not inhibited. Salt always speaks of permanency, while oil speaks of the Holy Spirit. Let us look at the life of the Lord Jesus. There is always that open fragrance about Him. It cannot be hidden; it is always there. Wherever He is, with whomever He is in contact, in whatever He does, there is always a fragrance coming out. He cannot help it. There is also that permanency in Him—everything He does, everything He says, is eternal. And it is all done in the power of the Holy Spirit.

Yet, in a meal offering there are two ingredients prohibited: one is leaven and the other is honey. Leaven speaks of wickedness or corruption, either in teaching, in doctrine, conduct or manner. Honey, on the other hand, speaks of natural sweetness. There is not a natural but a supernatural, divine sweetness in Christ Jesus.

A meal offering is for God's pleasure. Therefore, when the Lord Jesus was on earth, heaven was so pleased that it opened up and declared: "This is My beloved Son, in whom I am well pleased and delighted" (see, e.g., Matthew 3:17, 17:5). He, like the meal offering, is for God's pleasure. Is it not wonderful that when the Lord Jesus entered this world to be a man, His whole life was a pleasure to God? Actually, the whole creation— including man—was created for God's pleasure (see Revelation 4:11). We were created for God's pleasure, but we gave Him much sorrow. But thank God, through Christ Jesus, mankind has again become a pleasure to God. Is that not marvelous? It is the grace of God.

Peace Offering

The third offering, which is the peace offering, speaks of Christ as our peace. Having been justified by faith, we have peace with God through our Lord Jesus Christ (see Romans 5:1). Christ is our peace (see Ephesians 2:14a). He has not only made peace between us and God by reconciling us to God, but He has also effected peace among us human beings. He has brought both Gentiles and Jews together and has taken away the middle wall of partition so that we may be brought into one new man: having peace and approaching God together (see Ephesians 2:11-15 AV). Christ is our peace offering.

In a peace offering, the fat of an animal is removed and completely burned to God for Him to consume. Fat, in Scripture, speaks of the inward abundance, the abundance—spiritually speaking—of inward life. Today, we do not like fat, but fat actually means that there is so much life that it becomes like fat stored within a person. And so, in the abundance of our Lord's inward life and energy He has so satisfied God's righteousness that He has reconciled us to God.

Then, of course, we know in the peace offering that not only God has His part but also the priest has his part, the offerer and his family have their part, and even the strangers and the neighbors have a portion in it as well. This speaks of communion and fellowship. But how can we have fellowship with God and have fellowship with one another? Clearly, the basis of such fellowship is Christ, our peace offering.

Sin Offering

The fourth offering is the sin offering, and I think this is very clear. "He who knows no sin, our Lord Jesus, is made sin for us that we may become the righteousness of God" (see II Corinthians 5:21).

"Christ bore our sins in his body on the tree, in order that being dead to sins, we may live to righteousness" (see I Peter 2:24).

When we were yet sinners, Christ died for us (see Romans 5:8). It is because of His death, because of the blood of the Lord Jesus that is brought into the holiest of all to atone for sins, that our sins are all forgiven. Therefore, Christ is also our sin offering.

TRESPASS OFFERING

The fifth offering is the trespass offering. Everything surrounding this offering not only speaks of Christ dying for us once for all and cleansing us from our past sins, but also speaks of His daily cleansing us.

"If we walk in the light as God is in the light, we have fellowship with one another, and the blood of Jesus Christ, his Son cleanses us from all sin" (see I John 1:7).

We have an Advocate with the Father, Jesus, the Righteous (see I John 2:1b). So whenever we fall into sin in our daily life and we become defiled, Christ Jesus—our trespass offering— is there cleansing us day after day in order that our fellowship with God may not be interrupted.

In these five offerings we find the basis of worship: it is through Christ. When we see Him as our offerings, when we appropriate Him as all of this, then praise and worship will come forth from within us. *Worship* actually means "worth-ship." In other words, worship simply means an acknowledgment that Christ is worthy; and because we see that He is worthy, therefore, we worship Him, praise Him, appreciate Him, and we love Him. The ground of worship is Christ—all that He is and what He has done for us.

LAWS OF THE OFFERINGS

Leviticus 6:8—7 discusses the laws of the offerings. The offerings themselves speak of *worship*; the laws governing the offerings have reference to the *worshipers*. In the offerings we see the *sacrifice*, but in the laws we see the *offerers*: what the offerers should do with these offerings, and what participation they have in them. Therefore, in the laws of the offerings we find the act of identification. First of all, the offerer is identified with his offering. Whenever something was to be offered, the offerer placed his hand on the head of the animal to show that he was identified with the offering.

Let us realize that we become worshipers because we are identified with Christ. He is the reason for our worship. We appreciate Him and appropriate all that He is to us, and that makes us worshipers.

Then we also see in the laws that there is the necessity for participation. These offerers participated in all these offerings except the burnt offering, the latter of which was all for God. For instance, in the meal offering, the priests burned a portion to God and then they ate the rest. In other words, we share in and enjoy what Christ is to us, and the same with the other offerings. There is a participation, a sharing, and a communion involved in these offerings.

PRIESTHOOD OF BELIEVERS

In Leviticus 8—10 there is described for us the consecration of the priests; in Leviticus 11—22 there is discussed the separation of the people. Let us bear in mind that we today are God's priests as well as God's people. In the Old Testament period this division came into being because of the Israelites' sin. After God delivered the children of Israel and brought them to Mount Sinai, He said to them: "If you will keep My commandments and My covenant, you will be a peculiar people to Me. You will be My people, a people of My possession and a kingdom, a nation of priests" (see Exodus 19:5-6). They were not only people but also priests. So, today, through the finished work of Christ which is a complete and perfect redemption, we are *both* God's priests and God's people. For us, there is no more such division. In the Old

Testament era there was indeed this division—the priests were priests and the rest of the people were the laity. Today, we cannot divide the people from the priests. There are to be no priesthood and laity categories anymore. All believers are priests as well as being the people of God. Every believer is a priest as well as a part of the people of God. Therefore, we will not try to divide them; we instead will put these chapters together and live out the reality which lies behind them.

HOLINESS

In these chapters there is one characteristic which stands out over all things mentioned. Whether it concerns the priests or concerns the people, the one word which stands out above all others is *holy*. Hallowed, separated, consecrated—these various meanings all convey the same thought. God is seeking for true worshipers who worship Him in spirit and truth; but in order to worship God we have to have in ourselves a certain character. And what is that supreme overall character which God requires of His worshipers? It is holiness, separation. God himself declared repeatedly: "Be thou holy because I am holy" (see, e.g., Leviticus 11:44-45, 19:2, 20:26). There must be a sameness—a suitability, a correspondence—between God and the worshiper. As a matter of fact, it is always true that who or what we worship gradually characterizes us. If we worship an idol, gradually we will become like that idol. If we worship the living God, gradually we will become like Him. You and I are taking up His character. That is the reason why, in worshiping God, the character of the worshiper is very, very important. If we want to be true worshipers, God requires that we be a separated people, a holy priesthood.

The reason for holiness is quite simple. Again and again we find that this explanation appears throughout these chapters. The Lord repeatedly declared: "I am the Lord Thy God." That is the reason for holiness. It is because He is our God. He is the One whom we worship. Therefore, He demands that we worship Him in holiness. "Worship the Lord in the beauty of holiness," the Scriptures tell us. Indeed, that is what the psalmist said (see Psalm 29:2b, cf. I Chronicles 16:29). We have to worship God in the beauty of holiness. Otherwise, our worship will not be accepted; it will bring reproach to God, and God will not be pleased.

The opposite of *holy* is not *sin*. The opposite of *sin* is *righteousness*. The opposite of *holiness* is *commonness*, to be common or ordinary. God wants us to be special. In essence He declares to us in His word that, "you are My peculiar people" (see Titus 2:14; I Peter 2:9a). God has separated us from the world because He demands separation. We need to be separated not only from the world but even from the religious world. We also need to be separated from ourselves, the old flesh. We need to be separated from anything that is not of God, so that we can be dedicated to God. Separation or holiness has two sides to its basic meaning: the one is a separation *from* and the other a separation *unto*. We are being set apart *from* all that is not of God, and we are being set apart for all that is *unto* God. That is holiness. Therefore, it requires that all those who worship God must take upon themselves the character of holiness. Again we say that the only reason why we must be holy is because God is holy.

With the children of Israel it was more the case of an outward separation. There were certain things they should not do and certain things they must do, and that separated them from other peoples. They were also separated from the world because of what they ate and what they did not eat. In the book of Leviticus we are told that there were unclean things the Israelites should not eat and, accordingly, that was to separate them from others. Indeed, that is the reason why the Israelites considered the Gentiles as dogs because they ate all these unclean foods. With the children of Israel it had more to do with outward things which thus governed their separation; but of course, with us today our separation is an inward matter: it is the life of Christ in us that separates us, and as the life of Christ begins to grow in us, we become more and more separated. It is no longer a matter of outward things anymore. Of course, it will overflow towards these outward things, there is no doubt about that; but it has to begin with an inward life; and once that occurs then, gradually, we take upon ourselves the character of Christ. And as Christ is being formed in us, the wall of separation from the world and from anything that is not of God rises higher and higher until, finally, in the New Jerusalem we shall have never seen such a high wall in the whole world (see Revelation 21:10-17). At that moment we shall experience complete separation. Holiness is therefore most important for the people and house of God.

SET FEASTS

From Leviticus 23 to 26 we learn of the set feasts. Worship is more than simply a personal, individual matter; it is also a corporate act. So the children of Israel had certain seasons in which they were called to assemble together to draw near to God, to worship Him and to serve Him together as a nation. And these convocations, as it were, are the set feasts.

It is true that we do not worship God only corporately without there also being that individual, personal experience of worship. Today, the problem is that many people make this matter of worship a place they go to on Sunday morning for worship, but during the rest of the week they never worship. That is not worship, because worship is a daily life experience. True worshipers worship God in spirit and truth continually. In other words, it is no longer a matter of time and space; it has transcended these limiting factors. So whether we are at home, in the office, or working—wherever we are and whatever we are doing—our whole life ought to be one continual worship unto God. That is worship. It is no longer limited to a certain place and time.

Unfortunately, today many people are still doing that,

thinking that Sunday morning is worship and Sunday afternoon is recreation. Too many shelve worship; they relegate it to an insignificant place in their lives. On the other hand, we realize worship is corporate, which is good. Unfortunately, there are people who do not worship with others anymore. They say, "I worship God, I don't need anybody else, just God and me." So they stay at home and worship. And some others simply turn on the radio or the television and worship by that means. They do not assemble and meet with other people anymore. On this issue, however, the word of God is very clear: yes, worship is personal, but it is also corporate. It is the will of God that we should come together from time to time to worship God together (see Hebrews 10:25; cf. Acts 2:42).

SABBATH

These set feasts the children of Israel had were simply fixed times for them to draw near to God together—holy convocations. It is very interesting that in Leviticus 23 Sabbath is mentioned first, and yet it is not listed in the set feasts that follow. Actually, Sabbath *is* a set feast, no doubt about that, but it is not grouped with the other seven. This is because Sabbath is the basis for all the other seven feasts; it provides the foundation for all the other feasts.

What is Sabbath? Sabbath signifies rest. Why can a person rest? It is because the necessary work has been done. The work of Christ is already finished, and we are in the good of that finished work of Christ. Therefore, we can come together to restfully celebrate. Assembling together is not trying to come and obtain something in order to pacify ourselves or to induce ourselves to rest. On the contrary, we all are to come with a Sabbath spirit because we have already rested in Christ. Hence, we all come to celebrate and glorify God. Therefore, Sabbath is the basis of all the other set feasts, all of which speak of Christ and what Christ has done for us.

PASSOVER

Christ is our Paschal Lamb (see I Corinthians 5:7). As it was at the first Passover Feast in Egypt when the blood of slain lambs had been sprinkled and the angel of death had passed over the homes of the Israelites, even so for us today, it is because of Christ, *the* Paschal Lamb—whose blood has been shed, has been accepted by us and sprinkled on our hearts—that we have come out of death into life. Christ is indeed our Passover Lamb, and thus death's angel has passed over us. Let us thank God for that!

FEAST OF UNLEAVENED BREAD

In relation to the Passover Feast there is the feast of unleavened bread. We have to celebrate this feast with unleavened bread—that is, in sincerity and truth, and not with leavened bread—a symbol of wickedness and malice. Once we accept Christ as our Paschal Lamb, we then begin the feast of unleavened bread for seven days, and seven speaks of fullness. Which is to say that after we are saved by the blood of the Lamb, from then on our whole life is to be lived in the reality of the feast of unleavened bread as we celebrate, live and work. Our whole life from then on, personally and corporately, is a feast of unleavened bread. There should be no malice or wickedness, but all of life should be characterized by sincerity and truth. That is the way we should live before God.

FEAST OF FIRSTFRUITS

The third set feast is the feast of the firstfruits that centrally involves the waved sheaf. At the beginning of the Jewish year there is the barley harvest. When the people harvest the barley, they take a sheaf of the harvest and bring it to the temple and offer it to God. By this symbolic act they celebrate the feast of the firstfruits. When we apply this to the New Testament time, it speaks of resurrection—the resurrection of our Lord Jesus (see I Corinthians 15:20, 23). Christ is raised from the dead as the firstfruits of those who have fallen. He is the firstfruits of resurrection, and after Him shall come those who believe in Him. Our Lord Jesus has not only lived a life of purity, He has not only died on the cross and become our Passover, He is also raised from the dead. Therefore, one day, we all shall be raised.

PENTECOST

Firstfruits is followed by the feast of Pentecost; and of course, Pentecost has its spiritual counterpart in the New Testament book of Acts in chapter 2. We are told that there were one hundred and twenty believers who on the day of Pentecost had gathered in the upper room and were praying; and suddenly, there was a hard blowing that filled the house. They were filled with the Holy Spirit, and that was the beginning of the church. The one hundred and twenty became a body of one hundred and twenty members. This body continues to grow, until one day, when the body of Christ—the church—is fully grown, Christ will come back and receive the church to be His bride.

The first four set feasts are celebrated during the beginning months of the year, and then there is a lapse of time until the end of the sacred year. For the Jewish people, July is towards the end of the sacred year. At the beginning of the civil year, there are still three more set feasts.

BLOWING OF TRUMPETS

First is the feast of the blowing of trumpets. On the first day of the seventh month (beginning of the civil year) the priest will blow a horn. Of course, this has application to the Jewish nation, but here we would like to apply it to Christ and to us. So we can probably say that the blowing of horns speaks of reformation. After the church had its beginning on the day of Pentecost in the first century, it had continued on and on until, gradually, the church lost its testimony and sank into the world. Then the awakening began; so, historically speaking, probably the blowing of horns refers to the Reformation that occurred in the sixteenth century. There was a great awakening among God's people and various aspects of this have continued on and on up to the present day.

DAY OF ATONEMENT

On the tenth day of the seventh month there is a day of atonement, which is a very important day. It is a day of repentance, a day of humiliation before the Lord, a day of great significance because this is the day of atonement. How can we today apply this in relation to ourselves? Probably, this set feast refers to the last days as God's people begin to appreciate more and more the work of our Lord Jesus. They begin to see more and more of God's eternal purpose with His people, and because of this, how it humbles them. How they repent before God!

The more we see God's purpose the more we are humbled because we do not find ourselves in the right place. How we need to repent before God! And because of this repentance, by the grace of God, He will raise up a remnant—an overcoming people—that will answer to God's heart. So, probably, the set feast of atonement has its application in our day to the closing days of the age of grace..

FEAST OF BOOTHS

The last of the feasts is the feast of booths when the children of God assembled together for a period and began to live in booths. It was a time of great joy because they were reminded of what God had done for them through the years. Probably, this refers to the kingdom age. One day, the kingdom shall come and God's people can truly rejoice. Today is the day of our humiliation, but one day there shall be a day of glory when Christ shall be glorified and shall lead many sons into glory.

Hence, here are all these set feasts—signifying corporate worship. We come together to appreciate the Lord together and to celebrate and worship Him.

VOWS OF DEVOTION

A very fitting end to the book of Leviticus is found in chapter 27. It is concerned with the vows of devotion. Leviticus begins with an offering—which speaks of Christ. Leviticus ends with speaking of the people who are so touched by the mercies of God, who have been so affected by all that God has done for them, that they make vows of devotion. In other words, they want to devote themselves to God—not only their possessions, their houses and their lands, but even themselves. Surely that is the right thing to do.

When we realize how much God has done for us, when we realize what Christ is to us, and as we are gradually maturing in the Lord, is it not the most spontaneous, natural thing for us to devote ourselves to Him? We want to give ourselves to Him. The love of Christ constrains us, knowing that One died for all, and we all died. And now we live for Him, who lived and died for us (see II Corinthians 5:14-15). Therefore, like the children of Israel in olden times, there shall be people today who want to devote their lives to the Lord and give themselves totally to Him.

Indeed, worship *is* a life of devotion. Worship is simply devoting your life to the Lord. You live for Him; you let Him live in you; you allow Him to do whatever He wants with you; you give up your right over yourself and let Him have the rights over you. It is not how you want to serve or what you want to do for Him. No. It is what *He* wants to do with you. That is worship. How can we say we worship Him when we want to do what we want to do? How can we say we serve Him when we do what we feel is good? It is only in a life of devotion that He has full rights over us. Anything that is devoted to God loses its right. The right then belongs to God. He can do anything He likes. If He wants to throw it away, fine. If He wants to use it, good. It is up to Him. It is devoted to God.

However, we find in Leviticus 27 that even in this matter of the people devoting their lives to God, there was established a gradual scale of value. When a person back then devoted himself to God, the priest would check with him and say, "How old are you?" If the priest learned that the devotee was over sixty years old, the price, the value of his devotion, went down. In other words, the usefulness of such a devotee was diminished. But if a devoted person was twenty or thirty, he obtained the highest estimation. It was all determined according to the shekel of the sanctuary. We all need to be devoted to God, but not all devotedness is the same in value. Back then, it was evaluated according to the shekel of the sanctuary, but in our day that speaks of spiritual growth. How we need to grow in the Lord! Paul said, "I am what I am by the grace of God" (see I Corinthians 15:10a).

How do we grow? Of course, we grow by the grace of God. If grace is taken away, we amount to zero. But the grace of God is always sufficient: it is abundant, never ending. Accordingly, if the grace of God is towards us day by day, then we ought to be those who are growing continuously. Unfortunately, sometimes we waste the grace of God; we may even despise His grace; we may step away from it. And if we do so, we will not measure up: our devotedness will diminish in value because God does not have us as He should have us.

Is not this something which we should consider before God? What am I worth to Him? He is worth everything to me, and that causes me to worship Him. But after He has done all that for me, am I worth anything to Him? Am I of some value to Him? Am I of some value to His kingdom, of some value to

His purpose? This is what God is looking for in His people, that we may be of great value to Him. But let us never forget that whatever value we have is by His grace; there is nothing of which to boast: I am what I am by the grace of God. And this is the message of the book of Leviticus.

Let us pray:

Dear heavenly Father, Thou art seeking for true worshipers, those who worship in spirit and truth. Oh, how we praise and thank Thee for all the provisions Thou hast provided for us in Christ Jesus that we, today, may be worshipers, true worshipers; and we do desire to be true worshipers. We do want to worship Thee in spirit and truth. So Father, we do pray that Thou wilt use these few words, if Thou please, to touch our hearts and bring us into that place where we can truly worship Thee and be true worshipers. Oh, how we praise and thank Thee, knowing Thy worth, and we do want to be worth something to Thee; and it is all for Thy glory. We ask in the name of our Lord Jesus. Amen.

NUMBERS

THE WALK OF GOD

Numbers 1:1-4—And Jehovah spoke to Moses in the wilderness of Sinai in the tent of meeting, on the first of the second month, in the second year after their departure from the land of Egypt, saying, Take the sum of the whole assembly of the children of Israel, after their families, according to their fathers' houses, by the number of the names, every male, according to their polls; from twenty years and upward, all that go forth to military service in Israel: ye shall number them according to their hosts, thou and Aaron. And with you there shall be a man for every tribe, a man who is the head of his father's house.

Numbers 9:15-23—And on the day that the tabernacle was set up, the cloud covered the tabernacle of the tent of testimony; and at even it was upon the tabernacle as the appearance of fire, until the morning. So it was continually: the cloud covered it, and at night it was as the appearance of fire. And when the cloud rose from the tent, then the children of Israel journeyed; and at the place where the cloud stood still, there the children of Israel encamped. According to the commandment of Jehovah the children of Israel journeyed, and according to the commandment of Jehovah they remained encamped; all the days that the cloud dwelt upon the tabernacle they encamped. And when the cloud was long upon the tabernacle many days, then the children of Israel kept the charge of Jehovah, and journeyed not. And if it were so that the cloud was a few days upon the tabernacle, according to the commandment of Jehovah they encamped, and according to the commandment of Jehovah they journeyed. And if it were so that the cloud was there from the evening until the morning, and that the cloud was taken up in the morning, then they journeyed; or a day and a night, and the cloud was taken up, they journeyed; or two days, or a month, or many days, when the cloud was long upon the tabernacle, dwelling upon it, the children of Israel remained encamped, and journeyed not; but when it was taken up, they journeyed. At the commandment of Jehovah they encamped, and at the commandment of Jehovah they journeyed: they kept the charge of Jehovah according to the commandment of Jehovah through Moses.

Numbers 26:1-4—And it came to pass after the plague, that Jehovah spoke to Moses and to Eleazar the son of Aaron the priest, saying, Take the sum of the whole assembly of the children of Israel, from twenty years old and upward, according to their fathers' houses, all that go forth to military service in Israel. And Moses and Eleazar the priest spoke with them in the plains of Moab by the Jordan of Jericho, saying, From twenty years old and upward ...; as Jehovah had commanded Moses and the children of Israel, who went forth out of the land of Egypt.

Numbers 26:63-65—These are they that were numbered by Moses and Eleazar the priest, who numbered the children of Israel in the plains of Moab, by the Jordan of Jericho. But among these there was not a man numbered by Moses and Aaron the priest, who numbered the children of Israel in the wilderness of Sinai. For Jehovah had said of them, They shall surely die in the wilderness. And there was not left a man of them, save Caleb the son of Jephunneh, and Joshua the son of Nun.

Let us pray:

Dear heavenly Father, how we do praise and thank Thee that through the blood of Thy beloved Son and the new and living way which He has opened for us through His flesh, we may have such grace and boldness to enter the holiest of all, behind the veil, and to behold the glory of the Lord with unveiled face. We thank Thee that we may hear Thy voice, that we may see Thy glory and be transformed according to Thy image by the Lord the Spirit. So our Father, as we come together this morning, our hearts are full of joy knowing that Thou art good, so good to us. In Christ Jesus. Amen.

The book of Numbers is the fourth volume of the Pentateuch, the five-volume book of Moses. Genesis shows us the *will* of God. His will is to have a man, the man after His own heart; and, of course, that man is none other than the Lord Jesus Christ; and through Him there comes into being the corporate man, the church. Exodus tells us of the *work* of God. Because man failed and sinned against God, He began to undertake the work of redemption. Redemption is not only rescuing people from the pathway towards hell, it also is drawing people to God himself so that this redeemed people may become the dwelling place of God. Then the book of Leviticus is the *way* of God. After a people have been redeemed, God calls them to come to Him to worship Him. They are to be worshipers because He has opened the way for them to himself. And, now, this is followed by what is recorded in the book of Numbers, which speaks of the *walk* of God. God calls us to walk with Him until we reach His destination for us.

The title for this book of Numbers was derived from the fact of the two numberings of the children of Israel. At the time of the beginning of this book the first numbering of the children of Israel occurred at Mount Sinai, and then again, in the time of chapter 26, there is the second numbering of the children of Israel, who were preparing their way to enter the Promised Land. Hence, this is the reason why the book is called Numbers. Let us briefly contrast this book with Leviticus.

The book of Leviticus tells of the believer's worship whereas the book of Numbers speaks of the believer's walk. In Leviticus the sanctuary—the tabernacle—is most prominent.

In Numbers, however, it is the wilderness that is mostly in view. We are told in Leviticus that God calls His people to come and fellowship with Him, but in Numbers the call of God to His people is that they may be faithful to Him in their walk. And, finally, the book of Leviticus speaks of our privilege whereas the book of Numbers speaks of our responsibility.

This book of Numbers tells us the story of the children of Israel from the time they began to journey from Mount Sinai up to the time they arrived at the plains of Moab—roughly thirty-nine years. God had delivered the Israelites out of Egypt and brought them to Mount Sinai. And by the time at the end of the book of Exodus, which was in the first month of the second year, they had set up the tabernacle. With the tabernacle having been set up, God began to speak to the children of Israel out of the tabernacle, calling them to come and worship Him; and as we saw previously, that is the book of Leviticus. Then, at the time of the beginning of Numbers, which was in the second month of the second year after their departure from the land of Egypt, God again spoke out of the tabernacle or tent of meeting to the Israelites and said, "Number the children of Israel." So, if one counts from that day on up to the moment when they arrived at the plain of Moab ready to enter the Promised Land, the period covered approximately thirty-eight to thirty-nine years. That will provide some idea of the history of the book of Numbers.

Before we go into this book, it will help us if we know briefly what this book is all about. It can be outlined as follows:

The first ten chapters (Numbers 1—10:10) tell us how God prepared the children of Israel for their journey from Mount Sinai toward Canaan.

From Numbers 10:11 through Numbers 14 we are told of their journeying from Mount Sinai up to Kadesh-barnea, which is at the southern border of the Promised Land.

Chapters 15—19 give us some incidents which happened during their thirty-eight years of wanderings because of their rebellion. There is no record of the itinerary of these thirty-eight years. So far as God is concerned these years were wasted. Therefore, nothing is recorded of their itinerary during those thirty-eight years. Only a few other incidents are recorded.

From chapters 20 to 25 we are told that the Israelites started out again from Kadesh-barnea. After those wasted thirty-eight years of wandering, they had returned to Kadesh-barnea and launched forth again. Their history picks up from there and these chapters tell us of the last year, the thirty-eighth year. They had wandered for thirty-seven years and this was now the thirty-eighth year during which they would arrive at the plains of Moab.

Chapters 26 to 36 tell of the preparations for entering the Promised Land.

If we keep this outline in mind, it will probably help when studying this book of Numbers.

GOD'S FULL PURPOSE

This book tells us of the journeys of the children of Israel, and their journeying through the wilderness was according to the commandment of God. In this book we see the movement of God: He is moving on, leading His people forward. He does not lead His people out of Egypt only to let them stay in the wilderness. That is not God's purpose. His intent was to move on toward the ultimate end He had in mind for this people which was Canaan. God was moving on towards His full purpose, leading His people to walk with Him—to travel and journey with Him—until His tabernacle would be set up in the Promised Land and His people would be settled there. All of their journeyings were according to the commandment of God. He commanded them to move on; and if they were faithful and followed His commandment, they would move on with Him and arrive at His intended destination for them.

In a sense, is this not true with us today? We know that after

God has redeemed us and delivered us out of the world and out of sin, His purpose for us is not that we remain in the wilderness but that we move on into His full purpose for us. God is always moving on. He does not want us to halt in our Christian walk. Unfortunately, after they are saved, many of God's people simply stay put somewhere in a wilderness situation. They do not move on with God into His full purpose. We must understand that God's purpose for us is to move forward towards His ultimate end and purpose, and that is Christ and His riches; for Canaan, spiritually speaking, betokens the riches of Christ because Canaan was a land flowing with milk and honey. Spiritually speaking, it is an environment that is not lacking in anything, for Canaan symbolically speaks of the unsearchable riches of Christ. God's purpose for His people is always that. He does not want to barely save us, like a brand plucked out of the fire (see Amos 4:11; Zechariah 3:2; Jude 23; I Corinthians 3:15). Rather, God wants to save us abundantly into experiencing the unsearchable riches of Christ, and He is always moving forward towards that end. He is always leading us in that way and it is our responsibility to move on with Him, from station to station, until we enter into the fullness of Christ. Indeed, what after all, is the *church*? Is it not the body of Christ, which is the fullness of Him who fills all and in all (see Ephesians 1:22-23; Colossians 1:18-19; 2:9-10a). It is therefore the fullness of Christ that is in view here; and it is towards this fullness of Christ that God continually moves forward; and that, in short, constitutes our journey.

THE WILDERNESS JOURNEY

In one sense, wilderness is a necessity. When the children of Israel came out of Egypt, they had to pass through the wilderness in order to enter Canaan. The wilderness is part of God's ordained way of entering Canaan; but according to His word the days the children of Israel needed to spend in the wilderness should have been within a mere two years. From the time God had delivered them out of Egypt and brought them to Mount Sinai was a year. And then, if they were faithful to God, the distance from Mount Sinai (Mount Horeb), by way of Mount Seir to Kadesh-barnea, would actually have only been eleven days. In other words, within two years they should certainly have been out of the wilderness and into the Promised Land. Unfortunately, it took them forty years because of their unfaithfulness. On the one hand, the wilderness journey was a necessity; on the other hand, it should have been two years at most and not forty years in length.

Why was the wilderness journey a necessity for the Israelites? Deuteronomy provides us the answer and describes the experience of the wilderness:

"And thou shalt remember all the way which Jehovah thy God led thee these forty years in the wilderness, to humble thee, and to prove thee, to know what was in thy heart, whether thou wouldest keep his commandments or not. And he humbled thee, and suffered thee to hunger, and fed thee with the manna, which thou hadst not known, and which thy fathers knew not; that he might make thee know that man doth not live by bread alone, but by everything that goeth out of the mouth of Jehovah doth man live. Thy clothing grew not old upon thee, neither did thy foot swell, these forty years. And know in thy heart that, as a man chasteneth his son, so Jehovah thy God chasteneth thee; and thou shalt keep the commandments of Jehovah thy God, to walk in his ways, and to fear him" (8:2-6).

KNOWING OURSELVES

Speaking spiritually for us today, the wilderness journey is a necessity because it provides us with some important, necessary experiences. We are to experience a number of things in our own wilderness situation. First, we must have the experience of coming to know ourselves. At the beginning we do not really know ourselves; in fact, nobody knows himself or herself. Of course, before we believed in the Lord Jesus we did not know ourselves: we thought much better of ourselves than we actually were; we were sure we could please God; we believed we had righteousness—until finally we were convicted by the Holy Spirit and brought down to dust and ashes. We immediately repented and acknowledged that we had no goodness nor righteousness of our own, that all our righteousnesses were as filthy rags, and that that would not do (see Isaiah 64:6a). And because of all this, we humbled ourselves and accepted the Lord Jesus as our Savior. This does not mean, however, that because of this experience of salvation we know ourselves.

Unfortunately, after we are saved, we assume we are now a better person; we now have changed. It is true, we are a new creation; we have received a new life. But so far as our flesh— our natural life—is concerned, we have not changed a bit. Yet we do not realize this because we do not know ourselves; and because we do not know ourselves, we believe that since we have now been saved we are different—that what we could not do before we surely can do today: that previously we could not obey God but now we can, that previously we could not keep the commandments of God but now we can, that we could not please God before but now we can. Instead of sinning we try to please God with our flesh, that is to say, with the energy of our old flesh and in the power of the natural life. Instead of living by the new life that has been given to us by which to live, we go back and live according to the power of our old life and say, "Now we are able; we will keep God's Law, we will do it." Which is just like the children of Israel who had said, "We will do everything which God has commanded. You do not need to speak directly to us; we are afraid of that. Rather, speak indirectly and we will follow everything You say" (see Exodus 20:19).

This was not only the attitude of the Israelites, this is also our attitude. Because of this, in our own wilderness experience we are to be humbled. God uses our wilderness journey to humble us that we may know what is truly in our heart, that we may come to see that there is absolutely no good in us, that is, in our flesh. That is why our old man was crucified with Christ; but we do not realize that. So the wilderness journey is in that sense very precious. God gives us opportunity after opportunity to know ourselves as to what is truly in our heart; to discover that our heart is deceitful above all things; to discover how unfaithful and unbelieving we are, how prone to sin and rebellion we are, that we have not changed one whit except for the fact that we have the redemption of the Lord.

KNOWING GOD'S CARE

Through the wilderness journey we also have the opportunity to know the care of God. We come to know not only our weaknesses and our impossibilities; we also come to know the all-sufficient, loving, faithful care of God. That is why God sometimes allowed the Israelites to be in hunger in order for Him to shower manna upon them and thus be able to show them that man does not live by bread alone but by every word that proceeds from the mouth of God. Our own wilderness experience enables us to know God, to know His care, to realize how dependable and faithful He is. On the one hand, we come to know our undependability; on the other hand, we come to know the dependability of God. We come to know our unfaithfulness, but we also come to know the faithfulness of God; and thus we will not lean upon ourselves anymore but will henceforth cast ourselves completely upon Him. What an important lesson to learn!

KNOWING GOD'S CHASTENING

By means of the wilderness experience we additionally are to be disciplined and chastened by the Lord: whom the Lord loves He chastens (see Hebrews 12:6). Because He loves us, therefore, He has to discipline us. We are wild. We need to be chastened in order to have all this foolishness in us removed so that we may grow from babyhood and childhood into manhood and womanhood. In other words, God's chastening is purposeful: to make us sons and daughters of God; and hence, through these chastenings many lessons are to be learned in our personal wilderness journey.

After we believe in the Lord Jesus and are saved, we find that God is moving us onward. He does not want us to stay put anywhere because if we do so, we remain in the wilderness. He wants us to move on from station to station until, finally, we know ourselves, we know Him, and we begin to grow up and enter into the unsearchable riches of Christ. The quicker we enter into His riches, the better. We do not need to linger in a wilderness situation for forty years; two years should be enough. Of course, I am not speaking of physical years; I am speaking here in a spiritual sense.

THE WORLD

What we have just now considered has been a discussion of the wilderness in spiritual terms; but what, physically speaking, is the wilderness for us believers today? In His redeeming us, God has delivered us out of Egypt—that is, out of the world; but we obviously are still in the world. Physically, we are indeed still in the world, even though, spiritually speaking, we are out of it. Therefore, to us believers today, physically speaking, wilderness speaks of the world. Before we were saved we thought of the world as being like Egypt of old, a place of riches and wealth: indeed, the storehouse of the world. However, after we are saved, our viewpoint, estimate and outlook towards the world are entirely changed. We no longer see the world as Egypt, a land rich with corn, with leaks and garlic, with fishes and all such other savory and fragrant foods;

instead, we begin to view the world as a barren wilderness. In other words, we now do not see anything in the world that can satisfy us.

The world to us today is a wilderness, no longer our home anymore. We are simply traveling through the world and journeying towards our eternal home in God. And because we are not *of* the world but are still *in* the world, therefore so long as we live here we shall have many trials, testings, afflictions, sufferings and tribulations. These are the things which we can expect. Do not think that suffering is strange to a believer; suffering is common to a believer. We live in a hostile wilderness situation, and what, then, can we expect in such an unfriendly environment?—sufferings, testings, trials, afflictions. But thank God, out of them all He is teaching, educating and maturing us so that we may grow up and enter into the riches that are in Christ. As long as the Lord wants us to live in this world, let us not think of dying. Living is most worthwhile, yet not because the world is attractive but because God has much to teach us and to mature us as long as we are in this world. As a matter of fact, this world is a training place. We are being trained for our future vocation. One day we shall serve God as He has ordained for us, and today, we are simply being trained to do so. And hence, if we consider this matter more deeply, we shall see that it is a wonderful thing that God has arranged that we continue to live on earth till our training be completed.

Another point we need to remember is that this traveling, this journeying, is not only a personal matter. It is true that each and every Israelite was journeying, but the whole idea of journeying back then was corporate in nature. God was moving His people onward towards His goal for them. Oftentimes we speak of spiritual pilgrimage as a very personal experience, and that is true: each one of us believers is on a spiritual pilgrimage and it is very personal: at times we feel as though we are the only one on the road. All of that is quite true. Yet let us not forget that simultaneously God is moving us all together as an assembly of saints, even as He did with the assembly—the congregation—of the children of Israel. God today is moving His people towards His end. If we look back through the past twenty centuries we shall find that God has been moving His church onward, step by step, station by station, towards that ultimate end of His. This is something very exciting, and which ought to motivate us to move on together with our Christian brothers and sisters.

THE NUMBERINGS

In this book of Numbers, there is first of all the numbering of the children of Israel. In the book's first four chapters there are actually three different numberings recorded, but the main one was the numbering of the children of Israel. Out of every family and tribe, all the males, twenty years old and upward who would go forth into military service, were counted. That was the main numbering. The numbering of the firstborn from one-month-old and upward, and the numbering of the Levites from one-month-old and upward, these both speak of all the firstborn belonging to God. We remember how back in Egypt the angel of destruction had struck all the firstborn; so God said, "All the firstborn belong to Me" (see Exodus 13:2b). That is why you find here the numbering of the firstborn from one-month-old. In other words, through the firstborn God was telling His people that all of them belonged to Him. Those who are redeemed are no longer their own, they belong to Him. This numbering of the firstborn from one-month-old corresponds to the numbering of the Levites of one-month-old because the Levites were called to serve God instead of the children of Israel. So if we put this together in spiritual terms, it means that all of us who are redeemed of the Lord belong to Him— that we are all Levites and all are to serve God from the very beginning. You and I do not need to wait until we are twenty years old before we begin to serve God. As soon as we are born again, from one-month-old and upward, we are to serve Him. This has to do with service.

KEEPING THE TESTIMONY OF GOD

Let us notice that as believers we have many hats to wear. We are the redeemed children of God and we belong to God; and as such, we are all Levites and priests, and we are to serve Him. Then, too, we are soldiers in military service who are the army of the Lord. So, the numbering here of the children of Israel was that of those who were to be the soldiers. The children of Israel were going to travel through the wilderness; but before they started traveling, God numbered all the males twenty years old and upward who would go forth into military service as the army of the Lord. In order to go forth into battle a person needs to grow up somewhat. The one-month-old could not fight; he needed to be twenty years old. It thus means that a maturing, a growing up is required; and as the person begins to mature, he is then able to bear arms and fight the fight of God.

Spiritually speaking, those who were numbered from twenty years old and upward and who would go into military service actually represented the whole congregation. Each and every believer is not only a redeemed person, not only a priest and Levite to serve God, but is also supposed to be growing up and become strong enough to equip himself or herself as a man or woman of God to fight the fight of the Lord. If we apply all this to us today, it means that everyone is called into such spiritual warfare.

When the children of Israel came out of Egypt and started their journey, they were a disorganized, motley multitude. They were not in the least organized, and furthermore, a mixed multitude came out with them. Everything was confused and quite messy; but then, at Mount Sinai, God covenanted with His people and this people became a holy nation, a covenanted nation.

As a covenanted nation they were to be that corporate vessel of the testimony of God. And here in the book of Numbers it is very, very interesting that the tent of meeting—the tabernacle—is called the tabernacle of testimony (or, witness KJV). This is very special because only once is this term used in Leviticus (see 16:13), but here in the book of Numbers the tabernacle is called the tabernacle of the testimony (see 17:7-8; 18:2b).

As a covenanted people of God to whom God had committed himself, they were no longer like the rest of the nations. They were a nation taken out of the nations to be a peculiar people, a possession of God. As God called them to himself, He covenanted with them, and He committed himself to this people. In other words, the testimony of God was entrusted to this people. They were to testify that God is their God ... that God is in their midst ... that He is unique ... that He is living ... that He is the only God. This was to be their testimony as they traveled through the wilderness into the Promised Land. This is the reason they had to be organized into an army of the Lord. As the army of God they were to encamp around the tabernacle in order to protect it. They were to march in formation with the tabernacle in the midst of them. In other words, they had a responsibility to keep the charge of the commandment of God. They were a people to bear the testimony of God, and this was their battle. Of course, the nature of that battle changed as they went from the wilderness and towards the Promised Land. In the wilderness their battle was mainly a battling against the world, their flesh and sin, because these things would affect their testimony. They were in the wilderness as the army of God, fighting against the world, against the flesh and against sin so that the testimony of God might be maintained in their midst. But after they entered Canaan, they fought for possession; they fought for inheritance; they fought against the evil forces of the air, those unseen forces that lay behind the seven tribes of Canaan.

In a sense, is this not true of us today? We are God's covenanted people. At the Lord's Table, the cup is the cup of God's covenant. God covenanted with us a new covenant, and today the testimony of Jesus is entrusted to us as His people. We bear the testimony of Jesus as we travel through this world, and how that is very much attacked by the world's enticement: the lust of the flesh, the lust of the eyes, the pride of life. The things of the world try to affect and attack the testimony of Jesus in our midst. We find that our flesh and others' flesh try to attack and destroy this testimony of Jesus. Sin affects the testimony of Jesus. We Christians are daily battling against all these forces in order to keep the charge, to maintain the testimony of Jesus intact among us. This is a tremendous responsibility!

That is why the children of Israel had to be organized into an army in order to keep the testimony of God through the wilderness. After they were organized, then, of course, the center was the tabernacle. The tribes were encamped according to their standards—all according to God's ordering. No one could choose his place, but every position was ordained by the commandment of God and they stayed where He had put them.

Now if we transfer all of the above to our New Testament age, how good it is! Christ is our center, is He not, and we are all, as it were, encamped around Him. Christ is the Head and we are all the members of His body. We are all surrounding Him, and everyone is placed according to His ordering. You and I do not choose which member of the body of Christ we are. God has set us as members in His body, and wherever He sets us—that is the best place for us. How we need to be fitly framed and joined together even as the children of Israel were as they camped around the tabernacle. What a beautiful divine order! However, for us today, it is not a matter of an outward organization; it is an inward, organic ordering of the life of God in us. And as we center upon Christ, we will be fitly framed and joined together, and together we will keep the testimony of Jesus.

THE PILLAR OF CLOUD

When we come to chapters 9 and 10 we learn that God began to move the Israelites forward, and their journeyings were according to the commandments of God. Yet they were not moving all the time. If, with the numerous children and women among them, God's army were to be on the move constantly— even for but eleven days—many would die. So, we see how God moved them step by step towards the Promised Land by means of the cloud. After the tabernacle had been set up, the pillar of cloud for the first time descended upon the tabernacle. That, of course, speaks of the presence of God in their midst. As long as the cloud covered the tabernacle and remained there, the children of Israel remained encamped around the tabernacle and kept the charge of God; but, when the cloud began to lift and move, then they broke camp and moved on accordingly. Their movement was governed by the pillar of cloud. In other words, the presence of God governed all their journeyings. Sometimes the cloud was upon the tent one day and the next day it was lifted; accordingly, they started moving. At other times, they might stay put for a few days or even a month. They had no choice, saying, "Well, we have stayed here too long and we want to move." No, they remained encamped as long as the cloud stood still, and only moved when the cloud itself moved. They could not say, "We want to stay here a little longer." The cloud governed their journey.

How true it is today for us! Our spiritual journeying is governed by the presence of God. Today, God's presence in His church is through His Spirit. The Holy Spirit dwells in the church and He is responsible to move His people onward. Sometimes there will be an occasion for rest, a time for consolidation, and so the Holy Spirit will remain unmoved. Then there will be a time for journeying, for going forth; and as the Spirit leads, the people of God shall follow the Spirit and go on. In our spiritual journeying this is very important because sometimes we become impatient: "We have stayed here too long; we want to move." But if the Spirit of God does not move, how can we move? To where will we move? We will be out of God's order, out of God's way. But at other times, we become so cozy and so comfortable that we just want to stay put forever. If, for example, we come to an Elim, with all its fountains and palm trees, we would like to stay there longer, but God says, "No, you have to move on." And if, on the other hand, we come to a Marah, we say, "Oh, we do not want to stay here; we want to bypass it." But the Lord says we need to stay there. We cannot make our choice. We have to learn to follow the Holy Spirit. The presence of the Lord, as represented by the Spirit, will govern our journeying together as God's people.

THE SILVER TRUMPETS

The children of Israel were not only governed by the cloud, they were also governed by the blowing of the silver trumpets by the priests. The cloud gave them the general impression that the next move was about to begin, but the trumpet gave them the details—which camp would break up first, who would move first, who would be next. This was all governed by the silver trumpets and this was the way they moved on together.

Today, as God's people, our journeying must be governed by the Spirit of God, by the presence of the Lord; but at the same time, it is being reinforced, as it were, by the blowing of silver trumpets. Silver trumpets speak of prophetic ministry, because according to the New Testament, when a trumpet was blown with a specific note, the people would know what to do (see I Corinthians 14:8; cf. Numbers 10:9). Such a situation speaks to the fact that those who were near to God, such as the priests who were very close to the tabernacle, watched the cloud very carefully. When the cloud began to lift, immediately they responded and blew the trumpet and declared that it was time to move. In the body of Christ there are those close to the Lord who can discern the moving of the Spirit, and they will prophetically give utterances to the church. This is the way that the people of God will move forward.

THE DISCIPLINE OF GOD

Unfortunately, as soon as the children of Israel started to move, they began to murmur. During that whole journey, they murmured and rebelled against God, from Mount Sinai to Kadesh-barnea, an eleven-days journey (which, of course, took them much longer because of things happening). Even Miriam and Aaron became jealous of Moses. Murmur and rebellion had set in not only among the people but even among the leaders. All these rebellions and murmurings and unfaithfulness culminated in the negative report of the spies. The spies came back and said: "Indeed, this is a very, very good land; *but*, the people there are so tall. Both we and they looked upon ourselves as grasshoppers. The cities are walled up to heaven, and it is a land that devours people. We cannot go there; they will eat us up" (see Numbers 13:27-33).

Then the people cried and rebelled against God, and so He declared in response: "You have tested Me ten times, and now, this is the end. You will not be allowed to enter the Promised Land" (see Numbers 14:22-23).

There is one thing which we must notice here. After God took them out of Egypt, from Egypt to Mount Sinai they murmured and sinned against God, but He never chastened them. When they murmured, He catered to their every whim and gave them whatever they needed. He never said a word because that trip was governed totally by grace. But after they became a covenanted people with God, from then on to Kadesh-barnea and afterwards, whenever they murmured and rebelled and sinned against God, His discipline came upon them. In other words, God's dealing with His people had changed. It was not simply a matter of grace any longer. They were a covenanted people now and God had to deal with them according to His covenant. He disciplined them in order to restore them, and to make them grow; but when they refused to grow, then one day God said, "That is enough. This whole generation that does not believe in Me cannot enter the Promised Land. They think that their women and children will become hostages." So God said, "I will instead bring those children in." Yes, there was still the mercy, the grace and the faithfulness of God. None of that aspect of His relationship with the Israelites was affected, but the discipline of God did come upon that people, and consequently that whole generation was not able to enter the Promised Land.

These words are recorded for our education. You may recall how, in I Corinthians 10:1-12, the apostle Paul especially mentions those things which had happened to the Israelites in the wilderness—how the people had murmured and rebelled, how they had sinned against God, and how discipline had come upon this people as a result. And then the apostle Paul wrote this: "All these things are recorded for our sake, for our admonition, for those of us who live in this last age, so that we may learn these lessons."

Let us not think that we can stand in and of ourselves. If anyone thinks he can stand, beware lest he fall (see v. 12). We need to trust the Lord, depend upon Him and His grace, and upon His faithfulness all the time because there is no good in us. We cannot depend upon ourselves, but He is trustworthy and able to keep us if we commit ourselves to Him. So these events from the book of Numbers are lessons for us to learn. We need to learn these lessons. Yes, there is grace; but remember, because God loves us and we are His covenanted people, therefore, He will chasten and discipline us. I often say, "God does not punish us, but He disciplines us." There is a difference. Punishment is for the sake of some damage inflicted, but discipline is for recovery, for maturing. God

loves us and He does discipline us, but this is where we need to
learn to follow the Lord. When He disciplines us, let us submit
ourselves under His mighty hand and learn the lesson so that
we will not be like the children of Israel who did not believe
and rebelled against God until He had to say: "This generation
cannot enter the Promised Land."

PREPARATION TO ENTER THE PROMISED LAND

For thirty-eight years the children of Israel wandered from
Kadesh-barnea until they came back to Kadesh-barnea, and
during that period there is no record of their itinerary. You
cannot find it in the book of Numbers, even in the summary
given in its chapter 33 concerning all the stations to where they
had gone step by step. The record is completely silent. So far
as God was concerned, these were lost years.

We need to be careful before the Lord that we may be
faithful to Him. As He moves forward, we must move with
Him in order that we may not be unfaithful to Him and begin to
wander and wander. Otherwise, the days in which we wander
shall be lost days; they will not count; there will be no record of
them in heaven. May the Lord therefore have mercy upon us.

Thank God, after thirty-eight years, the Israelites came
again to the plains of Moab. God brought them back to the
border of Canaan and called Moses to number the children of
Israel the second time. When they finished the numbering, they
discovered that none of the first generation was there. Every
one of that generation who did not believe in God had fallen in
the wilderness except two—Joshua and Caleb.

God's purpose is to lead us into the unsearchable riches of
Christ that we may be the fullness of Christ. This is true. And
God will do this because He is faithful; He cannot deny himself.
But whether we are able to enter into that fullness now depends
upon our faithfulness to Him. If we are not faithful, if we do
not believe in Him, we may fall in the wilderness and may not

be able to inherit our inheritance. But if we have an excellent spirit, a spirit that follows the Lord all the way, believing in Him no matter what, like Joshua and Caleb, then in that spirit God will lead us into His purpose—into the fullness which is in Christ. So we see that God raised up a new generation. In this second numbering it was a new generation which possessed the spirit of Joshua and Caleb, and God brought them into the Promised Land.

We do not need to look at this merely historically. Yes, unfortunately, it is often true historically. We may find a generation that has heard the call of God and they have come to know Him in a certain way; yet somehow they do not believe and enter in. But thank God, He raises up the next generation who do enter the Promised Land. Yes, in history that is oftentimes true; but spiritually speaking, we do not need to wait for the second generation because the first generation can be renewed. In other words, if we repent and humble ourselves before God, if we listen to Him and have a spirit that follows Him, then God can renew us and make us that new generation that enters the Promised Land.

The last chapters of Numbers record the preparations for entering the Promised Land. These chapters demonstrate how faithful God is. In spite of our unfaithfulness, God is still faithful to himself. He prepared that people to enter the Promised Land and there was a renumbering of the people. He even apportioned the land before they went into it. God said, "This land is yours. I will apportion it and let you have it." The land was divided up by tribes, but in the tribe of Manasseh, Zelophehad did not have any sons, so his descendants were not apportioned any land. Thank God for the daughters of Zelophehad! These daughters came to Moses and said, "Our father died in the wilderness, not because of the sin of Korah, but because of his own sins. He had no son, but does that mean we should have no inheritance?"

Here we see in the daughters of Zelophehad a desire for

possession. Wonderful! They had the desire and they wanted to possess their portion of the Promised Land. So they asked the question, "How about it?" And God said, "What they say is right. If there is no son, give it to the daughters."

Then the chief fathers of the tribes said, "But if the daughters marry into the other tribes, the land will go to them." So God said, "All right, if they marry, they must marry within the tribe, and thus the land will stay within the tribe." This reveals to us that in this new generation there was a new spirit. They were not like the old generation who despised the Promised Land, but they were a new generation that desired the land and treasured it. Even though they did not have it, they desired it; and God honored that. That is very beautiful.

Even so, unfortunately, there were two tribes that would rather stay on the eastern side of the Promised Land rather than cross the Jordan. In other words, they lived for their cattle, they did not live for the purpose and glory of God. This also is a warning to us.

So the whole book of Numbers is very relevant for us today. We are journeying towards the fullness that is in Christ as a people. May the Lord have mercy upon us that we may be faithful to Him.

Let us pray:

> *Dear heavenly Father, we do praise and thank Thee for delivering us out of sin, out of death, out of Satan, and that Thou art bringing us into Christ, the fullness that is in Christ. Oh, our Father, we do thank Thee that even though we need to travel through the wilderness, yet Thou art teaching us, educating us, developing us. We pray that we may not be so stubborn that we will not believe in Thee; but Lord, we pray that we may be a humble people, that we may truly humble ourselves before Thee and look to Thy faithfulness to lead us into the Promised Land—the fullness which is in Christ. We ask in Thy precious name. Amen.*

DEUTERONOMY

THE WORD OF GOD

Deuteronomy 1:1-5—These are the words which Moses spoke to all Israel on this side the Jordan, in the wilderness, in the plain, opposite to Suph, between Paran and Tophel, Laban, Hazeroth, and Dizahab. There are eleven days' journey from Horeb by the way of mount Seir to Kadesh-barnea.

And it came to pass in the fortieth year, in the eleventh month, on the first of the month, that Moses spoke to the children of Israel, according to all that Jehovah had given him in command to them; after he had smitten Sihon the king of the Amorites, who dwelt at Heshbon, and Og the king of Bashan, who dwelt at Ashtaroth and at Edrei. On this side the Jordan, in the land of Moab, began Moses to unfold this law.

Deuteronomy 6:4-15—Hear, Israel: Jehovah our God is one Jehovah; and thou shalt love Jehovah thy God with all thy heart, and with all thy soul, and with all thy strength. And these words, which I command thee this day, shall be in thy heart; and thou shalt impress them on thy sons, and shalt talk of them when thou sittest in thy house, and when thou goest on the way, and when thou liest down, and when thou risest up. And thou shalt bind them for a sign on thy hand, and they shall be for frontlets between thine eyes. And thou shalt write them upon the posts of thy house, and upon thy gates. And it shall be, when Jehovah thy God bringeth thee into the land which he swore unto thy fathers, to Abraham, to Isaac, and to Jacob, to give thee: great and good cities which thou buildedst not, and houses full of everything good which thou filledst not, and wells digged which thou diggedst not, vineyards and olive-yards which thou plantedst not, and thou shalt have eaten and shalt be full; then beware lest thou forget Jehovah who brought thee forth out of the land of Egypt, out of the house of bondage. Thou shalt fear Jehovah thy God, and serve him, and shalt swear by his name. Ye shall not go after other gods, of the gods of the peoples that are round about you; for Jehovah thy God is a jealous God in thy midst; lest the anger of Jehovah thy God be kindled against thee, and he destroy thee from the face of the earth.

Deuteronomy 29:1—These are the words of the covenant that Jehovah commanded Moses to make with the children of Israel in the land of Moab, besides the covenant that he made with them in Horeb.

Let us pray:

Dear heavenly Father, how we praise and thank Thee that Thou hast given us Thy word and Thou hast given us Thy Spirit that through the quickening of Thy Spirit, through the interpreting of Thy Spirit of the word, we may touch Thee, the living Word. So we come today to offer this time to Thee and ask Thee to bless us. In the name of our Lord Jesus. Amen.

Deuteronomy is the fifth volume of the five-volume book of Moses. It is called Deuteronomy because the word in Greek means "second Law," or "the second Law-giving," or "the second edition of the Law" (of course, without amendment). This is the summing up of all four books which precede it; and, actually, this book raises the whole record to a higher level. Genesis tells us of the will of God; Exodus, the work of God; Leviticus, the way of God; Numbers, the walk of God; and now Deuteronomy tells us of the word of God.

"On this side the Jordan, in the land of Moab, began Moses to unfold this law" (Deuteronomy 1:5).

God gave the Law to the children of Israel at Mount Sinai; but on the plains of Moab, Moses began to unfold and declare, explain and expound, this Law. Fundamentally, Deuteronomy does not give us any new revelation; essentially, it is the repeating of the Law that had already been given by God at Mount Sinai. Nonetheless, there is a difference. At Mount Sinai the Law was given without comment, but here the Law is unfolded, explained and expounded. At Mount Sinai it was God who spoke: both directly to the people himself and also indirectly to them through Moses. But in Moab it is Moses who speaks; even so, he is basically repeating what God had already spoken. Yet we shall see that Deuteronomy not only repeats the Law—the letter of the Law—that was given before but also introduces the spirit of the Law. And out of the spirit of the Law there comes forth a new application and new interpretation; nevertheless, there is no redundancy. So even though Deuteronomy is not a new revelation, it is nonetheless new. And it is therefore just as inspired as when the Law was first given.

THE PRINCIPLE OF REPETITION

The principle to be found in Deuteronomy is a very important one and which appears often in the Scriptures. It is the principle of repetition. For instance, in Job 33:14 we read: "God speaketh once, and twice,—and man perceiveth it not." Again, in Psalm 62:11: "Once hath God spoken, twice have I heard this, that strength belongeth unto God." And in the New Testament, in II Peter, Peter declared that what he wrote to them was nothing new. Before his departure from the earth he was most diligent and careful in reminding his readers of various things in order that they might recall them afterwards. They knew of these things already but he was simply writing to remind them.

God speaks once, and He speaks twice. Why is this so? It is not because God himself needs such repetition; it is because of our hard hearing. If God speaks only once, we may not hear it; but out of His love towards us, He condescends himself to speak again that we may finally hear what He wants us to hear.

And we do thank God for this repetition. At Mount Sinai God spoke himself, but on the plains of Moab it was Moses who spoke on God's behalf.

In a sense, this principle of repeating is true with us today. God has spoken, and we know this because we have the Bible in our hands. What is the word of God? What is the Bible? The answer is: *God has spoken*. God has spoken in the past to our fathers through the prophets in pieces and fragments, here and there; but now, God has spoken in His Son—fully and completely. God has spoken, and all that He has spoken has been written down and recorded in the Scriptures which we now have in the Bible. However, as we read the word of God, the Spirit of God will speak again, yet He does not speak anything new. There is no new revelation outside of the Scriptures. What He speaks is consonant with the Scriptures; and yet, when He speaks again to you and to me it gives a new meaning, a new application. The written words become living and very real to our present-day life experiences. We need to store the word of God richly in our hearts, and then the Holy Spirit can take hold of these words, unfold them to us, explain and expound them to us and apply them afresh. Therefore, even though there is no new revelation outside of Scripture, so far as we are concerned, it is new and it is living. And that is the principle of Deuteronomy.

THE THREE COMMANDS ISSUED

This book is very, very important. Moses not only spoke these words to the children of Israel, he also wrote them down. And because of this there were issued three commands. First, if we carefully read this book of Deuteronomy, we will find that it was commanded of any king who would ascend to the throne of the nation of Israel that he copy this book by and for himself and read it every day as long as he lived. Second, it was commanded that after the children of Israel entered the Promised Land, they were to write these words on huge plastered stones. And third, it was commanded that every seventh year, at the time of the Feast of Tabernacles, this book must be publicly read aloud and explained to the people (see 17:18-20; 27:2-8; 31:10-13). So we can see from all this how important this book is.

DEUTERONOMY IS QUOTED IN THE NEW TESTAMENT

Deuteronomy is quoted a number of times in the New Testament. The Lord Jesus himself testifies to the authenticity of this book; for at the time when He was tempted in the wilderness, He quoted from this book's chapter 8 and chapter 6. Again, in Matthew 22, when the Pharisee lawyer tried to tempt Him, Jesus quoted again from Deuteronomy 6: "Thou shalt love the Lord thy God with all thy heart, and with all thy soul, and with all thy understanding." This is the greatest commandment of all. Hence Jesus quoted from the early part of Deuteronomy. Then, too, we learn how the apostle Peter (see Acts 3) and the first martyr Stephen (see Acts 7) both quoted from the middle part of Deuteronomy 18. And the apostle Paul (see Romans 10) quoted from the latter part of Deuteronomy 30. This book is quoted again and again in the New Testament and thus validates the authenticity of it; and we do thank God that we have this book in our hands.

THE NEW GENERATION

Practically speaking, it was necessary for Moses to repeat the Law because when the Israelites arrived at the plains of Moab it was a new generation that was assembled there. The old generation that had come out of Egypt had all fallen in the wilderness throughout the many years of their wanderings because of their unbelief and rebellion. So that many years after God had originally given the Law to the grown-ups among the children of Israel, those people had all died; only their children—now adults—remained. Some of these children, when very young, might have indeed heard God speaking to them at Mount Sinai, but many others of them were later born in the wilderness and had never heard God speaking. Having a new generation before Moses, there was a great need of repeating the Law, of letting them know and understand what had previously been given. Actually, this new generation was in a better mood and spirit to receive the Law, because although the older generation had in fact heard the Law when originally given to them, they did not quite understand it—they did not quite see the significance of it. But now, at the plains of Moab, with thirty-eight years of past experiences, this new generation was in a better position to understand the Law.

The same situation is true with us today. We have the word of God in our hands, but when we read many of its words, we do not quite understand them; they do not make a deep impression upon us until we experience something. Experience is very necessary to understanding; it helps us to understand what God has spoken. Without experience we do not have any precedent in sight; and, therefore, it is hard to understand. But if we have personal experiences to look back upon and then we return to the word of God, we shall find that His word is opened up to us in a new way. It requires that we have some experience in order for us to understand certain words of God.

SEEING THE LAND

Let us realize, furthermore, that when the older generation among the children of Israel were at Mount Sinai, they had just come out of Egypt but they had not seen Canaan yet. Now, though, at the plains of Moab, this new generation was poised to make entrance at the very border of the Promised Land. In other words, they had Canaan in view, and that enabled this later generation to understand the Law much better than their parents because the Law had much to do with the land. And, spiritually speaking, I believe this is true with us today. If we see and have "the land" in view—that is to say, if we see the eternal purpose of God and His ultimate destiny for us, then that will enable us to understand God's word in a much better way. Oftentimes we read the word of God and do not understand because we do not see "the land"; we do not have before us the ultimate purpose of God. But when we have *that* in our vision, then the whole Bible is opened up to us. And hence, that new generation of Israelites was in a much better position to understand the Law because the Law was very much in relation to the Promised Land.

Hopefully, we too are a new generation. I mentioned in an earlier message that a new generation does not necessarily have to be an actual physical one. We can be renewed by the Spirit of God at any time and thus, spiritually, we become a new generation before God. We can have the spirit of Caleb and Joshua—a believing spirit instead of an unbelieving one. I do believe, today, that we are in a much better position to understand the word of God: we have some past experiences which can shed light upon the word of God, and we also have "the land" in view.

In the days of the book of Deuteronomy the Promised Land was very much in view as the people listened to the rehearsal of the Law. By contrast, during the time of Numbers the Israelites were in the wilderness and for them the wilderness was what was in view. But in the days of Deuteronomy, and even though they had not yet gone into the land, they could see it, and everything in the Law was related to it. So the Law was given that they might be able to enter the Promised Land and remain there. Now because the land was very important, it is not surprising that Deuteronomy contains three portions of text wherein the land is described in some detail. The Israelites have not come into the Promised Land yet, but the Holy Spirit through Moses describes the land to them in order to stir up their hearts to be eager to enter and possess it. Here, then, are these three descriptive passages concerning the land of Canaan.

A VERY GOOD LAND

"And it shall be, when Jehovah thy God bringeth thee into the land which he swore unto thy fathers, to Abraham, to Isaac, and to Jacob, to give thee: great and good cities which thou buildedst not, and houses full of everything good which thou filledst not, and wells digged which thou diggedst not, vineyards and oliveyards which thou plantedst not, and thou shall have eaten and shalt be full" (6:10-11).

"For Jehovah thy God bringeth thee into a good land, a land of waterbrooks, of springs, and of deep waters, that gush forth in the valleys and hills; a land of wheat, and barley, and vines, and fig-trees, and pomegranates; a land of olive-trees and honey; a land wherein thou shalt eat bread without scarceness, where thou shalt lack nothing; a land whose stones are iron, and out of whose mountains thou wilt dig copper" (8:7-9).

"For the land, whither thou enterest in to possess it, is not as the land of Egypt, from whence ye came out, where thou sowedst thy seed, and wateredst it with thy foot, as a garden of herbs; but the land, whereunto ye are passing over to possess it, is a land of mountains and valleys, which drinketh water of the rain of heaven, a land which Jehovah thy God careth for; the eyes of Jehovah thy God are constantly upon it, from the beginning of the year even unto the end of the year. And it shall come to pass, if ye hearken diligently unto my commandments which I command you this day, to love Jehovah your God, and to serve him with all your heart and with all your soul, that I will give rain to your land in its season, the early rain and the latter rain; and thou shalt gather in thy corn, and thy new wine, and thine oil; and I will give grass in thy field for thy cattle; and thou shalt eat and be full" (11:10-15).

In summary, then, this land that God had promised to Abraham, Isaac and Jacob is a very good land. It is a land flowing with milk and honey. It is a land of plenty, of abundance. It is a land where everything is already prepared—cities already built, houses already filled with good things, wells already dug, and vineyards and oliveyards already planted. It is a land full of waterbrooks, of streams, of springs. It is a land with copper and iron. It is a land with corn, wheat, barley, pomegranates, figs, olives, and all such other good things. Furthermore, the eyes of the Lord are constantly upon this land, and He rains upon it with early rains and latter rains. In other words, it is a land of such abundance that God's people can enjoy and be full. Who would not want such a land?

Yet what, today, is our land? We have a land that God has promised to us as well. It is even better than the land of Canaan, far better! We too have a land wherein everything is prepared for us. We do not need to dig any well, build any house or plant any vineyard. God has already done it all for us. We have a land that is full of water of all kinds; we have a land of plenty; we have a land upon which the eyes of God are constantly fixed; and, of course, we know Who that land is—our Lord Jesus. The Lord Jesus Christ is that land. In Him God has provided everything for us. All the fullness of the Godhead dwells in Christ bodily, and we are complete in Him (see Colossians 2:9-10).

It is as though God has said to us: "You do not need to do anything. I have done it all. I have prepared everything for you in Christ Jesus, and there you can find every expression, every activity of the Holy Spirit. The Spirit's expression may be like waterbrooks—very quiet—so that you may drink and rest. Or, it may be like springs which spring forth with water, or like mighty rivers. Everything needful and desirable is there. All the activities of the Holy Spirit are in Christ Jesus." The Lord Jesus is not only our food to meet all kinds of need, but He is also our strength—as it were, our iron and our copper. Surely the eyes of God are upon the Lord, and if we love and serve Him, then we will have no lack of any kind and we shall be full. In fact, He is the fullness of life.

What is the church? The church is the body of Christ, the

fullness of Him Who fills all and in all (see Ephesians 1:22b-23). How good is our Promised Land! Are we eager to enter in? Are we anxious to explore its extent and depth? Are we desirous of enjoying everything that is in Christ? Thank God, we are in Christ; we are in our Promised Land. For of God are you in Christ Jesus, says the Scripture, and God has made Him our wisdom, righteousness, holiness, and redemption (see I Corinthians 1:30). How we therefore need to treasure our land of promise, the Lord Jesus!

THE THREE DISCOURSES OF MOSES

Moses spoke the words of this book of Deuteronomy on the plains of Moab by the side of the Jordan River. The time that is covered by this book is approximately two months. We know this by comparing Deuteronomy 1:3 with Joshua 4:19. Within these two months Moses unfolded and expounded the Law—the word of God—to that new generation of the children of Israel. The whole book of Deuteronomy is very easily divided into three sections according to the three discourses which Moses gave to the children of Israel.

The Historical Discourse

The first discourse is found in Deuteronomy 1—4. These particular words which he spoke are historical in nature. In other words, Moses reviewed the past history of the Israelites. He began with Mount Sinai, then discussed the wilderness experience up until the time when the children of Israel had arrived at the plains of Moab. This historical review was very, very important because it created in the people a right attitude. It was important for them to be reminded of what had occurred in the past. In other words, the emphasis in this first discourse was to recollect the past. Moses helped the children of Israel to recall what had gone before lest they might have forgotten. He reminded them of the fact that they were not a great people, that they also had not been a good people. Actually, they had been a stiff-necked and rebellious people. The reason God had delivered them out of Egypt with a mighty hand and had brought them through the wilderness and dispossessed their enemies in order to give them their possession was not because of *their* greatness or *their* power. In reality, they were the smallest and weakest of peoples on the earth; their enemies were much greater and more powerful than they were. Indeed, the reason they were now at the plains of Moab waiting to enter the Promised Land was not because of what *they* were; it was because of the love of God. Moses told them this: "Because God loved you, therefore, He did all these things for you. Let me remind you of this: that you have been an unfaithful people; you have rebelled against God again and again; you have no right to be here, and yet it is His love and faithfulness which have brought you to this point." He wanted the children of Israel to recall all of this, for it would humble them and prepare their hearts to receive the word of God with more readiness.

Is this not true and needful with us today? We must ever keep in mind that we are what we are today not because of our greatness nor because of our goodness. As a matter of fact, we too were a stiff-necked and rebellious people: we too had been unfaithful continuously; but thank God, He loves us. He loves us not because we are lovable; we are not. Moreover, our enemies are greater and mightier than we are. Yet God in His love towards us has delivered us out of the world; He has dispossessed our enemies and given us "the land"—everything that we need in Christ our Promised Land. We are full, but let us beware lest, being full, we forget. Unfortunately, when even this new generation of the children of Israel were filled, they—like their elders—forgot God. They began to go their own way as though they had gotten and accomplished everything by themselves. They departed from God and began to worship false gods. And the result was that God's discipline came upon them. Therefore, we feel Deuteronomy—even with respect to this historical discourse—is very important for us to learn from and heed.

How we need the Holy Spirit to remind us again and again of the love of God in Christ Jesus; that we are what we are today by the grace of God. This should always humble us. The greatest danger for God's people is that we become proud when we are blessed by Him. Unfortunately, this happens all the time. When we are in affliction, we humble ourselves; but when we are in prosperity, we become arrogant. We think we obtain everything because we are good, that we are better than everybody else. Whenever that kind of pride enters our heart, let us beware; for the next step is to fall, because pride always precedes a fall (see Proverbs 16:18). In such situations we need to recall the goodness of God and remember our unfaithfulness; yet not to discourage us but to humble us in heart and spirit. For humility is the spirit of the Lamb. We need the spirit of humility, and only in that spirit are we ready to hear and receive what God by His Spirit has to say to us individually and to His church corporately.

THE LEGISLATIVE DISCOURSE

The second discourse of Deuteronomy is legislative in nature (see Deuteronomy chapters 5—28). In this lengthy section of the book we learn that Moses repeated the Law of God which had been given at Mount Sinai, but he also brought the people into the spirit of it and applied it in a new way. First, he repeated the Ten Commandments (see chapter 5), and then from chapter 6 onward he began to separate these commandments one from the other. In other words, having initially summed up all Ten Commandments in *the* commandment of loving God (see Deuteronomy 6:5). Moses then commenced dividing them up and applying them afresh to various situations in the people's lives with new interpretation.

With respect to this second discourse we would like to emphasize two points. First, that when Moses began to unfold the Law to the children of Israel he said again and again, "Hear, O Israel, hear." Hearing is very, very important. The older generation had heard the Law, and yet, they did not hear because their hearts were hardened. To this new and younger generation Moses now said, "Hear, O Israel; hear what God is going to say to you." And the Spirit of God graciously interprets this for us today in Hebrews 3:7: "As says the Holy Spirit, Today if ye will hear His voice, harden not your hearts, as in the provocation, in the day of temptation in the wilderness."

In other words, the reason why that older generation of Israelites had not heard was not primarily because of their ears; it was entirely because of their heart. In reality, our heart and our ears are connected. Yes, it is quite true, we use our ears to hear, but if our heart is not there, we may not hear what God says. If our heart is hardened, and no matter how loudly God's word may come forth, even like thunder, we will hear nothing. So the issue is the heart. God always refers back to the human heart. If our hearts are hardened, then our ears will be filled with oil and fat—and consequently, we cannot hear.

How we therefore need a circumcised heart! (cf. 10:16) Moses promised the children of Israel that one day God would circumcise their hearts (see Deuteronomy 30:6). What does that mean? It simply means that our natural, fleshly, selfish will needs to be taken away and crucified on the cross in order that our hearts may be tender, soft, willing, ready, and humble to hear what God has to say. Our greatest problem is our heart. Oh, that the Lord would circumcise our heart, that He would remove the fat surrounding and covering our heart—that is to say, that He would cut away the unbelief, the stubbornness, the selfish will and pride and make our heart tender, soft, willing, ready, and humble to receive what God has to say. If the heart be softened, then the ear will hear. The most important issue is for us to hear what God has to say.

The second point to be emphasized about this discourse is the fact that Moses led the children of Israel from the letter of the Law to the spirit of it. He tells them, "Hear, O Israel ... thou shalt love the Lord thy God with all thy heart, and with all thy soul, and with all thy strength." The spirit of the Law is love. If we only see the letter of the Law, that creates fear; but if we see the spirit of the Law, such will create love. God wants us to love Him because He is love. He wants us to love Him with all our heart, with all our soul, and with all our strength. If we couch this emphasis in New Testament terms, we may say that He wants us to love Him with all our spirit, with all our soul, and with all our body (cf. I Thessalonians 5:23; Hebrews 4:12). In short, our whole being is to love Him. And if the reason He gives the Law is because He loves us, and if we therefore love Him in return, then the Law is no longer burdensome (see I John 5:3). That is the secret.

One day, God said to the Israelites through Moses: "I will circumcise your heart and cause you to love Me" (see again 30:6). God will do that to His people; and in a very real sense, He has already done it to us because He has taken away that stony heart and given us a heart of flesh (see Ezekiel 11:19; 36:26). He has given us a new covenant, and in that new covenant He has caused us to love Him (see Deuteronomy 30:6). We love Him because He first loved us (see I John 4:19). For us today, His Law, His commandment, is no longer grievous or burdensome (see again I John 5:3). It is just as the Lord Jesus once said when He was on earth—quoting David in the Psalms: "Lo, I come to do Thy will, and Thy Law is inscribed upon my heart; it is the delight of My heart and I love to do it" (see Hebrews 10:5-7 and cf. with Psalm 40:6-8).

THE PROPHETIC DISCOURSE

Moses' third discourse is prophetic in nature, and the major point in view is the covenant (see Deuteronomy 29—34). God made a covenant with the new generation at the plains of Moab by the side of the Jordan River. Let us bear in mind that this covenant was extra to the one God made at Mount Sinai with the children of Israel— which was the Sinaitic Covenant, the covenant of Law. On the plains of Moab, however, God made another covenant in addition to the one made at Mount Sinai—and it is the Moabic Covenant, a covenant of Law *and mercy*. The Law is still there; indeed, it is even repeated; but the people are now under the mercy of God. The older generation had already manifested their unfaithfulness and had been disciplined; and now the mercy of God has brought the new and younger generation to the border of the Promised Land. And by His mercy He will be bringing them into the Promised Land, but on condition that they obey God. Obedience is the key.

God made this additional covenant with the younger generation of the children of Israel. It was a covenant of both Law and mercy. God demanded obedience from the people, and if they obeyed, they could enter the land, possess it, and continue to live in it. But if they should disobey, if they should break the covenant of Law and mercy, God would discipline them. Yet, when we come to chapters 29 and 30, we learn that God said, "I will circumcise your heart." That is, "After I have scattered you all over the world because you will have foresaken My covenant in going after other gods, but if you then turn back to Me, I will circumcise your heart and cause you to love Me and keep My word. My word is not far from you. You do not need to go up to heaven to bring it down, nor do you need to go to the bottom of the earth to bring it up. It is in your mouth and it is in your heart" (see 30:1-6, 11-14). This is a prophecy of the new covenant. Even in that covenant of Law and mercy issued on the plains of Moab, God was already promising them the covenant of grace. He was anticipating what He would say at the time of the prophet Jeremiah.

For in Jeremiah 31 we learn this which God said, "One day I will not take their hands and lead them as it was before because they did not obey Me. The old covenant is annulled. I will make a new covenant with the house of Israel. I will write My Law in their hearts; and I will be their God, and they shall be My people. No one needs to teach his neighbors to know the Lord, but from the least to the greatest they all shall know Me in themselves, and I will forgive their sins and remember them no more." The seed of the new covenant was already planted there at the plains of Moab.

The children of Israel are still to this day under the Moabic Covenant, the covenant of Law and mercy; but today, the church of God is already in the new covenant of grace. On that Passover night when gathered with His disciples, the Lord Jesus took the cup and said, "This is the cup of the new covenant sealed by My blood; drink it, all of you" (see I Corinthians 11:25; Luke 22:17, 20).

The Lord Jesus Christ has taken that new covenant spoken of prophetically in Jeremiah and brought it to the church. We are under the new covenant of grace today. He has inscribed His Law upon our hearts. He causes us to love Him; He enables us to do His will. And He has forgiven and forgotten all our iniquities. Thank God for that! But the children of Israel, today, are still under the Moabic Covenant—Law and yet mercy, mercy and yet Law. But one day in the Millennium, when the Lord Jesus shall return, the whole nation of Israel will enter into the covenant of grace that we experience today.

After the Moabic Covenant was made, Moses was moved in heart by God to write a song not only to testify against the children of Israel but also to testify of the faithfulness of God. God knew what would happen because He knows humanity so well. And as in the days of Moses, so today, He warns us; yet, He never gives us up. He still promises. And He will yet restore His people as He has planned because His purpose never changes. Thank God for that.

Following this, there is the blessing of Moses recorded in chapter 33. Before Moses died he gathered to himself the elders of all twelve tribes (see 31:28) and blessed every tribe of the children of Israel. When Jacob had died, he too pronounced a blessing, in his case, upon his sons; but these two blessings, though both were prophetic, were different. Jacob blessed his sons as he envisioned what would happen to them at the end of their days. But Moses blessed the twelve tribes of Israel as he envisioned the sovereign grace of God and the assignment and arrangement He had in mind concerning these twelve tribes and what would happen to them in the land. These tribes' elders who were gathered before Moses were there representing

God's chosen people, being a testimony to the greatness of God. Such was the blessing of Moses. Thank God, the song of Moses warns us and the blessing of Moses encourages us.

Today, we thank God, that even though we know we are unfaithful, yet He is so faithful and that whatever He has planned He will bring it to pass. Therefore, it behooves us to cooperate with Him and to obey. It is not hard to obey today because we have the life of the obedient Son in us. It is quite true that it is difficult for us, in and of ourselves, to obey. For within us, that is, in our flesh, there is always present a tendency to rebel: we in ourselves are inclined to rebel against anything and everything that is of God, for that is human nature. But thank God, we have the life of the Son in us, and the life of the Son is one of obedience. Though He were a Son, we are told in the New Testament, yet He learned obedience through the things which He suffered so that He might become the Leader of eternal salvation to us who believe (see Hebrews 5:8-9). We have the obedient life of the Son in us, and it is therefore not hard for us to obey. If we love God, obedience is a pleasure and a delight.

This, then, is Deuteronomy. It actually sums up all four preceding books and elevates them to a higher level, in order that we may learn to hear Him, love Him and obey Him so that we may enjoy Christ our Promised Land.

Let us pray:

> *Dear heavenly Father, we do praise and thank Thee that Thou hast not only promised us the good land, but Thou hast already given it to us, even Thy beloved Son. We do praise and thank Thee that we are in Him and He is in us. Father, do enable us to hear Him, to love Him and to obey Him that we may remain in Him, that we may enjoy Him to the fullest. And it is all to be a testimony to Thee and a glory to Thy name. Father, we acknowledge that we are unfaithful, stiff-necked, rebellious; but Thou art faithful, loving, trustworthy and good. What Thou hast purposed Thou wilt perform it to Thy glory. In the name of our Lord Jesus. Amen.*

JOSHUA

POSSESSING THE LAND

Joshua 1:1-9—And it came to pass after the death of Moses the servant of Jehovah, that Jehovah spoke to Joshua the son of Nun, Moses' attendant, saying, Moses my servant is dead; and now, rise up, go over this Jordan, thou and all this people, into the land which I give unto them, to the children of Israel. Every place whereon the sole of your foot shall tread have I given to you, as I said unto Moses. From the wilderness and this Lebanon to the great river, the river Euphrates, the whole land of the Hittites, to the great sea, toward the going down of the sun, shall be your border. None shall be able to stand before thee all the days of thy life: as I was with Moses, so will I be with thee; I will not leave thee, neither will I forsake thee. Be strong and courageous, for thou shalt cause this people to inherit the land which I have sworn unto their fathers to give them. Only be strong and very courageous, that thou mayest take heed to do according to all the law that Moses my servant commanded thee. Turn not from it to the right or to the left, that thou mayest prosper whithersoever thou goest. This book of the law shall not depart from thy mouth; and thou shalt meditate upon it day and night, that thou mayest take heed to do according to all that is written therein; for then shalt thou have good success in thy ways, and then shalt thou prosper. Have I not commanded thee: Be strong and courageous? Be not afraid, neither be dismayed; for Jehovah thy God is with thee whithersoever thou goest.

Joshua 5:13-15—And it came to pass when Joshua was by Jericho, that he lifted up his eyes and looked, and behold, there stood a man before him with his sword drawn in his hand. And Joshua went to him, and said to him: Art thou for us, or for our enemies? And he said, No; for as captain of the army of Jehovah am I now come. Then Joshua fell upon his face to the earth, and worshipped, and said to him, What saith my lord unto his servant? And the captain of Jehovah's army said to Joshua, Loose thy sandal from off thy foot: for the place whereon thou standest is holy. And Joshua did so.

Joshua 13:1-6—And Joshua was old, advanced in age, and Jehovah said to him, Thou art old, advanced in age, and there remaineth yet very much land to take possession of. This is the land that yet remaineth: all the districts of the Philistines and all the Geshurites, from the Shihor, which floweth before Egypt, as far as the borders of Ekron northward, and which is counted to the Canaanite; five lordships of the Philistines: of Gazah, and of Ashdod, of Eshkalon, of Gath, and of Ekron; also the Avvites; in the south, the whole land of the Canaanites, and Mearah which belongeth to the Sidonians, unto Aphek, to the border of the Amorites; and the land of the Giblites, and all Lebanon, toward the sun-rising, from Baal-Gad at the foot of Mount Hermon to the entrance into Hamath; all the inhabitants of the hill-country from Lebanon to Misrephoth-maim, all the Sidonians; I will dispossess them from before the children of Israel. Only, partition it by lot to Israel for an inheritance, as I have commanded thee.

Joshua 23:1-6—And it came to pass a long time after that Jehovah had given rest to Israel from all their enemies round about, and Joshua had become old, advanced in age, that Joshua called for all Israel, for their elders, and for their heads, and for their judges, and for their officers, and said unto them, I am become old, advanced in age; and ye have seen all that Jehovah your God hath done to all these nations because of you. For Jehovah your God is he that hath fought for you. Behold, I have divided unto you by lot for an inheritance, according to your tribes, these nations that remain, from the Jordan, as well as all the nations that I have cut off, as far as the great sea toward the sun-setting. And Jehovah your God, he will expel them from before you, and dispossess them from out of your sight; and ye shall take possession of their land, as Jehovah your God hath said unto you. And be ye very courageous to keep and to do all that is written in the book of the law of Moses, that ye turn not aside therefrom to the right hand or to the left.

.

Let us pray:

Dear heavenly Father, how we do worship Thee that through Thy beloved Son we can call Thee "Abba Father." And we know that Thy pleasure is upon us because Thou hast accepted us in Thy Beloved. Our Father, we do praise and thank Thee that Thou dost speak to us through Thy word. So we are here; open our heart and our ears that we may hear what the Spirit says to the churches. We ask in Thy precious name. Amen.

The Lord Jesus divided the Old Testament Scriptures into three parts: the Law of Moses, the Prophets, and the Psalms (see Luke 24:44). We are going to begin today with the prophets, and as was mentioned earlier, the prophets section includes both historical writings and prophetic writings. The same Spirit who moved the prophets to set down the prophetic writings likewise moved those who recorded the historical writings. Although there were those moved by the Spirit of God to write histories, they were not just historians. Their writings were not simply secular histories concerning economic and political developments of the nation of Israel. On the contrary, these men were moved by God to write the history of the nation of Israel as it related to God. In other words, they selected from the history of that nation only those events, developments, and personalities that related to the unfolding of the kingdom of God upon the earth. Because of this, these historical books are numbered among the writings of the prophets. We are not merely studying a history of a nation on earth, however interesting that might be or however disappointing at times it might also be, but additionally, by means of the various historical narratives of that nation, we are enabled to see how God's promise of the seed of Abraham is brought to fruition on the earth to bring blessing upon all nations.

The historical writings of the prophets are the books of Joshua, Judges, Ruth, I and II Samuel, I and II Kings, I and II Chronicles, Esther, Nehemiah, and Ezra. These historical writings cover a very long period. They begin with the death of Moses and end some four hundred years before the birth of Jesus. So, roughly, the period covered runs to about one thousand and fifty-five years.

This long history can likewise be divided into three sections. The first extends from the death of Moses to the ascension of King Saul, a period of about three hundred and fifty-five years. We would call this the age of theocracy because God himself ruled over His people as their King.

The second section extends from the ascension of Saul to the overthrow of the nation of Judah, a period of nearly five hundred and ten years. This has been called the age of monarchy because during that time the children of Israel had earthly kings.

And the third section describes the nation under foreign rule through to the end of all prophetic voices—which probably came to a close around 396 B.C. and covered a period of some one hundred and ninety years. This period has been termed the age of dependency because the nation was under foreign rule as a dependency.

The book of Joshua is a continuation of the last book of Moses, Deuteronomy. It begins where Deuteronomy ends. The latter tells us of Moses' death, and so, in Joshua, we read how God said to Joshua: "Rise up, for My servant Moses is dead; therefore, enter the land that I promised to the children of Israel." In short, what Moses commenced, Joshua finished. Moses was used by God to lead the children out of Egypt and Joshua was used to lead them into Canaan, the Promised Land. Concerning the leadership of Moses, the one most prominent event which probably everybody remembers is the crossing of the Red Sea, and that speaks figuratively of deliverance from bondage. With regard to Joshua's leadership, everybody remembers the crossing of the river Jordan, which speaks of the entering into the blessing of God.

JOSHUA REPRESENTS GRACE

We can view Moses and Joshua from various angles. Some people say Moses represents law because he was the law-giver. But law cannot bring people into the full blessing of God. It was Joshua who led the people into the Promised Land; and hence, in contrast to Moses, Joshua can be said to represent grace. By the grace of God, we are able to enter into the full riches and blessing of our Promised Land—Christ.

That is one way to view Moses in relation to Joshua; on the other hand, we can view Joshua in relation to Moses as the continuation of the work begun by Moses. In other words, what Moses began, Joshua finished. So in that sense, they both can represent the Savior. Our Savior Jesus (as pictured for us by Moses) not only delivered us out of curse and bondage and out of death and the dominion of Satan, thus setting us free, but He (as pictured for us by Joshua) is also the One who has led us into His unsearchable riches. Accordingly, I believe that as we look into this book of Joshua we shall see that there is indeed such a continuation by Joshua of what Moses had begun, and both are a portrayal of Jesus as Savior.

This book is entitled Joshua, and the reason is because Joshua is the hero. According to Jewish tradition, which has been shown to be correct, the materials in this book came from Joshua himself. The entire book can be divided into three parts. The first can be found in chapters 1-5 and covers the entering into the Promised Land. The second part is covered in chapters 6-12 and tells about the conquering of the land. The third part can be found in chapters 13-24 and chronicles the possessing of the land. If we can remember this outline it can help us in our private study of the book of Joshua.

FIGHTING SPIRIT

Joshua's name was formerly Hoshea which means "deliverance" or "salvation," but Moses changed that name to Jehoshua or Joshua (see Numbers 13:16), meaning "Jehovah-savior." Of the tribe of Ephraim, he was born in captivity and bondage back in Egypt. So when the children of Israel came out of Egypt, Joshua was a young man at that time. The first mentioning of this young man is found in Exodus 17. After the children of Israel came out of Egypt and crossed the Red Sea they traveled through the wilderness area where the Amalekites attacked them. So Moses chose the young man Joshua to lead the people to fight against the Amalekites.

There must have been thousands and thousands of young people among the children of Israel at that time. So why was Joshua the one chosen to lead the people to the fight? Evidently, Moses must have been noticing and observing this young man. There must have been something qualitatively positive in him which stood out. Later on in the Scripture we read that Joshua had "another spirit" (or, different spirit, i.e., different from that of the ten other spies; see Numbers 14:24 and cf. with 14:6-9). In short, he had the Spirit of God with him. There was a spirit in him which marked him out as a worthy young man. We may say that it was a fighting spirit which this young man possessed. Someone would never choose a person to go out and fight who lacked a fighting spirit.

This was a very strange battle involving the Amalekites because even though it was indeed a physical conflict that saw them coming out to attack the children of Israel and Joshua leading the children of Israel to fight against the Amalekites, the result of the battle did not fundamentally rely upon the men who were doing the fighting. On the contrary, Moses had gone to the top of a hill and had raised up his hands that held up the rod of God. Whenever his hands were raised, the children of Israel prevailed, but whenever his hands became weary and dropped to his sides, the Amalekites prevailed. Accordingly, the Israelites had to bring a stone for Moses to sit on, and two persons—Aaron and Hur—had to hold his hands up until the Amalekites were overwhelmed. In other words, there were actually two battles going on: one on the plain and one on the hill; and yet, these two battles were one. And it was because of what occurred on the hill that the battle on the plain was ultimately won.

Now for us today, the spiritual significance of this strange battle is that the attackers—the Amalekites—represent the flesh. Figuratively speaking, when we come out of Egypt, we are delivered from under the curse and out of death, but we then find ourselves in the wilderness. We have not arrived in the Promised Land yet; and when we are in that kind of position, our greatest enemy will be our flesh. As a matter of fact, the whole wilderness history is one of exposing the flesh in the children of Israel as well as around them. We have already mentioned how in Deuteronomy chapter 8 we are told that God tested them those forty years in the wilderness in order to bring out the flesh in them so that they would know they were fleshly and unable, in and of themselves, to enter the Promised Land. So, spiritually, the Amalekites represent the flesh.

Do we have a fighting spirit against the flesh, or do we give in to the flesh? There are many believers who are very passive, even neutral on this matter. But with the flesh we cannot be neutral; we cannot be passive, because the flesh will prevail over us. It is the will of God that we must have a fighting spirit in order to fight against the flesh to the very end. Let us recall what God has said: that this battle will go on until the name and remembrance of the Amalekites be completely removed from the earth. It will not be only one battle but the conflict will go on until the name of Amalek is completely erased from the earth (see Exodus 17:14). So far as the flesh is concerned, there can be no negotiation, there can be no compromise. It is a fight to the finish—to the very end.

Do we have such a fighting spirit in us? Oh, how God's people yield to their flesh! How we love ourselves! How we cater to the desires of our flesh! How we give in to it! We do not want to see our flesh suffer. Rather, we want to satisfy it, gratify it, indulge it, give everything to it. How true it is that when we give in to our flesh, we may experience enjoyment somewhat so far as our flesh is concerned; but the result is spiritual death.

ABIDING SPIRIT

This young man Joshua, we are told, had another spirit in him: a fighting spirit. He fought against the flesh to the very end. But we must never forget that in fighting against the flesh, it is not by might nor by power but by the Spirit of God (see Zechariah 4:6). In other words, no one can fight against himself. How can a person fight against his flesh and prevail? It can only be done through the work of the Lord Jesus. In Joshua's day it was there on the hill that the battle was won. And this is a spiritual illustration of how the Lord Jesus won the battle on Calvary's hill. Our old man was crucified with Christ on the cross. So Paul was inspired to write: "I am crucified with Christ, and no longer live, I, but Christ lives in me; but in that I now live in the flesh, I live by faith, the faith of the Son of God, who has loved me and given himself for me" (Galatians 2:20).

So let us remember that there is a constant battle going on within us. It is a battle against the flesh, but it is not fought with our hands or our feet or with our natural strength. We are not able to do that. It is only possible because the Lord Jesus has taken this old man of ours and crucified him with himself on the cross. It is on the basis of that event and that fact that we can deliver the flesh unto death. That is how the battle is won.

This young man Joshua was an attendant to Moses. We too often think only of Moses and what a great man he was, but we tend to forget his attendant. When Moses went up the mountain to receive the Ten Commandments, he remained there forty days and forty nights. The Scriptures tell us that while he was on the mountain receiving the Ten Commandments, the children of Israel ended up worshiping the golden calf down on the plain. God therefore told him to go down because the children of Israel had sinned. Moses went down carrying the two tablets of stone on which the Ten Commandments had been inscribed by the hand of God, and when he saw their sin, he broke the tablets.

Yet where was Joshua when this entire episode was taking place? Joshua was not on the plain among the people who worshiped the golden calf nor was he on the top of the mountain with Moses receiving the Ten Commandments. He was somewhere in between. He certainly climbed up with Moses, but he probably stayed behind somewhere along the middle area of the mountain while Moses went up farther to receive the Ten Commandments. Can you imagine what it must have been like for a young man to be all by himself for forty days and forty nights? Moses had the presence of God with him, but Joshua did not; neither did he have the people with him. Hence, he was totally alone there; yet, this young man, even though he was all alone somewhere at the middle level of the mountain, was able to remain there faithfully for forty days and nights. What, then, was Joshua doing? In his spirit he was abiding. Yes, this young man had a fighting spirit, but it was accompanied by an abiding spirit.

Some young men have a fighting spirit but lack an abiding one. If you have only a fighting spirit, sooner or later, you will fight with people who should not be fought with; but if you also have an abiding spirit, then you have no problem. In this young man, there were both qualities of spirit. He was able to abide, seeing no one; and yet, by faith, he was there communing with God.

This commendable characteristic in Joshua was revealed in yet another instance. After Moses came down the mountain, he broke the two tablets of stone; and we will recall how the people were disciplined. Moreover, when Moses saw that the camp had been defiled, he moved his tent and placed it at a far distance from the camp. This was the tent where God had always met with His people. But every time Moses now met with God, he would go to that tent that was relocated to a place far apart from the camp. There God would descend in a pillar of cloud and speak to him because the camp was now defiled. But because Moses was the leader, he would of necessity be required to go back to the camp again; but the Bible says that the young man Joshua remained in the tent and did not depart from it (see Exodus 33:11). This young man had learned to abide. He remained in that tent because that was where God was and he did not depart from it. He had a life with God.

"He that dwelleth in the secret place of the Most High shall abide under the shadow of the Almighty" (Psalm 91:1).

We need to dwell in the secret place of the Most High. Then we will abide under the shadow of the Almighty, for only thus will there be might and power attained. This young man Joshua had that kind of spirit: a fighting spirit against all flesh and an abiding spirit in the Lord.

FAITH

Joshua was one of the twelve spies who had been sent to spy out the land. Only he and Caleb—having a different spirit, another spirit, an excellent spirit—gave a good report. The ten other spies gave a bad report (see Numbers 13 again). All twelve saw the land; they all came back and said the land was good, that it was truly flowing with milk and honey as God had said. But the ten spies added this: "We see that the people are giants there. They look upon us as grasshoppers and we look like grasshoppers in our own sight. Their cities are walled up to heaven; it is a land that swallows up people. We cannot go in; we will all be devoured." They thus gave a very bad report, but

Joshua and Caleb said: "No; it is a good land as God has said, and if God is pleased with us, if it pleases Him, He will give that land to us. These people are our food. We are well able to possess the land because God is with us." In other words, Joshua not only saw the good land, he saw God; and because he saw God, there was faith in him.

What is faith? Faith is not looking at environment; faith is not looking at yourself; it is not looking at problems; faith only looks at God. You must therefore look away towards Jesus, the Author and Finisher of faith (see Hebrews 12:2a). Sometimes you wonder why you have no faith. Sometimes you try to create some faith, but you find it does not work. The secret is to look away; look away from yourself and from anybody else, look away from your problems and circumstances. It does not mean you do not see or do not know and realize these things. You do recognize them for what they are, but you must look away from them and look to Jesus, and when you do that, all things become possible with Him.

JOSHUA REPRESENTS THE SPIRIT OF GOD

We have already mentioned that Joshua represents grace in contrast to Moses who represents law. But further in this typology, Joshua, in relation to the land, represents the Spirit of God. It is His Spirit that leads us into our possession. When we first believed in the Lord Jesus, God put His Holy Spirit in us, and now the Spirit of God in us has one very important task to do, which is to lead us into our possession.

Here, though, we need first to understand that the land of Canaan does not represent heaven as such. In some hymns about heaven that are often sung, there is the distinct view put forward that if you gain entrance into Canaan (by crossing the river Jordan to the other shore), you have reached heaven. On the contrary, that is very sentimental and not true. In the Scriptures, Canaan does not represent heaven as we commonly think of it. Canaan represents the unsearchable riches of Christ in the heavenlies. If, nonetheless, you still believe Canaan to be representative of heaven, then make it the heavenlies; for Canaan does not symbolize heaven, as such, but speaks of the heavenly places; and in the realm of the heavenlies, you will find there the unsearchable riches of Christ, even the fullness of Christ. But, of course, in these same heavenly places, you will find that the enemies of Christ are also there; nevertheless, that is not something of which to be afraid. This will be touched upon later.

God has given His Spirit to us as a pledge or down payment, and the Spirit of God in us is to assure us that the fullness in Christ is our possession. Now, though, we have only tasted a little of our possession; for example, we have tasted the forgiveness of our sins. If we will recall, when our sins were forgiven, how sweet that was. We have only tasted a little of the freshness of that eternal life. We begin to feel we are living; that we are no longer dead. We begin to taste of our relationship with our heavenly Father; indeed, we cry, "Abba Father." We begin to taste a little of the preciousness of Christ. The very mentioning of His name brings tears to our eyes. We begin to taste something of Him and His preciousness. The Holy Spirit is in us telling us that all this is ours, but it is only a taste.

In Deuteronomy we are given descriptions of the land, but in Joshua we are told how God's people entered and possessed the land. The Spirit of God in each one of us is moving us, urging us, beseeching us, working in us, drawing us, revealing more of Christ to us, and saying to us: "Now rise up and enter the Promised Land and take possession." In other words, there is much, much more in Christ our Promised Land that God wants us to possess. Why, then, delay? Why stay where you are? Why be so self-contented? Go on. Enter, possess, and continue to possess. That is the work of the Spirit of God. Hence, it is Joshua who leads the people into and possession of the Promised Land.

SPIRIT OF SONSHIP

In relation to us today, Joshua can also represent the kind of spirit that is one with the Spirit of God. Let me call it the spirit of sonship. God has renewed our spirit, and under the influence and the work of His Spirit, there should be manifested in us the spirit of sonship. We read in Galatians that in the fullness of time Christ came, born of a woman under the curse of the Law that He might deliver us from under that curse so that we might receive sonship (see 4:4-5 and cf. with 3:13). In other words, the Holy Spirit in us is renewing our spirit towards sonship, and hence, the spirit of sonship simply means that we want to be placed as sons in God's kingdom. We are not satisfied to merely being babies in Christ.

Let me ask: Is that spirit of sonship in you? Or would you rather remain as babies? Now there is nothing more comfortable than being a baby with no responsibility. As a baby you do not need to think of anybody else; everybody thinks of you. In fact, you are the center of the universe. Many children of God like to remain as babes in the church, and if they are not immediately served, they begin, as it were, to cry and kick. But God has given us the spirit of sonship, and this spirit in us is that we are never satisfied with being babies. We want to grow up, we want to mature and bear responsibility; we want to have fellowship with our Father and be useful to Him.

The spirit of Joshua is one of sonship, and it is this kind of spirit that inherits the land. Do we have this kind of spirit in us? Do we desire to grow up? Do we want to possess our possessions? Do we want to enter into the riches of Christ? This is what the church ought to be, for it is the body of Christ, the fullness of Him who fills all and in all (see Ephesians 1:22b-23). And with this kind of spirit in us we may enter and possess the land.

POSSESSING OUR POSSESSIONS

Crossing the River Jordan

As you open the book of Joshua, you very soon read of God speaking to Joshua: "Rise up and enter the land. I have already given it to you. Wherever you put your foot down, it is yours." In other words, this land had been given to the children of Israel long ago. God had promised Abraham this land, and when He promised it to him, it was already a fact. With us, however, there is a time factor: there is first the promise, and later on, it becomes a reality. But with God, He is timeless: when He promises, it is immediately done. God had already given that land to Abraham, but after many hundreds of years, the children of Israel came out of Egypt, and forty years after that, God said: "Now go in, put your foot down, and it is yours." Is this not true of us today?

"Blessed be the God and Father of our Lord Jesus Christ, who has blessed us with every spiritual blessing in the heavenlies in Christ" (Ephesians 1:3).

God has blessed. It is not that God *is going* to bless or that God *will* bless; to the contrary, the passage declares that God *has* blessed. He has blessed all of us who are His with all spiritual blessings—every spiritual blessing we can think of in Christ Jesus in the heavenlies. He has blessed us with all of these. They all are ours; for God has given His Son to us in full. Everything that is in Him is for us, and God says that Christ His Son is ours. Therefore, everything about Him is ours. All of Him is given. It is all waiting for us to simply step in, put our foot down, claim it, and take it by faith, and whatever we take by faith is ours. Please take note that three times God said, "Be strong and very courageous" (Joshua 1:6, 7, 9). Hence, let us not be afraid, let us not draw back. Let us be strong and very courageous.

This Joshua spirit in us needs to be encouraged to "be strong and very courageous" because, first of all, God has promised; and second, because the word of God is with us. God repeated to Joshua His promise made to the Israelites and also told Joshua to meditate upon His word, keep the commandments, and he would be very successful and prosperous; indeed, said God, nobody would be able to stand against him because His word would be with him. And third, God himself is with us: "My presence is with you" (see Joshua 1:1-9). Think of that! We today, like Joshua of old, have the promise of God, the word of God, and the presence of God with us. Why, then, should we hesitate? Let us "be strong and very courageous."

The first thing in possessing the land back then was to cross the river Jordan. I think we all understand this. When the children of Israel came out of Egypt, they had to cross the Red Sea, and then they had to cross the river Jordan. After they crossed Jordan, they were in the Promised Land. But speaking spiritually, these two waters are actually one, for they represent two sides of one act. In other words, one symbolizes a coming out, the other betokens a going in; yet they represent but one reality. And if we read the New Testament carefully, we shall discover that they both speak of baptism.

BAPTISM

What is baptism? "As many as have been baptised unto Christ Jesus, have been baptised unto his death" (Romans 6:3).

Now the first side of baptism—from the perspective of the Old Testament—is represented by the Red Sea. When the children of Israel passed through the Red Sea, they were baptized unto Moses (see I Corinthians 10). Before that, they had belonged to Pharaoh. After the baptism, they belonged to Moses, and that is what baptism signifies with respect to believer's baptism. When we were baptized, we were baptized out of Egypt unto Moses. Hence, spiritually speaking, we no longer belong to the world but to Christ. We were baptized unto Christ. Baptism does not mean we are baptized into a particular church membership. The Bible never teaches that. We were baptized out of the world and out of Satan's domain unto Christ. God has translated us from the power of darkness into the kingdom of the Son of His love (see Colossians 1:13). That is what baptism signifies on the one side.

The other side of baptism is represented by the river Jordan. Figuratively speaking, in the Jordan we were baptized unto His death. When the children of Israel came out of Egypt and crossed the Red Sea, it was with the rod of God. Moses lifted up the rod of God over the water, and it divided the sea. But in crossing the river Jordan, it was the ark of God which went into the river, and the children of Israel went with the ark through the river. This event thus speaks of identification; that is, it speaks of our co-death, co-burial and co-resurrection with Christ. That is the reason why, after we are baptized, we can declare: "It is no longer I, it is Christ who lives in me." We are baptized unto Christ—unto His death, His burial, and His resurrection. That is what crossing the Jordan signifies. Once they crossed through Jordan, not only was the world—Egypt—behind them, the wilderness of the fleshly self-life was also behind them.

CIRCUMCISION

After the Israelites crossed the river Jordan, in Gilgal they had to undergo circumcision. This represents the subjective side of the cross. The objective side is what Christ himself has done for us: He has died, and in His death, we also died; He was buried, and in His burial, we too were buried; He was raised from the dead, and in His resurrection, we likewise were raised in Him and with Him. It was all His doing, we having done nothing.

On the other hand, on the subjective side, the stone-knife is applied to our flesh and cuts it off. And by this action the reproach of Egypt is completely rolled away (see Joshua 5:2-9). We are completely new in Christ Jesus, and we begin to possess our possession. So far as God's purpose is concerned, the possession is ours; but so far as our experience is concerned, we need to know the working of the cross in our lives; and Jordan speaks of the cross—the death of Christ. As we experience the working of the cross in our lives, we shall possess more and more of the riches which are in Christ. The cross will cut our flesh off, but it will also add Christ to us.

SPIRITUAL WARFARE

After the children of Israel entered the Promised Land, the second experience was the battling, because they found the seven tribes of Canaan there. Let us bear in mind that in the wilderness the battling was against the flesh, but in the Promised Land the battling was against the Canaanite tribes, which speak spiritually of the evil powers of darkness in the heavenlies. We are not able to fight the evil powers of darkness if the flesh has not been subdued in us. Many believers try to fight the evil powers of darkness by themselves. They are very brave, but the flesh in them has not been dealt with. And if that be the case and we try to fight against the enemy, we shall find that we have a quisling within us; indeed, a fifth columnist is inside us. The enemy therefore has an ally in us, and hence we will never be able to overcome him. But if we know how to overcome the flesh by the cross, then we are in a position to fight against the evil forces of darkness in the heavenlies. They always try to stand in the way of our possessing our possessions in Christ, but the battle is the Lord's.

Joshua went to the vicinity of Jericho, and as the Israelites' commander-in-chief he was planning his strategy on how to take that city. As he was looking about and surveying that city a man suddenly appeared before him with a drawn sword, and Joshua said: "Are you for us or for our enemy? Are you with us or with our enemy?" And the man replied: "No, I am neither for you nor for your enemies. I have come as the captain of the army of the Lord." Joshua immediately bowed down and worshiped, and said, "Lord, what have You to say?" And the Lord said, "Take off your shoes, you are standing on holy ground" (see Joshua 5:13-15). The fight against the seven tribes of Canaan was not fought with human power; it was God who fought for the Israelites; and thus, victory did not depend upon them. God planned all the strategy and all the details, and told His people what to do. All they had to do was obey and follow, and the enemies were defeated. No one could stand before the children of Israel because the Lord was fighting for them. So far as Joshua was concerned, the battling continued for about seven years before he wiped out the enemies.

Spiritually speaking, as we are possessing our possession in Christ we shall encounter opposition. The evil powers of darkness are there trying to hinder us from possessing all the riches that are in Christ. But remember, we have a Captain; His sword is drawn; and He has already overcome. He has already routed all enemies—the opposing principalities and authorities in the heavenlies—and has made a public show of them, having triumphed over them by the cross (see Colossians 2:15). He has crushed the head of the serpent; He has defeated the enemy (see Genesis 3:15b; cf. Hebrews 2:14b). Hence, the war is already won and we are engaged in a mopping-up operation. We do not really have to battle. The only fighting we undertake is the mopping-up work: an enemy may be hidden in a corner or behind a door, and we are simply required to dispose of him in a mopping-up operation. That is all we need to do. The victory is already won.

In spiritual warfare, it is not a matter of fighting *to* victory but is a going *from* victory to victory. If we think we are fighting to victory then we will be defeated, because Satan is much older than we are. He is much wiser, more experienced, more intelligent, and more powerful than we are; and accordingly, we will never be able to defeat him. But thank God, Christ has already overcome on the cross, and hence it is for us from victory to victory. He is before us, leading us and fighting the battle. All we need to do, therefore, is trust and obey. All we need to do is do what He wants us to do. It may appear very strange to be told what occurred at Jericho. The ark led the children of Israel in surrounding that city once a day for six days and seven times on the seventh day. I wonder if those citizens of Jericho atop the wall looking down upon that scene were shaking their heads and saying, "What are they doing?" It may have appeared most strange, indeed, but the Lord knew what He was doing: "Not by might, nor by power, but by my Spirit, saith Jehovah of hosts" (Zechariah 4:6). It is in the might of the victory of Christ that our battles are won.

THE DIVIDING OF THE LAND

After seven years or so of battles, God told Joshua to divide the land. Even though all the land had not yet been conquered, they were to divide it. They divided the land by faith, as though it were already theirs.

Let us understand that though we are to inherit Christ, no one person is big enough to inherit all of Him. He as our Promised Land has to be apportioned among His people. You will have a portion, I will have a portion: each of us will have a portion, and yet we possess together. You do not take your portion and go your way. No; we possess our possession *together* because Christ is not divided. What is given to you is for the good of the whole. Some may inherit the hilly areas, some may inherit the plain, others inherit the valley, and still others inherit the seacoast; some others may be able to plant corn, others may have to dig mines, others may have to hunt, and still others may have to fish; but, spiritually speaking, whatever you or I have or do, it is all for the glory of God and for the welfare of the whole body of Christ. If you keep what you have of Christ all to yourself, you may have to eat "fish" all your life and nothing else. God loves variety. The church is a matter of unity in variety, not unity in conformity. Everyone has a portion of the riches of Christ to possess and make fruitful, and then we all can bring our fruit to the house of God to offer it to Him and enjoy together. Such is the life which God has ordained for His church.

Are we who are in the church enjoying this kind of life? Or are we still wandering in the wilderness of the flesh and self? Have we known the cross working in our lives so that we may be delivered from our flesh? Are we beginning to see the riches and the glory of Christ our Promised Land? Have we received and are possessing our portion of the unsearchable riches of Christ? And do we share that with our brothers and sisters? Or do we merely keep it to ourselves and walk away? This book of Joshua figuratively speaks of possessing our possession in Christ. Thank God, He has provided for us the New Testament counterparts to the Old Testament book of Joshua, and they are the letter of Ephesians and the book of Acts. The first part of Ephesians, chapters 1—3, is, as it were, a vision of the land; chapters 4—6 is a vision of the possessing of the land; and the book of Acts is the story of the battle of the Lord: how His gospel goes forth everywhere and conquers and overcomes. So may the Lord help us to enter into and possess our possession in Christ—and all done for the upbuilding of His body.

Let us pray:

> *Dear heavenly Father, we do praise and thank Thee that Thou hast not only promised us the good land, but Thou hast already given it to us, even Thy beloved Son. We do praise and thank Thee that we are in Him and He is in us. Father, do enable us to hear Him, to love Him and to obey Him that we may remain in Him, that we may enjoy Him to the fullest. And it is all to be a testimony to Thee and a glory to Thy name. Father, we acknowledge that we are unfaithful, stiff-necked, rebellious; but Thou art faithful, loving, trustworthy and good. What Thou hast purposed Thou wilt perform it to Thy glory. In the name of our Lord Jesus. Amen.*

JUDGES

POSSESSING ALL THE POSSESSION

Judges 2:1-23—And the Angel of Jehovah came up from Gilgal to Bochim, and said, I made you to go up out of Egypt, and have brought you to the land which I swore unto your fathers; and I said, I will never break my covenant with you; and as for you, ye shall make no covenant with the inhabitants of this land; ye shall throw down their altars: but ye have not hearkened unto my voice. Why have ye done this? Wherefore I also said, I will not drive them out from before you; but they shall be scourges in your sides, and their gods shall be a snare unto you. And it came to pass, when the Angel of Jehovah spoke these words to all the children of Israel, that the people lifted up their voice and wept. And they called the name of that place Bochim; and they sacrificed there to Jehovah.

And Joshua dismissed the people, and the children of Israel went every man to his inheritance to possess the land. And the people served Jehovah all the days of Joshua, and all the days of the elders whose days were prolonged after Joshua, who had seen all the great works of Jehovah, which he had done for Israel. And Joshua the son of Nun, the servant of Jehovah, died, a hundred and ten years old. And they buried him in the border of his inheritance in Timnath-Heres, in mount Ephraim, on the north side of the mountain of Gaash. And also all that generation were gathered to their fathers; and there arose another generation after them, which knew not Jehovah, nor yet the works which he had done for Israel. And the children of Israel did evil in the sight of Jehovah, and served the Baals. And they forsook Jehovah the God of their fathers, who had brought them up out of the land of

Egypt, and followed other gods of the gods of the peoples that were round about them, and bowed themselves to them, and provoked Jehovah to anger. And they forsook Jehovah, and served Baal and the Ashtoreths.

And the anger of Jehovah was hot against Israel, and he delivered them into the hands of spoilers that spoiled them, and he sold them into the hands of their enemies round about; and they could not any longer stand before their enemies. Whithersoever they went out the hand of Jehovah was against them for evil, as Jehovah had said, and as Jehovah had sworn unto them; and they were greatly distressed. And Jehovah raised up judges, and they saved them out of the hand of those that spoiled them. But they did not even hearken to their judges, for they went a whoring after other gods, and bowed themselves to them; they turned quickly out of the way that their fathers had walked in, obeying the commandments of Jehovah; they did not so. And when Jehovah raised them up judges, then Jehovah was with the judge, and saved them out of the hand of their enemies all the days of the judge; for it repented Jehovah because of their groanings by reason of them that oppressed them and crushed them. And it came to pass when the judge died, that they turned back and corrupted themselves more than their fathers, in following other gods to serve them, and to bow down to them: they ceased not from their own doings, nor from their stubborn way. And the anger of Jehovah was hot against Israel; and he said, Because this nation hath transgressed my covenant which I commanded their fathers, and hath not hearkened unto my voice, I also will not henceforth dispossess from before them any of the nations that Joshua left when he died; that through them I may prove Israel, whether they will keep the way of Jehovah to walk therein, as their fathers did keep it, or not. Therefore Jehovah left those nations, without dispossessing them hastily, neither delivered he them into the hand of Joshua.

Judges 21:25—In those days there was no king in Israel; every man did what was right in his own eyes.

Let us pray:

Dear heavenly Father, as we are gathering together in the name of Thy beloved Son, the Lord Jesus, and in Thy presence, we do praise and thank Thee because we have the confidence that Thou art here with us. Our Father, we do pray that by Thy Holy Spirit Thou wilt open Thy word to us and speak afresh to each one of us. Our Father, Thou knowest that we cannot live without Thy word. We long for Thy word. Speak to us that we may live. We commit this time into Thy hands, and may Thy name be honored. In the name of our Lord Jesus. Amen.

A SAD BOOK OF THE BIBLE

This book is entitled Judges because of the characteristics of the time. During this period—between the death of Joshua and the kingly ascension of Saul—God raised up judges in the nation of Israel to deliver them from the oppressions they had to endure from their enemies both within and without. Judges is one of the saddest books in the Bible because it narrates the apostasy and rebellion found among God's people. Because of their rebellion and apostasy, the wrath of God descended upon His people and He allowed their enemies to oppress them. Under that oppression they groaned and moaned and cried and wept before the Lord, and the Lord, in His mercy, raised up ruler-judges or saviors to rescue them from their enemies. And during the time of a given judge there was peace, but after that judge died the people again went back to rebellion, and God once more allowed their enemies to overcome them. Again they cried to the Lord, and God, in His mercy, raised up another judge. This continued on and on for hundreds of years—a very sad history, indeed.

The book of Judges is a continuation of the book of Joshua, but what a difference there is between these two books. In Joshua there is victory, but here in this book we see defeat.

In the book of Joshua we find progress, but in Judges there is declension. In Joshua there is faith, but here is unfaithfulness. In the book of Joshua there is the song of joy and of victory, but in Judges there is the sobbing lament of sorrow. In Joshua we read of the Spirit of God, but here in Judges we read of people living according to their flesh, and thus, they come under great oppression. It is one of the saddest narratives in the whole Bible.

A BOOK RELEVANT TO OUR DAY

Nevertheless, this book is relevant to our day and very important, because there is quite a similarity between the history of the children of Israel during the time of the judges and the history of God's people throughout the centuries. On the one hand, God led the people of Israel into the Promised Land and promised to give the entire land to them as their possession, but they failed to accomplish His purpose. Instead of possessing all their possession, they repeatedly came under oppression by their enemies, both those living among them and those living around them. In short, they failed to possess their possession. On the other hand, God, in His mercy, has today put us in Christ, our Promised Land. By God, we read in the Scriptures, we are in Christ Jesus, and God has made Him our wisdom, righteousness, sanctification, and redemption (see I Corinthians 1:30). It is all of God. It is His mercy that has placed us in Christ. All who have believed in the Lord Jesus not only have Christ in them, they also are in Christ. Christ is in us, the hope of glory, that is quite true; however, we must remember that at the same time we are in Christ. Christ is our Canaan—our Promised Land. He is the land that flows with milk and honey. In other words, as soon as we believe in the Lord Jesus, God puts us in Christ; as it was with the children of Israel and Canaan, so God has given Christ to us as our inheritance. All the riches which are in Christ, God has given to us.

"Blessed be the God and Father of our Lord Jesus Christ, who has blessed us with every spiritual blessing in the heavenlies in Christ" (Ephesians 1:3).

This passage reads: "who *has* blessed us"; not, who *is going to* bless us. In the heavenlies God has blessed us with every spiritual blessing which He has in Christ Jesus. God has given us all the unsearchable riches of Christ to be our possession (see Ephesians 3:8b), and all we need do to possess it is to take our Promised Land, as it were, put our feet down, claim it, and enjoy it to the glory of God.

The church should be in great blessing. She should be enjoying all the spiritual blessings which are in Christ Jesus; unfortunately, like Israel of old, God's people in the New Testament age have also failed. We find that throughout the centuries of church history God's people have been in deep spiritual poverty instead of having entered into the fullness which is in Christ. This is not because God has not promised to give them and us His blessing; rather, it is because they and we have not been faithful. Our hearts and our eyes have not been single towards God. We all have had other interests and have been distracted. We all had begun to love other things— even the world. We all had begun to walk according to the flesh instead of according to the Spirit (see Romans 8:4; Galatians 5:16, 25). And because of all these things, the enemy has had his hand upon God's people down through these many centuries.

REVIVAL COMES WHEN GOD'S PEOPLE CRY OUT

Yes, God's people have been under oppression many, many times through these past centuries. But thank God, when they began to cry out to the Lord, He would grant a revival, and with that revival, there would come a time of refreshing—a time of joy, peace and rest. It might have continued for ten years or even a hundred years; unfortunately, however, God's people would begin to fall away again from following the Lord with singleness of heart. And, accordingly, God's discipline would come upon them and He would allow the enemy to oppress them again, depriving them of spiritual food, and so they would cry out once more to the Lord. But, then, still another revival would come and with it another time of refreshing. Such an experience has been occurring repeatedly throughout church history. Sadly, we shall find towards the end of the book of Judges that the Israelites never fully possessed their possession. And hence, there is quite an analogy which can be discerned between the history of God's people recorded in the book of Judges and the history of the Christian church of God today. Therefore, that is the reason why we must study this book and learn from it the lessons God wants us to learn.

THE WAY GOD COMPUTES TIME

This book of Judges covers roughly four hundred and fifty years, as is indicated in the book of Acts: "After these things he gave them judges till Samuel the prophet, to the end of about four hundred and fifty years" (13:20).

Let us note, though, that I Kings 6:1 states the following: "And it came to pass in the four hundred and eightieth year after the children of Israel were come out of the land of Egypt, in the fourth year of Solomon's reign over Israel, in the month Zif, which is the second month, that he began to build the house of Jehovah."

Here it says that it was four hundred and eighty years from the time the Israelites came out of Egypt until the fourth year of King Solomon's reign when he began to build the temple. Now if the book of Judges covers some four hundred and fifty years, if the wilderness experience covers forty years, and if both Saul and David were each king for forty years, and if Solomon was king for three years—all of which thus comprises for more than four hundred and eighty years, how can we reconcile this with the four hundred and eighty years number stated in I Kings 6:1?

The secret is that God's way of computing time is different from ours. Historically or physically speaking, we know that, time-wise, it is considerably more than four hundred and eighty years from the time God's people came out of Egypt until the time when Solomon began to build the temple; but in terms of accounting spiritually, it is only four hundred and eighty years. The period covered in the book of Judges is four hundred and fifty years, but during part of that time the children of Israel had been under the oppression of the enemy. In other words, they were not what God had wanted them to be; for they had come under the oppression of Mesopotamia for eight years, the oppression of the Moabites for eighteen years, the Canaanites twenty years, the Midianites seven years, and the Philistines for forty years. Moreover, there were eighteen years in which they had come under the Ammonites but those years had run parallel with the forty years of the Philistines, and hence those years are not to be counted. Accordingly, if we add up all the years the children of Israel were under the oppression of these various enemies, they total ninety-three years. And if we deduct these ninety-three years from the sum total of the forty years in the wilderness, the four hundred and fifty years of Judges, Saul's forty years, David's forty years, and Solomon's three years, the result is four hundred and eighty years.

Such, then, is the way God computes time, and there is a lesson here for us to learn. We may recall the instance when Moses had prayed to God that He would teach him how to number his days so that he might be wise (see Psalm 90:12). We need to be wise in numbering the days. Many days that are historically or physically present time-wise are not counted in the sight of God. If they do not contribute to His purpose, they are discounted. And that is a serious matter. Our spiritual history as a person or as a people may not be as long as our physical years. We may be seventy years old, but in the sight of God we may perhaps be only two years old. We may be together as His people for twenty years, but in the sight of God it may perhaps be only eight years in length. Who knows?

Whatever time does not contribute to the purpose of God, whatever time does not stand for the testimony of Jesus—these are wasted times; they do not count before God. How sad it was with respect to the children of Israel! They were led into the land of promise to fulfill God's purpose: they were to be a testimony of God in the world; but when they were in the Promised Land, ninety-three years were completely discounted by God because His people were not where they should have been. May this be a lesson for us to learn: that we be wise to number our days so that none of them will simply end up being wasted.

THE THIRTEEN JUDGES

Now from the book of Judges we learn that God raised up thirteen judges altogether. Some of them were contemporaries who judged during the same period; and some judgeships were consecutive. No judge judged the whole land of Israel. A judge would do so over some part of the Promised Land but not over the whole of it. To say the least, nothing was perfect during the time of these judges. The names of these thirteen were Othniel, Ehud, Shamgar, Deborah and Barak (both are one), Gideon, Abimelech, Tola, Jair, Jephthah, Ibzan, Elon, Abdon, and Samson.

Before we look more closely into this book of Judges, there is another point we need to consider which will provide for us a panoramic view of God's counsel. These judges served as a transition between the two ages of theocracy and monarchy. When God began with His people, it was a theocracy, God himself being their King. God ruled over them; He brought this people out of Egypt and brought them to himself; and thus He became their King. During this period of theocracy, the most important function exercised was that of the priest because the priesthood was the intermediary between God and man. Therefore, under theocracy, it was the priesthood that was most prominent in the history of the children of Israel; yet the priesthood failed. It did not bring people to God, nor was He able to reach His people through the priesthood. So God raised up judges as an emergency temporary measure.

Judges did not constitute a permanent measure in the economy of God. In the latter, theocracy with its priesthood is a permanent measure that was then followed by monarchy or kingship: one day, God would raise up kings to rule over the children of Israel as His representative. But in between the time of the failure of priesthood and the introduction of kingship, God invoked an emergency measure which came in the form of judges. Because the latter was not God's permanent measure but an emergency one, nothing was perfect, nothing was complete. It was short-lived, and it would soon be eliminated. And that, in essence, is the book of Judges.

During the time of Judges, the people would be delivered and they would then have a time of rest and peace. It was a good time, but unfortunately, it never lasted very long. Spiritually speaking, this Old Testament phenomenon of judges or saviors whom God raised up from time to time speaks, figuratively, of revival. When God's people are under oppression or are very depressed and low spiritually, God, in His mercy, does bring in revival. But let us realize that revival is not God's permanent measure; it is His temporary work. I will explain more about this later on, but we need to bear this fact in mind because it is important to understand the Scriptures.

Now the book of Judges can be divided into three parts. The first section is from chapters 1:1 to 3:6. It tells us the reason for the people's condition. Why were they oppressed? Why were they in such a low state? The part from chapters 3:7 through chapter 16 gives the history of the children of Israel during the time of the Judges and chapters 17—21 give us some details concerning the inner condition of the people during the time of Judges. In other words, historically speaking, time-wise, the history actually ends at chapter 16, but chapter 17 to the end of the book reveals the inner spiritual state or condition of the children of Israel.

THE REASON FOR DEFEAT

The first part or section of the book tells us the reason for the situation among the children of Israel, and it can be found in chapter 2. When the children of Israel first came into the Promised Land under the leadership of Joshua, no enemy could stand before them. They won battle after battle. They wiped out enemy after enemy, and they were able to take possession of a great number of cities and lands. Therefore, Joshua was able to divide up the land to all the tribes of the children of Israel. After Joshua died the Israelites continued on with possessing their possession. In the first chapter, we find them asking the Lord concerning who should go first to take the land that had not been captured yet, and God said the tribe of Judah should go first. So Judah told the tribe of Simeon that if they would go with him, he later on would help Simeon to get their possession. The Israelites did in fact begin very well to take their possessions, but even from reading only the first chapter, we can begin to see how, when they were going out to possess their possessions, weakness had already manifested itself: there were some cities they could not take, some lands they could not capture, and some enemies they could not drive out.

Let us remind ourselves here that God had promised the land to the children of Israel: "No enemy can stand before you." God was with them and was faithful to them. He was well able to drive out all their enemies so that His people might possess their possession. Why were the children of Israel not able to fully possess it? Some of their enemies were too strong for them, and if we read very carefully, we shall learn that some enemies lived in their midst, and in some places they even lived in the midst of their enemies. Immediately, therefore, we see weakness shown in the lives of the people of God. Why?

Well, in chapter 2 we read that the angel of the Lord went up from Gilgal to Bochim and delivered a message to the children of Israel. Now, if we read the book of Joshua carefully we shall discern that Gilgal was *the* place in the Promised Land just as Sinai was *the* place in the wilderness. After crossing the Jordan River the children of Israel came to Gilgal, and there they underwent circumcision (see Joshua 5:2-9). The Bible declares about this event that the reproach of Egypt was rolled away from them. *Gilgal* means "rolling" or "rolled away." It simply means that Gilgal, having become the site where the flesh-cutting knife had been applied to God's people, was the place where the reproach of their Egyptian slavery had now been rolled away. In other words, symbolically speaking, God's people back then were now completely delivered from the world and the flesh and thus God by His Spirit could lead them forth to one victory after another over their enemies: "Not by natural might nor power of the flesh, but by My Spirit," declares the Lord (see Zechariah 4:6). The Israelites went out each time from Gilgal to fight their enemies, and after they overcame them, they always returned to Gilgal. Indeed, from the very outset Gilgal served as the people's headquarters, and from there they went forth to gain victory in the land again and again. Gilgal, therefore, represented the proper place where God's people experienced victory over all adversaries.

However, we next learn that the angel of the Lord had to go up from Gilgal to Bochim because God's people were no longer based at Gilgal. Bochim means "weepers" because the angel of the Lord had to deliver a very stern message there which caused the people to weep. Through the angel God had said: "Why do you not keep My covenant? Why do you do these things? Why do you leave Me? Why do you begin to mix with the inhabitants of the land? Why have you entered into a league with those inhabitants? Why do you begin to worship their gods? And so, because you have done all this, I am not going to drive out all your enemies." And so the children of Israel wept. They wept bitterly because of their weaknesses and consequent defeats. Hence, "from Gilgal to Bochim" can explain the entire book of Judges.

Whenever we leave the place of the cutting off of the flesh, that is to say, the place of the cross—and even if such occurs when we have been blessed with every spiritual blessing in the heavenlies in Christ—we will be defeated. And like the Israelites of old we, too, will have cause to weep because of such defeats. The children of Israel were not faithful to God, and because of their unfaithfulness, they were weakened before their enemies. Their enemies were able to live in their midst, and in certain places they even ended up having to live among their enemies. And from time to time their enemies would overcome them and put them under great oppression—perhaps for eight years or twenty years or for as long as forty years. Then they would cry out to the Lord, and the Lord, in His mercy, would send judges to deliver them. But even when the judge was living, they did not heed the voice of God. Therefore, when the judge died, they would return to the same old habit, and the whole scenario would repeat itself all over again. What a depressing story!

CHURCH HISTORY

We need to take note of something here. In the history of God's people under the new covenant, church history during these past two thousand years has been very much like the time of the book of Judges. At the beginning all seemed to have gone well with the church, but then, gradually, she became spiritually weakened because of unfaithfulness to God. She was weakened because of the believers' love for the world; indeed, the church began to mingle with the world. God's people were weakened because they began to have other loves, other objects of dependence, other relationships—in short, they catered to their flesh. And hence, the enemy began to gain ground and oppress God's people, and so they cried to the Lord, and the Lord brought in revival. He gave His people some great man and brought in a great revival to grant them some refreshing. But these revivals were only occasional, and they were not universal in scope: here a revival, there a revival, but not a revival of God's people all over the world. Moreover, these revivals never lasted very long. Some were longer and some were but for a few short years and then they were gone, and the cycle has repeated itself again and again down to our present day. Unfaithfulness is the reason. God is faithful, but we are unfaithful. Yet even in our unfaithfulness, God still shows His mercy and now and then He grants us a time of refreshing, but it seems that we never learn.

THE HISTORY OF THE JUDGES

The second part or section of this book is the actual history; and so we learn that during this long four-hundred-and-fifty-year period, God raised up thirteen judges whose call to leadership represents a continuous repetitive cycle of declension, oppression, repentance and revival. In fact, there were altogether seven such cycles of declension which are recorded in Judges. The description of the first cycle is found in chapter 3:7-11. The Israelites were under the oppression of Mesopotamia for eight years, and God raised up Othniel as a judge, and there was peace for forty years. The second cycle is narrated in chapter 3:12-31 that describes the oppression by the Moabites, Ammonites, and Amalekites lasting eighteen years, with God raising up Ehud to deliver the people. Shamgar's judgeship is contemporary with that of Ehud, and the peace was eighty years in length. The third cycle is related in chapters 4:1—5:31 and involved the oppression by the Canaanites lasting twenty years. On behalf of the Israelies God raised up Deborah and Barak as deliverer-judges, and there was peace for forty years. The fourth cycle's description can be found in chapters 6:1—

8:32 and tells of the Midianite oppression lasting seven years. Here God raised up Gideon to deliver the children of Israel, and there was peace for forty years. The fifth cycle is described in chapters 8:33—10:5 and relates the wicked usurpation of leadership by Abimelech for three years, prompting God to raise up Tola as judge for twenty-three years and Jair as judge for twenty-two years. The details of the sixth cycle can be found in chapters 10:6—12:15 and tell of the oppression by the Ammonites that lasted eighteen years, with God having to raise up Jephthah as judge for six years, Ibzan for seven years, Elon for ten years, and Abdon for eight years. The seventh and final cycle is described in chapters 13 through 16 and involved the Philistine oppression of the Israelites for forty years, and God raised up Samson to deliver the people for twenty years.

THE INNER CONDITION

The third and final section runs from chapter 17 through chapter 21 and reveals the inner history of the children of God during the time of the judges. The condition was so low that a Levite priest from the tribe of Benjamin in the house of Micah sold himself to the tribe of Dan to be the priest there. Think of that! The moral state was so low that the people sinned without manifesting any shame. Moreover, there was open public self-righteousness on display: the other Israelite tribes deemed themselves more righteous than the tribe of Benjamin which led to fighting among the brethren and even the killing of each other. Furthermore, even one of the judges was found to be in sin: think of Samson! In sum, the people were divided, fought against each other, and were under the near-constant oppression of the enemy. It was only by the mercy of God that they still existed and were not completely annihilated. Such was the abysmal inner history of God's people.

OBSERVATIONS GLEANED FROM CHURCH HISTORY

SECOND-GENERATION TRADITION

With all the above as background, we need to make several observations. We are not simply reviewing the history of another nation here, but we also want to take stock of ourselves in the light of that history as is presented in the book of Judges. First of all, then, let us realize that as long as Joshua and the elders with him of the first generation were living, the children of Israel kept God's commandment—His covenant—and were faithful to God. But after Joshua and the elders of that first generation died who had witnessed the great works of God and knew Him personally, another generation came forth. They did not know God nor His great works and something happened— they drifted away from God: they began to mix with the heathen, to worship their idols, and to do other things that the heathen did. And very soon they found themselves under the oppression of their enemies. In brief, they were defeated.

Do we not find the very same thing when we read church history? God raised up a people, a body of believers, the church—just as He had done with Joshua, the elders and the rest of the Israelites. They knew God; they had seen the work of God; they had personal experience of Him; they had received revelation from Him; they had seen Him; and because of that, there was spiritual strength. They were able to enter their Promised Land—Christ—and to possess all of His unsearchable riches. Indeed, no enemy could stand before them; they were invincible. But when that first generation passed away and the second came forth, the latter did not have that firsthand revelation which the first generation had received. In other words, with the first generation, it was revelation, but with the second it had become tradition. The second generation did not see for themselves; they only heard of these things. For the second generation it had become a matter of tradition, and tradition can never deliver; it can never set people free; rather, tradition binds people. It is revelation that sets people free. Hence, at the beginning, what is raised up is organic in nature. The life of the church is an organic life, but now the life of God's people has become organizational. And when the church becomes organizational, the life is gone. The more life there is, the less organization is needed; but the less life there is, the more organization is required to support it and maintain it.

What do I mean by the first generation? Please understand that I do not mean those who are over sixty years old but those people who have a personal relationship with the Lord, those people who have seen the Lord, those who have caught the vision, those who know the purpose of God, those who have received revelation. These are people of the first generation. No matter how old physically, they never need, spiritually speaking, to descend into the second generation. They can always remain in the first. Even though another generation is raised up, these too can be a part of the first generation. Unfortunately, however, people sit back and take it easy: they do not need to fight to retain what they had seen and received as the first generation; on the contrary, they now merely receive what is handed down to them and think they have it. Yet they do not have it because they do not have a revelation.

What these believers have is a tradition, and they find themselves without life and depending on an organization. What a pity! And whenever God's people come into that kind of situation, the enemy has the upper hand. Let not anyone be surprised or wonder why he or she suddenly becomes overcome by the enemy. There should not be any surprise since the life is not there anymore.

HOLDING FAST THE HEAD

The second observation which ought to be set forth here is that during the time of the judges the commentary pronounced in the Scriptures by the Holy Spirit concerning the kind of situation described in Judges was that during those times of declension there was no king, and, therefore, everyone did what was right in his own eyes. Why was the situation like that? Quite simply, because there was no king—no unifying force—in Israel to bind the people together. There was no direction, no government. Hence, everybody did whatever he or she thought was right; each one always thought that he or she was right and that whatever each person did was right and that the other people were wrong. Accordingly, I will go this way and you can go that way. God's people also fought against each other and naturally, they were overcome by the enemy. There was no unity and no love; there was no power that really bound them together.

Has this not been the history of God's people in our own day? True, in reading God's word we learn that we do have a King—even Christ; and the church is His body under His headship. And with Christ being our Head and King, He is the One who unites us together. And if we hold fast to Him as the Head, we will be fitly framed together and will minister one to another; and the body will build itself up in love (see Colossians 2:19; Ephesians 1:22-23; 4:15b-16). That is what God has ordained for us to be. Unfortunately, however, God's people today do not hold fast the Head. Everyone is a king to himself or to herself. Instead of holding fast the Head, we are scattered. We do what we each think is right in our own eyes; we fight for what we think is right; and so we fight with our brethren.

Is Christ divided? (see I Corinthians 1:13) If we see Christ and really hold to Him as our King, we will be one, and in that unity there is strength. But when we are divided, we are scattered: we are doing things according to what we think is right, and thus we become easy prey for the enemy. Divide and destroy—that is the tactic of the enemy.

We therefore need to learn this lesson: that only when God's people hold fast the Head—even Christ—and let Him have complete rule over us do we honor Him as our King. Indeed, this is what the church is to be: "Where two or three are gathered together unto My name," said Jesus, "there am I in the midst of them" (see Matthew 18:20). In other words, when we put ourselves under His name, when we let Him be our Head and let His authority be over us, then He is present, and we are invincible; otherwise, we are defeated.

REVIVAL OR RECOVERY?

One final observation to be gleaned from church history as it relates to the book of Judges is that it is a book of revivals. This is what the book is if we wish to view the book from the positive side. If, though, we consider the negative side, Judges is a book of declension. Thank God for the positive side, for revival; but let us realize that revival is not God's permanent measure. People today are praying for revival as though this is the one thing which the church of God needs above all else. No; we most of all need recovery, not revival.

What actually is revival? Revival is that which always looks back. We have fallen, so we need to be revived and go back to where we were before we fell. That is revival. Recovery, on the other hand, always looks forward; yet not only to restore all which has been lost but also to push ahead to the full purpose of God. We thank God for the revivals which have been sent to the world throughout the centuries. These have been times of refreshing, even glorious times; but unfortunately, one revival comes and then it goes, and so we need another revival. But thank God, sometimes He does send recovery.

Let me illustrate. I believe the Reformation was a recovery and not a revival. One can say, in effect, that it was universal in scope. Something was restored and brought into the path of God's eternal purpose. That is what a recovery is. I believe the Brethren movement that occurred in the nineteenth century was likewise a recovery because the effect of it was world-wide.

Truth was recovered and that brought the church forward. The Welsh Revival was most glorious, but it was only a revival, not a recovery. It affected Wales, a part of the world, but it was not universal. It did not seem to bring the church further on in God's eternal purpose.

What we need today is recovery. We need the Lord to recover us; not only for Him to restore all which has been lost in the past, but to lead us forward into the full realization of God's eternal purpose. And we thank God, He is doing this very work of recovery in our day. He is moving on, and we need to move on with Him. So may the Lord help us.

Let us pray:

> *Dear heavenly Father, we do praise and thank Thee that Thou hast not only promised us the good land, but Thou hast already given it to us, even Thy beloved Son. We do praise and thank Thee that we are in Him and He is in us. Father, do enable us to hear Him, to love Him and to obey Him that we may remain in Him, that we may enjoy Him to the fullest. And it is all to be a testimony to Thee and a glory to Thy name. Father, we acknowledge that we are unfaithful, stiff-necked, rebellious; but Thou art faithful, loving, trustworthy and good. What Thou hast purposed Thou wilt perform it to Thy glory. In the name of our Lord Jesus. Amen.*

RUTH

RECOVERY OF THE INHERITANCE

Ruth 1:16-17—And Ruth said, Do not intreat me to leave thee, to return from following after thee; for whither thou goest I will go, and where thou lodgest I will lodge: thy people shall be my people, and thy God my God; where thou diest will I die, and there will I be buried. Jehovah do so to me, and more also, if aught but death part me and thee!

Ruth 2:8-12—And Boaz said to Ruth, Hearest thou not, my daughter? Go not to glean in another field, neither go from here, but keep here with my maidens. Let thine eyes be on the field which is being reaped, and go thou after them; have I not charged the young men not to touch thee? And when thou art athirst, go to the vessels and drink of what the young men draw. Then she fell on her face, and bowed herself to the ground, and said to him, Why have I found favour in thine eyes, that thou shouldest regard me, seeing I am a foreigner? And Boaz answered and said to her, It has fully been shewn me, all that thou hast done to thy mother-in-law since the death of thy husband; and how thou hast left thy father and thy mother, and the land of thy nativity, and art come to a people that thou hast not known heretofore. Jehovah recompense thy work, and let thy reward be full from Jehovah the God of Israel, under whose wings thou art come to take refuge.

Ruth 3:9-11—And he said, Who art thou? And she answered, I am Ruth, thy handmaid: spread thy skirt over thy handmaid; for thou hast the right of redemption. And he said, Blessed be thou of Jehovah, my daughter! Thou hast shewn more kindness at the end than at the first, inasmuch as thou followedst not young men, whether poor or rich. And now, my daughter, fear not: all that thou sayest will I do to thee; for all the gate of my people knows that thou art a woman of worth.

Ruth 4:9-10—And Boaz said to the elders and all the people, Ye are witnesses this day, that I have bought all that was Elimelech's, and all that was Chilion's and Mahlon's, of the hand of Naomi; moreover Ruth the Moabitess, the wife of Mahlon, have I purchased to be my wife, to raise up the name of the dead upon his inheritance, that the name of the dead be not cut off from among his brethren and from the gate of his place: ye are witnesses this day.

Let us pray:

Dear heavenly Father, we have just read Thy word and now we ask Thy Holy Spirit to open Thy word to our hearts. Speak to us, Lord, and draw us closer to Thyself because Thou art our Redeemer, our love, our all. We do commit this time into Thy hands. In the name of our Lord Jesus. Amen.

In the whole Bible there are only two books which bear the name of a woman: Ruth and Esther. We know there are remarkable differences between these two women. Ruth was a Moabitess, and therefore a Gentile, but she was sovereignly brought into the covenant people of God. Esther was a Jewish woman, but she was sovereignly placed in the court of a Gentile kingdom. Nevertheless, there is one thing that is common to both of them; they were both used to fulfill God's purpose.

This book of Ruth follows the book of Judges. In the ancient Jewish canon of the Scriptures, Ruth and Judges had actually been put together as one book. The event that is recorded in this book of Ruth happened during the time of the Judges, although we do not know for sure under which judge it had taken place. Some people think it occurred during the time of Gideon, because before Gideon was raised up by God as a judge, the children of Israel had come under oppression and were being deprived of their food. There was famine in the land. So probably, what is recorded in the book of Ruth happened during the time of Gideon as judge.

There is a great difference between the book of Judges and this book of Ruth. In Judges we notice the tragic, sad history of God's people. They were unfaithful to God and because of that, they were oppressed by the enemies who were among them and around them. Not only were they unable to fully possess their possession; they also were in danger of losing their possession. It was a very depressing record; but when we come to the book of Ruth, we see the bright side of the history of the children of Israel. Here we learn that through God's sovereign grace everything seemed to have been restored. There was redemption, and there was recovery of the inheritance. Hence, Ruth actually gives us the bright side of the history of God's people during the time of the judges.

The book of Ruth is one of the Jewish festive rolls that is read during feast days at festival time, and we are told that this book is read at the time of Pentecost. It not only is a very beautiful story, it also is a book which displays for us the principles of grace and redemption.

Ruth was a Moabitess, and we learn from Genesis 19 that Moab was the son born out of terrible sin. The very word Moab translated from the Hebrew means "from the father"; which is to say, what is of the flesh is flesh. According to Deuteronomy, the Moabites, even to the tenth generation, were not able to become part of the congregation of the Israelites (see 23:3). In other words, the Moabites were completely excluded from the promises of God; and Ruth was of this Gentile tribe. Yet, through sovereign grace, she was brought into the covenant people of God. Not only that, we find that it was through her that David the future Jewish king was born. In the genealogy of Jesus recorded in Matthew 1 she is one of the four women mentioned: indeed, the Lord Jesus came through her. That demonstrates for us the tremendous, sovereign, amazing grace of God.

Ruth stands between the books of Judges and I Samuel. We will recall how at the end of Judges the Holy Spirit gave His explanation for why there was such an abysmal state of affairs in the history of God's people during this period. It was because at that time there was no king and everyone did what was right in his own eyes. But, then, in the time of I Samuel, God introduces His king to His people. It is the commencement of the history of kingship, and in between there is Ruth. Ruth is the link between Judges and I Samuel because, through Ruth, David came into this world. This book of Ruth is therefore very important in God's word. It is not only a beautiful story, it also paints for us a picture of the Lord's redemption.

DISCIPLINE OF GOD

As we have mentioned earlier, during the time of Judges there was a famine in the land, and that land, of course, was the Promised Land. In Deuteronomy 8 we read that this land was a good land. It was full of springs, waterbrooks and rivers; it was a land of barley, wheat and corn; a land of olives and vineyards; and a land of iron and copper. It was thus a land richly blessed by God, flowing with milk and honey. And if the children of Israel would keep God's word and His commandment, then God's eyes would be upon that land most favorably. He would bless the heaven and heaven would bless the earth, and the earth would continually yield up bountiful harvests and thus there would be no scarcity in that land. Yet, we learn that there was famine in the land, which was therefore something out of the ordinary—it was not what should have been. What was the reason for it? The children of Israel had rebelled against God: they had not kept the covenant; they had not kept the commandments of God; instead, they had committed one abomination after another and had worshiped idols. In short, they had totally left God. Accordingly, that was the reason the land was cursed. It was the disciplinary hand of God upon that land.

When the discipline of God comes upon a people, what should they do? They should humble themselves under His mighty hand and repent. If they would repent, then He would forgive them and restore them to His blessings. Instead of doing that, however, this man Elimelech had taken his family and had left the land of promise—the land of his inheritance— and had gone into the land of Moab. This man had avoided the discipline of the Lord. This is all very ironic because in Hebrew the very name Elimelech means "whose God is king" and his wife's name, Naomi, means "my pleasantness." They had gone from Bethlehem, meaning "the house of bread," to the land of Moab, "of the flesh."

Let us ask ourselves: Are we in any position to judge that man? Is it not so that often this is the very way we ourselves react to the discipline of God? Too often, when God disciplines us, our first reaction is to try to escape from it instead of acknowledging our sin, humbling ourselves before God and repenting of it, just as we are told to do in I Peter: "Humble yourselves therefore under the mighty hand of God, that He may exalt you in... [due] time" (5:6). Instead of doing that, though, we flee from God's discipline. And yet, do we realize that avoiding His discipline means losing our inheritance?

The disciplinary hand of God followed that man to the land of Moab. He could not escape God's discipline. There is no way for that to happen, and ultimately he died. His two sons married Moabitish women against the plain word of God, and so the discipline followed them as well. Both of the sons died. There was no hope for that family to regain their inheritance because all the men had now died. They had tried to flee from the discipline of God.

Permit me to inquire: Does God ever discipline us? If He has never chastened us, then we are not His sons; we are bastards (see Hebrews 12:8). He chastens us because He loves us. Are we so perfect that we never sin against Him, that we never do anything wrong? And if God should discipline us out of His love, is it not His desire to restore us? He has no desire to punish us. It is not God's will for us just to suffer. He disciplines us because He wants to restore us to himself and to our inheritance. But if we escape from discipline—and even if it may appear to be so—can we really escape God's chastening? Probably, the hand of God will be even heavier than upon those who remain where they are. But for those who try to escape from discipline, they should remember this one thing: they have the danger of losing their inheritance. Discipline is for the purpose of inheriting our inheritance. There is so much in Christ that God wants us to inherit, and through discipline we grow up and are able to possess our possession in Christ Jesus.

RESTORATION

Let us see that in all of this, God is merciful. When the children of Israel were under oppression, they finally cried out to the Lord. From Judges 6 we learn that they were oppressed for seven years, and yet, strangely, it was not until toward the very end of that seven years that they began to cry to the Lord for help. And when they cried to God, He sent His messenger to tell them why they were in such a poor situation. In other words, God convicted them so that they might repent of their sins, and thereafter, in His great mercy He raised up a judge in the land of Israel to deliver them out of the hand of their enemies.

Meanwhile, Naomi was left in the land of Moab with her two daughters-in-law—altogether, three widows. They were there for about ten years. Then she heard in the country of Moab that God had visited His people back home in Israel and was providing them food. This woman, Naomi, was under the disciplinary hand of God, but let us notice her attitude. She was not like her husband who had continually fled from God's discipline to the very end. By contrast, Naomi realized that she was under her God's discipline. She told her two daughters-in-law that she was in more pain and suffering than they because the disciplinary hand of God was upon her very heavily (see Ruth 1:13, 20-21). In other words, she was a woman who had been submitting herself under the discipline of the Lord. So far as she herself was concerned she had lost all hope of regaining her inheritance; for now there was no man left in her life. But when she heard that back home God had visited the land to give the people bread, her heart was stirred because, even though she was under discipline, she had a heart's desire for God and for the inheritance. So she decided to go back to the land of promise. She attempted to send her daughters-in-law away because it was a hopeless case for them to follow her into the land of Israel. They being Gentiles, there was no hope there for them. Nevertheless, there was Ruth.

How was Ruth to be brought into a relationship with the covenant people of God? It was not because she had been married to Mahlon; it was really through Naomi that Ruth was to be brought into that relationship. Naomi was a person under discipline, and because she had been submitting herself under the chastening hand of God, there came forth such beauty from that kind of attitude. Indeed, it attracted Ruth to cast herself for refuge beneath the wings of the God of Israel.

How very true it is that when we see a person under God's discipline and who has a submissive spirit, a testimony is there. It shows not only faith, it shows as well how living and how real is the God to whom a person submits. We do not see this kind of attitude in the world; rather, what we see is rebellion. On the other hand, when we witness in a person that kind of submissive spirit which treats it all as from the Lord, causing that person to bow under the hand of God, to acknowledge that He is right in all His doings, and to look only for His mercy, then it reveals that God is real. It shows that one's relationship with God is real, and that attracts people because they are looking for reality.

Yet that spirit attracted Ruth not only to Naomi but also to the God of Naomi. So when Naomi tried to send her away, Ruth declared: "Do not intreat me to leave thee, to return from following after thee; for whither thou goest I will go, and where thou lodgest I will lodge: thy people shall be my people, and thy God my God" (Ruth 1:16).

She cast her lot with the people of God. She took the God of Israel as her God. She was willing to leave her native place, her own people and her gods and simply entrust herself under the wings of the living God.

THE VIRTUES OF RUTH

Ruth in Hebrew means "beauty." Some people say Ruth means "satisfied" or "friendship." As we read this book of Ruth we can easily discern how beautiful this woman was. There were so many virtues in her. Let us look, for example, at her relationship with her mother-in-law. Usually, the relationship between a mother-in-law and daughter-in-law is very difficult because both want to have the exclusive right over the man, and invariably, there will be conflict. It is very difficult for a mother-in-law and daughter-in-law to get along well, but here was a beautiful example of a good, intimate relationship between a mother-in-law and her daughter-in-law. This mother-in-law was concerned about everything for the daughter-in-law. We may recall how Naomi had said, "Is it not time that I should do something for her?"

Likewise, the daughter-in-law had great love towards her mother-in-law. How willing she was to serve her, to work for her, to support her. There was such a beautiful relationship here. And I do believe that if the life of the Lord is truly being lived out, this should always be the case. Sometimes, though, we find this is not the case because we are living by our own fleshly life instead of living by the life of Christ. If His life is truly living in both the mother-in-law and daughter-in-law, there will be a harmonious, loving, beautiful relationship. That is bound to be so.

Another virtue in Ruth was that she was a very diligent person. She worked long and hard in the fields, and even the servant of Boaz observed that "this maiden has worked here from morning until now, and she very seldom rests." She was continually working and working and working. She was a diligent, industrious woman, and when she was given some food to eat, she left some for her mother-in-law: she was not selfish in any sense. Hence, there are many good things which we can say about Ruth, but I believe we ought to concentrate on but one point here: she cast herself under the wings of the God of Israel.

Let us repeat what was said earlier. She was a Moabitish woman. Therefore, as a native of Moab she was excluded from the commonwealth of Israel and barred from the promises of God. She had no part whatsoever with God; yet she was drawn to Him. She placed herself beneath His wings. Legally, she had no part forever, even to the tenth generation; yet God did not deal with her in a legal manner. He dealt with her through grace. One Christian brother has commented about Ruth as follows: "The children of Israel did not love God and they were in danger of losing their inheritance, but here was a Moabitess who loved God, and because of her love for Him, she gained the inheritance." God will never refuse a lover no matter what one's past history may be.

We will remember from Luke 7 how the Lord Jesus on one occasion said to Simon the Pharisee concerning the formerly sinful woman who had come in to anoint Jesus: "She is forgiven much because she loves much." In her heart, Ruth was drawn to God through Naomi. She said, "Your people are my people; your God is my God." Because of that, the blessing of the Lord came upon her. This should teach us a lesson that above all things else there must be love. If we love God, He will never refuse us.

OUR KINSMAN

A third person came into the picture: Boaz. The name Boaz means, "In him is strength." A kinsman of the family of Elimelech, Boaz was a rich man possessing many fields. He was a generous person and very observant. And it so happened that Ruth was gleaning in the fields of Boaz. Now according to the Levitical Law, when you are reaping your harvest and overlook a sheaf of grain, you are not allowed to go back and collect it. This was to be left for the widows, the strangers and the poor. It was the practice among the children of Israel that whenever there occurred a harvesting or a reaping of fields there would be poor people, widows and strangers following the reapers and picking up whatever was left behind so that they might have food to eat. That shows the character of God who always has a compassion towards the poor, the widows and the strangers. God in His Law reminded the children of Israel that once they too were strangers—in the land of Egypt—and that they were to do to others what they wished others to do to them.

In accordance with this compassionate law and custom, therefore, Ruth asked permission from her mother-in-law to go and glean in the fields. Again, how obedient this daughter-in-law was. And Naomi said, "Go." There were many fields around Bethlehem, but by the providence of God she was directed to the fields of Boaz. She herself did not know that, but God knew. And when Boaz came out to the one particular field of his, he noticed Ruth and asked the people who she was. They told him that she was a Moabitess who had come back with Naomi and that she had been working until now; and Boaz was kind to her. He said to Ruth: "All that you have done has been told me. You are a woman of worth. You are willing to leave your land, your own nativity and your own people and come under the wings of God. God will recompense you; He will reward you." This which he said about Ruth is the reason why Boaz was so kind to her. We can see here that Boaz represents Christ. He is a type of Christ.

The Lord Jesus is our Kinsman. How can God be our Kinsman? He is our Creator, our Maker. We are His created beings. The Scriptures tell us that we are like clay in the hands of the potter. And figuratively speaking, God is the Potter. The Potter has every right to make whatever vessel He wishes out of us the clay, and there is therefore nothing we can say about it. How, then, can God be our Kinsman? It is because there is a relationship there due to the fact that the Word became flesh—even Jesus himself—and tabernacled among men, full of grace and truth. On the one hand, God is far, far above all of us a very great distance. There is no relationship of an intimate kind there. On the other hand, thank God, Jesus His Son came into this world.

"For both he that sanctifies and those sanctified are all of one" (Hebrews 2:11). It is because we are of flesh and blood that, therefore, Jesus took part in the same so that He might die for us and through His death annul the one who has the power of death, the devil, and deliver us out of the fear of death (see vv. 14-15). He thus can become our Kinsman. He is rich, full of grace and truth, and He is willing and kind.

Boaz said to Ruth: "Stay in my fields, do not go anywhere else. Just glean in my fields." Even the *gleanings* from the fields of Boaz were plentiful. Let us take note of the fact that even before we really came to know the Lord, perhaps we merely had a kind of desire for Him. We had not actually come to know Him yet, but God in His providence will lead us, as it were, to His fields. I do not know if you have ever had that kind of experience. Although you did not yet know God, you had a desire, and strangely, you found yourself gleaning in the fields of Boaz and picking up blessings from God. God did bless you in many ways even though at that moment you did not truly know Him yet.

It reminds me of the Syrophoenician woman who besought the Lord Jesus on behalf of her child, and the Lord told her that it was not right to give the children's (i.e., the Jews') bread to the dogs. Nevertheless, the woman responded with, "That is right, but the pet dog picks up the children's crumbs from beneath the table" (see Mark 7:24-30). This was the situation with Ruth the Gentile in her own day. She was a dog so far as the Jews were concerned, but so far as God was concerned, she was a pet dog, not a wild dog; and thus, like this Syrophoenician woman, Ruth was allowed to pick up all the "crumbs" in the fields of Boaz.

Unfortunately, some people are satisfied just to pick up bits and pieces. They think it is grand just to be under the table picking up something. They do not want to sit with the King and eat from His table. Yet there is so much more that the Lord is willing to give us.

RIGHT OF REDEMPTION

Ruth was brought to the fields of Boaz and because of that her livelihood was solved. Even her mother-in-law's livelihood was solved; but is that all? Is that all you want? Do you merely desire some blessing from God? God will surely bless you, but is that all you want? Not so with Naomi; she knew better. When the harvest was over, she told Ruth that Boaz was their kinsman. And because of that, he had the right to claim redemption.

In God's word, specifically in Leviticus 25, we read that if an Israelite became poor and had to sell his land, the next of kin had the right to redeem it. We must not forget that the land actually belonged to God, and He apportioned to each person a parcel of it. That portion of land was meant to be kept in the family forever. So if a person became so poor that he had to sell his land, then according to the law, the next of kin had the right to buy it so that the land would remain in the family. This kept it from going to the other Israelite tribes or possibly even to foreigners. That was one law.

There was another law, stated in Deuteronomy 25, which

reads that if a man died without a child, his brother, who lived with him, should take his wife in order to bear children for his deceased brother. That was so the inheritance would continue on. Inheritance was a very important issue to the children of Israel.

Boaz had the right of redemption but it had to be claimed. So Naomi said: "Tonight, Boaz will eat and drink and be very happy because the harvest is over, and he will probably lie down on the threshing floor. You must therefore go in and claim the right of redemption." So Ruth went in and lay at Boaz's feet, and when he awoke, he asked her who she was. And she replied: "I am Ruth, cover me with the skirt of your garment. You have the right of redemption."

THE CROSS

This entire episode happened on the threshing floor—the place where was separated the wheat from the chaff. Spiritually speaking, threshing floor speaks of the cross because there is a separating or dividing of everything: what is of God (the wheat) from what is not of God (the chaff) (see I Corinthians 3:12; cf. Jeremiah 23:28). As happens at the threshing floor, there was a great dividing which occurred at the cross; and it was at the threshing floor where Ruth claimed her right of redemption.

Let us always remember this, that it is at the cross of the Lord Jesus that we lay our claim to the right of redemption, because the Lord Jesus has died on the cross for us and where He proclaimed: "It is finished." The work of redemption is finished, and therefore, we lay claim to our right of redemption there. We as it were say: "Redeem us, Lord."

Let us recall the parable which the Lord Jesus taught concerning the two men who entered the temple to pray. One was a Pharisee and the other, a publican or tax collector. The Pharisee, being self-righteous, was praying loudly to be heard by everybody (except God who did not hear his prayer); and he prayed, saying: "God, I thank You because I am so good, I am

not like that sinner over there." And the sinner—the publican—
did not even dare to come forward towards the altar. Instead,
he stood back and beat his breast and prayed: "Oh, God, have
mercy upon me" (see Luke 18:9-14). Another translation says,
"Oh, Lord, allow me to be atoned." The publican was looking
at the altar. He saw the sacrifice burning there and he said:
"Allow me to be atoned. I claim my right of redemption."
And he obtained it. It is at the cross of the Lord Jesus that
we claim our right of redemption, and what a right it is! It is
a double redemption. It not only redeems the land (i.e., one's
inheritance), it also redeems the person.

THE LAW CANNOT REDEEM

Unfortunately, there was one person even closer in
relationship to Elimelech than Boaz. So Boaz said: "Yes, I
will do it; I will be glad to do it because you are a woman
of worth. Everybody knows this; but there is one closer, and
if he wants to claim it, I have to let him. If he does not lay
claim, then I will do it" (see Ruth 3). The name of this closer
kin is not mentioned. Spiritually speaking, who can be that
one to us? Who is closer to us, in a sense, than even the Lord
Jesus? It is evident from Scripture and history that before grace
came through the Lord Jesus, God had given the Law through
Moses. In other words, the Law came first and then grace (see
John 1:17). Do we realize there is one that is closer to us in
time, and that is, the Law?

Yet, can the Law redeem us? If we keep the Law, we may
live, that is true; yet who is able to keep the Law? The Law
is holy, but we are in the flesh; we are weak and unable to
meet the demands of the Law. The Law, as represented here
by the unnamed closer kinsman, cannot redeem us because if
he should try, it would jeopardize his inheritance. This means
that if he (the Law) says that everything is okay, then he would
become lawless. So he (the Law) cannot do that. There is no

way for the Law to redeem us. The Law says if you keep every facet of the Law, then you live; but if you break any one of the Laws, you die. With the Law, there is no compromise, there is no negotiation, there is no way through to redemption. Law cannot do it. So that the unnamed closer kinsman said he was unable to redeem the land, and accordingly he took off his sandal and gave it to Boaz as a sign of his inability. That was the custom at that time for any transaction which a person could not undertake and fulfill.

Thank God, the Law cannot redeem us. Unfortunately, oftentimes, even in the Christian world, there are many people who still try to keep the Law in order to be redeemed, but the Law tells us they cannot do it. It is a hopeless case; no one is good enough to be saved and redeemed except through the redeeming blood of the Lord Jesus.

Boaz not only had the right of redemption now, he also had the will to redeem. He had the willingness and the readiness; he was even anxious to redeem, and Naomi knew that; for she said to Ruth that Boaz would not rest until he had done it (see Ruth 3:18b). Sure enough, early in the morning, Boaz went to the gates of the city. He called that unnamed kinsman to be present and called the witnesses and the elders together, and immediately, he wanted to have the transaction made (see Ruth 4:1ff.).

HIS BELOVED WIFE

Is that not like the Lord Jesus? He not only has the right and the means to redeem us, He not only has the will and is willing to redeem us, He is even anxious to redeem us. Oh, how truly anxious He is! Why, then, are you not anxious about it? Let Him redeem you, and not only the lost inheritance is recovered, the person himself is also redeemed. For Boaz declared: "I will purchase the land and I will purchase Ruth to be my wife."

Do we know that we have lost our inheritance through sin? All of what God originally meant for us to possess for eternity we lost through sin. We not only have lost our inheritance—God's intended grace for us—but we ourselves are also lost. To lose an inheritance is one thing, but to lose oneself is another and far worse thing. We had lost both: we were lost and we lost our inheritance. We had no hope: our portion would be with the devil in the fire that always burns. But thank God, through the Lord Jesus He has redeemed us and bought us for himself—yet not to be His slaves but to be His beloved wife.

UNION WITH CHRIST

Redemption is more than having our sins forgiven. It is more than simply having our lost inheritance restored. Redemption is such that we as people are so redeemed that we are brought into union with Christ. Too often our vision is limited to the idea that when we are redeemed we obtain something—that we obtain forgiveness of sin, that we obtain eternal life, that we obtain this and that blessing of God; but let us see that there is much, much more than that involved in redemption. When we are redeemed, we are brought into union with Christ. And if that be so, then all that is Christ's is ours: all the fullness and all the riches which are of Christ is now ours, and it is all because we are united with Him in one. And being thus united with Him, everything which God had originally designed to give us as heirs of God and co-heirs of Christ become reality for us. We are now entering into the fullness of God, and that is what redemption is—that is how vast is the scope of our redemption. And the Lord declares that He has done it, for let us note that Boaz declared before the people: "Today, I have done this; you are witnesses." The Lord has done it. Now let us enter in.

KINGSHIP

At the end of the book we find that Ruth, a Moabitess, was not only brought into a relationship with God's covenant people but was also brought into union with Boaz. And out of that union eventually came David (see Ruth 4:17-22). In other words, the king of Israel, was brought in and also, eventually, the King of all kings. As we learned earlier, Elimelech means "whose God is king." His name was so, but his life was a far different testimony: he did not allow God to be King over his life. Had he done so he would have remained in the Promised Land in spite of the famine. He would have humbled himself before God, trusting God and submitting himself under His disciplinary hand, and thus he would have been restored. But he did not let God be his King. And that is the summation of the entire book of Judges: nobody had allowed God to be their King. They themselves were kings, and they did things according to their own will. But through the union of Ruth and Boaz came the king.

Let us recognize and ever remember this: that it is through the redemptive work of the Lord Jesus Christ that we are brought into union with Christ, and in our union with Him, the kingship of Christ is brought into being. Let the whole world know that our Lord is King, for in this union we not only enjoy everything that He has for us, but we also declare that He is our King and that He is the King of the whole world. Such is the book of Ruth.

Let us pray:

> *Dear heavenly Father, we do thank Thee for this book of Ruth because it does show us Thy amazing grace, the greatness of Thy redemption. Lord, we do acknowledge that we are like Ruth having at one time no part with Thee, and yet in Thy great love and mercy, in Thy sovereign grace, Thou hast brought us into that covenant relationship with Thyself. We thank Thee that Thou hast redeemed us through the cross of our Lord Jesus. We thank Thee that we are now united with Thee. We thank Thee that we do acknowledge that Thou art our King and there is none else. To Thee be the glory. In the name of our Lord Jesus. Amen.*

I SAMUEL

EPOCH-MAKING VESSEL

I Samuel 3:1, 19-21—And the boy Samuel ministered to Jehovah before Eli. And the word of Jehovah was rare in those days; a vision was not frequent... And Samuel grew, and Jehovah was with him, and let none of his words fall to the ground. And all Israel, from Dan even to Beer-sheba, knew that Samuel was established a prophet of Jehovah. And Jehovah appeared again at Shiloh; for Jehovah revealed himself to Samuel at Shiloh by the word of Jehovah.

I Samuel 7:1-6—And the men of Kirjath-jearim came, and fetched up the ark of Jehovah, and brought it into the house of Abinadab on the hill, and hallowed Eleazar his son to keep the ark of Jehovah. And it came to pass, from the day that the ark abode in Kirjath-jearim, that the time was long; for it was twenty years. And all the house of Israel lamented after Jehovah. And Samuel spoke to all the house of Israel, saying, If ye return to Jehovah with all your heart, put away the strange gods and the Ashtoreths from among you,   and apply your hearts unto Jehovah, and serve him only; and he will deliver you out of the hand of the Philistines. And the children of Israel put away the Baals and the Ashtoreths and served Jehovah only. And Samuel said, Gather all Israel to Mizpah, and I will pray Jehovah for you. And they gathered together to Mizpah, and drew water, and poured it out before Jehovah, and fasted on that day, and said there, We have sinned against Jehovah. And Samuel judged the children of Israel in Mizpah.

I Samuel 12:1-5,18-25—And Samuel said to all Israel, Behold, I have hearkened to your voice in all that ye said to me, and have made a king over you. And now behold, the king walks before you; and I am old and grey-headed; and behold, my sons are with you; and I have walked before you from my youth up to this day. Here I am: testify against me before Jehovah, and before his anointed. Whose ox have I taken? or whose ass have I taken? or whom have I defrauded? whom have I injured? or of whose hand have I received any ransom and blinded mine eyes therewith? and I will restore it to you. And they said, Thou hast not defrauded us, and thou hast not injured us, neither hast thou taken aught of any man's hand. And he said to them, Jehovah is witness against you, and his anointed is witness this day, that ye have not found aught in my hand! And the people said, He is witness! ... And Samuel called to Jehovah; and Jehovah sent thunder and rain that day. And all the people greatly feared Jehovah and Samuel. And all the people said to Samuel, Pray to Jehovah thy God for thy servants, that we die not; for we have added to all our sins the wickedness to ask for ourselves a king. And Samuel said to the people, Fear not: ye have done all this wickedness; yet turn not aside from following Jehovah, and serve Jehovah with all your heart; and turn ye not aside; for it would be after vain things which cannot profit nor deliver; for they are vain. For Jehovah will not cast away his people for his great name's sake; because it has pleased Jehovah to make you his people. Moreover, as for me, far be it from me that I should sin against Jehovah in ceasing to pray for you; and I will teach you the good and right way. Only, fear Jehovah, and serve him in truth, with all your heart; for see how great things he has done for you. But if ye do wickedly, ye shall perish, both ye and your king.

Let us pray:

Dear heavenly Father, how we do praise and thank Thee that we who were once sinners, rebels, who deserved nothing but death, that through Thy beloved Son, our Lord Jesus Christ, because of the shedding of His blood and the breaking of His body, we can come to Thee, accepted in the Beloved. With boldness we can behold Thee, the glory of the Lord, with unveiled face. So Father, we do thank Thee for this privilege that Thou hast given to us, and as we are in Thy presence, we do pray that Thy word would be opened to our hearts. Speak to us, Lord. Deliver us that we may be wholly Thine, and to Thee be the glory. In the name of our Lord Jesus. Amen.

The first book of Samuel is one of transition in narrating the history of the nation of Israel; for this book records the change from judgeship to kingship. The children of Israel had been living under the judges for some time, and it had developed into a very unsatisfactory situation, with the people of Israel having rebelled against God again and again. And because of their rebellion, God had allowed their enemies to oppress them. But while they were under oppression, they would cry to the Lord, and God, in His great mercy, would raise up judges or saviors to deliver them from their enemies. But whenever a given judge would die, the children of Israel would return to sinning again, and the whole sorry scenario would begin all over and would repeat itself time after time. During all those days there was no king, and everyone did what was right in his own eyes. Above all else, they did this: they rejected God as their King.

Yet in this book now before us we find that God took the occasion of their sin and turned it into good. That is to say, having rejected God as their King, the children of Israel perpetrated an evil act: they asked for a king like that of the nations. But thank God, He took the occasion of their sin and raised up a kingship that would be according to His purpose. For God ultimately gave them a king after His own heart, and eventually, through that king God would bring in the King of kings and the Lord of lords, even the Lord Jesus Christ.

In the ancient manuscript, what we know of today as I and II Samuel were one book. It was simply entitled Samuel, because Samuel was the central figure in the whole book. He was not only the last of the judges, he was the prophet raised up by God; and through him, God brought in the king and the kingdom. However, in reading through I Samuel we shall see that there are actually three leading figures: Samuel, Saul and David. So we can very easily divide I Samuel into three parts: chapters 1—7, Samuel; chapters 8—15, Saul; and 16—31, David. Now of course, their personal histories overlapped one another, and their influence overlapped one another as well, but we can see very clearly that these three men are the leading persons in the book.

According to Jewish tradition, chapters 1—24 were written by none other than Samuel himself. But since we learn at the beginning of chapter 25 that Samuel died, he could not have written the rest of I Samuel. Instead, this remaining part of the book was written by Nathan the prophet and Gad the seer, and this fact we know from I Chronicles 29:29.

FROM JUDGESHIP TO KINGSHIP

As we have already said, I Samuel is a book of transition from judgeship to kingship. As a matter of fact, in God's original order, judgeship was not included. Judgeship was merely God's temporary emergency measure. God had raised up the priesthood, and through the priesthood the people were to be brought to God, but the priesthood failed. And because of its failure, God instituted an emergency measure and raised up the order of judgeship. Nevertheless, God's permanent order had always been kingship. But before kingship was brought in, God undertook an emergency measure in terms of judges. However, under the judges the children of Israel never really returned to the Lord. Under the judges they came back to the Lord for a short time, but it was only for deliverance. For after each episode of deliverance they returned to sinning again because their hearts did not turn to the Lord. And that, as we saw earlier, was the book of Judges. But now with I Samuel we shall see that God is going to change the era from one of judgeship to that of kingship.

Another facet to this change which can be noticed is that in turning from judgeship to kingship God raised up another order—that of leadership: the prophets. Through the prophets God brought in the change from the judges to the kings. From Acts 3 in the New Testament we learn that Samuel was considered to be the first of the prophets. Of course, we acknowledge that in one sense Abraham himself had been a prophet but, strictly speaking, the Scriptures have deemed Samuel to have been the first of the prophets. And then from Samuel there was a succession of prophets for a thousand years until it ended with John the Baptist. These are the Old Testament prophets, and through them God made the change. The priests represented the people before God, but the prophets spoke for God to the people. And it was through the prophets that the transition to kingship was finally made.

THE FIRST STAGE OF SAMUEL'S LIFE

PREPARING A VESSEL FOR THE TRANSITION

Samuel was raised up by God as the vessel to bring in the transition. He was the last of the judges and the one to introduce the kings. He was an epoch-making vessel of God. We find that during that period Eli was also the last of the judges. Historically and chronologically speaking, he was probably a judge at the same time as Samson. Let us recall that the judges did not rule over all Israel; each judge only ruled part of it. So very likely Eli was judge at the same time as Samson. But although these judges were raised up by God to deliver the people and God did use them to do that work, let us look at these judges themselves. In the book of Judges we read what a sorry character Samson was; his life was a failure—and Eli, too.

True, Eli seemed to be a good man, but he was very old, feeble, and very weak. He could not see very well because his eyes were nearly blind, and he honored his sons more than he did God. He had two sons who were priests, and they were very wicked. They made sacrifice an abomination, an abhorrence in the eyes of the people (see I Samuel 2:12-17). They drew the people away from God instead of helping them to know Him, and Eli allowed his sons to go on like that. Indeed, he honored his sons more than God; and in a sense, that very partiality was representative of the spiritual condition of the people at the end of the period of the judges.

We also learn that during this period the word of God was very rare (see I Samuel 3:1b). God rarely spoke. Now we know that our God is One who speaks. Although He is not talkative, He nonetheless likes to talk. He never talks nonsense but speaks the truth. Yet the condition of God's people was such that they nearly shut the mouth of God. He could not talk to them because they did not have ears to hear. At that time it was no use speaking to them. And the Bible adds further that a vision was not frequent in those days (see 3:1c). In other words, God did not appear to them very often, yet not because He did not want to; on the contrary, God would have loved to communicate and commune with His people. He would have loved to show himself to His people, but their spiritual condition was so repulsive that He had to withdraw himself: He had to hide himself. Such, then, was the condition of the children of Israel during the period of the judges. It is true that from time to time they did experience some deliverances from their enemies, but their hearts were never turned towards God. It was a pitiful condition. And God's judgment was already upon Eli. He said, "Because you honor your sons more than Me, therefore your time will come to an end." Everything was dark, very dark. There seemed to be no hope for the people; but in His great mercy God was going to do something glorious. He was going to bring in the kingdom with *His* king.

A NAZARITE

Secretly, God was preparing a human vessel. Whenever He wants to make a move, whenever He wants to do something on this earth, He will first prepare a vessel. So, secretly, He was preparing a vessel for this dark time, and to effect that transition it all began with a woman named Hannah. The name *Hannah* means "grace." God shut her up to such a degree that she had to travail in prayer, and out of her travailing prayer, a son was born. His name was Samuel, meaning, "asked for of God." This son was born out of the travail of Hannah, and even when he was in his mother's womb he was already destined to be a Nazarite.

In Numbers 6 we are told that a Nazarite is a person who is devoted to God. During the period of his vow a Nazarite could not drink anything of the vine, he could not let the razor touch his head, he had to let his hair grow long, and he could not go near a dead body lest he be defiled. All this signifies but one thing: that such a person is wholly devoted and dedicated to live for God. And Samuel was a Nazarite for life. Even while in his mother's womb he was a Nazarite because Hannah could not drink any wine. Samuel was therefore born devoted and completely dedicated to God; and when he was weaned, he was sent off to the tabernacle in Shiloh because the temple was not yet built. As a little boy he was sent there to minister to God.

This little boy Samuel ministered to God under Eli because Eli was both priest and judge at this time. The two sons of Eli were wicked men when Samuel was just a little boy; and we know how a boy could have easily been influenced to imitate and follow the older brothers. But even though he was a little boy and living in that kind of evil environment, Samuel kept himself pure towards God. He was not affected by the evils around him. He ministered to God faithfully under Eli.

DILIGENCE

Of course, Samuel could not do much, but as a little boy he was to open the tabernacle doors. That responsibility was important because if nobody opened the tabernacle entrances, the people could not come in and worship. The doors had to be opened very early in the morning, and for a little boy to do that kind of work demanded some kind of diligence on his part. Samuel did all such small things in the house of God diligently, and he did them very faithfully.

AN EAR TO HEAR

Because of Samuel's faithfulness, God noticed him, and one night He called to him. Samuel did not know it was God calling him because he had never heard from God before. He thought it was Eli calling him, and so he went to Eli and said, "Here I am; you called me." And Eli said, "I did not; go back to bed." He returned to his bed and God called him again. He went to Eli a second time and Eli said, "No, I have not called you; go back to bed." Then God called the boy a third time and he went to Eli once more. Suddenly, Eli realized it was God who was calling him. Unfortunately, Eli was very weak now, but he had had experience, so he told Samuel that if he heard the call again he was to say, "Lord, here am I; speak, thy servant heareth." And God stood by him and called him, "Samuel, Samuel"; and God began to speak to him and appear to him. The Bible says, "The child grew in favor of God and of man" (see I Samuel 2:26). He grew in his knowledge of God, the word of God began to come to him, and whatever he said came to pass. So all Israel, from Dan to Beersheba, knew that God had established Samuel as His prophet. And God's word began to come to the people through him, and God once more began to appear to the people by appearing to Samuel (see I Samuel 3:15-21). God had raised up a vessel prepared for the Master's use.

EPOCH-MAKING VESSEL

Do we realize that we, too, are living in a period of transition? The children of Israel back then were living in the time of transition from judgeship to kingship, and it was a huge transition. Under judgeship everybody had been doing what was good in his own eyes. There was no unity, no strength, no peace. But under kingship the people would all be united into one and there would be peace—a great difference. We today are living in a time of transition. What characterizes our time at this moment? Thank God that this is the time and dispensation of grace: "You are saved by grace through faith and this not of yourself; it is the gift of God" (see Ephesians 2:8). But even this current time of grace is coming to an end. One day, the period of grace will be over and the time of righteousness will appear upon this earth. One day, the kingdoms of this world will become the kingdom of our God and of His Christ. In other words, one day, the kingdom of God will come upon this earth. When that happens, then righteousness shall rule over the whole earth. Today, lawlessness is ruling all over this earth, but one day, righteousness shall rule. The King of righteousness shall arrive; and we know that that day is coming soon.

However, when God makes that great transition, He will need a vessel. Indeed, God is preparing an epoch-making vessel to effect this change. Where is this vessel? Who is this vessel? It is true, God's thought is concerning His church because the church is supposed to be that vessel by which to conclude this age of grace and bring in the age of righteousness. The church is supposed to be that vessel to prepare for the coming of the King, but unfortunately, the church has failed; it has fallen into the world. Therefore, God is raising up in the church a remnant people—what the Bible calls "overcomers." God is raising up a people from among all His redeemed ones, who will be prepared just as Samuel had been in his day.

TRAVAILING PRAYER

How was Samuel brought into this world? It was through the travailing prayer of Hannah. According to spiritual principle, we know Hannah represents grace. It is through grace that we are born into the kingdom of God. It is through the travailing prayer of some people that we are saved. If we look back upon our personal histories, it can be said that we probably came to the Lord through somebody who had been praying for us. Perhaps it was our mother, father, husband, wife, or even our children. Perhaps some of our friends were praying for us. It is usually through travailing prayer that people are brought into the kingdom of God.

NAZARITES

In a sense, we are all children of grace as was Samuel; but that is not enough. We must also be Nazarites in the spiritual sense. Today God does not want us to do all those physical things as the children of Israel had done because they were God's earthly people. In our day we are God's heavenly people. So with us everything is on the spiritual level; but the principles are the same. God's purpose is that we who are children of grace should also be Nazarites. In other words, because our lives are redeemed, therefore, we are to be devoted to God, to live for Him, to live for His interest no matter what profession we may be in.

As Nazarites we are supposed to be separated from the world; which means that the vine and all the produce of the vine which figured in the Old Testament Nazarite's vow of negation speak of what the world can offer us in terms of the pleasures of sin (cf. Hebrews 11:24-26). We are to be separated from the world because we have been joined to the true vine, our Lord Jesus. We receive all our resources from Christ Jesus, the true vine, and not from the world anymore (see John 15:1).

A Nazarite of old was also supposed to let his hair grow long; and according to the Scriptures, this, in spiritual terms, is a symbol for covering. In other words, we need to cover our head before our God: therefore, let Christ be our Head (see I Corinthians 11:3ff.). We are His body to carry out His will.

And finally, the Nazarite vow of old called for a Nazarite not to touch any dead body lest he be defiled, and in the Scriptures a dead body symbolizes the flesh. We as modern-day Nazarites are not to touch our own flesh—that is, we are not to give in to our flesh nor to the flesh of other people, because the flesh is very defiling and always brings in death. So in a very real sense, we are all supposed to be Nazarites who are separated and devoted to God. Now are we?

FAITHFULNESS

In spiritual life, there needs to be time to grow. In physical life we were not born from our mother's womb a full-grown man or woman. As a matter of fact, only one person came into this world that way, and that was Adam. When God created him, he was a full-grown man. By contrast, everyone of us began as a babe, and, gradually, we grew. Even so, spiritually, it is the same. We need to grow in favor of God and man (see Luke 2:52 and I Samuel 2:26). We not only need to grow up spiritually, we also need to learn to minister and serve God under apprenticeship. Perhaps at the beginning we do small things such as opening the doors; yet in these small things, as we are learning to minister to God by ministering to God's people, our faithfulness shall be proven.

Are we faithful? God is looking for faithful people, not for talented people; and if we are faithful, then God will choose us. Let us recall from God's word that to one, God gave five talents and to another, two talents, but the difference in talents is of no consequence to God. What is of consequence to Him is being faithful or unfaithful. We need to be faithful in the small things, because if we are faithful in small things then God will entrust us with more and greater things (see Matthew 25:14-30).

Then we need to hear the call of God. In other words, there needs to be a personal relationship with God. Our relationship with Him must not be indirect. We have to have a direct

communication with God. He has called each of us to do what
He has placed us in the body of Christ for; and if we are faithful,
then the word of God will come to us, and He will appear to us.

Let us realize that such will be the vessel that God will use
in these last days to make the change—to conclude this age
and bring in the age to come which is the kingdom age. God
is looking for such a vessel. Every one of us can be included.
Some of us may not currently be included, but we all can be
so if we are like Samuel; that is, if we are truly separated and
devoted to the Lord and are faithful even in small things, if we
grow up in the Lord and are hearing from Him and seeing Him
in our spirit. Today, that epoch-making vessel is a corporate
vessel. It is no longer only one man called Samuel; it will be
a number of people: it will be a company of overcomers, and
through these overcomers, the manchild (see Revelation 12)—
the King with His kingdom—shall be brought in. Now this first
stage of Samuel's life we have clearly seen in chapters 1—6.

SECOND STAGE OF SAMUEL'S LIFE

The second stage of Samuel's life is provided us in chapters
7—12. The children of Israel were in such poor condition that
when the Philistines came forth to war with them, they could not
fight because God was not with them. They were so superstitious
that they thought if they could bring the ark of God into their
midst, then God would fight for them. This was because the
ark of God had fought for them before. For instance, on the
occasion when they had surrounded Jericho and Jericho fell, the
ark had been in their midst. Hence, they thought if they brought
the ark of God into their midst, He would fight for them and
the Philistines would be defeated; but God never respects any
superstition. Their life had become so rebellious that He was not

with them: He was no longer for them. Even though they now brought the ark into their midst, they put their faith in the ark thinking that because the ark represented the presence of God, surely He would fight for them. But God did not fight for them; on the contrary, He even allowed His ark to be taken captive by the Philistines. The testimony of God and the glory of God had departed from Israel. And when the news came to Eli that the ark had been taken, he fell backwards, breaking his neck, and he died. It was at this time that his godly daughter-in-law gave birth to a boy. She called that boy *Ichabod*—meaning "no glory": signifying that the glory of the Lord had departed from Israel because the ark had been taken captive (see I Samuel 4:12-22). The children of Israel did not know how to protect God's glory, but God knows how to protect His own glory.

The ark would be in the land of the Philistines for seven months, and during that period the Philistines could not tolerate any longer what had begun to take place in their midst. There were plagues upon the land and plagues upon the people. They also had placed the ark in the temple of their god, Dagon, whose image was a fish. And at one point Dagon fell down upon the threshold, bowed before the ark of God, and broke its neck. Therefore, the Philistines were so frightened at this that they had to send the ark back to the children of Israel, but the latter had no heart for God or for the ark of God. So they let the ark remain in the house of Abinadab in Kiriath-jearim, to be hidden away there in the forest for twenty long years. No one asked after the ark.

DELIVERANCE FOR THE CHILDREN OF ISRAEL

Samuel, the prophet of God, now began to speak, and through his prophetic labors the hearts of the children of Israel began to return to God; and then deliverance came. Oftentimes people do indeed look for deliverance, but their hearts are not for God; so even if God, in His great mercy, sends deliverance, it will be short-lived. For what is more important to Him is the heart: it must return to God. When the Israelites were under the judges, the latter were not able to bring the people's hearts back to God. These judges were used by Him to bring deliverance from time to time, but now God raised up the prophet Samuel, and through His speaking through him, the hearts of the children of Israel began to return to God. They acknowledged that they had sinned against Him, so Samuel prayed for them. And when Samuel prayed, God fought for them and the Philistines were defeated; there was deliverance. Samuel called that event an Ebenezer— "Hitherto has God helped us" (see I Samuel 7:1-12).

REQUEST FOR A KING

Samuel was their last judge, but we shall notice from chapter 7 that while he was judging them, he had built an altar; and that is very important.

Gradually, Samuel grew old, and even though his sons were not as wicked as Eli's, they were not as good as Samuel. So the children of Israel came to Samuel and said, "You are old; give us a king to rule over us like the rest of the nations." And Samuel was grieved because he discerned in such a request that they had rejected God as their King. The children of Israel had been a theocracy from the time they had come out of Egypt when God had made a covenant with them at Mt. Sinai right up to this moment. God had been their King, for through the priesthood God had become linked with His people, but He himself was their King. But at this moment in their history, the children of Israel rejected God as their King, because in their asking for a king to rule over them like the rest of the nations, it revealed that they had rejected God as their King. So for this reason, Samuel was grieved. Indeed, it was more than a rejecting of Samuel; it was a rejecting of God himself. Samuel therefore prayed to God, and God said: "They are not rejecting you, they are rejecting Me. Give them a king that they may know what life will be like under a king like that of the nations." Even though Samuel did not like the idea, he obeyed God and said to the people, "All right, God will give you a king" (see I Samuel 8).

SAMUEL'S FAITHFULNESS

Then Samuel challenged Israel thusly: "I have now lived before you from my youth up till today. If I have done anything wrong, if I have defrauded anybody, have taken anything from you, done any unrighteousness or judged unrighteously, tell me and I will pay it back." And the children of Israel said, "You have never done anything wrong." He had lived such a pure life before the people. Then he said, "You asked for a king and that was wrong because you rejected God; so I will show you that your wickedness is great in God's sight in asking a king for yourselves." Now it was the harvest time, and during the harvest season one does not expect rain, but Samuel said, "I will pray to God and He will send rain and thunder." So rain and thunder came upon the people and they immediately realized that they had truly done a wicked thing in asking for a king. So they said, "We have sinned; besides all our other sins, we have added this sin of asking for a king like the nations." And Samuel said: "Yes, you did a wicked thing, but you have already done it; from now on, be faithful to God. If your hearts are towards Him, He will still bless you, but if you turn away from Him, then you will perish. But as for me, God forbid that I should cease praying for you and teaching you the good and right way." Think of that! Samuel was actually rejected by the people when they asked for a king; nevertheless, he was able to be faithful to the people to the very end.

A SERVANT OF THE LORD

There are a few things during this second stage of Samuel's life which I would like to repeat and emphasize; and firstly is the work of Samuel the prophet. What is prophetic ministry and what is its aim? Prophetic ministry is not only giving to the people the mind of God, it is also aimed at turning the hearts of the people back to God. A prophet is to speak for God, but the speaking is with such authority that it will touch the hearts of the people and not their minds and turn their hearts to God. You may remember that at the end of the Old Testament the Scriptures declare that God will raise up the prophet Elijah once again. And he will turn the hearts of the fathers to the children and the children's hearts to the fathers (see Malachi 4:5-6a). So the work of a prophet is to touch the hearts, and this is what Samuel did. His ministry was not only a physical, outward deliverance; it was also an inward turning. Any outward deliverance is temporary; only an inward turning of the heart is permanent; and that is the work of a prophet.

Secondly, at the same time, Samuel was a judge, and while he was a judge, he built an altar. What does this act signify? An altar is the place where one calls upon the name of the Lord. So we see that Samuel did not judge according to his own wisdom; he judged the people by praying and calling upon the Lord; he judged with the judgment of God.

Thirdly, Samuel was a man flexible in the hands of God. Even though he was not happy with the request made by the children of Israel because he knew it was wrong, nevertheless, when God said do as they had asked, he did it. To be used by God, one has to be flexible. On the one hand, the servant of God has to be firm; he cannot compromise the truth. On the other hand, God's servant has to be so flexible that whenever God wants to bend him, he will bend in that direction.

And then, fourthly, even though Samuel was rejected by the people, he was still faithful. He not only told them they were wrong, he also said, "I will pray for you without ceasing." Now that is a true servant of the Lord.

THIRD STAGE OF SAMUEL'S LIFE

ANOINTING OF SAUL

The third stage of Samuel's life can be found in chapters 13—24. That was the period in his life when God used him to make the transition from judgeship to kingship. First of all, we learn that he anointed Saul. Because the people had asked for a king like the nations, God gave in to their request but sent leanness to their souls. Oftentimes, when we ask God for something that is really not His will, He will let us have it; but let us at the same time realize that there will be leanness in our souls. It is not good to force God to hear us. It is much better if we hear Him than to ask Him to hear us.

In this connection, I can never forget the story told about Miss Margaret Barber. A servant of the Lord in China, she was a very strong character, not a weak person in the least. One day God revealed His mind to her about something in her life, and she did not like it. She had her own idea about it and struggled with God, as we all do. Ultimately, she prayed this prayer: "Lord, don't give in, don't give in; I will yield." That is the attitude we all need to have.

Unfortunately, the children of Israel asked for a king like that of the nations. What kind of king would the nations have? The world naturally looks at appearance, so God gave them a king according to outward appearance, and that was a man called Saul. Now the name Saul means "asked for." The people of Israel "asked for" a king like the nations, and that is what they got. We will recall that the meaning of Samuel's name is: "asked for of God"; and it is in fact better if we "ask for of God," for then you will obtain it from God. But if you "ask for of men," you obtain it from men.

Actually, Saul was not a bad man. Indeed, from the standpoint of the world he was a very good specimen. He was tall, a head above all the other people, and he was handsome.

Moreover, Saul was a humble man because when Samuel told him that God had chosen him, he said, "Who am I? I am the smallest in my family, and my family is the smallest in the tribe of Benjamin, and Benjamin is the smallest of the twelve tribes. Who therefore am I?" (See I Samuel 9:21) And when they cast lots and the lot fell on him to be the king, they could not find him because he had hidden himself among the baggage (see I Samuel 10:21-23). Furthermore, after he was anointed king, some wicked men said, "Who is he?" They would not follow him, and some of the people who were for Saul therefore wanted to kill them. But Saul said, "Don't do it" (see I Samuel 10:27; 11:12-13). He was a good man; in fact, he had a very good beginning; but he was a man of the flesh.

In the sight of God there is no good in our flesh but we do not see it. In our eyes there is much bad in the flesh, but there is also much good in it. Do we think ourselves to be fairly good? Yes, we acknowledge that there are many bad things in us, but we believe we are not that bad: Are we not sometimes kind, sometimes gentle, sometimes generous? There is definitely some good in us. Now that was Saul. He was a man of the flesh. There was obviously some good in him, but the flesh can never obey God. The things of God are foolishness to the man of the flesh. He will not and cannot do the will of God.

GOD'S REJECTION OF SAUL

The test of this man of the flesh came. Samuel told Saul, "You wait in Gilgal for seven days, and I will come and offer sacrifice." The Philistines were gathering there, and Saul was with his people. He waited and waited and waited until the seventh day, but Samuel did not come. So before the seventh day was out, Saul could not wait any longer. He thought that the Philistines would come upon him and he had not prayed to God yet. He was religious but legalistic in his religion; so he forced himself to offer sacrifice. Even so, that was something he should never have done because he was not a priest; but he did it anyway. It was just after he had finished sacrificing that Samuel arrived: it was still within the seven days, but right at the very last. Nevertheless, Saul could not wait; and because of that, God declared through Samuel that the kingdom would be taken away from him and given to a person more worthy—a man after God's own heart (see I Samuel 10:8; 13:5-14).

Later on, as related in chapter 15, God gave Saul another chance and told him through Samuel to wipe out all the Amalekites and destroy all their possessions. Saul killed all the people, but he took King Agag alive. He slaughtered the sheep and the cattle, but he also kept the best of them alive. He thought he had done God's will. He even made a great thing out of it and put up a monument for himself. When Samuel came, he went out to meet him and said, "I have done what God asked me to do." But Samuel replied: "What do I hear? Is it not the bleating of sheep and the oxen lowing?" Saul explained to him that the people had wanted to keep the best to sacrifice to God. And we will remember what Samuel said in reply, "To obey is better than sacrifice." God rejected Saul from being king. Even so, Samuel loved Saul: he moaned and lamented before God for him. He truly loved Saul. But God said: "That is enough. Go to Bethlehem and anoint another one" (see I Samuel 16:1).

A Man After God's Heart

We remember the story of Jesse's eight sons and how when Eliab the firstborn came—who like Saul was also a tall man— Samuel looked at him and immediately thought this certainly must be the man God now wanted to be king. He had looked at the outward appearance but God said: "No, I look at the heart, not at the appearance. It is none of these sons." Finally, the eighth one came—David. David was the one, so God said, "Anoint him." Samuel anointed David, and from that day forward, Samuel protected David, loved Saul, and loved God's people to the very end of his life. And in chapter 25:1 we learn that Samuel died.

This faithful, obedient vessel had been used by God to bring about the transfer from judgeship to kingship. Now it is quite true that although the first king was Saul, he was not the right one, even though his kingship—like that of David's—had come through Samuel, too. It is very strange but it often happens this way: that the flesh will come first and then the spirit, just as the Law had come in first and was then followed by grace. And here we find that Saul came in first and then David. Let us understand that Saul was in the *plan* of God but not the *purpose* of God. There is a difference here, and I trust we can see it. In God's purpose His kingship is according to David, and one day, a Son of David shall sit upon His throne. That is God's idea of kingship. God's purpose was not in Saul being king but the latter, to be sure, was an integral part of God's plan. God had planned it that way in order to show the contrast between the kings of this world—the kings according to the nations—and the king after God's own heart. What a difference that is!

I have only shared with you about one person—Samuel; but there are two more prominent persons in this book. I will add a little further here about Saul and then leave David to the next discussion because II Samuel is actually the story of David. So we can combine the rest of I Samuel with the book of II Samuel in discussing the life of David in the next message.

I believe one brother has put it very well when he observed this about Saul: "If you look at the life of Saul, one can say that his beginning was bright, but soon, very soon, it became overcast and his sun set amidst the blackest clouds." I think that about sums up Saul's life. He began bright but then his life became overcast. He became muddled and he ended up a very dark individual. He not only persecuted David and attempted to murder him, but also at the very end, because God would not answer him, he even tried to consult a witch—a spirit medium—and fell upon his own sword on the battlefield and died. Such was the tragic life of Saul.

As we read in the Scriptures about Saul it should truly warn us today that if we live according to the flesh we shall be no different from Saul. He had been anointed, to be sure, but he did not live under the anointing; instead he lived according to the flesh.

We Christians are anointed. The very word *Christian* means "anointed one." We are all anointed, for the Holy Spirit dwells in us. He is the anointing within us, and if we live under that anointing and let the Holy Spirit within us teach us in all things, we will abide in Christ (see I John 2:20-27 ASV). But if we are not listening to the Spirit, we are not living under the anointing. Instead, we are living according to the flesh: we seek to have our self-will, and the result shall be that we will end up like Saul. May God have mercy upon each one of us.

Let us pray:

Dear heavenly Father, we do thank Thee for Thy precious word. We pray that these words may not be merely history to us, but we ask that Thou wilt by Thy Holy Spirit illumine us, examine our hearts that we may be like Samuel, a vessel fit for the master's use. We pray that Thou wilt not allow us to fall into the way of Saul. Oh, deliver us, Lord. Only Thy grace can keep us from falling. So we just look to Thee for Thy keeping, and not only for Thy keeping but for Thy working in us, that we may be walking in the way of David to serve Thee and Thy purpose. In the name of our Lord Jesus. Amen.

II SAMUEL

A MAN AFTER GOD'S HEART

II Samuel 5:4-5—David was thirty years old when he began to reign; he reigned forty years. In Hebron he reigned over Judah seven years and six months; and in Jerusalem he reigned thirty-three years over all Israel and Judah.

Acts 13:22—And having removed him [that is, Saul] he [God] raised up to them David for king, of whom also bearing witness he said, I have found David, the son of Jesse, a man after my heart, who shall do all my will.

Let us pray:

Dear heavenly Father, we do want to praise and thank Thee that through the blood of Thy beloved Son we have ready access to Thy throne of grace; and how much grace we do need in this time more than ever. So we just look to Thee that Thou wilt be gracious to us in opening Thy heart and Thy word to us, that we may be drawn closer to Thyself and closer to Thy will. We do commit this time into Thy hands and trust Thy Holy Spirit to perfect the work which Thou hast already begun in each one of us, to the praise of Thy glory. In the name of our Lord Jesus. Amen.

First and Second Samuel were originally one book. It tells us of the development of the people of Israel into a national kingdom. In I Samuel we saw the transition from judges to kings, and from priests to prophets. We know that, formerly, the children of Israel were under the judges, and as we mentioned before, the order of the judges was an emergency measure of God. It is not God's permanent order. It came because of the affliction of God's people due to their unfaithfulness; and so, because of the mercy of God towards His people, He raised up judges to deliver them from their enemies. But as we learned from the book of Judges, no judge was ever raised up over all the tribes of Israel. Furthermore, even under the judges the times and the periods of all the judgeships were short; they were temporary, not permanent. The people were never united as one nation and kingdom under any judge. And eventually, God took them from the order of judges and brought them into a permanent order—that of the kings. And this is what we find in I Samuel.

Formerly, the people of Israel had their link with God through the priests. The priests were His chosen ones to bring the people to himself; but again, we see that the priesthood failed terribly. And because of the failure of the priests, God raised up prophets to be that link between himself and His people. We can see this very clearly when we review again the beginning of I Samuel. Eli had been both priest and judge, yet he failed God terribly, and thus in him the whole priesthood and judgeship failed God's purpose. So God began the change from judges to kings, and from priests to prophets. He raised up Samuel as a prophet, and that order of prophets continued on for a thousand years until John the Baptist. Hence, we can say that I Samuel actually speaks of transition while II Samuel speaks of establishment. In other words, the kingdom of Israel was firmly established under the rule of King David.

Chapters 1—24 of I Samuel were most likely written by Samuel himself, because we know from Scripture that Samuel wrote, and he left a record. Chapter 25 of I Samuel through the whole of II Samuel is most likely the works of Nathan the prophet and Gad the seer. How do we know that?

"And the acts of David the king, first and last, behold, they are written in the book of Samuel the seer, and in the book of Nathan the prophet, and in the book of Gad the seer" (I Chronicles 29:29).

So the entire story of David actually was recorded by these three prophets: Samuel, Nathan and Gad.

ISRAEL AS A KINGDOM

God was intent on establishing the children of Israel as a kingdom. It is very much God's will for His people. It is not His will that His people should be scattered, divided or weak, but that His people should be united and strong as His kingdom upon the earth. But before God will do anything to realize His will and purpose, He always first looks for a suitable vessel. To put it another way, God is more interested in man than in the work. God does have a work to do, but if He cannot find the right man He will wait until He obtains the right person to do the right work. This, in fact, is an established rule of God. By contrast, men are very impatient. When we see a need, when we want to see a work done, we are in such a hurry that we think if only we can get the work done it does not matter who is doing it, whether that man is suitable or not. We emphasize work rather than man, and because of this, the result is that a work is done hurriedly, but then it will be destroyed just as quickly and will leave a tragic end in its wake. This is what we found in I Samuel.

It was God's will to give His people a king who would represent God as their King; however, the children of Israel were so anxious to become a kingdom after the manner of the nations around them that they could not wait for God's king. So they indeed got a king, but they got King Saul, a man of the flesh; and how incredibly tragic that was! What a disaster it became to them! Yet, during all that time God was actually preparing a suitable vessel, but unfortunately, the children of Israel could not wait.

THE KINGSHIP OF CHRIST

"Ye are a chosen race, a kingly priesthood, a holy nation, a people for a possession, that ye might set forth the excellencies of him who has called you out of darkness to his wonderful light" (I Peter 2:9).

Let us fully understand that we who are the Lord's—we who are the church—are called to be a chosen race, a holy priesthood, a holy nation. And it is for us to set forth the excellencies of Him who has called us out of darkness into His marvelous light. The church is also a kingdom. In reality, the church of God is the kingdom of God on earth at this time. It is His will that we should be one and not scattered and divided. It is His will that we should be strong and not weak. It is His will that we should be able to proclaim the excellencies of Him who has called us out of darkness into light. That is to say, it is the will of God that we as His church and as His kingdom should bear a good and strong testimony to the world as to what a God we have. This is His will.

Now in order for God's will to be accomplished, there is One who has been sent as the Son of David and yet He is a greater than David, He being the Lord of David—even the Lord Jesus Christ. He is the One whom God has ordained and provided for that kingdom. In other words, under Christ's kingship this kingdom of God shall be established; but unfortunately, we are so impatient that we cannot wait. How often we try by fleshly means to build up that kingdom: we try to follow man, or man even tries to set himself up as the king: man tries to gather people under him and around him, and the result is that *man's* kingdom is built instead of God's kingdom. We cannot wait patiently to put ourselves under the kingship of Christ. Yet it is under the kingship of Christ that this kingdom of God shall be established on earth as it already is in heaven.

DAVID

We mentioned before that in I Samuel there are three persons in view: Samuel, Saul and David. We spoke at length on Samuel and then touched a little on Saul, but we did not say anything about David because II Samuel is all concerned with him. Nevertheless, as we consider David, we must return to I Samuel since the personal history of David has its beginning in that book's 16th chapter. David's life can be roughly divided into three stages: David as a shepherd, David as a fugitive, and David as king. The first two stages are recorded in I Samuel and the last stage is provided in II Samuel.

DAVID AS SHEPHERD

We will recall that God had removed Saul because, as a man of the flesh, he did not and could not obey God. The will of God was foolishness to him, and because of this, God removed him. Then God said that He had given David to the people as their king, and He bore witness to David. He said, "I have found David, the son of Jesse, a man after my heart, who shall do all my will" (see Acts 13:22b). God declared: "I have found a man." God is always seeking and searching. Do we know that He is still searching and seeking today? His eyes go to and fro throughout the whole world for the purpose of finding a man whose heart is perfect towards Him. And if He can find such a man, imagine what He can do with him! Imagine what work He shall be able to do with such a man! God's interest is always in man, and it is very difficult for Him to find the right person. Out of all the children of Israel, God looked and looked and looked until He finally found David.

David is first mentioned in the Scriptures in I Samuel 16, and at that time David was probably around fifteen years of age, a teenager. He was just a lad; yet what counts spiritually is not a matter of one's physical age but a matter of one's heart towards the Lord. Of all those among the children of Israel, old and young, God looked and looked and looked, and He found one fifteen-year-old lad; and what is more, he was the youngest of the eight sons of the man Jesse. This lad was neglected by his father because he could not see anything great in the boy; and furthermore, he was despised by his older brothers. They misunderstood him completely, and so he was sent out to the fields and the wilderness to watch over a small flock of sheep which belonged to the family. In the eyes of Jesse and his family this lad was good for nothing, so they sent him out to the pastures to watch over a few sheep. They thought that was all he was good for. Such was the boy David in their eyes.

THE HEART OF DAVID

This lad David was unknown to all and even to his family, but he was very well known to God. There in the wilderness, as he was watching those few sheep in solitude and in that tranquil environment, David turned his heart to God. He opened his heart to Him, and because of this, God opened His heart to David. They had a heart-to-heart relationship. On the one hand, he began to touch God's heart; on the other hand, the boy began to understand God's heart. Of course, as a youth, his understanding was limited, but it grew as he grew older and as he spent more time with God. But the fundamental reason David was chosen was because as a teenager he had opened his heart to God; and as God looked upon him, He saw a pure and perfect heart. It was definitely not because of his outward appearance that David was chosen by God but because of this youth's commendable inward condition.

Now David's oldest brother Eliab must have been a big man because when Samuel saw him, he said to himself, "This must be the man of God's choice." Why? Because Samuel had Saul in his mind. Saul had been a big man, standing a head above all the other people; so evidently, Eliab must have been a tall, handsome and appealing man. As a young lad of fifteen, David was probably small, but God did not choose him because of his outward appearance, nor did He choose him because of his ability or talents. Simply put, God chose him because of his heart. This is always the criterion of God's choice. We look at outward appearance which includes one's features, one's eloquence, one's talents, perhaps also one's experience, status, and relationships. Mankind always looks at outward appearance in choosing people, but that is not God's way of choosing. He looks upon the heart as His basis for making a choice. Therefore, if we want to be chosen by God, we must realize that it is our heart that matters with Him and not our natural appearance.

When God sent Samuel to the family of Jesse to anoint one of his sons to be the future king, the father did not even bother to call David back from the fields. What could this boy do? Instead, he called his seven other sons because apparently they all had some aspect of outward appearance that was attractive in one way or another. So, one after the other of these sons came before Samuel. Eliab was the first one who passed before him, and so Samuel said, "This must be the one," because he was so like Saul. But God said, "Now, Samuel, do not look at this in this manner. That is not the way I choose." The second one passed by and the third, and so forth, one after the other; but Samuel finally said: "God has not chosen any of them. Is that all of your sons?" To which the father replied: "There is another one in the field watching the sheep; he is nothing, a nobody." However, Samuel declared: "We have to wait. Call him here." And when David appeared, God said, "This is the one; anoint him."

DAVID'S HIDDEN LIFE WITH GOD

David was indeed anointed by God, and the Spirit of God came upon him; even so, he was sent back to the field to watch the sheep. Evidently, it was during this period, and now under the anointing of God, that David witnessed the deliverance of God. On one occasion a lion and then a bear appeared, and David rose up and tore apart the bear and the lion and saved the sheep in the power of God. That was such a tremendous feat which David did out in the field: here he was, a mere lad, and yet, barehanded, he was able to kill a lion and saved the sheep from a bear; and yet, nobody knew about it! David did not come back and boast before his parents and brothers in order to gain their favor. "You see what I have done? You looked down upon me, but now, see what I have done!" He did not do that. He did not tell anybody until he was compelled by circumstances to do so later when Saul could not believe that this lad before him could do the job of fighting against Goliath. So David said, "I can," and he mentioned the lion and bear experiences (see I Samuel 17:31-37). But prior to this, nobody ever knew.

We are so different; we want to prove that we are somebody. If God has favored us with an ability to do something, we want everybody to know that we are such a great person. But not David. David did not try to push or elevate himself before man. Even though he was now anointed to be king, he was content to continue watching over the sheep, awaiting God's time and not trying to do anything for himself. We do not know how long he continued guarding the sheep, but we do know one thing: that while he was out there in the field, he had sweet communion with God; He had a hidden life with God; a life unknown to man but known to God.

How unfortunate that we tend to live before man. Actually, our life before man is more than what we truly are. We put on many airs which are not real in order to give people a good impression, but we have very little of a secret, hidden life with the Lord. How we appear before man does not matter, for man's estimate is not accurate; but how we live before God alone counts. Do we therefore have a hidden life with

God? Do we spend time with Him in the closet? Is our life a completely public one to be seen by people, and behind all that there is nothing? Or is there much true life behind, within and secret—hidden with the Lord? Even if men do not know it or have not seen it, that does not matter, because sooner or later the effect will be seen.

A SHEPHERD'S HEART

It was out in the fields and out in the wilderness that David also developed a shepherd's heart. In order to watch over the sheep you need a shepherd's heart. If you are only a hireling, working for wages, then, of course, you are only interested in yourself, and when the lion or the bear appears, you will run away. You will leave the sheep because you feel you are more important than they; you have to save your own life. David, however, developed a shepherd's heart as he watched over the sheep. He loved the sheep that he tended, and he was willing to sacrifice his life for them. That is why he fought against the lion and the bear: he had a true shepherd's heart. In fact, these were preparations for the future tasks which God would call him to do. Without a hidden life with God, how could David be a good king ruling over a nation? If he did not know the will of God, he would rule the nation according to his own will and make a mess of God's people. He had to have a hidden life with God, and he had to develop a shepherd's heart because God's people are like the sheep of the pasture. They are God's sheep, and if He raises you up as a shepherd, you will need to have a shepherd's heart. You will need a love for the sheep, a willingness to lay down your life for them. You cannot be self-centered or self-interested or concerned only with preserving yourself, but you must be willing to sacrifice yourself for the sheep of God's flock. That kind of shepherd's heart has to be developed, and here we shall see that God was preparing the vessel of His choice: David the youngest son of Jesse.

PRESENTED TO THE NATION OF ISRAEL

Then the day came that God would present him to the children of Israel. At this time there was an ongoing battle between the Philistines and the Israelites, and the Philistines had a challenger, the giant Goliath. He challenged the army of the Israelites by declaring: "Choose a man, and let's fight!" The issue was over this matter of who was to be servant to whom. Were the children of Israel to be servants to the Philistines, or were the Philistines to be servants to Israel? Who will be in control? And as it turned out, the issue was to be settled by this fight with Goliath. However, no one in the army of Israel was able to meet this challenge. And if there were none, then the children of Israel would become servants to the Philistines.

David was not in the army; he was still out in the fields tending the sheep, but three of his brothers were. In God's providence, the father called David back from the field and said, "Go to the battlefield to see how your brothers fare." He was sent to the battlefield and thus became aware of this challenge laid down by Goliath. David rose to the occasion and went forth to fight against the Philistines. He proclaimed: "You come with sword and spear and javelin; but I come to thee in the name of Jehovah of hosts, the God of Israel, to prove to the world that there is a God in Israel. Let the congregation of Israel know that God saves not by sword or spear or javelin" (see I Samuel 17:45-47). And David killed Goliath. That is the way God's choice was presented to the nation of Israel, and that event concludes this first stage in David's life in which he became overnight a national hero.

ONE GREATER THAN DAVID

Yet, we have One greater than David: He who is the Son of David but who is also the Lord of David, even the Lord Jesus Christ. When God sent His beloved Son into this world,

He was born in a stable manger; for at His birth there was no place in the inn for Him; He had no house and He had no home. Moreover, He was hidden away in Nazareth until He was nearly thirty years old. Those were hidden years for Jesus. The only thing we know is that at the age of twelve He was brought to Jerusalem to be presented to God as a Son of the Law. We well remember how He had then stayed behind because—as He later said—He ought to be in His Father's house and occupied with His Father's business. But being a minor, the boy Jesus went back to Nazareth with His parents, being obedient to them and submitting himself under their rule. And there He spent the rest of those hidden years still unknown to man. In the eyes of man was there anything good to come out of Nazareth? Nothing good (see John 1:45-46). Nevertheless, He was known of God.

When Jesus was at the age of about thirty, God presented Him to the children of Israel. And the way that God presented Him to the nation of Israel was through baptism. At that time John the Baptist was calling the nation to repent: "Repent, for the kingdom of the heavens has drawn nigh. You cannot go on as usual. Do not think that you are all right. You need to repent; you need to turn around completely because the kingdom of God is coming." The Lord Jesus came to John the Baptist to be baptized, but John—sensing such character and such consciousness in this Person—said to the Lord, "No, I cannot do it." Why? Because Jesus was a Man who did not need to repent. There is no person in the whole world who does not need to repent. In fact, we need to repent continuously; yet here was a Man who had nothing of which to repent. In those thirty years on earth, hidden somewhere in the hilly country of Galilee, there had been nothing for Him to repent of because He had pleased the Father all the time. Even so, the Lord Jesus replied to John this way: "Let us fulfill all righteousness." The Lord allowed himself to undergo the baptism of repentance because He offered himself to be a sacrifice on humanity's behalf. He offered himself to the children of Israel. He offered himself on behalf of the whole world and took our place of repentance and our place of death and burial. And when He came up out of the waters of baptism, the heavens opened and the Holy Spirit descended upon Him and abode on Him as a gentle dove, and the voice from heaven declared: "This is my beloved Son in whom I am well pleased." And thus in this manner was Jesus presented to the nation of Israel as the Lamb of God.

Then He was led into the wilderness to be challenged by the prince of this world. In the Garden of Eden Adam had been challenged by Satan and the first man failed. The Lord Jesus, under the power of the Holy Spirit, was urged—even driven—into the wilderness, and there He was tempted and challenged by the enemy. The Son of Man completely gave himself to God, obeying and worshiping and serving Him alone, and denying himself and the world. And the result: He defeated the strong man and was now in a position to set the world's prisoners free; and from there He came forth to preach the glad tidings. Such was Jesus' presentation to the world.

DAVID AS A FUGITIVE

OBEDIENCE THROUGH SUFFERING

Returning to the life of David, we will notice that very soon, David's triumph over Goliath turned into persecution because of the jealousy of Saul (see I Samuel 18:5-9). When David and the others were returning from having killed the Philistines, the ladies went out to meet the triumphant procession singing as they did so a song that praised Saul for killing his thousands but David his ten thousands. This was true that they sang, but it was very unwise for them to have done so, and because of that, jealousy entered the heart of Saul. Instead of being glad for what David had done, Saul became jealous of David and commenced persecuting him. So from chapter 18 of I Samuel all the way to the end of that book we find narrated the fact that David had to flee as a fugitive for over ten years. He hid in caves and dwelt in strongholds out in the wilderness. He changed his place ever so often in order to escape Saul who was hunting him down to kill him. During those ten years, David's sufferings were so great. This we learn from many of his psalms which date from that period. In those poems he poured out his heart; and there we read about the tremendous sufferings he went through; yet it was through these sufferings that he learned obedience.

Interestingly enough, God put Saul into David's hands twice. In I Samuel 22 and again in chapter 24 we learn how God had purposely placed Saul in David's hands in order to test this youngest son of Jesse; and we read how David dared not touch God's anointed. David would rather wait for God's time than to do something to help himself. Think of that! He learned obedience, he learned to obey God in spite of his advantage over Saul. By contrast, we always try to gain if there is opportunity for us to gain and in doing so say that God gave us the opportunity; that we therefore have every right and every reason to do it. But David was willing to lose rather than to gain, to obey rather than to be profited. He learned obedience through the things which he suffered (see Hebrews 5:8).

God was going to install David on the throne to be in authority and to represent God's authority. Think of what a tremendous thing it is to represent the authority of God and not the authority of man, to exercise God's authority over His property and His possession! How can anyone assume such a position without having undergone strict discipline? The way to authority is obedience and submission. If we do not know how personally to obey God, how can we exercise His authority over others? This is a basic spiritual principle. Unless we know how to be *under* authority, we are not qualified to *exercise* authority. And on this point we clearly see that David learned this tremendous lesson of being under authority in order that one day God may put him in authority.

KNOWING THE FRAILTY OF MAN

Outwardly, those ten years were years of suffering, and yet they were necessary because during those ten years, David began to know himself. It is not when we are in times of peace and prosperity that we come to know ourselves but when we are under pressure, when we are in distress, under adversity or in need or in lack. These are the times wherein we begin to know ourselves—in fact, to know the frailty of man. During those years David began to know himself much more thoroughly than he had known himself before. How do we know this to be true? We may recall what David said to Saul after Saul had hunted him down and found him: "Why do you come out to seek after me? Who am I? I am but a dead dog. I am nothing but a partridge. I am merely a flea. I am nothing, not worth your hunting." David could confess this before his enemy!

We may sometimes pretend to be humble and say, "I am nothing, I am just a flea." But suppose somebody tells you that you are a flea. Perhaps before your friends you would be able to say "I am but a dead dog," because you know your friends will not accept that. If, though, you declare that before your enemies, they will accept it. They will really think you are a dead dog. Would you actually do that? David, however, after those many years of suffering, came to the conclusion that he was indeed a nobody—that he was nothing, just a dead dog or a flea. And he was not afraid even to confess it before his enemies. His heart attitude was: "Let people look upon me as a flea because that is what I am." How can anyone learn *this* lesson unless one suffers? Suffering is very good medicine.

LEARNING TO KNOW GOD IN A FULLER WAY

As David endured those years he not only learned authority through obedience and learned to know himself; he also learned to know God in a much fuller way. To discern this as having occurred in David we only need to read his various psalms and notice the many different ways by which he addressed God. For he addressed Him with many different descriptions and titles. For instance, in Psalm 18:2 alone, he declared the following one after another: "My God, who are You? You are my strength, You are my rock, my fortress, my high tower, my God, my shield, the horn of my salvation." God had become everything to him. And these were not just words. Behind these words there lay numerous personal stories and experiences. When he was weak, he found God as his strength. When he was low, he discovered God to be his high tower. When he was fleeing, he experienced God as his fortress. When he was attacked by the enemy, he took God as his shield. In other words, David experienced God in a variety of ways, all of which brought him to know God in a far greater measure.

That is precisely what we need, is it not? We need to experience Christ in such ways that He truly becomes everything to us. It is easy to *say* that Christ is everything to us, but is He really? It has to be tested. And when it is tested, then we will see whether He is everything to us or whether other things mean more to us than Christ. It is only through testing that we will be brought into that place where Christ will be everything to us. Then our testimony will be real. So these were preparations for David's future rule on behalf of God. They were necessary preparations for David, and they are likewise necessary ones for us to experience if we, too, are to rule in God's kingdom.

Transition of the Kingdom

In the days of his tribulation David fled to the cave of Adullam, and his brothers and his family heard about it and went to join him (see I Samuel 22). In addition, all those who were in distress, who were in debt, who had a dissatisfied and bitter spirit, they, too, went to join David. In fact, he became captain over those people—some four hundred of them. And when we come to chapter 23, we learn that two hundred more joined them, and thus David had six hundred people with him. Furthermore, by reading I Chronicles 12 we shall find that when David was in Ziklag, and later when in Hebron, even more men from all the tribes of Israel went forth to join him for the purpose of transferring the kingdom to him.

How very similar all this is to the One who is greater than David. The Lord Jesus, when on this earth and after He had been presented to the world, went all around doing good, healing the sick, feeding the poor, setting the captives free, calling the dead to life, and preaching the gospel to the poor. Jesus did nothing but good; yet, He was despised, rejected, persecuted and finally crucified on the cross. But there on the cross He accomplished the greatest thing of all which He had ever done: He finished the work of redemption. He gave hope to everyone by opening heaven's door and closing the gates of hades. He rose from the dead, ascended on high, and God has anointed Him and crowned Him with glory and honor. Even now, He is seated at the right hand of God waiting for His enemies to become His footstool. But on earth it is a different story. In heaven He is in glory, but on earth He is still despised, rejected and persecuted. Nevertheless, God is gathering a people to himself, those of His family. Thank God, we who are Christians are His family.

Let me inquire, Do we think we should go out and join Christ who is outside the camp? (See Hebrews 13:12-13) Or do we think that this is a time we should compromise and win the world? That we should court the favor of the world? Is this the time for our glorification? Or do we realize that this is the time of our humiliation? Should we not go out and join Christ because He is to be found outside the camp? If we are indeed His family, then that is where we who are in distress should go. Why, back then, should the children of Israel have been in distress? They were supposed to be the kingdom of God, but they were under Saul. No wonder God's people were in distress, in debt, and dissatisfied.

Are you satisfied with the world today? Are you satisfied with the religious world? Do you feel that you are in lack, that there is a lack of spiritual supply? Are you in distress over what is happening in the world and especially among God's people? If this is the situation you are in, then you should go outside the camp and join our Greater than David. Gradually, more and more people are coming out of the establishment and joining Christ. They are willing to bear His reproaches rather than enjoy the riches of Egypt (see Hebrews 11:26); and it is through such people as these that God is going to transfer the kingdom of this world into the kingdom of God and of His Christ (cf. Revelation 11:15). Veritably, this is what He is doing today.

DAVID AS KING

The last stage of David's life is when he became king and reigned over Israel; and this is all recorded in II Samuel. David was thirty years old when he became king in Hebron and ruled for seven years and six months, and during that time there were constant battles between the house of David and the house of Saul. The house of David became stronger and stronger whereas the house of Saul became weaker and weaker, until finally, David was crowned king over all Israel in Jerusalem and served as king for thirty-three years. And thus he was king for forty years altogether. During his rule David united all the people of Israel into one nation, one kingdom. He possessed all the land from the Mediterranean to the Euphrates, from the Red Sea to the river Orontes (in what is today North Syria). In other words, what God had promised to Abraham, Isaac and Jacob came under David's rule. For the first time the children of Israel had possessed their possession.

Jerusalem the Place for God's Name

After David came to the throne, three significant actions would mark his reign. As soon as he was crowned king over all Israel, the first thing he did was to capture Jerusalem (see II Samuel 5). Ironically, if we look at geography or study past political history, we shall discover that Jerusalem was actually not a strategically positioned place. Indeed, it was not a site for establishing a future world center. Even so, as soon as David became king, the first action that he took was to capture Jerusalem and make it the capital of the nation. Why? It was not for political reasons, nor was it for geographical reasons; it was purely because David was a man after God's heart. Somehow he had received revelation from God that this was the one spot in the entire world where He wanted to put His name. We may remember from Deuteronomy 12 that through Moses God had told the people of Israel that after they entered the Promised Land they should not do any longer what they had been doing in the wilderness. Because they were pilgrims and strangers traveling through the wilderness, they had offered sacrifices to God wherever they happened to be. But God had now said: "After you enter the Promised Land and possess it, this habit shall no longer be so. You cannot offer sacrifices anywhere you want to. I will appoint one place, and there I will put My name. You must go to *that* place and offer sacrifices and nowhere else." Yet, after the children of Israel had entered the Promised Land and for hundreds of years thereafter, nobody knew what or where that place was. It was not to be known until David appeared and learned from God that Jerusalem was to be that place. He only had God's interest in his heart. He did not become king for his own benefit, as the kings of the world would do. When men of the world have that kingly position, they benefit only themselves; but not so with a king representing God. In God's kingdom, the king's heart is to serve only God's purpose because God wants a place to put His name on earth. So David captured that place so that the name of God might be sanctified and be on this earth.

ARK OF GOD

The second action David took was to bring the ark of God into Jerusalem (see II Samuel 6). The ark represented the glory and presence of God, but it had been captured by the Philistines. When the ark came back to the children of Israel, they were not ready to receive it. They no longer cared about the ark, so it was hidden in Kirjath-jearim out in the fields of the woods there for twenty years until Samuel persuaded the people, he gradually having brought their hearts back to God. But even after that, the ark remained at Kirjath-jearim. Nobody asked about it. And during the forty-year reign of Saul, he himself never once inquired before the ark. By contrast, when David was a fugitive, he was inquiring where the ark was and trying to find it. In Psalm 132:6, 8 he said this: "We finally found it in the fields of the wood where it was hidden for so many years." During all those years nobody had looked for it, nobody had treasured the presence of God nor sought the glory of God. But David did. And as soon as he took Jerusalem, the next thing he did was to bring the ark back to Zion and to what the Scripture in II Samuel 6:17 describes as the tabernacle or tent of David, so that the presence of God might be the center of the kingdom and that God might be the King over all Israel; for David acknowledged that he was but His representative.

HOUSE OF GOD

The third action David endeavored to do is told about in II Samuel 7. He was in his palace resting on his couch one day, and he said to himself: "I cannot rest. I must build God a house, a temple, a permanent place. How can I continue to live in a cedar palace while the ark of God is in a tent? This cannot be. I have to build God a temple, a house." Even though he was not allowed to build that temple because he was a man of war and had shed too much blood, God did allow him to prepare for the house. Out of his love for God, David prepared materials for it. God even gave him the pattern for the house, and gave him a son, Solomon, to build it. Throughout the entire kingship of David his interest was God's interest, not his own, in order that God might be God over Israel. And under God, the people of Israel became a strong and united kingdom; and the testimony of God spread forth far and wide. That was David as king.

DAVID'S MISTAKES

Also from II Samuel we learn that David made two huge mistakes—he committed two serious sins. One is recorded in chapters 11 and 12, which begin: "At the time of war..." In those olden days, there were times of wars and times of rest. Most likely, back then, when spring or summer came, the people would get excited and want to go to war, but when winter would come, they all wanted to rest. At the time of war, all the nations would begin to mobilize and then they would fight. As king, David was supposed to lead the army and go out to war, but on one occasion, instead of doing that, he decided to take it easy. So he sent Joab his general out to lead the troops while he remained behind and rested in his palace. On this occasion of not fulfilling his duty and while at leisure, he committed a serious crime. He took the wife of Uriah the Hittite, one of David's mighty men, and then he had Uriah killed at the battlefront (see II Samuel 11 and 23:39).

David had a perfect heart towards God, but he was not perfect. And because of that, God's discipline came down heavily upon him. David repented, as we read in Psalm 51. He cried; his heart was torn and broken before God. He prayed: "God, I am willing to do anything, to offer sacrifice, but I know You will not accept it. But You will accept a broken and contrite heart." Because of his repentance, God forgave him. Yet, even though he was forgiven, discipline followed him and his household. But thank God, in judgment there is mercy. Yes, God took away the first son born of Bathsheba; for in spite of his prayer and fasting, God did not hear. But at the birth of the second child, God said, "I love that child." This was *Solomon*, whose name means "peace."

Then, towards the end of his rule, David committed another error, a huge mistake. Out of his pride, he wanted to number his people. He wanted to know how strong his kingdom was. God had promised that he would bless the children of Israel as the stars of the heavens and as the sands of the seashore; but somehow, David's pride took hold of him and so he numbered the people to see how strong he was. He sinned against God, and punishment came upon the nation. A plague came upon Israel for three days, and David repented. David said to God: "It is all my fault, not my people. Kill me, not the people." He repented, and God sent him down to Mount Moriah. At the threshing floor of Araunah God said to David, "Build an altar and the plague will stop." David did so, and that very place became the site of the temple to be built (see II Samuel 24:10-25; and cf w/ II Chronicles 3:1). Mercy and grace came out of discipline and punishment.

ONE GREATER THAN DAVID

Having reviewed together the remarkable life of David, we nonetheless find that we have One who is greater than David, the Lord Jesus Christ. God has anointed Him King, and what has Christ done and what is He doing? First of all, He has put His name in us. You remember His prayer found in John 17: "Father, I have given Your name to them; keep them in Thy name." Today, not only does the Lord Jesus have God as His Father, but also the Lord Jesus shared His Father with us so that we can call God, "Abba, Father." He gave the name of the

Father to us and now we are in the family of God (see Mark 14:36; Romans 8:15; Galatians 4:6-7a). Christ also gave His own name to us. He said, "From now on, you can pray in My name, and if you ask in My name, My Father will answer you" (see John 16:23-24).

Let us acknowledge today that God has the name of Father upon this earth and that name has been put in the Jerusalem above; moreover, that name is in the church; and this name unites us into one. The children of Israel had to go three times a year to Jerusalem to show that they were one people; and is it not the name of the Father that has joined all of us brethren in Christ together into one? We are one. We are all called by that name of Father; therefore we are one. God's name is in our midst, and how we need to honor that name: "Hallowed be Thy name."

Next, we see that Christ makes His presence known to us. "Where two or three are gathered together unto my name, there am I in the midst of them" (Matthew 18:20). We who are believers in Christ are called by His name, we gather together in His name, and we are one: we are united in His name and experience His presence with us. There is nothing more precious than Christ's presence. If His presence is not with us, all our church gatherings are in vain.

Then we find that Christ is building us together into a house, yet not with dead stones but with living stones. He said: "I will build my church upon this rock and the gates of hades shall not prevail against it" (see Matthew 16:18). He is building us together into a house so that God our Father may rest among His people. This is what the Lord is doing today. Thank God for that. In the building up of the church—even the house of God—the kingdom is being established. "Thy kingdom come" is to be our constant prayer. Thanks be to God that our David is not like David, the son of Jesse. Even though he had a perfect heart, he was nonetheless imperfect. But Christ our David is perfect, for He has never committed any error, mistake or sin.

Everything He does is good and is best. In fact, He does all the will of God. "Thy will be done on earth as it is in heaven." So today, we are God's kingdom, we are God's church, and Christ is putting God the Father's name in us, Christ's presence is with us, and His promise to us is that He is building the house of our Father God.

Let us pray:

> *Dear heavenly Father, we do praise and thank Thee because Thy Son is the Son of David and also the Lord of David. We do praise and thank Thee, Thou hast anointed Him King and we are His kingdom. Oh, rule over us. May Thy name be hallowed in our midst. May Thy kingdom come to our midst, and may Thy will be done in us as it is in heaven. And to Thee be the glory. Amen.*

I KINGS

WISDOM AND PROPHETIC MINISTRY

I Kings 4:29-34—And God gave Solomon wisdom and very great understanding and largeness of heart, even as the sand that is on the sea-shore. And Solomon's wisdom excelled the wisdom of all the sons of the east, and all the wisdom of Egypt. For he was wiser than all men; than Ethan the Ezrahite, and Heman, and Calcol, and Darda, the sons of Mahol; and his fame was in all the nations round about. And he spoke three thousand proverbs; and his songs were a thousand and five. And he spoke of the trees, from the cedar-tree that is on Lebanon even to the hyssop that springs out of the wall; he spoke also of cattle, and of fowls, and of creeping things, and of fishes. And there came of all peoples to hear the wisdom of Solomon, from all the kings of the earth who had heard of his wisdom.

I Kings 17:1—And Elijah the Tishbite, of the inhabitants of Gilead, said to Ahab, As Jehovah the God of Israel liveth, before whom I stand, there shall not be dew nor rain these years, except by my word.

Let us pray:

Dear heavenly Father, we do praise and thank Thee that through Thy beloved Son we can approach Thy throne of grace with boldness. We do praise and thank Thee knowing that Thy presence is with us, and we just desire that we may see Thy face. We pray that as Thy word is explained, Thy Holy Spirit would reveal Thy Son to us. And to Thee be the glory. In the name of our Lord Jesus. Amen.

Before we enter into the book of I Kings, I think it is necessary for us to have a little background. First of all, it would be helpful to see the connection between I and II Kings, or The Kings, and the two books of Samuel. We know that I and II Samuel and I and II Kings give us the history of the kingdom of Israel. In I Samuel we notice a transition—how the nation's leadership was transferred from the judges to the kings and from the priests to the prophets. Then in II Samuel we learn how the nation was established as a kingdom under the reign of David. On the other hand, in I Kings we begin to see the disruption of that kingdom and how it was divided into two kingdoms. And in II Kings we witness the downfall of both the kingdom of the north, Israel, and the kingdom of the south, Judah. And finally, let us note that in the Hebrew Bible, I and II Kings are but one long book, and that one book, practically speaking, covers the whole history of the kingly rule among God's ancient people Israel.

Now a kingdom is naturally centered upon the king. The government of the king determines the fate of the kingdom. That is the reason the content of the book of The Kings is mainly the history of these kings. And in knowing the history of these kings, we come to know the history of the kingdom.

We do not know for sure who was the writer or composer of this book of The Kings. Of course, we do know the ultimate author: the Holy Spirit. And most probably, this book was composed during the latter part of the Babylonian Captivity. We know this because when one comes to II Kings 25, which is the end of that book, the writer mentions how—at the hands of the Babylonian king, Evil-Merodach—King Jehoiachin received his freedom, after thirty-seven years as a prisoner. That was in about 562 BC. Hence, it had to have been during the second part of the Captivity that this book was composed.

This one book of The Kings presents to us three different periods. The first period details the forty years of the reign of King Solomon running approximately from 1015 to 975

B.C. The second period covers the time from the division of the kingdom to the termination or destruction of the northern kingdom of Israel, which, roughly, was from 975 to 721 B.C. And the third period provides the history of the remaining kingdom—Judah in the south—until the Babylonian captivity, a period dating roughly from 721 to 588 B.C.

As was mentioned before, we do not know who the writer or composer really was. According to the Jewish Talmud, the composer was Jeremiah. In one sense there seems to be some justification for thinking this because when one compares Jeremiah 52 with II Kings 25, one finds that they are the same. Furthermore, when we read II Kings 17, which is a commentary by the writer of the book, we see that the expression and sentiment resemble that of Jeremiah. However, we are confronted with a great difficulty here because Jeremiah was exiled in Egypt, not in Babylon; and evidently, this book was composed in Babylon and not Egypt since the latter is not even mentioned. Some people think Baruch, the scribe, might have been the writer; but we have the same difficulty. Most English-language commentators, however, believe that this book was composed by Ezra.

Whoever the composer may have been, it is believed that he was a kind of prophet because he drew his material from what—when delved into more deeply—are three different prophetic sources. One is the book of the acts of Solomon (see I Kings 11:41); the second is the book of the chronicles of the kings of Judah (see I Kings 14:29); and the third source is the book of the chronicles of the kings of Israel (see I Kings 14:19). Now in comparing all this with Chronicles, these three sources are described differently because in Chronicles they are mentioned as being the writings of the prophets. For instance, concerning the citation pertaining to Solomon which one finds in II Chronicles 9:29, instead of mentioning there the book of the acts of Solomon, it says, "Are they not written in the words of Nathan the prophet, and in the prophecy of Ahijah the Shilanite, and in the visions of Iddo the seer?" Accordingly, when comparing Kings and Chronicles together, we come to the conclusion that the book of Chronicles was mainly the writings of the prophets, and it is generally agreed that the prophets were the historians in the nation of Israel. Therefore, what they presented in their writings is not just history; rather, it is both historical and prophetical in nature.

Why was this book of The Kings written? It was written not only as a history, it was also written with a specific purpose to a people who were in captivity. It was during the time when the children of God were captured as slaves, were far away from their land, and humiliated. So the prophet composed a history of the nation, beginning with the glorious time of Solomon and ending with the Babylonian captivity. The reason he presented this picture to the people in captivity was to remind them that they were the covenant people of God. And that when they had been faithful to God, He had blessed them, but whenever they had been unfaithful to Him, then judgment most surely followed upon them. Thus, the reason behind the writing was to convince the people of God and to show them that the way back to His covenant blessing was through repentance and a returning to faithfulness towards God.

It is interesting to see in this book of The Kings that not only are the stories of these kings told, but also the prophets are shown to have occupied a very prominent place in the history. This is a reflection upon the love of God because the prophets became prominent when these two nations were in declension. God so loved His people that when they were falling away, He raised up prophets and sent them to His people, calling them to return to Him in repentance. It is very interesting to see that even though God did send prophets to the nation of Judah, they performed no miracles. All the miracles performed by the prophets were done to the nation of Israel. In other words, the lower the people fell, the greater the mercy and love of God were shown. Unfortunately, even though God sent His prophets again and again to the children of Israel, they did not listen. And eventually, both the northern kingdom and the southern kingdom were destroyed.

What does this history say to us today? We have already mentioned that what we have in the Old Testament is not just secular history; it is also prophecy—that is to say, it is the revelation of God. Therefore, through this book of The Kings God is saying something to us. We, as God's people today, are the people of the new covenant just as the children of Israel were the people of the old covenant. They were a people under law and we today are a people under grace. Yet there is a similarity between the history of the ancient people of God and the history of God's people today. When we open the New Testament book of Acts, which is the history of the church—the people of God today—it is so glorious. From the day of Pentecost the Holy Spirit was at work and the name of the Lord Jesus was constantly being uplifted. God's people were one, they loved one another, and God added to the church daily. It was almost like the reign of Solomon in that glorious time. But then, gradually, declension came in. We can see this in the last writing of the apostle John—the book of Revelation. For there in the letters to the seven churches we learn that God's people had begun to decline and to leave their first love. And because of that, all kinds of corruption had begun to come in.

Indeed, throughout the centuries since the time of John's book of Revelation, God's people have seemed to have always been drifting further and further away from God; yet God in His mercy had continually sent His prophets calling His people back. From time to time, there have been revivals in the history of the Christian church, but such revivals have come and gone. It seems as though in more recent times that the people of God have been sinking lower and lower. We can certainly say that the church is in a Babylonian-like captivity. In other words, God has delivered the church out of the world. He has gathered us out of the world unto himself. That is what the church is; but the church, by itself, has gone into Babylonian captivity, which is a falling into the religious world. It is still the world, but it is the religious world. Even so, there is a way for coming back, and that way is through repentance and a returning to first love. This is the lesson God is teaching us from the entire book of The Kings.

I Kings itself can be divided into four parts. The first part is the passing of David, from chapter 1 to 2:11. The second part covers the reign of Solomon, chapters 2:12-11. The third part is the division of the kingdom, told of in chapters 12-16. And the last part relates the story of Elijah, recounted in chapters 17-22. Now we are not able to discuss all the kings and all the prophets, so we will take up but one king and but one prophet—Solomon and Elijah.

SOLOMON THE KING

Solomon means "peaceful." He was born after David had repented of his sin with Bathsheba and was disciplined by God. When Solomon was born, God loved him very much and gave him a special name, Jedidiah, "beloved of God." Therefore, he was a son of grace. And David promised the boy's mother, Bathsheba, that her son would sit upon his throne. His elder brothers, Absalom and Adonijah, tried to take the throne away from Solomon, but God gave it to him. He inherited the kingdom from his father David, who had been a man of war and who had fought many battles; whereas Solomon was a man of peace. He loved God and sacrificed to Him at Gibeon. God appeared to him in a dream and said, "Ask what you would like to have." And Solomon asked for an understanding heart that he might judge the people, that he might discern between the good and the bad. He did not ask for riches, nor for glory, nor for the lives of his enemies; he simply asked for an understanding heart. In other words, he did not ask anything for himself; what he asked for was only for God's sake. God had put him on the throne but Solomon said he was just a little child. He did not know how to go in and out among God's people or how to rule them according to God. So he asked only for an understanding heart that he might rule God's people for God, and God was pleased with that request. God promised to give Solomon wisdom and an understanding heart, but He also said He would give him riches, glory, and all the many other things he did not even ask for.

Solomon has become the synonym for wisdom. His wisdom exceeded that of the East and all the wisdom of Egypt; indeed, Solomon was wiser even than Ethan, Heman, Calcol, and Darda. Now we know that the wisdom of the East was philosophical, mystical and speculative in nature. The wisdom of Egypt, on the other hand, was mechanical, scientific and materialistic. And the wisdom of Heman, Ethan, Calcol, and Darda was in essence poetical and spiritual. Nevertheless, the wisdom of Solomon exceeded them all. His wisdom was divine in nature; for God gave him an understanding heart. In the original the phrase, "an understanding heart," signifies a heart that hears. In other words, God gave him a heart that can hear Him, and that is true wisdom. Let us not think wisdom is a matter of the mind; that is knowledge. Wisdom is a matter of the heart. If our hearts can hear God, we have the greatest wisdom in the whole world.

Solomon heard God. He wrote three thousand proverbs and a thousand and five songs. He spoke about all the trees: from the cedar-tree in Lebanon to the hyssop that creeps upon the walls; and he also spoke about the cattle, fowl, fishes, and creeping things. Yet let us be clear that he did not speak of all the trees as a botanist, nor of all the cattle as a zoologist; he spoke of all these things as a man of God; meaning that he could see God's power and creative genius in everything; and *that* is wisdom.

Solomon was not only a man of wisdom; he was also, through God's gifting, a man of great wealth. It was under Solomon that the promise of God to Abraham was fulfilled for a time because King Solomon's dominion extended from the great river Euphrates to the little stream of Egypt. Moreover, he received tribute from all the different nations. His table was so rich. He had in great abundance silver in Jerusalem as though stones and cedars as though sycamores in the lowlands. He was not only rich, but in his lifetime he also did a work that nobody before him had ever done: he built the temple of God. Solomon had the wisdom to understand the pattern which God had given to his father David. He was able to mobilize many people to build the house of God, and he had the wisdom to use all the various materials for its construction. Not only that, after he finished the building of God's house, he offered it to God, and He accepted it. The glory of God filled the house and fire came down from heaven and burned up the offering. That is a most glorious thing.

Unfortunately, however, in his old age Solomon loved many foreign women, and they enticed him away from God to worship idols. God was highly displeased with him, but for his father's sake, He would not allow the nation to be divided under Solomon, but under his son.

Now that is the history side of this portion of the book of The Kings.

"ONE GREATER THAN SOLOMON"

In a sense, we know King Solomon is a type of Christ because He is the One who is greater than Solomon. We will remember how in the Gospels of Matthew and Luke it is said that the queen of Sheba came from the south, traveling a long distance to hear the wisdom of Solomon; but the Lord Jesus had said, speaking of himself: "Here is One greater than Solomon, but who will hear Him?" (see Matthew 12:42, Luke 11:31) By comparison in a number of different ways with Solomon the son of King David, we find:

(a) that the Lord Jesus is the Son incarnate, full of grace and truth (see John 1:14);

(b) that Christ is the Prince of peace, for when He was born, the angels sang, "Glory to God in the highest, peace on earth, goodwill towards men" (see Luke 2:13-14; see also Isaiah 9:6);

(c) that Christ on earth was the Beloved of the Father: throughout His life He pleased His Father, doing the Father's will without exception, so that again and again heaven opened and declared, "This is My beloved Son in whom is My delight" (see Matthew 3:17, 17:5);

(d) that there is no one who can compare with Christ Jesus with regard to wisdom since He is wisdom—He is the very wisdom of God (see I Corinthians 1:30a);

(e) that, therefore, how blessed it is for anyone who stands before Christ and hears Him;

(f) that there is no one who can compare with Christ as to His riches, for we are told in the New Testament that all the fullness of the Godhead dwells in Him bodily and that we who are His disciples are made complete in Him, we having been blessed with every spiritual blessing in the heavenlies in Christ Jesus (see Colossians 2:9-10; Ephesians 1:3); and

(g) that there has been no other who has done such a marvelous work as Christ has done. Did not the Lord Jesus declare: "I will build My church upon this rock, and the gates of Hades will not prevail against it" (see Matthew 16:18)? The chief accomplishment which Solomon did in his life was to build the temple of God, but he built it with lifeless stones—beautiful stones, yes; massive stones, yes—but all dead and lifeless, nonetheless. And eventually, that temple was completely destroyed, with not a stone left upon another (see e.g., Mark 13:1-2). But the One greater than Solomon has built a living temple with living stones, that is to say, with people such as we—not beautiful in ourselves, but God made us beautiful in Christ. And Christ is building us together into a holy habitation of God for eternity, and it can never be destroyed (see Ephesians 2:22). What a marvelous work He has done, indeed!

But finally, it needs to be noted that the One greater than Solomon is most unlike Solomon who had loved many foreign women. Christ, though, has but one love. He loves His Father, and He loves His church and gave himself up for her.

Now *that* is *our* King Solomon; and we know that one day Christ—the King of all kings—shall come back and establish His kingdom upon this earth, and righteousness shall rule over the whole earth.

In one further though smaller sense, Solomon can also represent us, because of our union with Christ. Are we not sons of grace? We are. Are we not children of peace? We are, because Christ is our peace (see Ephesians 2:14). He has made peace for us with God and with one another, and He has brought us together into one new man, one body (see Ephesians 2:15). Are we not called children or sons of wisdom? (see Luke 7:35) We are; yet not because we are wise in ourselves, but because Christ is our wisdom (see I Corinthians 1:30a). Is it not true that the one work God has commissioned us to do is to build the house of God? The foundation is laid in and by the Lord Jesus, but every one of His followers is building upon that foundation. And because we who are His followers are building the house of God, let us not build with wood, stubble, and hay but build with gold, silver, and precious stones, so that our work may remain and God be glorified (see I Corinthians 3:10-15). So, spiritually speaking, such is Solomon to us personally.

ELIJAH THE PROPHET

The name Elijah means "whose God is Jehovah." This is very, very meaningful when it is understood that Elijah lived in the days of apostasy. In his time the whole nation of Israel fell into apostasy under King Ahab, and Ahab was under the influence of the Gentile woman, Jezebel. So the whole nation was led away from God. But here was Elijah, whose God was Jehovah. His very name is a testimony. Elijah the Tishbite stood alone for the rights of God in a nation of apostasy. So far as can be determined today, as a Tishbite Elijah must have been a native of upper Galilee, but he became an inhabitant of Gilead, which was on the other side of Jordan. Why did he flee to Gilead? It must have been that his testimony was too "hot" for the nation. He stood for God, but the king and the whole nation rebelled against God. He must therefore have been persecuted and had to flee for his life.

When one reads I Kings 17, it may seem as though Elijah the Tishbite suddenly appeared out of nowhere, because there is no mention there of his past history. Suddenly, he had appeared and declared to Ahab the king, "As the Lord liveth, before whom I stand, there will be no dew or rain except by my word" (v.1). Even though Elijah's past history was not given, we can assume what that history must have been. He was a man zealous for God. He was so hurt by what he had seen that he cried out against the abomination of the nation, and because of that, he had to flee for his life. But did he give up? No. There in Gilead he was praying. How do we know this? In the New Testament book of James it is said, "Elijah was a man of like passion to us, and he prayed and there was no rain for three years and six months. And he prayed again and rain came, and the earth caused its fruit to spring forth" (see 5:17-18). Here was a man who was zealous for God, who stood for God's right, who was hurt by what he saw in the nation, who cried out against the sin and abomination of the nation, who had to flee for his life; nevertheless, he did not give up. He gave himself to prayer. He prayed for God's kingdom; he prayed for God's right; and as he prayed, he was so burdened that he even prayed and asked God to withhold the rain. He had the assurance that Jehovah had heard him, and so He sent him to Ahab to proclaim His judgment. And, hence, we can be sure there was a hidden history of that prophet with God.

In essence Elijah had declared to Ahab, "As Jehovah liveth ... You think that Jehovah is dead, but Jehovah liveth. He is still living. He is the God before whom I stand. I am His servant. I wait upon Him and I do His errand. There will be no dew or rain except by my word." He was so one with Jehovah God that he could say, "Except by my word." That was Elijah.

But strangely, immediately after he made the proclamation, God hid him. At the first, God had pushed Elijah into the limelight, but then He took him away into seclusion; for we learn that after that proclamation Ahab wanted his life; so God had to hide him. More than that, in praying that there would be no rain, Elijah had forgotten about himself, in that he would be in need of water, too. Let us ask ourselves, Do we ever pray to the extent of forgetting ourselves? Thank God if we do. Unfortunately, too many of us think first of ourselves, and that is why our prayer is impure (see James 4:3). But Elijah was so zealous for God that he forgot himself completely, but God remembered him. So God sent him to a little stream, which happened to be the source of the river Jordan. One should always go to the water source; and in this instance God also supplied Elijah miraculously with ravens there. Ravens certainly like meat, but these ravens brought their meat to Elijah. Is not that wonderful? God supported Elijah throughout the years, yet not only with ravens but also with a widow who lived in the Gentile city of Zarephath, and who was a Gentile woman. God's provision is always higher and often different than what we would think. That really should increase our faith.

Now after three years and six months God said, "It is enough." Not that the nation had repented, but it was as though God repented. He changed His mind, because in judgment there is always mercy; God therefore sent Elijah back.

We will remember the story of that confrontation on Mount

Carmel. Elijah gathered the whole nation together and said, "Why do you waiver, halting and hesitating between two opinions? If Jehovah is God, follow Him. But if Baal is God, then follow Baal" (see I Kings 18:21). That seemed fair. So there was a challenge, and fire came down and consumed the sacrifice that Elijah offered. It not only burned up the sacrifice, it burned up the water and the stones. So everybody said, "Jehovah is God" (see I Kings 18:21-39). There was a great victory, as if the whole nation would now return to God. Unfortunately, it was not so.

The next day Jezebel threatened Elijah and declared: "Before tomorrow I will have your life." And Elijah realized that the nation had not returned to God. He was so disappointed that he fled in despair. But God was so merciful. He supplied him with angel food so that he was able to walk forty days and forty nights until he arrived at Mount Sinai and entered into a particular cave there. For in the original it reads: "*the* cave," which is where Moses was when he received the Law. We should always go back to the source of things. So Elijah went back to that cave waiting to hear from God. God appeared to him and inquired, "Elijah, what are you doing here?" And Elijah replied: "I am zealous for You, but the nation killed the prophets, tore down the altar, and left You, and I am the only one left—and it did not work. So let me die. What is the purpose of living anymore?"

How gracious God is! He did not blame Elijah, for He knew his heart. God said, "Go back; anoint Hazael as king of Syria, anoint Jehu as king of Israel, and anoint Elisha as prophet. I have left Myself seven thousand who have not bent their knees to Baal nor kissed him with their mouth. Do not think this is the end. I still have many agents around, and I am going to continue working" (see I Kings 19).

That nearly brought the history of Elijah to a close. He went back and did a few things more, but not much; and God in His very gracious way even took Elijah and raptured him away.

Nevertheless, Elijah's service was not finished yet. For let us recall that on the Mount of Transfiguration Elijah appeared with Moses. And the last words of the Old Testament book, Malachi, declares this: "Elijah shall return to turn the hearts of the fathers to the children and the hearts of the children to the fathers lest they be cursed" (see vv. 5-6). We know from prophecy that Elijah will yet come. John the Baptist came in the *spirit* of Elijah, but we know that he was not Elijah because John denied it. Yet we know that Elijah is coming. Before the return of Christ, Elijah shall first come and prepare His way; for in the book of Revelation, we learn of the future appearance of the two witnesses, Moses and Elijah (11:3). So Elijah's work is not finished yet. God has something for him to do yet, and Elijah will eventually finish all the work that He has sent him to do. Now that is the story of Elijah.

THE LESSON FROM ELIJAH

What can we learn from Elijah? I think Elijah is the representation of prophetic ministry. He is the greatest prophet and the representative of all the prophets. That is why we find on the Mount of Transfiguration Moses representing the Law and Elijah representing the prophets—the Old Testament. They came together to discuss with the Lord Jesus about His departure from the earth. We see in Elijah the making of a prophet, how a prophetic ministry comes about. Here was a man zealous for God, a man who stood for God's rights amid the scene of apostasy, a man of prayer, a man with burden, a man who waited upon God, and a man who received a message from God.

We must realize that we are living today in the end days. It is prophesied in God's word that in the end days the whole church will sink into apostasy, and hence this is the time that there is a tremendous need for prophetic ministry, that God will raise up people with a prophetic ministry to call His people back.

What is a prophet? And what is prophecy? A prophet not only foretells the future, a prophet forthtells the mind of God. As a matter of fact, it is more a forthtelling of God's mind than a foretelling of the future. A prophet is one who receives a word from God for His people at a particular moment in time. He will tell God's people what God thinks about them and what He requires of them, and he will also reveal to them God's ultimate purpose regarding His people. Now that is prophetic ministry.

In the life of Elijah we do not see much in the way of foretelling the future, but we do see a lot of forthtelling of the mind of God. What we need today are people who hear from God and who can tell His people what is wrong—what God thinks about them—and what He requires of them, not only for the immediate but also for the ultimate, informing them of the eternal will of God concerning His people. That is prophetic ministry, and that is the most needful work in the church today.

But where are the prophets? We need people who are zealous for God, zealous for His rights. We need people who are willing to lay down their lives for that. We need people who will be burdened to enter into travailing prayer. We need people, as they wait upon God, to hear from Him. The life of a prophet is a difficult one because a prophet is lonely. He stands against the tide. He will be rejected, ridiculed, persecuted, even killed. But we need such people. God's church needs such prophetic ministry. A prophet is one who is selfless: God can push him into the limelight and God can also pull him back into seclusion: he will serve God in secret as well as in public: for him there is no difference. The reward of a prophet is not here and now, it is there and then. We need to pray that God will raise up prophetic ministry for the church today. I feel this is the most needful service in today's church. Oh, that God would raise up prophets, send them to His people, who will call them back to repentance and to first love.

Let us pray:

Dear heavenly Father, as we study the history of Thy ancient people we are humbled. Thou art ever so merciful, so gracious, so kind, so loving, and so faithful; and yet we are always so selfish and so rebellious. Oh, our Father, we do ask for forgiveness. We pray that repentance may come upon Thy people. We pray that there will be a return to first love. Oh, how we do praise and thank Thee that even in the history of Thy people Thou dost not end with Babylonian captivity; Thou dost end with the freedom—the release—of King Jehoiachin. Lord, Thou dost always give us hope. We know that Thou art freeing us. We know that one day Thy kingdom shall come, and there will be the manifestation of the sons of God and there will be freedom and liberty on this whole earth. Oh, how we praise and thank Thee for Thy promise. We do ask Thee, Lord, that through observing the history of Thy ancient people we may be encouraged to go on with Thee. Thy will be done, Thy kingdom come. In Thy precious name. Amen.

II KINGS

SPIRITUAL LEADERSHIP

II Kings 2:9—And it came to pass when they had gone over, that Elijah said to Elisha, Ask what I shall do for thee, before I am taken away from thee. And Elisha said, I pray thee, let a double portion of thy spirit be upon me.

II Kings 18:1-7a—And it came to pass in the third year of Hoshea the son Elah, king of Israel, that Hezekiah the son of Ahaz, king of Judah, began to reign. He was twenty-five years old when he began to reign; and he reigned twenty-nine years in Jerusalem; and his mother's name was Abi, daughter of Zechariah. And he did what was right in the sight of Jehovah, according to all that David his father had done. He removed the high places, and broke the columns, and cut down the Asherahs, and broke in pieces the serpent of brass that Moses had made; for to those days the children of Israel burned incense to it: and he called it Nehushtan. He trusted in Jehovah the God of Israel; so that after him was none like him among all the kings of Judah, nor among any that were before him. And he clave to Jehovah, and did not turn aside from following him, but kept his commandments, which Jehovah commanded Moses. And Jehovah was with him; he prospered whithersoever he went forth.

II Kings 22:1-2—Josiah was eight years old when he began to reign; and he reigned thirty-one years in Jerusalem; and his mother's name was Jedidah, daughter of Adaiah of Bozcath. And he did what was right in the sight of Jehovah, and walked in all the way of David his father, and turned not aside to the right hand nor to the left.

I and II Kings, as was noted earlier, were originally one book. It covers practically the whole history of the kingly rule of the nation of God's chosen people. In I Kings we begin to see the disruption, and in II Kings we find the downfall.

After Solomon died, the kingdom was divided into two—the northern kingdom of Israel that comprised ten tribes, and the southern kingdom of Judah that possessed two tribes. In each kingdom we find nineteen kings. The nineteen kings in the kingdom of Judah were all the descendants of King David. Now we purposely leave out Athaliah because she was Ahab's daughter who tried to murder all the sons of David, usurping the throne for a few years; so we have eliminated her in our consideration. Therefore, in the kingdom of Judah there is only one dynasty. But in the northern kingdom of Israel, with its nineteen kings, there were different dynasties among them. One would take over the kingdom from the other and continue for perhaps three or four generations at most, and then another man would rise up and take over the kingdom and in so doing would establish a new dynasty. So these nineteen kings were not all of one dynasty but were comprised of a number of dynasties.

In the southern kingdom of Judah there were some good kings like Asa, Hezekiah, and Josiah; whereas in the northern kingdom of Israel there were no good ones at all; they were all bad. Now God in His mercy sent prophets to testify against the kingdom of Judah and the kingdom of Israel, calling the people to return to God, to repent, and to keep the commandments He had given them through Moses. Unfortunately, the people hardened their hearts, and eventually, both kingdoms were destroyed. The northern kingdom was destroyed first in 721 B.C. by the Assyrians, but the southern kingdom continued on for about one hundred and thirty more years because God remembered David and hence He tried to maintain a lamp there in that nation. But eventually, because of their continued disobedience, even the southern kingdom was destroyed—by Babylon around 588 B.C. So that is the history to be found in these two books of the kings.

We mentioned before that we are not merely studying ancient history here. We acknowledge that these histories are in the Bible: they are the word of God, and they therefore are meant for us today. But what are we to learn by reading and studying the history of the ancient people of God? First of all, we must realize that in a very real sense, God's people today— those who are redeemed by the Lord—are the kingdom of God.

"But ye are a chosen race, a kingly priesthood, a holy nation, a people for a possession, that ye might set forth the excellencies of him who has called you out of darkness to his wonderful light" (I Peter 2:9).

So in both a spiritual and a practical sense, God's people today constitute a holy nation and a kingdom of priests. Of course, we have only one King, and our King is none other than our Lord Jesus Christ. He is the perfect King. We are supposed to obey Him, to do His will, to be a witness and a testimony to Him; unfortunately, throughout the two thousand years of church history, God's people, like His chosen people in the Old Testament days, have failed Him again and again. We have repeatedly turned away from our Lord Jesus. On each occasion of apostasy which has occurred throughout church history right up to our own day, God's people at first begin to drift away and pay attention to other things than to the Lord, and as a consequence the world begins to come into the church. And eventually, the church on each such occasion has gone into apostasy, and yet God in His mercy has repeatedly sent to His people His servants. Indeed, even today He sends us revivals from time to time in an attempt to draw us back to himself, but unfortunately, as a whole, the condition of God's people has been going downward instead of upward. Nevertheless, thank God, in every age, He has reserved for himself a faithful "seven thousand" who have not bowed their knees to Baal. Elijah had complained to God: "I am the only one left for Thee." But God said, "No, I have My seven thousand."

During church history, and no matter what we have seen outwardly, we must acknowledge that the church has drifted away from God. Yet, God has had those who by His grace remain faithful to Him, and by means of these people, God has maintained His testimony throughout the ages. That is a real comfort.

II Kings begins with the passing away of Elijah and the coming of Elisha into ministry. We know that Elisha succeeded Elijah in prophetic ministry. The ministry of Elijah was judicial in nature, for he brought judgment to the nation. By contrast, we see that the ministry of Elisha was merciful in nature inasmuch as he brought life and resurrection to the people. And both these aspects of ministry must be included in prophetic ministry. In other words, on the one hand a prophetic ministry does bring judgment to the people of God, but on the other hand, it also brings in resurrection and life. We need God's judgment that we may repent, but thank God, after we repent there will be life and resurrection.

In chapters 1—13 we learn of the ministry of Elisha the prophet. In chapter 17 we are told about the destruction of the northern kingdom of Israel, and there then follows the commentary of the Holy Spirit concerning their history. In chapters 18—20, there is recorded a great revival under King Hezekiah. And in chapters 22—23 we learn of another revival—this one occurring under King Josiah. Now these are the highlights to be found in II Kings.

SPIRITUAL LEADERSHIP

For our consideration together today we will concentrate on one prophet and two kings: the prophet, Elisha, and the kings, Hezekiah and Josiah. Now we know that both prophet and king represent spiritual leadership. When we think of life in the body of Christ, we find that all members are equal. And because we are all members of the body of Christ, no member is more important than the other. The eyes need the ears, the hands need the feet, and so on. Even though we are all different, yet so far as life is concerned, we share the same life. There is no difference: we are all equal before God. So far as God's grace is concerned there is no reason one brother or one sister should receive more grace than the other brother or sister because God gives His grace equally to all. The reason some receive more and some receive less is not because God is partial in dispensing His grace; rather, it is because of our capacity. Some receive more of Him; others do not seem to be able to.

Therefore, so far as life is concerned, we are all equal before God. But so far as work in the church is concerned, we are as it is in the kingdom of God since we as believers are deemed to be the kingdom of God. And in God's kingdom there is not only divine order, there are also various positions. In the kingdom of God, our Lord Jesus is the King, but under Him the church has been given some apostles, some prophets, some evangelists, some pastors and teachers. These are those given for the ministry of God's word for the purpose of perfecting the saints. God also raises up elders and deacons for the government of the church in order to lead the people, to help them, and to build them up. So when we consider the work of God, we do find that there is leadership. Sometimes God's people are so democratic in their attitude that they feel there should be no leaders; or, that we are all leaders. It is quite true that when it concerns life, we are all equal, but when God begins to work to build up His church, He does raise up leadership. And we do need leadership because without it there can really be no building taking place. Apostles, prophets, evangelists, and pastors and teachers are raised up by God to perfect the body of Christ, to perfect God's people. And as God's people are perfected—that is, are matured and equipped—then every member of the body of Christ will begin to function and build up the body in love. These men are God's gift to the church. They are in spiritual leadership, leading God's people according to the word of God.

God also raises up elders and deacons in the church. These are people in certain positions of responsibility, and through them God wants to shepherd and help the people go on with the Lord. The first group of people mentioned are like the *prophets* in the Old Testament time because they minister God's word to His people. The second group of people are like the *kings* in the Old Testament time. They are concerned more with government and with service.

Leadership is very important for the growth of the church. We have seen how in ancient Israel, if the leadership was wrong, if the leaders were selfish, then the whole nation suffered. Such has been the history of the nation of Israel and that of Judah: when there was a bad king, then the whole nation came under curse; but if, by God's grace, there was a good king, one who ruled for God, then the whole nation was blessed.

We must acknowledge that God's people are like sheep. I think everybody loves sheep. They appear so loving, so gentle, so good, and thank God for that. Every child of God is loving. But sheep are most ignorant. If, for example, a sheep goes astray, it never knows how to come back, like dogs or cats. If also a sheep is caught among the thorns, it is never able to extricate itself; it has to be helped out. Moreover, a sheep does not know its pasture because it will eat anything that is before it; and hence, a sheep needs a shepherd to choose the pasture for it.

God's people are like sheep. They are so good, so innocent, and they are so ignorant. That is the reason why in church history, whenever God raised up the right leadership, God's people were blessed. But whenever there was bad leadership, God's people were led astray very quickly, almost overnight. They simply followed whoever was leading them. That is why it is so important that God gives His church spiritual leadership: leadership which truly comes from God and not from man, leadership that is not set up by man nor grasped after by ambitious people but is leadership that is ordained by God himself. And when God gives His church those leaders whom He himself has raised up and if they are truly leading the people in God, how blessed God's people will be.

So we definitely need to ask the Lord in prayer that He will raise up spiritual leadership in the church as we enter into this last phase of church history. We are at the end of the last days and are in a day of great apostasy—a great falling away. Many of God's people are being led astray here and there. They are innocent. We deeply feel for them, but this is the time we need to pray and ask the Lord to raise up spiritual leadership for His people. And that is the reason why II Kings is so important and relevant for us today because God raised up the prophet Elisha in the ministry of His word to His people and raised up King Hezekiah and King Josiah to lead the people back to God. Let us pray that God will do the same today.

ELISHA THE PROPHET

GOD'S CHOICE

The very name Elisha means "whose salvation is God." He was the son of Shaphat of Abel-meholah, and Abel-meholah was located in the valley of Jordan in the tribe of Manasseh. We find Elisha mentioned first in I Kings chapter 19. God had commanded Elijah to go back to anoint Elisha to succeed him as the prophet. So Elijah went to Abel-meholah and there he found Elisha and anointed him to be his successor.

So far as the assumption of prophetic ministry is concerned, it is a sovereign choice of God. It was God who told Elijah about Elisha. We may recall the words of our Lord Jesus recorded in John, chapter 15:16a: "Ye have not chosen me, but I have chosen you, and have set you that ye should go and that ye should bear fruit." Ministry is not a matter of what we want to do or that it is what we in ourselves are. God in His sovereignty will choose whomever He wants to choose. There is nothing for anyone to boast of or grasp after. It is a sovereign choice of God for anyone to assume true ministry among His people.

DILIGENCE

Why is it that out of the many young people in the nation of Israel God chose Elisha to be a prophetic minister? On the one hand, we have seen that everything surrounding this matter is based upon God's sovereign choice; on the other hand, we need to ask the question: Why does God choose this one and not the other one for the prophetic ministry? God must have seen something in the young man Elisha which made him different from the other young men. Or to put it another way, God must have seen something in that young man which made him worthy to be chosen. What was that young man doing when Elijah came to anoint him? He was plowing a field— an ordinary work—but he was plowing it with twelve yoke of oxen. Now have you ever seen a person plowing a field with twelve yoke of oxen? Usually, you will see men plowing a field with only one yoke of oxen, but Elisha was plowing with twelve yoke. It is evident that he must have come from a well-to-do family since only a well-to-do family could have possessed so many yoke of oxen. But then, too, if you are one who comes from a well-to-do family that has twelve yoke of oxen, you would probably not be the one doing the plowing. On the contrary, you would have hired people to do it, and thus you would be free to enjoy yourself and have a good time. But not this young man. Even though Elisha came from a rich family and could hire people to plow the field, he was the one doing the plowing. In other words, we may say that this young man was diligent—in fact, very diligent.

I think it was D. L. Moody who said, "God will never use

a lazy person." And he even said further, "God will never save a lazy person because that person is too lazy to believe in the Lord Jesus." God saw this young man Elisha as one who had the character of diligence and chose him. Not only that, God also noticed that while this young man was working, he did so wholeheartedly, not halfheartedly: he put all twelve yoke of oxen into the work. In short, his whole heart was in the work. Such a one was the kind of person God could use.

A HEART EXERCISED BEFORE GOD

When Elijah came to Elisha, without saying a word, he placed the prophet's mantle upon him. But what happened next? Elisha immediately ran after Elijah and said to him, "Let me go and say good-by to my mother and father and I will follow you." And Elijah replied, "What have I done to you?" Elisha returned home, killed the oxen, used the implements as firewood to boil the oxen, gave the food to the people to eat, and left and followed Elijah. Now how could this have happened so suddenly? It is evident to us that this young man, even while he was busily occupied with plowing his field, had been exercising his heart before the Lord for some time. It was not an accident. Elisha's heart was being exercised concerning the interests of God in the nation of Israel. He must have been praying, he must have been burdened before God, he must have been waiting upon Him to be called. He was ready, yet he did not go out on his own. He waited until God called him into the ministry. Even so, Elisha did not wait idly at home for the call. On the contrary, while he was waiting, he was diligently applying himself to whatever God had placed in his hand to do at that moment, and to do so with all his heart. That is why when Elijah placed the prophet's mantle upon him, Elisha immediately responded positively because his heart was ready. He simply burned all bridges behind him and wholeheartedly followed Elijah.

Let us ask ourselves, Are our hearts being exercised before God? When our hands are on the plow plowing the field and we are committing ourselves wholeheartedly to the work which God at that moment has put into our hands, is our whole interest and burden simply to have a hundredfold harvest from the field? Is that all? Or is it that when we are plowing the field, are we exercised with the interests of God upon this earth today? Are our hearts being burdened for His kingdom? Are we waiting upon Him ready to do whatever He may call us to do? In other words, we are not serving the world, we are serving God; even when our hands are on the plow, our hearts are with God. So that when the time comes to be summoned, are we ready to respond and to burn our bridges behind us?

On the other hand, if we do have a heart and a burden for the Lord's work, do we nonetheless step out on our own and assert, "Now that I am burdened, therefore I have to do it—I cannot wait anymore"? No, we must wait until God's call comes at His time. But when that time does come, let us not hesitate to respond, let us burn our bridges and follow the Lord.

THE SERVANT OF ALL

In I Kings 19:21 we read: "Elisha ministered to Elijah." To what does this refer? If we read II Kings 3, we will know; for there it tells us that he poured water on the hands of Elijah (see v 11b). Today, many of us do not know what that act signifies; but if we were to visit India, we would understand. People in India eat with their hands, and when finished eating, somebody will come and pour water on their hands to make them clean. In other words, it is the work of a servant.

Now Elisha was called to be a prophet. So we would probably expect him to open his mouth and prophesy; instead of that we find Elisha pouring water on the hands of Elijah. In other words, he was doing the work of a servant. We may likely think this is something beyond his dignity. He ought to be prophesying! But we do not find him prophesying; rather, he was serving Elijah as an apprentice, as a disciple. Indeed, this is how spiritual leadership is raised up. If God is to raise you up as a leader, you first have to be a learner. Before you can lead, you have to be a disciple to Christ. After all, leadership is not sitting on high and giving commands; leadership means to be the servant of all. Therefore, that spirit of servanthood has to be developed.

This was true with the twelve apostles who were with our Lord Jesus. The Lord called the twelve apostles, but first of all they were to be with Him learning of Him. They were not merely to learn the skills of preaching, they also had to learn to know the Lord, to learn His character, how He lived and how He acted. This today is what we need. We need to learn of Him. We need to learn His character and let His character characterize us; for only then are we able to minister life to people.

THE SPIRIT OF ELIJAH

Elisha ministered to Elijah for a period until God called Elijah up to heaven. One day Elijah told Elisha to stay in Gilgal, that he was going to Bethel. And Elisha said, "No, I will go with you." After they arrived in Bethel, Elijah said, "Stay here, I am going to Jericho." Elisha said, "No, I am going with you to Jericho." So when they were in Jericho, Elijah said, "Stay here, I am going over the Jordan." And Elisha said, "No, I am going with you." So they traveled all the way across the river Jordan, and then Elijah said, "I am departing from you; what do you want? You may ask." And Elisha asked: "Give me a double portion of your spirit."

Now what is the spirit of Elijah? It is the spirit of jealousy, the jealousy of God and a being jealous *for* God and His rights. And how do we know that this was the spirit of Elijah? It is especially revealed to us in the account of the episode of Elijah's greatest disappointment, even of despair.

When we are carefully watching ourselves, we will put up a front, resulting in nobody really being able to discern our spirit. Discerning another person's spirit is very difficult because the more civilized we are the more we hide ourselves. We will not allow people to know our spirit—our true person. But when we are in disappointment or despair, all the facade disappears and then our real person will be revealed. And such was the case with Elijah.

Now when do we see Elijah's real person coming out? It was when he was deeply disappointed and in utter despair—even of his life. He fled to Mount Sinai where God said to him, "Elijah, why are you here? What are you doing here?" And Elijah replied: "Lord, I am jealous for You. I am jealous for Your rights. And yet the whole nation is against me. They want to kill me" (see I Kings 19). So we can conclude from Elijah's words here that the spirit of Elijah is one of jealousy.

Let us understand that there is nothing wrong here with the use of that word jealousy. Today, it has a very bad connotation, but the word itself is not wrong. If someone is jealous for the right reason or for the right thing, that is something commendable. Our God is a jealous God, and we need His jealousy. We also need to be jealous *for* Him—so jealous for Him, in fact, that we do not want to see any portion of His rights being deprived. We want Him to be God in all things. We want Him to have everything which He deserves to have. And Elijah was so jealous for God that his very life was in danger. Now that is having a jealousy for God. And this godly prophet's disciple Elisha sought to have the same spirit of jealousy which his master had.

But we need to take note of something else about Elisha's coming to Elijah and asking, "Give me a double portion of your spirit." Truly, it can be said, this young man was not ambitious for himself in the least. And, again, we must observe that there is nothing wrong with this word ambitious, either. Some people think Christians should not be ambitious. Not so;

for Paul said, "I am ambitious." That is the very word he used in II Corinthians, but in the Bible it is not translated that way. Yet in the original we find Paul saying, "I am ambitious that I may please God in all things" (see II Corinthians 5:9). And like both Elijah and Paul, Elisha was not ambitious for himself but totally for God.

By Elisha asking for a double portion of Elijah's spirit signified that in wanting to be so jealous for God he was willing to take upon himself double trials and double afflictions. It would be costly, for in order to obtain that double portion of the spirit of Elijah, Elisha had to travel all the way from Gilgal to Bethel, on, then, to Jericho, and finally over the river Jordan. We know from Joshua 5:9 that Gilgal stands for the rolling away for the Israelites of the shame of Egypt—that is to say, the rolling away of the flesh, wherein the flesh is being completely dealt with. If we desire to have a double portion of the spirit of Elijah, the first thing needed is for us to have our flesh completely rolled away. Then we need to go to Bethel, which spiritually represents the house of God. We need to see in a positive way what the house of God really is, and there we will live under an open heaven. From Bethel we will go on to Jericho—so illustrative of spiritual conflict—and there we will experience the victory of Christ. And from there we will cross the river Jordan, which speaks of our being conformed to Christ's death. It was after Elisha had gone through all this in his journey with Elijah that he went back and was able to minister in life to every place which he would visit thereafter.

MINISTRY OF RESURRECTION LIFE

In reading these first thirteen chapters of II Kings we will learn that Elisha performed something like fourteen miracles altogether. There are different opinions about that, but we need not go into that. These many miracles simply underscore the fact of how God used that man immensely. In all these miracles

Elisha brought life and resurrection to the people. For example, he opened the waters of Jordan; he healed the waters of Jericho.

It is true, also, that he cursed the boys who came out of Bethel to poke fun at him. Yet in the original text describing this incident they are not presented as little boys but as teenagers. Bethel, at that time, was a place of idolatry; so evidently, the priests of that idolatry sent those teenagers out to ridicule and to mock Elisha, which was the same as their mocking the interests of God. For these teenagers had said: "Go up, baldhead, go up." In other words, since Elijah had gone up, why don't you also go up, and disappear? And of course, judgment came upon those teenagers.

Elisha also brought water into the desert for three kings that they might not die. Further, in order to maintain the life of a particular woman, Elisha multiplied the oil in a vessel to fill many empty vessels which the widow among the wives of the sons of the prophets had borrowed. Still other instances of Elisha having brought life and resurrection to the people were these: He restored the life of the little son of the Shunammite woman; he nullified the poison that was in that pot; he multiplied the cake of barley to feed a hundred people; he healed the leprosy of Naaman; he opened the eyes of his servant that he might see God's horsemen surrounding the city; and he proclaimed the victory over Syria. And even after Elisha died, when a dead body touched his bones, that body was resurrected. In short, the ministry of Elisha was truly one of resurrection life.

Oh, how we need such ministry! Yes, we need the ministry of judgment, but we also need the ministry of life and resurrection, and that is what the merciful side of prophetic ministry really is, to impart the life of Christ to God's people.

HEZEKIAH THE KING

GOD'S MEASURING ROD

Hezekiah came to the throne when he was twenty-nine years old, and he was on the throne for twenty-five years. The Bible says that Hezekiah followed the Lord and did everything which David his father had done without turning to the right or the left. In the Old Testament writings, especially in those dealing with the history of the kings, we read how God measured every king by the standard of David because David was *the* king. David represented the king after God's own heart. Indeed, he was a man after God's heart who did all God's will, and that is what a king in God's heart is. So God used David by which to measure every king mentioned in the book of The Kings. Some kings did not measure up in any way; they were utterly bad and did not do what David had done. On the other hand, other kings may have done some things which David had done, but not all things. And there were still a few others who did everything that David had done because their hearts were perfect towards God like David's, and Hezekiah was one of them. As a matter of fact, among the Jewish people, there were three kings who were considered to be most honorable. David was one and Hezekiah was another. Hezekiah followed the Lord with all his heart; he did everything that David had done. And hence, he measured up very well to God's standard.

Do you know that God has a standard by which to measure everything today, too? God will measure not only ministry, He will measure life, work, and every other relevant thing today by but one standard, and that standard is the One who is greater than David, our Lord Jesus. He will measure everything according to Him. In leadership, God will use the Lord Jesus as the measuring rod to see how much a person measures up to His leadership. Do we do what He has done? Or in some way do we deviate from Him? How God's heart will be pleased if He finds leadership that measures up to the Son of David, even the Lord of David! And Hezekiah was one who favorably measured up with David.

TRUST IN THE LORD

Hezekiah trusted the Lord. In his fourteenth year of reign, Sennacherib, king of Syria, seized the cities of Judah. He surrounded and laid siege over the city of Jerusalem and made unreasonable demands. Under that kind of situation, Hezekiah trusted God with his whole heart. He cried out to the Lord, and the Lord delivered him. We, too, need that kind of trust in the Lord.

A SIGN

In the prime of his years, when he was thirty-nine years old, Hezekiah fell sick unto death and God sent Isaiah to him to say, "Set your house in order, you are going."

Hezekiah turned his face towards the wall and wept and said, "God, remember, my heart was perfect towards Thee. I did everything for You and now in the prime of my years I am dying." Because he wept before God, God's heart was softened. So He sent Isaiah back to say to Hezekiah: "I have heard your prayer. I will give you fifteen more years. And on the third day you will go into the temple to worship."

Hezekiah responded with: "How can I know? Will I be given a sign?"

And Isaiah said, "Yes. Do you want the dial of Ahab to go forward ten degrees or backward ten degrees?" And Hezekiah replied, "I want it to go backwards."

So time went back ten degrees. Isn't that wonderful? We do not have the time here to try to prove this scientifically, but it has been proven. In the universe mankind lost twenty-four hours, and the report of these twenty-four hours can be found in the Scriptures (see Joshua 10:13), and the ten degrees are among them.

God gave Hezekiah a sign; the dial went back ten degrees and he was healed. How he trusted and believed in God. But unfortunately, his heart was not humbled by all which God had done. Instead, he began to be proud of himself. So that in those fifteen years two terrible events occurred. One was that when the king of Babylon heard that Hezekiah was healed, he sent an emissary to congratulate him. And Hezekiah was so proud of his country, his riches and his wealth that he was enticed by these emissaries. They were actually spies. He showed them all the things in his kingdom, and because of that, God told him that the whole nation, and everything he had, would be taken into captivity.

The second event which happened during those fifteen years was that he begat a son named Manasseh. This son turned out to be one of the worst kings ever, and because of his sins, God determined to destroy the nation of Judah.

There is a great lesson for us to learn from all this. If the Lord says your time is up, go gladly. If you try to persuade God—and He *can* be persuaded because our God is so soft, merciful and tenderhearted—it will not be good for you. It is better to submit yourself to God because everything He has ordained for you is the best for you—and for Him and His interests too.

Thank God, He did raise Hezekiah up as a spiritual leader, and under his leadership the nation did come back to God, at least temporarily. God also gave him Isaiah to help him in the work of restoration, even though at the very end, unfortunately, he fell into pride. And that is a great lesson for leaders to take to heart.

Leaders are especially exposed to this peril of being proud. If God does not use you, you have nothing to be proud of, but you may be jealous of other people. That is your danger; but if God should use you, then people will be jealous of you. You will not be jealous but you may be proud, and pride will be followed by a fall. So may the Lord have mercy upon us that, on the one hand, God will raise up spiritual leadership and, on the other hand, that the leaders will always keep themselves humble before Him.

JOSIAH THE KING

The great grandson of Hezekiah was Josiah and his name means "Jehovah heals or sustains." He was only eight years old when he began to reign, but even at such an early age, " he did what was just in the sight of Jehovah, and walked in all the way of David his father, and turned not aside to the right hand nor to the left" (II Kings 22:2). This is indeed most precious, as it can be a great encouragement to children. None are too young to love and follow the Lord: the earlier the better. In his eighteenth year, when he was twenty-six years old, Josiah repaired the house of God and found the book of the Law. "And it came to pass when the king heard the words of the book of the law, that he rent his garments" (v. 11). The response from the Lord through Huldah the prophetess was this: "Because thy heart was tender, and thou didst humble thyself before Jehovah … I also have heard thee, saith Jehovah."

"And the king stood on the dais, and made a covenant before Jehovah, to walk after Jehovah, and to keep his commandments and his testimonies and his statutes with all his heart, and with all his soul, to establish the words of this covenant that are written in this book. And all the people stood to the covenant" (II Kings 23:3). Josiah cleansed the temple, Jerusalem, all the cities of Judah, and even Samaria of idols as well as removed the necromancers and the soothsayers from the land of Judah.

"And before him there had been no king like him that turned to Jehovah with all his heart and with all his soul and with all his might, according to all the law of Moses; neither after him arose there his like" (v. 25). How we need a tender heart towards the word of God, and also a corresponding obedient action like that of Josiah.

In these men discussed here, whether prophet or king, we see the influence of good, sound leadership. Whether in prophetic words or in kingly actions, revivals can be brought in among God's people.

Let us pray:

Dear heavenly Father, we do commit these words into Thy hands and pray that Thou wilt make them living, even life to us. Lord, we do pray that Thou wilt raise up spiritual leadership in the church and pray that Thou wilt keep the leaders humble before Thee. We do look forward to the day when Thou shalt return and establish Thy kingdom upon this earth and to the day when righteousness shall reign over the whole earth. We ask in Thy precious name. Amen.

I CHRONICLES

A LOVE FOR THE HOUSE OF GOD

I Chronicles 11:4-9—And David and all Israel went to Jerusalem, which is Jebus; where the Jebusites were, the inhabitants of the land. And the inhabitants of Jebus said to David, Thou shalt not come in hither. But David took the stronghold of Zion, which is the city of David. And David said, Whoever smites the Jebusites first shall be chief and captain. And Joab the son of Zeruiah went first up, and was chief. And David dwelt in the stronghold; therefore they called it the city of David. And he built the city round about, even from the Millo round about; and Joab renewed the rest of the city. And David became continually greater; and Jehovah of hosts was with him.

I Chronicles 13:1-4—And David consulted with the captains of thousands and hundreds, with every prince. And David said to all the congregation of Israel, If it seem good to you, and it be of Jehovah our God, let us send abroad to our brethren everywhere, that are left in all the lands of Israel, and with them to the priests and Levites in their cities and suburbs, that they may gather themselves to us; and let us bring again the ark of our God to us; for we inquired not of it in the days of Saul. And all the congregation said that they should do so; for the thing was right in the eyes of all the people.

I Chronicles 17:1-2—And it came to pass as David dwelt in his house, that David said to Nathan the prophet, Behold, I dwell in a house of cedars, and the ark of the covenant of Jehovah under curtains. And Nathan said to David, Do all that is in thy heart; for God is with thee.

Let us pray:

Dear heavenly Father, how we do praise and thank Thee that we may gather together unto the name of Thy beloved Son, our Lord Jesus Christ; and because of this we know that Thy presence is here with us. In Thy presence there is fullness of joy and pleasure forevermore. We do worship Thee. Lord, as we linger in Thy presence we ask that Thou wouldst speak to us through Thy precious word. Do open Thy word to us and open our heart to Thy word, that Thy word will really become life and spirit to us, that Thou mayst be honored and glorified. In the name of our Lord Jesus. Amen.

Like I and II Kings, the first and second books of Chronicles were originally only one book. It appears in the Hebrew Bible in the third division called the Psalms. In the Hebrew Bible the title of these two books of Chronicles is *The Words of Days* or, alternatively rendered as, *The Events of the Times*. And in the Septuagint—the translation of the Bible from Hebrew to Greek accomplished by seventy men in Alexandria, Egypt—the title of that book is *Omission* because it is considered as supplementary to what has already been written. We know of this book under the title of *Chronicles*, and this title began to be known in the fourth century A.D.

A casual reading of the book of Chronicles will tell you that it is a compilation. The author collected and selected from different sources and then put them together into these writings. If we read I and II Chronicles very carefully, we are able to find these sources. For instance, in I Chronicles 9 it tells us the genealogy is according to the book of the kings of Israel. In chapter 29:29 we find that the history of David is according to the prophecy in the book of Samuel the seer, the book of Nathan the prophet and the book of Gad the seer. In II Chronicles 9 it says that the story of Solomon is according to the prophecy of Nathan and the vision of Iddo. So as we look through these two books of

Chronicles we learn that there are at least twelve sources for the material to be found therein.

THE PURPOSE OF CHRONICLES

We have the general history of the covenant people of God in the two books of Samuel and the two books of the Kings. Why, then, do we have I and II Chronicles? When the author gathered these materials together and put them into writing, he had no intention of giving us again a general history of the covenant people of God covering the kingdom from David until the time of the Babylonian exile. Rather, the history which is given here simply serves as a background for a specific purpose he had in mind. And against this background he is attempting to present a theme, a subject, a purpose—which is worship. In fact, the entirety of the history which is given in these two books of Chronicles is centered upon the temple and its Levitical worship. In other words, it is centered upon the religious life—the spiritual life—of God's covenant people.

Who is the writer of these two books of Chronicles? We know for sure that they could not have been written before the time of the decree of King Cyrus because in II Chronicles 36 the book ends with the decree of Cyrus. So it had to have been written by someone who was living after that decree was issued. Moreover, if we read I Chronicles 3 very carefully, we will see that it gives the genealogy of Zerubbabel to his grandchildren. So we know this book was composed during the time of Ezra. And finally, if we compare the end of II Chronicles with the beginning of Ezra, they are identical. In other words, the end of II Chronicles is the beginning of Ezra. So most people—including the rabbis, the early church fathers and the evangelical commentators—all believe that I and II Chronicles are the work of Ezra the priest.

The reason these two books of Chronicles were written was because at the time of Ezra the remnant of the children of Israel had already returned to Jerusalem, and the Levitical worship was being resumed. So Ezra composed these two books as a way of providing this remnant a history of what had gone before in order to strengthen their faith and their faithfulness to God in this area of worship.

In I Samuel we found that the kingdom had been formed under Saul according to the responsibility of man; whereas in II Samuel we learn that the kingdom had been established under David according to the purpose of God. Then with I Kings we have the history of the kingdom from the time of Solomon to the death of Jehoshaphat; and with II Kings we have the history of the remaining days until the time of the Babylonian Captivity. On the other hand, these two books of Chronicles begin with Adam and end with Babylonian exile. So they cover some thirty-five hundred years of history, and yet they do not give us a general history; instead, they give us the inner spiritual history of the covenant people of God. The Samuels and the Kings books were written from a prophetic viewpoint, but the two books of Chronicles were written from a priestly viewpoint. The two Samuels and the two Kings were written by prophets— Samuel, Nathan and Gad—but the two Chronicles were written by Ezra, a priest. As prophets, Samuel, Nathan and Gad looked at the history of the nation from a prophetic viewpoint—a nation under the rule of God. But as priests, Ezra and others looked at the nation as a holy priesthood to serve God. So the Kings and the Samuels books give us the outward history of God's people, whereas the Chronicles give us their inner history.

The church today is, on the one hand, a holy nation; on the other hand, she is a kingly priesthood. And in the church there are two things which are most prominent. One is the authority of God, the other is the worship of God. With this as a general background, let us consider I Chronicles.

The first ten chapters of this book give us the genealogy and also the history of the death of Saul. That serves as a kind of introduction because, for the remnant, such genealogy and history were very important, they providing the people a sense of continuity. For us today, however, we need not go into this genealogy. From chapter 11 onward, the main figure is David. In other words, David is the prominent person in the mind of the Spirit for delineating this period of history, but it is not David's personal history which is given here but the history of David as king in relation to worship and the temple. It is divided into three parts: chapters 11—12, 13—16, and 17—28.

KING DAVID

JERUSALEM

David was first king in Hebron, and then he was anointed king over all Israel. After he was anointed king over all Israel, the first action he took was to make Jerusalem the capital of the nation. So far as geography is concerned, Jerusalem is not a very strategic place. If one considers the matter from the political or even economic standpoint, this site is not strategically located because the major caravan trade route from east to west does not pass through Jerusalem but is to the north of it. Nor is Jerusalem situated on a high mountain. Actually, it is surrounded by high mountains. So from the rational human standpoint, Jerusalem would never be chosen as a capital of any nation. Strangely, however, after David became king, the first action he undertook was to take Jerusalem and make it the capital. Now why is this so? It is because this was the will of God.

After the children of Israel came out of Egypt and God brought them through the wilderness, but before they entered the Promised Land, God made it clear to Moses that when the people were in the wilderness they had worshiped wherever they were because they were traveling: there was no fixed place of worship. But after they do enter the Promised Land this was no longer to be so. God revealed to Moses that He would choose one place there to put His name, and to that place all the tribes of Israel would go. It was to be the only place they could offer sacrifices to worship God (see again Deuteronomy 12). Yet after the children of Israel entered the Promised Land, this place was never known, it was never revealed. The tent of meeting, or the tabernacle, was erected in Shiloh at one time and then moved to other places. There was no fixed place; for nobody knew the place of God's choice. Indeed, in the Bible we cannot find any reference to where it was situated. But wonderfully, there was a man after God's own heart who knew God's heart. David received revelation from God, and thus he came to know that the one place of His choice for worship in the whole land was to be Jerusalem. But at that time, it was occupied by the Jebusites. So after David was anointed king, the first thing he did was to take Jerusalem and make it the capital. He did not do it for himself; he did it for God, that there might be a place where He would be honored and would be known to all upon the earth.

Jerusalem, the city of peace, was the place where God put His name, and Jerusalem was also the place where the throne of David was set. It was to be the place where the children of Israel would go up together to worship. And if we read the Psalms, we will find that to those who loved God Jerusalem meant a lot.

"Jerusalem, which art built as a city that is compact together, whither the tribes go up, the tribes of Jah, a testimony to Israel, to give thanks unto the name of Jehovah. For there are set thrones for judgment, the thrones of the house of David. Pray for the peace of Jerusalem: they shall prosper that love thee" (Psalm 122:3-6).

Jerusalem was very precious to those who loved God. It was a city whose various parts were compacted together into a unified coherent whole, a place to where the tribes would go up together as a testimony to Israel. Jerusalem was also a place where the thrones were set.

When the children of Israel were in captivity, the same sentiment was being expressed by the psalmist in Psalm 137 as he sat by the rivers of Babylon.

"If I forget thee, Jerusalem, let my right hand forget its skill; if I do not remember thee, let my tongue cleave to my palate: if I prefer not Jerusalem above my chief joy" (vv.5-6). They had such love for Jerusalem because it represented God's will.

We are told, in Galatians 4:26, that Jerusalem above is our mother. The earthly Jerusalem is but a shadow of the real; it is a principle demonstrated in a shadowy way. The reality is the Jerusalem above, the holy city, the new Jerusalem. That is the true purpose of God. God desires a place where He can put His name, and this place in reality is the Jerusalem above. It is the new Jerusalem. And, of course, today, that is the church.

THE CHURCH

What is the church? It is the place where the name and Person of the Lord is centered. We will recall from Matthew 18 that our Lord Jesus declared: "Where two or three are gathered together unto My name, there am I in the midst of them." This is the simplest explanation of what the church is. The church is where the name of the Lord is the center and focus. Wherever people are gathered together to the name of the Lord Jesus, that is the church. God has called many out of every nation, tribe, tongue, and people and gathered them together to the name of the Lord Jesus and to no other name. And it is there that you have the church.

What does *gathered together to My name* mean? It means that these people who are gathered together take upon themselves the name of the Lord. I think the simplest illustration of this is that when a lady is married to a man, she takes to herself the name of that man. She joins herself to him, and they become one. So, *gathered together to the name of the Lord Jesus* simply means that these are a people who lay down their own name—who lay down themselves—and willingly subject themselves to the name of the Lord Jesus. They take His name as their name and let the Lord Jesus be their Head.

And hence, the church is the place where the Lord's authority is being known and where His throne is being set.

Do let us see that the throne of God is to be set not only in each of our individual hearts; it is also to be set corporately among His people. In each of our lives we need to have a throne set, and it is Christ who is to sit there. We usually sit on our own throne; we govern our own life. But if we are the Lord's, and if we know what salvation means, then we must get down from our throne and enthrone Christ. He should be on the throne in each of our lives because we are called by His name. And the same is true corporately. When God's people come together, it is the throne of our Lord Jesus that is set there and consequently His authority is being known. There is to be no authority among God's gathered people but the authority of our Lord Jesus. And that is what makes it the church.

What is Jerusalem? It is a place where the twelve tribes go to gather as a testimony. They live in different places, they each have their own inheritance, but they are not twelve different nations. They are but one nation because they come together to Jerusalem as one people. This is their testimony. That is what Jerusalem is all about. Jerusalem represents the one place where God's people flow together as one. There is only one Jerusalem; there is only one church; and all God's people— no matter where they are—flow together to Jerusalem as one people. Not only that, Jerusalem is a city that is compactly built; that is, it is organically knitted and drawn together.

We are not a scattered people but a people who have a center, and we flow together and are being unitedly built up together compactly, ministering one to another. That is our testimony. And because of this, God has a name that is known upon this earth. As long as Jerusalem was there God was called the God of the heavens and of the earth, but when Jerusalem lay in ruins during the period of captivity, He was no longer addressed as the God of the heavens and of the earth; instead, He was addressed simply as God of the heavens because His name was nowhere to be found upon the earth.

The church here on earth is to bear the testimony of God and of Jesus Christ. If the church were not here, who would know God? The name of God would be unknown. And it is the church that also bears the testimony of Jesus Christ. We uplift the name of the Lord Jesus so that He may be known throughout the whole world. Such is our Jerusalem.

Do we love the Jerusalem that is above as the godly people in the olden days loved the earthly Jerusalem? For to the ancient covenant people, Jerusalem was their first love. They loved her above everything else. The psalmist declared: "If I do not love Jerusalem above all things and make it my chief joy, then let my tongue cleave to my palate." In other words, I will be dumb. He also said: "Let my right hand forget its skill"—meaning, I will do nothing—"if I do not love Jerusalem." This city was so dear to the hearts of those godly people.

Is it true with us today concerning the Jerusalem above? Do we love the church as those earthly people loved earthly Jerusalem? If they loved her so dearly, how much more must we love the church! We love the church because it is God's desire. We love the church because this is the place where the name of the Lord is. We love the church because this is where God's people are built up together. We love the church because it is the vessel of the testimony of Jesus Christ.

Unfortunately, God's people today do not know much about the principle which Jerusalem represents. They are so scattered. They do not seem to have a center, a focal point or place. The condition of God's people today is like that during the time of the judges of old when everyone did what was right in his own sight because there was no king. Is it not a tragedy that God's people have become so scattered? Is it not true that God's people are not gathered together because they are not under one name? How important it is that we see the principle of Jerusalem! That is what David saw back in his day. We need to have in our hearts the spirit of David who knew in his heart that Jerusalem was God's will. God wants to have His name on this earth. He wants to have a place again on this earth where He can put His name. He wants His people to be built up together to bear one testimony. May this also become our passion and our desire.

THE ARK

From chapters 13—16 we learn that David did a second thing. Chapter 13 tells us that David consulted with his people. He said to them, "Let us bring the ark of the covenant of God to the city of David." We will recall that the ark in the Old Testament period represented the presence of God because His glory rested upon the mercy seat, which is the cover of the ark.

In the history of the children of Israel the ark occupied a very central position. It was on the mercy seat of the ark that their sins were atoned. Once a year the high priest would take the blood and the incense, enter behind the veil and make atonement for the whole nation. It was the ark which enabled them to have their sins covered. It was from the mercy seat between the two cherubim that God spoke to the children of Israel. They encamped around the ark, and it was the ark which led their way through the wilderness. And when they entered the Promised Land, it was the ark which fought for them. The ark was the center of their life and did everything for them.

Nevertheless, the children of Israel were unfaithful to God. During the time of Eli, and even though the ark was still in their midst, they behaved in contradiction to what the ark represented; so when the Philistines came against them, the children of Israel were defeated. But they thought they had been defeated because the ark had not been in their midst during the battle. Hence, they moved the ark from Shiloh to the battlefield. Surely, they now believed, the ark which had fought victoriously for them in the past would certainly fight for them again. Now that they had God's presence once more, they would certainly overcome the enemy. But God was not with them. He allowed the ark to be captured by the Philistines who kept it for six months. The children of Israel, who were supposed to be the guardian of the ark, did not guard the ark and so it was taken into captivity; nevertheless, the ark was capable of protecting itself; for during the entire period when the ark was in the land of the Philistines, the ark caused continual trouble for them. Consequently, the Philistines could no longer tolerate its presence among them, so they finally had to send the ark back. Yet even after the ark of God was returned to the children of Israel, they let it remain hidden in the fields of the forest in Kiriath-jearim.

For twenty long years the ark remained hidden there. And it was during those twenty years that Samuel began to encourage the people, and the hearts of the people began to return to God. Even so, the ark was still hidden there. During the time of Saul, who was king for forty years, he never once inquired at the ark. He had no heart for the ark, which is to say that he had no heart for God nor for His presence. He only wanted the blessings of God and not the presence of God. But along came David, who, even in the days of his affliction, often thought of the ark.

"Jehovah, remember for David all his affliction; how he swore unto Jehovah, vowed unto the Mighty One of Jacob: I will not come into the tent of my house, I will not go up to the couch of my bed; I will not give sleep to mine eyes, slumber to mine eyelids, until I find out a place for Jehovah, habitations for the Mighty One of Jacob. Behold, we heard of it [i.e., the ark] at Ephratah, we found it in the fields of the wood. Let us go into his habitations, let us worship at his footstool" (Psalm 132:1-7).

Because David had a heart for God, he had a heart for the ark. So, after he became king and had made Jerusalem his capital, the next action he took was to consult with his people concerning the ark: "Is it not time that we should bring the ark to the city of David and make it the center of our national life again?" All the people agreed with him. So they went to Kiriath-jearim and brought the ark back to Jerusalem. Unfortunately, David had consulted the people and his military, but he failed to consult the priests and the Levites. The people tried to bring the ark back on a new cart driven by oxen because this was the way it had come back from the Philistines. The Philistines had sent the ark back on a new cart driven by two milk cows. These were cows with calves. They had done it by this means as a test; for the Philistines had said among themselves that they would see if the ark was really God's presence or not. So they joined the two cows to the cart and kept the calves at home. They simply let the cows loose without guiding them where to go. In the natural course of things the cows would be expected to go back to their calves, but the Spirit of God controlled these two cows, for they went straight to the border of Israel. Yet as they went, they were lowing; they were moaning; they were suffering because they had to leave their young. Now that is the way the ark came back to Israel.

Probably, the people concluded among themselves that it was a good idea to have the ark on a cart pulled by the oxen. Indeed, how convenient! Was it not too heavy to place on the shoulders of the priests? It was an ingenious invention. The world is full of such inventions, is it not? So the children of Israel simply adopted the Philistine—that is, the worldly— way and tried by this worldly method to bring the ark back to Jerusalem. However, on the threshing floor, the oxen slipped and the ark was going to fall. So Uzza reached out and tried to hold the ark steady, but God smote him to death because no one was permitted to touch the ark. David was indignant: he thought he was doing God a great honor; yet he was also afraid. Who am I, he mused, to have the ark and presence of God? For David, the presence of God was a terrible thing. To bring up the ark was an honorable thing to do but it was also terrifying! So instead of bringing up the ark to Jerusalem, David took it aside and put it in the house of Obed-Edom. For three months the ark stayed there, and God blessed the house of Obed-Edom. When

David heard about that, he reconsidered and repented. He now realized that he had been wrong, so he consulted the priests. He let the priests, by means of poles, take the ark upon their shoulders, and so they brought it gloriously back to Jerusalem. The presence of God was once again in the midst of His people.

THE PRESENCE OF THE LORD

The ark represents our Lord Jesus. He is the ark; He is the mercy seat. In Romans 3 we learn that we have a mercy seat, and it is Christ. It is there that our sins are forgiven. It is there in Christ that God speaks to us and communes with us. It is there—in Christ—that we worship. He is the One who is the center of our gathering. He is the One who leads our way. He is the One who fights our battles. Such is our Lord Jesus. The Lord Jesus said, "Where two or three are gathered together unto My name, there am I in the midst of them"—this speaks of His presence. What makes the church different from any other group in the world? One thing only—the presence of the Lord. That is the one thing which makes the church different from every organization and every other group in the whole world.

Do we treasure His presence? We see how David treasured the ark. He treasured the presence of God and considered that as the most important thing in his life and in the life of the whole nation. Is this true with us today? We find God's people coming together; and thank God, we do come together to sing, to read His word, to fellowship. We come together to do many things, but do we not know that the one thing that makes us different from the world is His presence? If the Lord's presence is not with us, there is no reason for us to be assembled here. It is His presence which guides our steps. It is His presence which leads our way. It is His presence which makes us victorious. Without His presence we are defeated and lost. In short, His presence is everything to us. The reason we come together and place ourselves under Christ's name is because we know that this is where His name is—that is to say, where two or three or more are assembled together in His name. Such is where His presence is, and we love His presence. Indeed, Christ's presence is everything to us because all blessings come from His presence. This is true not only in our individual life but also in our life together. In either case, Christ's presence is the most important thing. Anything that would take the Lord's presence away, that thing has to go.

How do we obtain His presence? David had tried to bring the ark back in the way of the Philistines, but he failed by that means. One has to obtain God's presence according to His way. So here is another important lesson for us to learn. God's will has to be done in God's way. It is certainly the will of God that we have His presence, but how are we to have His presence? Not in the Philistines' way. Many try to obtain God's presence in many different ways. We try to have His presence by using the way of the world. Christianity, today, is full of the Philistines' ways. Groups in Christendom try to use different attractions. They use ingenious methods that are more convenient and without any cost personally. They use different activities and different methods and means, either through music or plays or parties or bazaars, whatever along this line it might be. They may bring people together, but can they bring in the presence of God? They may be able to attract people, but they cannot attract God. Let us realize and acknowledge that the ark—the presence of God—can only be brought in upon the shoulders of the priests. How we need to be sanctified! We are priests; not priests in name only but in reality as well. The universal priesthood of believers is the teaching of the New Testament. We are to be a holy priesthood, but are we holy? The priests who were to bear the ark upon their shoulders had to be sanctified. How we, too, need to be sanctified. We have to be separated and set apart for God. Oh, how we need to give our life completely to the Lord, so that the presence of God will be brought in upon *our* shoulders! Whenever people find consecrated believers coming together, such believers have the presence of the Lord there. This is the way to bring in His presence—not by method but by a sanctified holy people.

THE HOUSE OF GOD

From chapters 17—28 we learn that David undertook to do a third thing. As king he was dwelling in a house of cedars—his palace—but he could not rest. So one day he talked with the prophet Nathan: "Look, I dwell in a house of cedar, but the ark of God dwells in a tent. I feel uncomfortable about it." And Nathan replied, "Do whatever is upon your heart, for the Lord loves you." David had in his heart to build a house for God, to build Him a temple so that the ark might have a resting place. And God was pleased with his heart's desire.

After Nathan spoke he went out from David's presence; but God told him to go back and tell David what was in His heart in response to David's own heart desire. And if you read carefully what God said to David through Nathan you will be greatly moved: "Have I ever asked anybody for a house to live in? All these years I have been going from tent to tent, from tabernacle to tabernacle. I wander around with My people. I have never asked anything for myself and here you are wanting to build Me a house." God's heart had been deeply touched, but He then said to David: "No, you cannot build it for Me because you have shed too much blood. Your son who will be a man of peace, will build it for Me." But God next said, "Before My house is built I will first build your house." From this we see that we can never do anything which exceeds what God wants to do. He always does more than we can ever do. David wanted very much to build God a house but God said: "Wait a minute! Let Me build your house first, and then My house can be built." What a God He is! When David heard that, he went before God and said, "Lord, who am I? Who am I that Thou shouldst be so gracious to me? Nevertheless, do according to Thy word" (see

I Chronicles 17:16-27).

From chapter 17 of I Chronicles onward we find that God began to build David's house. He experienced victory after victory. God was building his house.

THE SITE OF GOD'S HOUSE

Then from chapter 21 we learn that something terrible happened. Out of his pride and faithlessness David wanted to know how strong he was. So he summoned Joab the captain of the host and sent him out to go through all the land and number his army. Now God had himself promised that He would make the seed of Abraham to be as the sand on the seashore and as the stars in the sky—that is to say, countless. Not only was David's action prideful, it also showed a lack of faith, and David knew he was wrong. Because of this transgression, God sent the prophet Gad to David, who said, "Because of what you have done, here is the discipline: three years of famine over the land or three months of the sword from your enemies or three days of pestilence: choose which one." And David replied: "It is very difficult to choose, but I would rather fall into the hands of God than of man." Man, as we all know, can be most merciless. So a great pestilence came upon the land for three days, and David beheld the angel of the Lord with his sword drawn over Jerusalem to destroy the city; so David prayed: "It is my fault, not the people's fault." And God's response was: "All right, you offer where that angel stood." So David went to the Mount of Moriah to the threshing floor of Ornan the Jebusite (which was where the destroying angel with drawn sword had been seen). There he bought the land, offered offerings to God, God heard him and consumed the offerings with fire, and the pestilence stopped. David said, "This is the house of God." Thus, the site of God's house was chosen. And some people have surmised that this was also the very site where Abraham had offered up Isaac.

THE GATHERING OF MATERIALS FOR GOD'S HOUSE

It was through repentance that God revealed to David the site of the house of God. From then on David began to prepare for God's house (see I Chronicles 22:1-5; 29:1-2). Even though he was not allowed to build the house, his love for God was so great that he prepared everything he could for it. He mobilized people—strangers for cutting wood and for cutting stones. He mobilized the Levites to be supervisors. He arranged the twenty-four courses of the priests and Levites to serve in the temple. Out of the spoils of his battles David dedicated to God the gold and the silver. Out of his affection for God he took in abundance from his personal treasure of pure gold and silver and dedicated that to God as well (see I Chronicles 29:3ff.). He made iron and silver in such abundance that it could not be counted. He did everything he could to prepare for the house. David even prepared for God's house the singers in twenty-four courses to sing praises to Him. God even revealed to David the pattern of the temple; said David: "All this have I been made to understand in writing from Jehovah's hand upon me regarding all the works of the pattern" (see I Chronicles 28:19). David loved God. He said, "Out of my affliction and out of my affection for God I give all these to Him willingly and gladly also," (see I Chronicles 22:14; 29:3, 17b). And he encouraged the people to give willingly and gladly also and they did (see I Chronicles 29:9, 17c).

God needs a place to put His name, He needs a place to put His presence and a place to be His dwelling place. This is God's will. Throughout the ages He has desired to have such a place. Now remember, the physical Jerusalem on earth is but a shadow or a type of the spiritual. And hence, the place which God wants to put His name is a spiritual place. It is a holy city, the new Jerusalem, the bride of the Lamb, the church, the body of Christ. That is the place where only His name is honored and no other. The will of God is that He wants to be present with His people. How He loves to be present with His people! How He enjoys having fellowship with His people! But unfortunately, He in a way has been limited, even shut out for the most part. How He desires that His presence and His blessing will be known! Indeed, this is what the church is—the place where God can bless His people with every spiritual blessing in the heavenlies in Christ Jesus—the One who said: "I am with you until the end of the world and I will not leave you nor forsake you" (see Ephesians 1:3; Matthew 28:20b; Hebrews 13:5).

We need to realize that God loves to be present with us, but oftentimes we lose His presence because we are not walking with Him. He desires to be present with His people, but even more so, He wants to dwell among His people. He wants a house, a home. I have often preached that God created the heavens and the earth, but these, as it were, are His office; but as God says in Isaiah: "The heavens are where His throne is; the earth is His footstool; but where is His house and what place shall be His rest?" The answer He gives in Isaiah is that He dwells among those of a poor, contrite and repentant spirit (see 66:1-2). It was out of the repentance of David that the site for the temple was discerned. It is in that contrite, repentant, broken spirit of His people that God can dwell in peace. Sad to say, God's people are fighting, and doing so not only against one another but against God himself. That gives Him no rest, for under those circumstances He cannot rest among His people. Yet this is what He still desires—to have a dwelling place where He may dwell in peace and in rest.

Do we have the spirit of David? The Lord Jesus is our David. He is greater than David, for He said, "I will build My church on this rock and the gates of Hades shall not prevail against it" (see Matthew 16:18). His love for His Father is so great. He wants to build that house for His Father. And He is building it, but are we building it together with Him who is our David? Do we, like the Lord Jesus, have this love for the house of God? David said, "In my affliction I gather the material for the building of the house" (see again I Chronicles 22:14-16). Do we realize that in and through all our trials, in and through all our afflictions, we, by the grace of God, may gather gold and silver to offer to God for the building of that house? Do we realize that all the spoils from our spiritual battles are for the building of God's house? Let us not think that all our afflictions and all our trials are in vain. Moreover, let us not think that our victories are ours. Not so (see I Chronicles 29:14b, 16); moreover, all such afflictions and all such victories are only opportunities given to us as the means of gathering materials for the building of God's house. In other words, these are opportunities by which we may know more of God's grace and know more of Him so that we may offer what He has revealed to us for building the house of God.

Yet David also said, "Out of my affection for God" (see again I Chronicles 29:3)—not only affliction but affection. How we need to love Him, and in love we are willing to give the best to Him. This is the way the house of God will be built. It is built with what we have gone through in life. His house is built with what He has done in our lives. It is built with the spoils gained from our battles and spiritual conflicts, but it is also built with our love. Such are the ways by which the materials are gathered together.

And David arranged the service of the house, the twenty-four courses of the priests, the Levites, and the singers. So under the guidance of *our* David, we are to serve the Lord as priests. Each one of us has a part in the priestly function. Each one of us is to serve Him as a Levite doing all the works of the temple, that is to say, all the manual work involved. And we are singers. We can all sing to the praise of His glory because the kingdom is His, the power is His, and the glory is His. May the Lord help us.

Let us pray:

Dear heavenly Father, we do thank Thee for Thy precious word. We do pray that Thy word may inspire us so that we, too, may have that longing, love, passion and desire for Thee, for Thy name, for Thy presence and for Thy dwelling. Lord, we do want to offer ourselves to Thee that we may be used of Thee to be the place where Thy name is honored, exalted, and spread abroad. We pray that we may be a people who know Thy presence. We pray we may be a people who give Thee rest. We ask in the name of our Lord Jesus. Amen.

II CHRONICLES

WISDOM TO BUILD THE HOUSE OF GOD

Our heavenly Father, we do want to worship Thee. We praise and thank Thee because Thou art the One who sent Thy beloved Son into this world, and Thou art the One who hast received Him in glory and hast crowned Him with honor and glory. And our Father, as we continue in Thy presence we do pray that by Thy Holy Spirit Thou wilt open Thy word to us and touch our hearts and draw us to thyself and to Thy beloved Son. We ask in Thy precious name. Amen.

As we mentioned before, I and II Chronicles were originally one book. They are different from I and II Kings. In the latter two books we have the general history of the nation of Israel and of their kings, but in I and II Chronicles we have presented an outline of history simply to serve as a background for a specific purpose which is, to unfold for us the religious life of the nation. Or to put it another way, I and II Chronicles concentrate on the house of God, the temple, its worship, the Levitical service—anything and everything having to do with the religious side of the nation's life.

Why is it that we need to study Kings and Chronicles? We would think that because these are histories of the past and of some other people, why should we study these books? We must bear in mind what the Bible tells us in the New Testament. In I Corinthians 10 we read: "All these things happened to them (the Israelites) as types for our admonition upon whom the ends of the ages are come" (see v. 11; see also v. 6). Accordingly, these things having happened as types, they are for our admonition who live at the end of the age. These books are relevant to us because we find in God's word that we, who are the redeemed of the Lord, are a holy nation, a kingly priesthood. Therefore, we can learn much from Kings and Chronicles. From them we can learn the spiritual principles which are to govern us as a holy nation and as a kingly priesthood. Such, then is the reason we need to study these books.

II Chronicles begins with the reign of Solomon and ends with Babylonian captivity, but nonetheless, ends on a positive note—the encouraging decree of King Cyrus (see II Chronicles 36:22-23). II Chronicles begins with the building of the house of God and ends with its destruction; but thank God, there is a ray of hope for restoration. In II Chronicles the first nine chapters are devoted to Solomon, and from chapters 10—36 we have the history of the Jewish kings of the nation of Judah. Yet all are concentrated on this matter of the house of God.

There is a difference in the history of Solomon which is recorded in Kings from that found in Chronicles. If we want to know the general history of Solomon from its beginning to its end, we have to go to I Kings because we do not find this in II Chronicles. In the latter the history of Solomon is concentrated upon just one thing, and that is the building of the temple. In I Kings we read about Solomon's sins and the prophecy concerning him, but we do not find these in II Chronicles because these two books are centered upon but one thing—the temple, the house of God. If we read II Chronicles, it seems as though Solomon had done nothing else but build the temple throughout his forty years' reign. Actually, we know from Kings that he did many other things, both good and bad; yet these were not recorded in II Chronicles; the latter books are focused upon one work only: the building of the house of God.

I think there is a lesson for us here. We may live a life upon this earth and be engaged in many things. There may be successes, there may be failures, but there is one thing God is really interested in in our lives, and that is our relationship to the house of God. Anything that is not related to His house does not seem to be worth recording.

SOLOMON

Traditional Faith

After Solomon became king, he loved God and demonstrated to Him his love by going to Gibeon where the brazen altar and the tent of Moses were. There he offered a thousand sacrifices to God. But we must understand that Solomon's expression of love for God was traditional in character. God had not spoken to him yet. He did not have a personal relationship with God, nor had he heard from Him. All he knew about God came from his father David. So his faith was traditional in nature. Yet, even though his faith was traditional, his love for God was real. He loved Him but in a traditional way. He did not yet have revelation, and that is the reason he went to Gibeon to offer sacrifices. We must recall from I Chronicles that David had already moved the ark to Zion to the tent of David. However, instead of Solomon going before the ark to offer sacrifices there, he went to Gibeon where the tabernacle was and offered sacrifices upon the brazen altar.

Do we discern what this means? We know the ark in the Scriptures represents the presence and the Person of God, but the tabernacle and all the things in it represent the things of God or His works. Which is more important—the ark or the tabernacle? the brazen altar or the mercy seat? In the first place, the tabernacle was built for the ark. All the things in the tabernacle were for housing, leading up to, and experiencing the ark. In other words, the ark gives meaning to the tabernacle; and consequently, the ark and the tabernacle should never be separated. Unfortunately, because of the sins of the people, the ark and the tabernacle *were* separated.

Not only were they separated; we learn from I Chronicles that David had to search out the ark because it was hidden at Kirjath-jearim in the fields of the wood. And because David loved God, he built a tent for the ark and brought it back to Zion. David truly loved God himself as a Person, but Solomon did not have that revelation. He knew God only traditionally, and because of this, he did not at first go to where the ark was. He did not treasure God himself as much as he treasured the things or works of God. So Solomon went down to Gibeon and there he expressed his love to God. Even so, God condescended himself to his level.

A HEARING HEART

After Solomon offered sacrifices in Gibeon, God appeared to him and said, "Ask what I should give to you." Solomon did not ask for long life, nor for wealth, honor or the life of his enemies; he asked God for only one thing: for wisdom and knowledge that he might rule the people according to God and His ways and judgments. In short, Solomon did not ask anything for himself. He only asked it for God; and if you carefully read I Kings 3, you will discern that the wisdom or understanding which he asked for was actually an understanding heart; that is to say, a heart that hears.

What is wisdom? We oftentimes incorrectly connect wisdom with the mind. In truth, knowledge is connected with the mind, whereas wisdom is connected with the heart. Yet what is true wisdom? It is nothing less than a heart that hears God. So in actual fact, Solomon asked for a heart that could hear God's voice, and in hearing Him, he would know Him and know His ways; he would know His judgments. That is what Solomon truly desired of God, and God was greatly pleased by what he asked. So God promised to give him wisdom and also added to it wealth, honor, and other things.

Now after God appeared to Solomon and gave him wisdom—a hearing heart, let us note what Solomon did next. He returned to Jerusalem and there he went before the ark and offered burnt offerings and peace offerings (see I Kings 3). We must acknowledge that it really takes revelation for a person to love God himself. If we do not have revelation, if our faith is traditional, we may indeed love the things and works of God, but we cannot love God himself. For instance, the brazen altar represents the atoning death of our Lord Jesus and because of His death our sins are forgiven. Surely we love this work of God in Christ because our sins are forgiven; but do we love God himself?

Or likewise, we love the brazen laver because in type that is where we are sanctified, are washed and purified. We even love the golden candlestick because it gives us light that we may know the will of God. We also love the golden table of shewbread because it represents Christ as the bread of life that we may be satisfied. Or we love the golden altar of incense because there we can pray and our prayer will be answered. We most certainly do love these things of God and all the works which God in Christ has done because it has all been done for us. But for us to love God himself is beyond us if we do not have revelation, because without revelation—without a heart which hears God—we shall always remain self-centered: we shall never be God-centered. If God is *for us*—fine. But what is it that we are *for Him*? Please note that after Solomon received revelation, after he was given wisdom, he went back to Jerusalem and the first thing he did was to worship at the ark. He loved God himself. And *that* is the sign of true wisdom.

Do you have a hearing heart? Can you hear God? Has He appeared to you? Do you receive revelation? If you do, you will love God himself more than the things and works of God.

HOUSE OF GOD

Now after God gave Solomon wisdom, he built the house of God. In Proverbs 9:1 we are told that "wisdom hath built her house." We cannot build the house of God if we do not have wisdom, and that is the reason the apostle Paul, in Ephesians 1, prayed for the Ephesian believers that the God of our Lord Jesus, the Father of glory, would grant to them a spirit of wisdom and revelation in the full knowledge of God (see vv. 16b-17). Paul prayed that the people there might receive wisdom in order that they would be able to build the house of God.

Why do we need wisdom to build the house of God? If we lack wisdom, how can we understand the pattern? Recall that God gave the pattern of the temple to David and David passed it on to Solomon. But it required wisdom to interpret and to convert the pattern into the temple.

I often laugh at myself because though I come from a family of builders, I knew nothing about building. My grandfather was a builder, my uncles were builders, my brother was a builder. I remember going to my brother's office and seeing those blueprints of his on his long table. I looked at them, but they did not mean anything to me: they were all filled with nothing but lines and odd shapes. But when my brother looked at these things, he saw a building. He was able to translate and convert these lines, points and odd shapes into a real building. But I did not have that kind of knowledge.

It needs wisdom to receive the pattern. In other words, today, the house of God is what He really wants, but who knows the pattern? Where is the pattern? Now we know that God has given us the pattern for His house. His pattern is in his word. God has revealed His purpose; He has revealed His will, mind and heart's desire. In short, He has revealed what He wants. And it is all in this book we call the Bible. The pattern of God's house is in this Book, but without wisdom, it is merely words on paper. To the uninitiated—that is, to those who lack wisdom—these words are nothing more than letters. Those who lack wisdom cannot understand, and thus they are not able to convert the Book's letters and words into a living house of God.

Today, many people are thinking of building a New Testament church. They realize that the churches are not New Testament enough, or that many of them are Old Testament churches—such as synagogues—instead of being New Testament churches. So people have begun to realize that they need to build New Testament churches. How, though, are they going to build them? We have been told to read the Bible, yes. There, we are told, it tells us in the book of Acts that Paul and Barnabas appointed elders, and in I Timothy we shall find elders and deacons being mentioned. And thus we can get the pattern: we see the lines and we see the points. So people say: "Let's organize a New Testament church. Let's have five elders, seven deacons. Now we have the New Testament church." Yet do they have the New Testament church? In reality, they are still ignorant, for they do not understand the pattern. Yes, they read and hear the words, but these are yet letters—dead letters. Oh, how we need a hearing heart to really see the pattern, to see that actually the pattern is nothing less than Christ Jesus himself. He is the pattern; but how do we convert that pattern into a building? That requires wisdom.

Solomon had the wisdom to do it. He knew how to read the pattern, and he knew how to convert that pattern into a glorious, beautiful temple. It took wisdom to mobilize thousands and ten thousands of people to work. It needed wisdom to put everyone in his right place. It required wisdom to coordinate the whole work, and wisdom to finish the work. Some people may begin but never finish. Not so with Solomon. And after the work was finished, the glory of God came down and filled the house. Solomon also had the wisdom not to change anything but did everything according to God's revelation. So God came in and took possession of that house: heavenly fire came down and consumed all the sacrifices. And this meant that God had accepted that house.

Afterwards, God appeared to Solomon again and said, "I have heard your prayers. My eyes will be open and My ears attentive to hear the prayers that are prayed in this house or towards this house. And I will do everything as I had promised David. But I warn you, if you and your seed should depart from Me and begin to worship idols, I will chasten and I will discipline, and there will come a time when this entire house will be destroyed and people will be astonished" (see II

Chronicles 7). Unfortunately, all this did finally happen after hundreds of years.

Now all this is the story of Solomon which was told us in II Chronicles.

WORK OF CHRIST ON EARTH

Today, we know One greater than Solomon and He is our Lord Jesus. And exactly what is His work on earth? We may think that His work on earth is to save sinners. Yes, He came to seek and to save the lost, but is that all? What was actually the work of our Lord Jesus while He was on earth? Or we can go even further: What is the Lord doing today in heaven? Or we may enlarge it even more: What has God been doing throughout the centuries? Or we can even go back to eternity: What did God have in mind in eternity?

We may recall that our Lord Jesus once said, "My Father worketh hitherto, and I work" (John 5:17). And what was and still is the Father's work and that of our Lord Jesus? It is singular in number. In other words, God in Christ does not have many works: He has only one work, and all the many works are to be found within that one work. Our Lord Jesus does only one work, just like Solomon. It is as though Solomon did not do anything else throughout his forty years' reign but the one work of building the temple, the house of God. And spiritually speaking, that is true.

What is the work of our Lord Jesus? His work is to build a home for God. God has been desiring a home. He created the heavens and the earth, but in Isaiah we read of Him saying: "Heaven is My throne, the earth is My footstool." Heaven and earth are God's office, as it were, but He went on to say: "Where is My home? And what place shall be My rest?" (see 66:1) Let us see that God wants to dwell among His people. He desires to make His people His home, which is the house of God; and that is the heart of God, for that is what He has continually been doing throughout the centuries. And that is why Christ came into this world, and that is also what Christ— ever since His resurrection and ascension—has been doing in heaven at the right hand of the Father, interceding for us. This is the one work which Christ has been doing. He said, "I will build My church upon this Rock, and the gates of Hades shall not prevail against it" (see Matthew 16:18). Even Abraham had looked forward to a city with foundations, which God is building (see Hebrews 11:10).

The work of God is the building of His house—a home for God and man—so that God may dwell with man and man may dwell with Him. There is love, harmony, worship, service, and glory there. And such is what God desires. We today have One greater than Solomon and He is building the real house. That ancient temple which Solomon had built was only a type. It was not the real thing; it was but a shadow of something to come. It could never compare with the reality which is the church of the living God that Christ is building with living stones—even with us who are His followers. And He is still building that church. Let us realize that He is calling each one of us to work together with Him in this work.

THE WORK OF THE CHURCH

What is the work of the church today? In other words, what is our work today? We may be engaged in different aspects of the work, but remember, there is only one work. We are all called to work with Christ in the building of God's house in order that God may have a dwelling place among us. On the one hand, we are the materials; on the other hand, we are also the workmen. Let us therefore be careful how we work. For this we need wisdom. We need wisdom to know the pattern, to convert that pattern into the building, to work together, and to know which part we are to play. Every one of us is called to do a part of it, and hence we need wisdom to know our place in the house of God. Do we have that wisdom? James in the New Testament wrote: "If anyone lacks wisdom, let him ask of God and doubt not and God will give it to him" (see James 1:5-6). Have we ever asked God for wisdom, or do we think we already have it? We may indeed think we know what God wants and we may also think we know what we are to do. But do we? Or do we really need to humble ourselves before God and say, "Oh Lord, I do not have wisdom. I need it so that my life upon this earth may be engaged in the building of Your house; I need it so that my life will not be wasted or ill spent but will be counted worthy in eternity; I need it so that my life on earth and my work here will contribute to the building of God's house and not to the tearing down of His house." To do that we need the spirit of Solomon—a spirit of wisdom and a heart to hear God.

REVIVALS AND DECLENSIONS

From chapters 10—36 we have the remaining history of the nation of Judah. Altogether it amounts to some three hundred and seventy years; but again, we need to note that II Chronicles does not give us a detailed history of the nation of Judah. It does not give us a description of all which the kings had done. On the contrary, the emphasis is on only one thing, and that is the house of God and these kings in their relationship to it. And God judged them accordingly: whether a given king was a good one and was accepted by God or whether he was a bad one and was rejected by God hinged upon their attitude and relationship to His house.

In Solomon's later years he was enticed by foreign women and began to worship all kinds of idols. As a result, the nation naturally began to drift away from God. There were times of frequent declension, but God in His mercy and in His promise to David gave them revival after revival, and in reviewing their long history we find reform after reform. We do not see that in the history of the northern kingdom of Israel, but only in the southern kingdom of Judah. And why? Because God remembered His promise to David. So we see through Judah's long history the failure of man but also the faithfulness of God. Altogether, there were five revivals or reforms, and during those times, it seems as though the people began to come back to God. They began to renew His house and rebuild it. They began to keep the Passover and the Law and the ordinances of Moses, but unfortunately, those revivals never lasted very long. Even *during* the time of a revival, the revivalist himself grew cold. There was revival upon revival, reform after reform, but finally came destruction. Nevertheless, thank God, there was the promise of restoration.

Does not this sound all too familiar to us today? Is not Christianity a history of similar revivals and declensions? Let us consider, for example, what occurred with the early church during the New Testament times. On the day of Pentecost when the Holy Spirit came and filled the upper room of the house, the one hundred and twenty souls there were baptized into one body, and so there was a glorious beginning of the house of God, which was the real house of God. God came and dwelt among these one hundred and twenty, for the heavenly fire came down, the glory came, and three thousand people got saved. Many more thereafter came to the Lord. The gospel began to spread and within thirty-three years, at the end of the book of Acts, the gospel had been preached, as it were, to the end of the world; which is to say was Rome, for it was the center of the known world of that day. (The book of Acts covered about thirty-three years of church history just as the life of our Lord Jesus had been about thirty-three years.) But then, before the apostles of those early days had passed away, even towards the latter part of the lives of Peter and Paul and John, there came in declension. The first love was gone, ritualism came in, and all kinds of false teaching, corrupt manners and worldly methods began to crowd in; and consequently, the church fell away.

And so has it been throughout her history ever since. But thank God, because of His love for His church, He has sent revival after revival. Indeed, if we look from the positive viewpoint, the history of Christianity has been one of revivals; but if we look from the negative viewpoint, it has been a history of declension. Yet God has continually sent revival upon revival, causing a return to God, a return to His word, and a rebuilding of His house. However, sadly, these revivals have never lasted very long—perhaps a generation, perhaps a little longer—but then, declension has come in once more. Nevertheless, God in His mercy, and because of His promise, would send another revival, and still another; but sadly, sadly, Christianity would repeatedly descend into a new Babylonian captivity. It would be captured again by the world.

Has the Church come out of the world yet? I use the word *Church* here in a general sense; I should rather say, Christianity. Has Christianity come out of the world yet? Or is it still in the grip of the world? Thank God, since the Reformation of the sixteenth century, we do find repeated instances of recovery, and that is a history which we will consider later.

Now in Judah's long history, about three hundred and seventy years, there were altogether five revivals or reforms which occurred under five kings. We shall review them very quickly here from II Chronicles 14—35.

ASA

The first king is Asa, whose story is found in chapters 14—16. Asa was the great-grandson of Solomon.

"And Asa did what was good and right in the sight of Jehovah his God; and he took away the altars of the strange gods and the high places, and broke the columns, and cut down the Asherahs; and commanded Judah to seek Jehovah the God of their fathers, and to practise the law and the commandment" (14:2-4).

Here, we find a revival, and because King Asa sought the Lord, the Lord blessed him. For instance, when the Ethiopians came against Judah with a great army, Asa trusted in the Lord and cried to the Lord in this manner:

"Jehovah, it maketh no difference to thee to help, whether there be much or no power: help us, O Jehovah our God, for we rely on thee, and in thy name have we come against this multitude. Jehovah, thou art our God; let not man prevail against thee" (14:11).

King Asa trusted in the Lord, so God destroyed the Ethiopian army and the king was encouraged after the victory by the prophet. Asa renewed the altar of the house of God, and God was truly with him. He was king for about thirty years, serving God; but unfortunately, in his later years, his love for Him began to grow cold. Therefore, Asa's trust in God was gone. So when the northern kingdom of Israel attacked him, instead of trusting in God, he tried to make an alliance with Syria, and God sent the prophet Hanani to reprove him. Said the prophet: "Why didn't you trust God? Ethiopia had a larger army, and you trusted Him then and He destroyed them. Why didn't you do the same here?" Instead of repenting, Asa became angry and put Hanani in prison. He even began to oppress some of the people, and when he came down with a disease of the feet, instead of seeking God, he sought only the physicians.

What is the lesson and the word which God wants to teach us here? "For the eyes of Jehovah run to and fro through the whole earth, to shew himself strong in the behalf of those whose heart is perfect toward him" (16:9).

God is looking for a perfect heart. If He can find such, He will show himself strong on that person's behalf. What exactly is a perfect heart? It is one that is single towards God: an undivided, pure heart; it is a heart of a man that loves God with all his heart. A perfect heart does not mean sinless perfection. David had a perfect heart towards God but he certainly was not sinless perfect. God's eyes go to and fro throughout the whole earth looking and seeking. He is watching, observing, trying to find one whose heart is pure towards Him, seeking to find one who is not double-hearted but loves God for himself and is pure, and without any selfish or ulterior motive. He has a perfect, undivided heart towards God. And if God can find such a man, His arm will display itself towards that man. Now that is the lesson here which we need to learn.

JEHOSHAPHAT

The narrative concerning King Jehoshaphat is found in chapters 17—20. He was the son of Asa.

"And Jehovah was with Jehoshaphat, for he walked in the first ways of his father David, and sought not unto the Baals; but he sought the God of his father, and walked in his commandments, and not after the doings of Israel" (17:3- 4).

Jehoshaphat sent out priests to teach the people the law of God. Then Moab and Ammon came with a great multitude to attack him, and Jehoshaphat prayed to God. And this is what God said in response: "Fear not, nor be dismayed by reason of this great multitude; for the battle is not yours, but God's. To-morrow go down against them: behold, they come up by the ascent of Ziz; and ye shall find them at the end of the valley, before the wilderness of Jeruel. Ye shall not have to fight on this occasion: set yourselves, stand and see the salvation of Jehovah who is with you!" (20:15b-17a).

So the people arose early in the morning and Jehoshaphat said to them: "Believe in Jehovah your God, and ye shall be established; believe his prophets, and ye shall prosper!" And he consulted with the people, and appointed singers to Jehovah. So they set the singers in front of the army, and as they were praising the Lord, He sent his liers-in-wait and killed the whole people (see 20:20-22). Under Jehoshaphat, there was a great revival. But unfortunately, there was one dark spot in Jehoshaphat. He would ally himself with King

Ahab of Israel—a very wicked king—by having his son marry Ahab's daughter, who was also wicked Jezebel's daughter; and so, because of that unholy alliance, Jehoshaphat nearly lost his life, and of course, in the process, he lost his business. For he had tried sending boats out to gather gold, but the boats broke. This was the one dark spot in Jehoshaphat's life.

What is to be learned from this? We need to believe and trust in the Lord. And we need to be careful not to be unequally yoked with unbelievers. If we are not careful, we will suffer for it.

JOASH

The third king's record can be found in chapters 23—24, and his name was Joash. After Solomon, there were altogether nineteen kings in the nation of Judah; just as the nation of Israel which also had nineteen kings. These nineteen kings of Judah did not include Athaliah, the daughter of Jezebel, because she had usurped the throne of Judah for seven years. Because she was not of the line of David, therefore, she cannot be counted.

Joash was a little baby when he was rescued from Athaliah's clutches by the high priest, Jehoiada, who hid him in the temple for six years (see 22:12). When Joash was seven years old, Jehoiada took him out and he began to reign. As a result, there was a revival because Joash renewed the house of God. The latter was in disarray and it had to be repaired. Joash had the desire to repair the house of God so that the worship might be resumed, and thus there was a revival during that time. All the days that Jehoiada the high priest remained alive, Joash served God, but after this high priest died, the princes of Judah came and Joash listened to their evil advice. He began to worship idols, and because of that, God's chastisement came upon him. He did not repent, and finally, he was murdered.

Joash was a weak person, and the lesson to be learned here is that for a weak person, his associations are most important.

Let us inquire, Who are we associated with? As long as Joash was under the advice of Jehoiada he was good, but the moment Jehoiada died, the princes of Judah came forth and led him astray. Let us never think that we are strong. Let us take care who we are with. If we are with godly people, they will help us to fear God, but if we are with evil people, we will not change them but they could change us.

HEZEKIAH

The fourth king's story of revival is found in chapters 29—32. "Hezekiah, in the first year of his reign, in the first month, opened the doors of the house of Jehovah, and repaired them. And he brought in the priests and the Levites, and gathered them into the open place eastward" (29:3-4).

Before Hezekiah came to the throne, even the doors of the temple had been closed. So he opened them and summoned the Levites and the priests in order that they might be sanctified and come and worship the Lord. Moreover, it was during Hezekiah's time that the observance of Passover was once again kept, even though they were not able to keep it according to God's law, which called for it to be held in the first month on the fourteenth day. This was because there were many who had not cleansed themselves, so they had to delay the keeping of it to the second month. Nevertheless, God forgave them for this in response to Hezekiah's prayer on their behalf (see 30:18). Furthermore, after they kept the Passover for seven days, their love for the Lord was so great that they wanted to keep it for yet another seven days. They kept the Passover twice over as a way of showing their love for God. And because of this, when Sennacherib, King of Assyria, came to destroy Judah, God answered the prayers of Hezekiah and destroyed the army of Sennacherib.

One day, Hezekiah became deathly sick and God sent the prophet to him and said, "Set your house in order; your time on earth is up." But he wept and said, "Lord, I have done so much for You; give me more time." And God, being so tenderhearted, was persuaded, and gave him fifteen more years of life. And He even gave him a sign, a fixed sign that He would do this: the sundial went back ten degrees. So Hezekiah was healed; but instead of being thankful to God, he began to be proud. And because of that, God's wrath came forth, but because he humbled himself, God's judgment did not come in his time. During those last fifteen years of his life Hezekiah committed two troubling things. One was that he fathered a son called Manasseh, and that was the son who destroyed the nation. And secondly, when emissaries of Babylon came to congratulate him on his having been healed from sickness, Hezekiah showed off to them all his riches out of great pride; and because of that, the nation was destined to be taken captive to Babylon.

The lesson to be learned here is that we should never try to force God. Do we know that God can be forced? We should rather let ourselves be forced instead of attempting to force God. Pride is the one thing we need to watch out for. If we are blessed by the Lord, that is something which we truly need to be very careful about. God gives grace to the humble, but He always resists the proud (see I Peter 5:5b).

JOSIAH

In chapters 34—35 we find the record of the fifth king and his revival. When King Josiah was only eight years old, he came to the throne of Judah. "And he did what was right in the sight of Jehovah, and walked in the ways of David his father, and turned not aside to the right hand nor to the left hand" (34:2).

Think of that—eight years old and he did what was right in the sight of the Lord! Eight years is not too young to know the Lord. It is not too young to walk in His way. Moreover, when he was sixteen years old, Josiah began to seek earnestly after the God of David his father. Furthermore, when he was twenty years old, he purged Judah and Jerusalem of all the idols, and when twenty-four years old, he purged the land and cleansed the house of God. It was there that the priest Hilkijah discovered the Book of the law of God given by Moses, and how tenderhearted Josiah was before God: He immediately humbled himself, repented and wept before God, and God heard his prayer on behalf of the nation, even though the destiny of Judah could not be redeemed. Even so, God said to Josiah through Huldah the prophetess that it would not happen in his time (see 4:14-28). When the king of Egypt came, and although he did not come to fight with Josiah, nevertheless Josiah went out against the Egyptian king (perhaps there was some pride there), and he was wounded by Egypt's archers and shortly afterwards died (see 35:20-24).

The lesson we can learn here is to serve the Lord in the days of our youth. When we are young, we still have the time to serve Him. If people do not serve Him when they are young, when they are old, they may indeed have the desire to serve, but where is the strength of will and determination?

So may the Lord use these lessons to encourage us. Moreover, even though there may be revivals and reforms which do not seem to last long, the lessons we learn from them are everlasting. May we truly learn these lessons, and if we do, it will help us when we are engaged in the work of the recovery of God's house.

Let us pray:

Dear heavenly Father, we do praise and thank Thee because Thou hast revealed Thy heart to us in that Thou dost desire to dwell among Thy people. And how it hurts Thee when Thy people forsake Thy house and forsake Thee. Lord, how we praise and thank Thee that in Thy mercy Thou art always sending prophets, Thou art always sending revivals, in order to draw Thy people back to Thyself; and yet Thou knowest our weaknesses. Lord, we are thankful for Thy faithfulness, and we know that because Thou art faithful, eventually Thou wilt have Thy house. So Lord, we do pray that by Thy grace we may learn all the lessons which we need to learn so that we may be able to persevere to the very end and be the house of God. To Thee be the glory; in the name of our Lord Jesus. Amen.

EZRA

REBUILDING AND BEAUTIFYING THE HOUSE OF GOD

Ezra 1:1-5—And in the first year of Cyrus king of Persia, that the word of Jehovah by the mouth of Jeremiah might be accomplished, Jehovah stirred up the spirit of Cyrus king of Persia, and he made a proclamation throughout his kingdom, and also in writing, saying, Thus says Cyrus king of Persia: All the kingdoms of the earth has Jehovah the God of the heavens given to me, and he has charged me to build him a house at Jerusalem, which is in Judah. Whosoever there is among you of all his people, his God be with him, and let him go up to Jerusalem, which is in Judah, and build the house of Jehovah the God of Israel—he is God—which is at Jerusalem. And whosoever remains in any place where he sojourns, let the men of his place help him with silver, and with gold, and with goods, and with beasts, besides the voluntary offering for the house of God which is at Jerusalem. And the chief fathers of Judah and Benjamin rose up, and the priests, and the Levites, even all those whose spirit God had stirred, to go up to build the house of Jehovah which is at Jerusalem.

Ezra 6:14-15—And the elders of the Jews built; and they prospered through the prophesying of Haggai the prophet and Zechariah the son of Iddo. And they built and completed it according to the commandment of the God of Israel, and according to the commandment of Cyrus, and Darius, and Artaxerxes king of Persia. And this house was finished on the third day of the month Adar, which was in the sixth year of the reign of king Darius.

Ezra 7:6-10—This Ezra went up from Babylon; and he was a ready scribe in the law of Moses, which Jehovah the God of Israel had given. And the king granted him all his request, according to the hand of Jehovah his God upon him. (And there went up some of the children of Israel, and of the priests, and the Levites, and the singers, and the doorkeepers, and the Nethinim, to Jerusalem, in the seventh year of Artaxerxes the king.) And he came to Jerusalem in the fifth month, which was in the seventh year of the king. For upon the first of the first month the project of going up from Babylon was determined on, and on the first of the fifth month he came to Jerusalem, according to the good hand of his God upon him. For Ezra had directed his heart to seek the law of Jehovah and to do it, and to teach in Israel the statutes and the ordinances.

Ezra 7:27-28—Blessed be Jehovah the God of our fathers, who has put such a thing as this in the king's heart, to beautify the house of Jehovah which is at Jerusalem; and has extended mercy to me before the king and his counsellors, and before all the king's mighty princes. And I was strengthened, as the hand of Jehovah my God was upon me; and I gathered together out of Israel chief men to go up with me.

Let us pray:

Dear heavenly Father, we do praise and thank Thee that through the blood of Thy Beloved Son, our Lord Jesus, and the new and living way which He has opened for us through His flesh, we dare to come into Thy presence, not only to come to Thy presence, but to remain in Thy presence. Oh, how we praise and thank Thee for this honor and privilege. And Father, we just pray that as we are continuing in Thy presence that the light of Thy countenance will shine upon our hearts and that Thy word will be spoken to our hearts. Make it life and spirit to us that Thou mayst be glorified. We ask in the name of our Lord Jesus. Amen.

The book of Ezra is a continuation of the history given in II Chronicles. We will find that the closing words in II Chronicles are the opening words of the book of Ezra. This, in a way, provides much proof to us that the same author composed these two different books. The book of Ezra begins with the return from captivity of a remnant of the children of Israel in the year 536 B.C. It ends with the second return from captivity of another remnant of the children of Israel under Ezra in 458 B.C. So, roughly, the history of this book covers around eighty years. Chapters 1—6 cover about twenty years of history. Then there is a gap of fifty-eight years between the time of chapters 6 and 7, and we know that that gap is filled with the story of Esther. Chapters 7—10 cover roughly one year. So that is the history which we find in the book of Ezra.

We know that the children of Israel were taken into Babylonian captivity because of their unfaithfulness to God. But God is faithful; before they were taken into captivity, God promised them through Jeremiah that the captivity would be seventy years, and after seventy years He would bring His people back to the land. "Thus saith the Lord: When seventy years shall be accomplished for Babylon I will visit you, and perform my good word toward you, in bringing you back to this place" (29:10).

THE ROYAL DECREE

The children of Israel were in the land of captivity. In the first year of the Persian King Darius, Daniel read the book of Jeremiah and understood that the captivity would be over within two years. So he gave himself to travailing prayer. He confessed his sin and the sin of the nation before God. He asked God to forgive and to bring the people back to the Promised Land (see Daniel 9). In answer to the travailing prayer of Daniel, a royal decree was issued in the first year of King Cyrus. And in that royal decree, he in essence said this: "God has given all the lands to me, and now all those who are of His people may go back to Jerusalem to build the house of God."

We will probably wonder how or why a Gentile king, Cyrus, who did not know God, would make such a royal decree. We must remember that Daniel was still there with King Cyrus at that time, and most likely he shared with the King what God had prophesied about Cyrus two hundred and fifty years before through the prophet Isaiah. Isaiah had lived around 800 B.C. In Isaiah 44:28 and into the beginning verses of chapter 45 we read that God prophesied and named Cyrus by name: "Cyrus is My shepherd; I have given all these things to him that he may do My will, that is, to rebuild My house." As Daniel shared this prophecy with Cyrus, and even though he did not know God, he must have been really touched. He himself acknowledged that it must have been God who had given him all the lands of his empire. So, in order to show his respect to God, Cyrus issued a royal decree allowing all the children of God who were then in captivity under his rule to return and build the house of God.

We must acknowledge, however, that it was not the faithfulness of the people; it was the faithfulness of God that initiated this return and the rebuilding of the house of God. Ezra, the scribe, put together the history of the return of the Jewish people from their captivity. And as he composed this book, he focused upon but one thing: to display the faithfulness of God to His own word. We may be unfaithful, but God always remains faithful. Ezra had also wanted to show the people of God that in order to fulfill His own promise, God is able to stir the hearts of even the Gentile kings—He is able to raise up instruments, human vessels, to fulfill His promise. Now that is our God, and this should encourage us.

In the book of Ezra there are in view two returns of the children of Israel out of Babylonian captivity. The first return occurred under Zerubbabel and the second, under Ezra. The first return to Jerusalem was for the purpose of *rebuilding* the house of God. But the second return was for the purpose of *beautifying* or *strengthening* that house—in other words, for strengthening the service of God's house.

GOD'S HEAVENLY CHOSEN PEOPLE

As we consider this book of Ezra, it is not merely an occasion for us to review a past history. We are to learn certain lessons which God wants us to have. In a way, the history of the children of Israel is a type of the spiritual history of the church, God's people today. Because the children of Israel were God's earthly chosen people and the church of God is His heavenly chosen people, the principles are often the same. I Peter 2:9 tells us that the church of God is a holy nation. Of course, this holy nation is different from all the other nations of the earth because it is heavenly and spiritual in nature. Nevertheless, it is a holy nation; and it is not only that, it is also a holy priesthood. Moreover, in I Peter 2:5 we are told that we are to be built up together into a spiritual house and into a holy priesthood so that we may offer up spiritual sacrifices acceptable to God through Jesus Christ. On the one hand, we are a holy nation; on the other hand, we are a holy priesthood; yet, like the children of Israel, we today have not been faithful to God.

THE CHURCH IN BABYLONIAN CAPTIVITY

As we look back into the two-thousand-year history of the church we find that, very quickly, the church left its original position. The church has degenerated and fallen into the world and thus, for the most part, it has been in Babylonian captivity ever since. If you read the history of the Reformation, you will find that Martin Luther and the other sixteenth-century reformers had observed that the church in their day was in Babylonian captivity. Even though God was calling His people at that time to return to Him, we are compelled to say that, generally speaking, the church is even today still in Babylonian captivity.

In Biblical typology Babylon is different from Egypt. God brought His people out of Egypt, which represents the material world. The riches of the world—the consequences of the lust of the flesh, the lust of the eyes, and the pride of life—that is all Egypt (see I John 2:16). God brought His children out of Egypt into the Promised Land of Canaan—a land flowing with milk and honey—which represents the fullness of Christ. Yet, later, the children of Israel, because of their gross unfaithfulness, fell into Babylonian captivity. Babylon is likewise a representation of the world, but it is a symbol of the *religious* world because all the world's religions can be traced back to Babylon. So we may say that the Israelites came out of the world as it was and then fell into the religious world.

How true this is with the church of God today! God has called us out of every nation, tribe, people, and tongue. He has called us out of the world and gathered us together as one under Christ Jesus, and it is His desire that we should remain in Christ and enjoy His fullness. But unfortunately, the church has not been faithful. And because of her unfaithfulness, the church was and still is in Babylonian captivity. In other words, the church today has become a religious system, not much different from the other religions in the world. *Babylon* itself means "confusion"; and we do find there is much confusion today among God's people.

Throughout church history, ever since she had gone into Babylonian captivity, God has been calling His people back—back to Jerusalem to rebuild the house of God. This calling has been going on for centuries and centuries. It was not only at the time of the sixteenth-century Reformation; we can even trace this calling all the way back to the second century. Again and again God has been calling His people back to Jerusalem—to the city of peace, to simplicity, to purity—and there, to rebuild His house and to reestablish His testimony. Now such is the history which we wish to explore by means of this book of Ezra.

SPIRITUAL REALITY

The two returns described in the book of Ezra did not signify a restoration of the nation politically; rather, they represented a recovery of the spiritual and moral condition of the people. They were not a free people; indeed, they were only permitted to go back to Jerusalem under the decree of the Gentile kings of Persia. As a matter of fact, after the Babylonian captivity, the nation of Israel would never be restored politically again until 1948, except for a short period of independence she enjoyed during the Maccabean era. So even though they would be back in their land following the Babylonian captivity, the Jewish people would never be free at all: they would be under the Gentile rule of different kingdoms and different reigns. And hence, these returns cannot be said to have represented a *political* restoration but, rather, a religious or moral recovery.

Why do I mention this? Because, according to God's principle, spiritual recovery precedes physical or political restoration. God always looks upon the heart whereas man always looks upon the outward appearance. What God is after is always the heart: the spiritual reality. And when there is spiritual reality present, then the outward appearance will be manifested sooner or later. Spiritual reality precedes outward manifestation, but we human beings think differently about this.

When our Lord Jesus came upon this earth two thousand years ago, the Jews rejected Him because they wanted a political recovery, but He sought a spiritual one first. So when considering this matter of the church, let us not look for a recovery of her outward glory following her plunge into Babylonian captivity; rather, let us be clear that what God wishes to do and is doing today is to first recover the spiritual reality among His people. Unless that is recovered, what is the use of recovering or having an outward appearance? Unfortunately, too many of God's people today are looking for outward glory instead of that inward spiritual and moral reality. One day, the glorious church—the bride of the Lamb—will indeed be manifested and will reign with Christ. So when considering the principle of recovery, let us clearly understand that what God is preeminently after is always the inward reality, not the outward appearance.

A REMNANT RETURNED

In the first year of his reign, King Cyrus issued a royal proclamation allowing the children of Israel who were in captivity within his kingdom to return to Jerusalem and rebuild the house of God. As was indicated before, the children of Israel in captivity were not free; they were slaves. Accordingly, they were not free to go back as they wished: they had to wait until the king allowed them to return. The proclamation had relevance to all of God's people who were in captivity; all could therefore return. And the decree was specific: they would be returning to do but one thing—to rebuild the house of God and nothing else.

Now we would think that when such a decree was issued, surely all the children of Israel in the land of captivity would rise up and return. For supposing we were in captivity, and one day we were allowed to go home. Would we not go home? Certainly we would. Strangely, however, this did not happen with the Jews here. Even though all Israel was allowed to return, only a remnant of them actually did so. The call ought to have stirred the hearts of all God's people, but unfortunately, only a remnant whose spirits were stirred by God actually returned. The rest of them did not return, as though they had not heard. They were not stirred, they did not care. Why was it so?

We know that after the children of Israel were taken into Babylonian captivity, and even though they were slaves for seventy years under the reigns of Babylon and Persia, they were actually given much liberty. They were allowed to build their own houses. They were allowed to build up their businesses—and we know how well they could do business. So many of these Israelites prospered greatly in the land of their captivity during those seventy years. They planted their roots down deeply in the land of captivity. More than that, they were even granted religious freedom. Had they not been given religious freedom, most probably they would all have wanted to go back; but this was not the case. As a matter of fact, it was the Babylonian captivity which finally liberated the children of Israel of their idolatry. For God, in having sent them into captivity, had in essence declared to them: "So you insist on worshiping idols, do you? All right, into the land of countless idols I shall send you!" And so the Jews were at last set free from their idolatrous tendencies.

THE SYNAGOGUE

Now in the land of captivity, the children of Israel had wanted once again to worship God. But they could not do so because Jerusalem had been destroyed; moreover, the temple no longer existed. How, then, could they worship? Here, human ingenuity came to the rescue. These Israelites were so clever; for they invented a most ingenious system that exists even to this very day. Wherever the Jews are today, you shall find this invention— which is, the synagogue. The synagogue was invented during that period because they did not have the temple and yet they wanted to worship God. Humanly speaking, they invented something better than God's plan. There had only been one temple, but there could now be countless synagogues. If in your community you could find ten Jewish men of leisure—which meant they were able and willing to spend some time for religious purposes— then you could have a synagogue. During this time of captivity, synagogues sprang up everywhere. It was so convenient: you could have a synagogue next door, and thus you did not need to travel too far, if at all. On the other hand, if you did not like certain people, you could organize your own synagogue: and if you did not like their way of doing things, then you could have your own synagogue. Even in the time of the apostles, there were synagogues based on a guild system. For instance, if you were a mason, you could have a masons' synagogue; if you were a mechanic, you could have one for mechanics. In other words, you could have a synagogue according to your own liking. Now was that not most convenient and ingenious?

In the synagogue the Jews read the Torah, the Law of Moses; they also read the prophets. In the synagogue, they also sang the Psalms and could likewise pray and even exhort one another. As a matter of fact, in the time of the apostles, how free they were! For whenever the apostle Paul, for example, came into a synagogue, the ruler there would approach him and say, "Well, sir, do you have anything to speak to us about?" You could say anything you wanted to because there was such liberty in the synagogue. What a marvelous development! The only activity you could not do in the synagogue was to offer sacrifices, for God had said you could not offer anywhere in the world but in the one place where He had put His name, which was the temple in Jerusalem. So these captive Jews could not offer sacrifices.

Yet the Law had said that without the shedding of blood there can be no remission of sin. There in the synagogue you could have everything religious but not the remission of sin. In other words, the most fundamental element was missing. Everything was there to satisfy or bribe your conscience and make you feel religious. But nothing was there which could restore your relationship with God.

The Jewish people in captivity who lived for themselves had everything they desired. They had all the good material things and also a religious system that bribed their conscience and made them feel religiously satisfied. And hence, if they were self-centered—and many of them were—then they were self-contented; and that is the reason why most of them did not feel any urge to go back to the land of Judah. Why should they be uprooted? Why should they face the danger of the journey? Why should they return to Jerusalem, to a ruinous situation?

Why should they build the house of God while living in tents there? Why should they do any of that? Their spirits were lulled to sleep by the material and religious benefits of remaining in captivity. They only cared for themselves; they did not care for God and His interests.

During these days of captivity God was no longer being referred to as the God of the heavens and of the earth. He was addressed simply as the God of the heavens, for He had been dismissed from the earth because He had put His name among His own people and they were now in captivity. There was no testimony of Him on earth anymore. Only those people whose spirits were still alert towards God, only those people who loved Him more than themselves and were interested in His interests rather than their own, were stirred in their spirits. They wanted to go back to rebuild the house of God in order that His name might again be known on the earth and that the testimony of God might once more be restored upon this earth. Now these were the people who returned.

FIRST RETURN

ZERUBBABEL

These Israelites returned under the leadership of Zerubbabel. The very name Zerubbabel means "born in Babylon" or "seed of Babylon." In other words, this young man had been born in Babylon, and thus he had never seen Jerusalem nor the old temple. How, then, was it that he wanted to go there? Zerubbabel had never seen his motherland nor the Jerusalem temple; instead, Babylon was his home. Why, indeed, had he desired to go?

We need to recall the fact that Zerubbabel was the grandson of Jehoiachin the king, and this king had been taken into Babylonian captivity. We must also note that the last few verses of II Kings 25 tell us that in the thirty-seventh year of

Jehoiachin's captivity, the king of Babylon set him free from prison and made him his friend. So in his later years Jehoiachin had actually lived in the royal palace and became a friend of the Babylonian king. Therefore, when Zerubbabel was born, he must have been born into a very good environment despite being in captivity. And hence, being in the royal court, he must have had social intercourse with one particular man—Daniel—who also was in the royal court at that time. By this time, of course, Daniel must have been an old man. Nevertheless, he must have shared with the young prince Zerubbabel concerning the purpose and will of God, His name, the house of God, and the glory of God. And as Daniel would share these things with the younger Zerubbabel, the latter's heart must have burned within him—so much so that he had a burning desire for God and for His glory. So when the decree of King Cyrus was published, Zerubbabel became the one who would lead the people back to Jerusalem to build the house of God.

All fifty thousand of those who returned with Zerubbabel had the same spirit. And upon their return to Jerusalem, the first action they took was to build an altar for calling upon the name of the Lord because of their fear of the enemies around them. Then, in the second year they began to lay the foundation of the house of God. The old men who returned with this remnant must have been seventy, eighty or even ninety years old. They were the ones who had seen the temple before it had been destroyed, and when they saw the foundation laid, they wept. But the young people among these returnees, those who had never seen the temple before, shouted aloud; and because of that, the surrounding enemies heard it. So these enemies tried by every means to stop the work; and in the remnant people's weakness, the work was stopped for about fourteen years. And we know what they did during those years until God raised up Haggai and Zechariah. Through the prophesying of these two prophets they returned to the work and, in four years, the house of God was rebuilt. Thank God for that!

THE CALL TO BUILD GOD'S HOUSE

There is a similarity between the recovery of the house of God in Jerusalem and the recovery of the testimony of Jesus today. We observed earlier that the church today is in Babylonian captivity; there is much confusion among God's people. Too many of God's people are seeking for earthly, material gains, just as do the people of the world. Too many are running here and there, seeking the perishable things, just as do the people of this world. We are continually thinking of building our own houses, businesses, our own welfare—everything for ourselves—though we know we are in captivity. How ingenious is the system we have invented!—God's people today do not need to worship as one; we can worship in whatever way we like; we can even have our own church. Is it not true that our conscience seems to have been bribed into sleep? We think we are religious, that we are worshiping God, but it is really done to fulfill our selfish desire. What about the testimony of Jesus? Where is it? Where is the oneness of the body of Christ?

God's people today are in great confusion, and yet the call is still there: Come out of Babylon: Return to Jerusalem and build My house. Is it not time that we begin to think of God's interests? Is it not time that we be God-centered instead of self-centered, even in religious pursuits and activities? Is it not time for us to be centered on the testimony of Jesus upon this earth instead of on our own welfare? Is it not time that we come out of all confusion and return to purity and to the simplicity that is in Christ Jesus? (see II Corinthians 11:3b) We have become too complicated, too sophisticated. We need to return to simplicity and sincerity in Christ Jesus (see II Corinthians 1:12), for it is there that we are to build the house of God. We *are* that house, and God desires to dwell among us who are His people. He wants to build us up together as living stones, to build us up together upon the one foundation, Christ Jesus.

The question therefore needs to be asked: Is our spirit

stirred? Can we remain in Babylon? Ought we not to rise up, be willing to face all dangers and return to our being almost nothing so that God's house may be built, so that Christ—the Head of the church—may be the center that God's people may be joined together as one, and that the name of Jesus may be glorified? It is true that we have never seen the glory of the early church, but we have heard about it through our having read of it in the Book. Is our spirit therefore stirred thereby? Can we continue any longer to be in lethargy and complacency, as though there is nothing needed further to be done? Where is the testimony of Jesus? Where are the people whose spirits are stirred up with the desire to return to simplicity and to rebuild God's house? Oh, may His altar be erected, may the foundation be laid, may His house be built.

Although such may never appear in an *official outward* history of the church, nevertheless, careful research into the past twenty centuries of her history will uncover the fact that there has been an *un*official inward *spiritual* history of the church. Thank God, that in every age there have been people who have heard the call: Come out of Babylon: Return to Jerusalem, and build the house of God.

SECOND RETURN

EZRA

Ezra was a ready scribe. As a matter of fact, by the Jews, Ezra was considered as *the* scribe. The name *Ezra* means "help." Fifty-eight years had passed when in 458 B.C he set his heart to seek the Law of God, to do it, and to teach it to God's people. He was an honored person, a scholar. He lived comfortably in the Persian court and was respected by all, even by the king; yet Ezra's heart was with the remnant people in Jerusalem. He wanted to go back there to teach them. So here we find a second return back to Jerusalem, this one under Ezra.

A few thousand people returned with him.

However, Ezra's return had a different purpose than that under Zerubbabel because by this time the temple was already built and the temple service had been going on for some time. But during those fifty-eight years the taxation had become very heavy upon the people, and because of this, even the priests and Levites had to make a living. They had to go out to the fields to till the ground. Moreover, the offerings were so meager that even though the temple service was going on, there were not sufficient sacrifices. In addition, there were not enough priests to handle all the temple work. In short, the temple was there and the service was going on, but the temple activity was very weak; and hence, the testimony of God was weak.

Ezra had the burden to return to beautify the house of God. *To beautify* in this context meant "to strengthen the temple service." Ezra was a person who knew *the word* of God by heart, and he was one who also knew *the hand* of God. A scribe was supposed to know God's word; but sometimes he would not know God's hand. Ezra, though, was a person who knew both the word and hand of God upon him; that is to say, he knew God himself. And so God answered his prayer, in that Ezra was allowed to return to Jerusalem to strengthen the temple service there. As a result, there would now be more bullocks, lambs, sheep, and resources. The Persian king had even said that his empire's treasury would back this up, and the Persian empire's treasury was almost limitless. The king also exempted the Levites and priests from having to pay taxes, and thus they could devote themselves to the temple service rather than having to continue to labor in the fields to earn a living.

THE PEOPLE PURIFIED

Ezra not only was able to build up the temple service but was also able to purify the people at the same time. Nevertheless, during those fifty-eight years God's chosen people—who were supposed to be separated from all the nations—had begun to intermarry with the surrounding countries. And because of that impurity, they were led away from God. So, while beautifying the temple, the people had to be purified by Ezra. So the people were purified and remained a pure people before God. This was very important because it was not only for the testimony of that time but had even greater future significance, since one day the Messiah was to come through them. God had to preserve a people for himself in order to prepare for the coming of the Messiah. Thank God, that in Ezra's time the temple service was strengthened, the people were purified, and God's testimony was recovered.

A HOLY PRIESTHOOD

We have mentioned before that the Bible tells us we are not only a holy temple—a spiritual house of God—but we are also a holy priesthood (see I Peter 2:5). With regard to our being God's spiritual house, it is His will that we should be built up together under one Head—Christ. We should be built together upon one foundation—Christ. We should be built and linked together with one cornerstone—even Christ—so that God may dwell among us and be satisfied. This being built up together is not merely to be an outward development; it is to be an organic one as well. The Holy Spirit is to build us together as one—being one in spirit, soul and love; and we are to bear and forbear one another, keep the unity of the spirit in the bond of peace, and grow together into the unity of the faith and of the knowledge of the Son of God (see Ephesians 4:3, 13).

But more than that, God wants us to be a holy priesthood in His house. The temple was to have been as our Lord Jesus declared: "Is it not written, 'My house shall be called a house of prayer for all nations'?" Yet, in Jesus' day the temple had degenerated into a house of merchandise and a den of robbers (see Matthew 21:12-13; Mark 11:15-17; Luke 19:45-46; John 2:13-16; Isaiah 56:7; Jeremiah 7:11).

We are to be a holy priesthood, in line with the Biblical understanding of the universal priesthood of believers. Even

Martin Luther, in his day, had preached the universal priesthood of believers. Can you believe that? Those sixteenth-century reformers knew it, but they did not put it into practice. Instead of there being the universal priesthood of believers, there has continued to be the sacerdotal system—a separation between the laity and the clergy—in Christendom.

Interestingly, according to I Timothy the church of God is referred to as the house of God and the church of the living God, as well as the pillar and base of the truth; and great is the mystery of godliness (see 3:15-16a). Yet by the time of II Timothy the church had become "a great house"—with vessels of honor and vessels of dishonor therein (see 2:20). Is it not the time for us to purify ourselves from being vessels of dishonor and become vessels of honor "fit for the Master's use" (see 2:21)?

Is it not also the time that all God's people come and beautify the house of God? Is it not the time that we all rise up and function together as members of the body of Christ, according to the gift and grace which God has given to each? (see Romans 12:5-6) There is no one who is not needed. There is no one who can do everything. Under the headship of Christ all the members of the body of Christ should function together as a holy priesthood so that God may be served.

This is what God wants to restore and to recover in His people. There are limitless resources because all the treasury of heaven is backing us up. All the spiritual gifts and all the grace of Christ Jesus are ours. There should be nothing lacking in God's house. But the point here is, Do we set our heart to seek the word of God and to do it? Otherwise, how can we teach people? Do we know the word of God? Do we know the hand of God in our lives? Otherwise, it is academic; it is not spiritual. God wants all of us to rise up and serve as a holy priesthood in His house. If such becomes a reality, how glorious that will be! How rich that will be! And how greatly God will be served! May the Lord help us.

Let us pray:

> *Dear heavenly Father, may Thy people hear Thy voice, and may the spirit of Thy people be stirred. Oh, our heavenly Father, we pray that Thy people will return to rebuild and to strengthen, that Thou mayst be exalted and that Thou mayst be served, because Thou art our God and our Father, our Lord and our King. Thou art worthy. We ask in the name of our Lord Jesus. Amen.*

NEHEMIAH

BUILDING THE WALL AND STRENGTHENING CORPORATE LIVING

Nehemiah 1:1-4—The words of Nehemiah the son of Hachaliah. And it came to pass in the month Chislev, in the twentieth year, as I was in Shushan the fortress, that Hanani, one of my brethren, came, he and certain men of Judah. And I asked them concerning the Jews that had escaped, who were left of the captivity, and concerning Jerusalem. And they said to me, Those who remain, that are left of the captivity there in the province, are in great affliction and reproach; and the wall of Jerusalem is in ruins, and its gates are burned with fire. And it came to pass, when I heard these words, that I sat and wept, and mourned for days, and fasted, and prayed before the God of the heavens.

Nehemiah 2:17-18—And I said to them, Ye see the distress that we are in, that Jerusalem lies waste, and its gates are burned with fire. Come, and let us build up the wall of Jerusalem, that we be no more a reproach. And I told them of the hand of my God which had been good upon me; as also of the king's words which he had said unto me. And they said, Let us rise up and build. And they strengthened their hands for the good work.

Nehemiah 6:15-16—So the wall was finished on the twenty-fifth of Elul, in fifty-two days. And it came to pass that when all our enemies heard of it, all the nations that were about us were afraid and were much cast down in their own eyes, and they perceived that this work was wrought by our God.

Let us pray:

Dear heavenly Father, as we are before Thee and before Thy word, we pray that Thou wilt give us the right spirit, the right attitude, that we may be those who tremble at Thy word, who love Thy word, and desire to do Thy word. We do commit this time into Thy hands and trust Thy Holy Spirit to grant us wisdom and revelation to the full knowledge of God. And to Thee be glory in the name of our Lord Jesus. Amen.

Nehemiah is the last of the historical books of the Old Testament. These begin with Joshua and end with Nehemiah. We would probably say it ends with Esther since it appears after Nehemiah; but time-wise, Esther is before Nehemiah. The time of Joshua to the time of Nehemiah covers roughly one thousand and twenty years of history—that is, from B.C. 1451 to B.C. 432. Many things happened during that time. The children of Israel had conquered the land of Canaan under Joshua. They then lived for over four hundred years under the Judges. Next, the kingdom was established under Saul, David and Solomon, and then it was divided into two from the time of Rehoboam to the time of Hoshea. The northern kingdom was taken into captivity and the single kingdom of Judah continued on from the time of Hezekiah to the time of Zedekiah. After that, there was the captivity in Babylon for seventy years, and thank God, after those seventy years, there was a return under Zerubbabel, a return under Ezra, and another under Nehemiah.

Even though Nehemiah is the last of the historical books in the Old Testament, it also provides a record of the beginning of God's special dealing with the city of Jerusalem and His people. For we read in Daniel 9 that as Daniel was seeking the Lord about this matter of the ending of the Babylonian captivity, the Lord sent His angel to Daniel and declared His plan for the city and for His people. But this plan covered much more than Daniel had prayed for or expected. God said He would set apart a period of time in history: a seventy weeks. Now the word weeks is actually not in the original. The original reads seventy sevens. Because seven is a week, that is why our Bibles read seventy weeks here. God has allotted in history a period of seventy sevens for the city and the people. And with that seventy sevens, God was going "to close the transgression, and to make an end of sins, and to make expiation for iniquity, and to bring in the righteousness of the ages, and to seal the vision and prophet, and to anoint the holy of holies" (9:24). Quoting Daniel again, we read that the seventy sevens began with this: "Know therefore and understand: From the going forth of the word to restore and to build Jerusalem unto Messiah, the Prince, are seven weeks [sevens] and sixty-two weeks [sevens]. The street and the moat shall be built again, even in troublous times. And after the sixty-two weeks [sevens] shall Messiah be cut off, and shall have nothing; and the people of the prince that shall come shall destroy the city and the sanctuary; and the end thereof shall be with an overflow, and unto the end, war,—the desolations determined" (9:25-26).

This seventy sevens commenced with the word going forth to rebuild the city of Jerusalem. This decree was given in the twentieth year of Artaxerxes Longimanus, and that is the time when Nehemiah received the order to go back to Jerusalem to build the wall and the city. So the seventy sevens began with the return of Nehemiah to rebuild Jerusalem. Then in troublous times, the city will be built again; and after sixty-two sevens, the Messiah will be cut off. The word *cut off* here is a very strong one. It means that the Messiah will not simply go away, He will literally be cut off; and that is a reference to the crucifixion of our Lord Jesus. So the book of Nehemiah is very, very important because it not only concludes the history of the Old Testament but also commences the recording of the special dealing of God with Jerusalem and with the people there.

All together, there were three returns to this city recorded in the Bible. The first was under Zerubbabel in 536 BC. He and about 50,000 people returned from Babylon to Jerusalem, and they rebuilt the temple. The second return was under Ezra, with a few thousand people going back with him in the year 458 BC. He and his brethren went back to beautify the temple—that is, to strengthen the temple service. And the third return occurred under Nehemiah in the year 445 BC; and his return was for building back the wall of Jerusalem and for strengthening the city life there.

THREE ASPECTS OF RECOVERY

THE HOUSE

We understand very well that the Old Testament history has been recorded for our admonition. In other words, the history of the Old Testament people serves as a type of the history of God's people today. We believe we are living in a time of recovery and that God's people need to return. In the recovery of God's people there are three distinctive aspects. First of all, we are told in Scripture, in I Peter 2:5, that we are as living stones being built up together to be a spiritual house. In other words, we believers today are the temple of God. But with regard to the children of Israel when they were in the land of captivity, they did not have the temple of God: all they had were synagogues; but God's heart was intent on seeing His house recovered because it was only in Jerusalem, in the temple there, that He had put His name. It was only there that people could offer sacrifices for the remission of their sins. Unfortunately, most of the people who were in captivity were content to continue living in captivity because they lived for themselves. Only those whose hearts were for God were willing to be uprooted from the land where they were sojourning and return to a ruined Jerusalem and there build the temple for God's name. The same thing is required of us today: there needs to be the rebuilding of the house of God. Living stones have to come together on the ground of purity, on the ground of Christ alone as the foundation, and to be built up together to be a habitation of God so that His name may be magnified.

THE PRIESTHOOD

The second aspect of the recovery work is the temple service. It was recovered under Ezra the scribe. How true it is that we are not only the habitation of God but we are also a holy priesthood; and this holy priesthood has to be recovered as well. In Christianity today there is a distinction made between the so-called clergy and laity. There is a certain group that is set apart to serve God, and the rest are laity—the common people. But all believers are priests, and we all are supposed to be a holy priesthood to serve the Lord together. That is likewise an aspect which has to be recovered in our day.

THE TESTIMONY

Furthermore, the church is not only a temple of God, it is not only a holy priesthood, the church is also a city that is built on the top of the mountain and thus cannot be hid. Christ said a city that is built on the top of a mountain cannot be hid; let your light therefore shine and be known to the world (see Matthew 5:14). Thus, God's people today are also a city, even a walled city. A city is a unit under one government; it is also a fellowship and is likewise a testimony. Hence, a city is the coming together of a people under the divine government of Christ. A city is additionally the fellowship of the saints living together in unity. And a city is also a testimony because it is to be known to the world as the vessel for the testimony of Jesus. The house needs to be recovered; the priesthood needs to be recovered; and the city as the testimony of Jesus has to be recovered. Now this latter aspect of recovery we find typified in the book of Nehemiah.

THE CUPBEARER

The book of Nehemiah reads almost like a personal diary. Nehemiah used the personal pronoun throughout. In short, it is a history of his own life; and yet, that life is so intertwined with the history of God's people that it becomes the last book of the history of the Old Testament era. *Nehemiah* means "the comfort of Jehovah"; and certainly, God raised up this man to be a comfort to His people.

We do not know too much about Nehemiah's past other than he was the son of Hachaliah; he lived during the time of Artaxerxes Longimanus in Shushan, the Persian empire's capital; and we also know he was the king's cupbearer. Evidently, Nehemiah came from the royal family of Judah; but we must remember that at that time, they were under foreign rule. They were slaves, and yet Nehemiah became the cupbearer of the king. The cupbearer was not a waiter in our modern sense. On the contrary, he was a very high official in the court because during those days, under that kind of absolute monarchy, the king or emperor was always fearful of being murdered. He had to have someone whom he could trust—his confidant. Usually, that man was one who was his companion and friend. Not only did the king love him, but the king was loved by that confidant to the point of his being willing to die for the king. And that is why, in the olden days, there was the cupbearer. This official would drink the wine first, before he handed the cup to the king, and if it contained poison, then the cupbearer would die for the king. Therefore, the cupbearer was one who was very close to the king. So even though Nehemiah was a slave, in God's providence he had become the king's close friend and confidant.

Nehemiah lived a very comfortable life in the court of Shushan; yet his heart and his concern were somewhere else. Even though he was in the palace and lived a very comfortable life and occupied a very high position in the Persian court, his heart was with the people who had returned from captivity to Jerusalem to stand for the name of God. He himself had not been able to go before that time, but his concern was nonetheless there. Even though he lived such a comfortable and privileged life, he never forgot his brethren who were attempting to stand for the name of God on this earth. His heart was there at Jerusalem.

THE UNWALLED CITY

One day Nehemiah's brother Hanani and some of the people came back from Jerusalem, and he inquired of them as to what had happened with the people there. He was told that the people of the captivity who had returned to Jerusalem and still remained there were in deep trouble. They were in tribulation and affliction, and suffering great reproach. Even though the remnant who had returned to Jerusalem were able to rebuild the temple and were able to resume the temple service, nevertheless, Jerusalem was still in ruins. The walls were destroyed and the gates were burned; there was no protection for the temple and for the remnant people whatsoever. And hence, the enemy around them could come in, day or night, to molest, harass, and attack them and reduce them to great distress. Life had become very difficult for God's people in that place. Because of that, many of them who had returned to Jerusalem had eventually gone back to the land of captivity because it was just too difficult. Fortunately, however, there were still some who remained in Jerusalem struggling to maintain the name of God in that barren land and in that unwalled city despite the fact they were in great affliction and suffered great reproach. Now when Nehemiah heard about all this, he was so deeply touched that he wept before God; and, sitting down before Him, Nehemiah fasted and prayed to the God of the heavens.

The news had come to him in November or December of that year. He prayed for several months thereafter, waiting upon God. He did not rush into anything on his own but earnestly sought the Lord. He prayed to God and offered himself to Him. It was not until March or April that God finally opened the door for him. Nehemiah was serving the king at the table one day, and when he lifted up the cup, the king noticed that there was sadness on his face. So the king said, "You are not sick. Why are you sad? There must be something in your heart."

Nehemiah was frightened because it was a very frightening thing if the king should notice there was something in one's heart. In other words, he might suspect that that person wanted to murder him, and that would be a very grave matter. Nehemiah had never shown a sad face before the king, but he could not help it anymore because his heart was so burdened. So quietly, he lifted up his heart to God and prayed. He then told the king, "How can I be happy when my city where my fathers are buried is in ruin?" The king asked, "What do you want?" And Nehemiah asked the king for permission to go back to Jerusalem to rebuild the city. The good hand of the Lord was upon him, and he was granted that permission. So that the royal decree which the king had now issued served as the commencement of the special dealing of God with the city of Jerusalem and with the people there.

THE UNWALLED CHURCH

In reading or hearing this story, are we touched by the Spirit of God in recognizing that the same situation is happening in our day? Most believers today are still in the land of captivity. Most believers today are continuing to build their houses and their businesses. Even though they do worship God, they nonetheless worship according to the way *they* think He should be worshiped, each according to his or her delight, just as was true during the synagogue system in the olden days of captivity. Is it not true, even in our day, that there are very few—a remnant—who are willing to leave Babylon? Instead, most remain in confusion—not only in the world but in confusion in the Christian world—rather than return to the purity and simplicity that are in Christ and there be built up together under the name of the Lord Jesus. Is it not true that there are few among God's people today who have seen the holy priesthood and who are willing to serve the Lord, each according to the gift and grace which God has given them (see Ephesians 3:7), instead of simply letting a few serve God for them? Is it not true, even today, that God's people are not separated from the world? There does not seem to be any wall separating the world from the church. Is it not true, even today, that there are very few who really live under the divine government of Christ? Is it not true, even today, that very few of God's people know the fellowship of the saints—how to live together in love and in unity? Is it not true, even today, that the testimony of Jesus is not spread forth, that the world does not hear Him nor see Him nor notice Him? Is it not true that this same situation is here with us today as it was back in Nehemiah's day?

Let us ask ourselves, Where is our heart? Where is our concern? Are we here merely living for ourselves? Are we here only for building our own houses and building up our own businesses? Are we here worshiping God, yes, loving God, yes, but each according to his or her delight? Do we serve God as a holy priesthood? Are we a city that is built on the top of the mountain—and thus a city which cannot be hid? Where is the testimony of Jesus in this world?

In the prayer of our Lord Jesus found in John 17 we notice that He prayed that we may be one as He and the Father are one so that the world may see that He was sent by God. How divided God's people are today! Even though there are attempts to bring God's people together, such an ecumenical movement is external: it does not work, it is not the real thing. How can we truly be one as Christ and His Father are one unless we are separated from the world? So in that prayer of John 17, on the one hand, the yearning of our Lord is that we may be one. That is the testimony which He desires of us. But on the other hand, how can we be one if we are not separated? So the Lord Jesus had said again and again to His disciples that they were not of the world: they were in the world but were not of the world. As we look at Christianity today, we can hardly discern any demarcation between the world and Christianity. Where does the world end and where does the church begin? There is no wall. And because there is no wall, those who desire to be the house of God, those who desire to serve as the holy priesthood, are continually being assaulted and attacked. They have no protection and are in affliction and suffer reproach. This is the day that many Nehemiahs need to be raised up by God.

Oh, how we need to see where our heart is! Is our heart with ourselves, seeking for our own welfare? Or is our heart with that little group of people who are struggling to stand for the name and for the testimony of Jesus? Where exactly are we? Are we concerned with the testimony of Jesus? If we are concerned, do we weep before God? Do we pray before Him? Do we offer ourselves to Him, that by His grace we may be used by Him for the building of the wall of the church?

The wall is of tremendous importance. At the very beginning, when God placed Adam and Eve in the beautiful Garden of Eden with all the trees and fruits, there was no wall. It was a garden, but there was no garden wall because God wanted Adam and Eve to be the wall of the garden. For God had said to them, "Watch it. You are the wall. You are to prevent the enemy from coming in. You are to preserve what God has done." Sadly, Adam and Eve failed. They did not watch. And the enemy came in and destroyed the work of God.

THE WALLED CITY

Nevertheless, throughout the centuries, God has been building that wall of separation with His redeemed people. That wall cannot be built by God alone because it belongs to the new creation. It has to be built with us and in us. God has been building that wall, and there will come a day when His people will behold the Holy City, the new Jerusalem (see Revelation 21:2). And what a city it will be! It will be a walled city, and that wall alone will rise 144 cubits (or 72 yards). A wall that tall has never been seen before (see Revelation 21:17). In other words, such a wall speaks of perfect separation. So, today, God is building that wall with His people.

How is that wall described in Revelation? It is a wall made of a most precious stone—jasper, crystal-clear (Revelation 21:18, 11). We are told in Revelation 4 that, when John saw the vision of God on the throne, he saw one like a jasper and a sardius. So jasper speaks of the life, glory and nature of God. Hence, that wall is to be built with the life of God, for it is God's life which brings in separation.

We need to be separated from the world, but what separates us? It is not rules and regulations. Such things may be able to keep us outwardly separated, but they cannot keep us separated inwardly. The children of Israel came out of Egypt, crossed the Red Sea, and yet, deep into the wilderness their heart was still back in Egypt. They did not forget about the garlic, leeks and onions and all other desirable things of Egypt. In short, the world was still in them. It is the life of God which separates us from the world. As the Holy Spirit begins to build up the life of God within us, automatically, that life will separate us from whatever is of the world. That wall will grow taller and taller and taller until it is complete and perfect. But the wall is not only a separation; it is also a protection and a preservation since all which is within the wall is being kept because of this wall. How we need to be kept because of that wall around us!

NEHEMIAH'S VISION

When Nehemiah heard about the situation in Jerusalem, his heart was burdened. He realized that the real need of the remnant who remained there was to rebuild the wall. So he prayed, and God answered his prayer, making it possible for him to go to Jerusalem and rebuild the wall. On the third day after he arrived, and without saying anything to anybody, he rose up in the night and with a few others he went forth to survey the ruin. He rode all around and observed how the wall was in great waste and ruin. The next day he gathered together

those who were there and said to them, "See what distress
we are in, and it is because we have no wall. So let us come
together and build the wall." He so inspired the people that
they said, "Let us rise up and build."

We need to have a deep concern for the *new* Jerusalem—
that is to say, the church. We need to have a deep burden for
the testimony of Jesus. But that burden alone is not enough. We
need to have a vision of the true condition of the people today.
Oftentimes we lack the vision of seeing what is really missing.
We sometimes think everything is rosy, that everything is
all right. We are so used to our environment that we become
accustomed to it. It is the genius of human beings that we can
get accustomed to anything; but it is also a danger because
we become *too* accustomed. We see things around us so often
that we do not take notice of their inadequacy anymore. In
other words, those people of the returned remnant who had
remained in Jerusalem saw the ruin every day, but it did not
mean anything to them anymore.

Is it not possible that we are in the same situation? We are
so accustomed to the ruins of God's people and to the weakness
of His testimony that it does not mean anything to us anymore.
Oh, how we need a vision! How we need to see in the night, as
it were, what a terrible and great distress the ruin continues to
cause. If God should give us a sense of that, I do believe that
He will also give us a desire to rebuild the ruined wall. And this
needs to be shared with all God's people. Oh, that we may all
rise up and say, LET US BUILD!

A CORPORATE BUILDING

The building of this wall as is told of in Nehemiah 3 is
very, very interesting. Although Nehemiah had the burden,
and though he went to Jerusalem to build the wall, it was not
a work which could be done by only one person. It was a work
which had to be done by all the people there. Everybody had

to be involved. It was a work too great for any one person. It is the same for us today, in that, in this building of the wall of the testimony of Jesus, everyone must be involved. It was not only the rulers of half the city of Jerusalem, not only the high priest and the other priests, but it was also the goldsmiths, the perfumers, the servants, and the children who were involved. Some people rose up and built with their sons, and there were some others who rose up and built with their daughters. Everybody was involved in the building of the wall. A goldsmith was involved in handling small but precious things. Then when he began to build the wall with all those stones and all the rubbish, it was a very different work. Now I especially pity the perfumers because their nose was so important. All the dirt and dust may have affected their nose, yet they did not mind because God's testimony was more important than their livelihood. The men, the women, the sons, the daughters, the younger, the older— everyone had to come to the work and build because each could only build the portion which God had given to him or to her. If anyone did not build, there would be a gap created there; and the enemy could thus come in. The people's names are all mentioned here, because God noticed. The nobles of the Tekoites thought it was beneath their dignity, so they let their servants do the job. They would not put their shoulders to the work (see Nehemiah 3:5), and God noticed that, too. But some of them loved the Lord so much that they built an extra portion of the wall.

The various works needing to be done in the building of the wall were all different. Some workers were engaged in building the tower or the gates. Some others were building in the valley and some were building at the corners. But whether it was difficult or easy, they all worked together as one person until, in fifty-two days, the wall had been built.

Is there not a lesson for us today? We are not to let our brothers and sisters put their shoulders to the work while we sit idly by, as though such work is beneath our dignity. If any one of us should not do his or her portion, not only will that wall have a gap, but the fact of that gap will even be recorded in the Book.

RESISTANCE OF THE ENEMY

They built the wall in great difficulty because the enemies of God's people were not happy with it. Their enemies the Samaritans mocked them, and when mocking did not work, they conspired to attack them. So the people had to work with one hand on a load of materials and the other hand on a sword. When the attack did not work, the enemy tried to effect something negative and divisive within and among the people. The rulers, the officers, were hard on the people, and the latter had to sell their sons and daughters to them as slaves. Because of that, murmurs and complaints arose, and these matters had to be straightened out. More than that, the enemy falsely accused Nehemiah of building the wall because he wanted to be king. They even bribed the prophet and the prophetess to prophesy falsely against Nehemiah. Think of that! But thank God, Nehemiah knew what he was doing: he would not let go of the work nor would he be threatened or diverted. Rather, he and the people continued on until the work was completed.

Why were the enemies so afraid? Because if the wall was completely built, the enemies could no longer do anything to God's people again. These enemies would be finished. And that was the reason they were so furious about the building of the wall. And when the wall was finally finished, they knew it was the work of God, and they grew even more afraid.

Who are the ones afraid today? Are we, or are the enemies? If the wall—that is, the testimony of Jesus—is rebuilt, we need not be afraid. The enemy will be afraid because he is defeated.

REVIVAL OF FIRST LOVE

The building of the wall is recorded in chapters 1-7 of Nehemiah. In chapters 8-10 we are told that after the wall was built, Nehemiah gathered the people and had Ezra read the book of the Law. The men, the women, and all those children who could understand were there listening to the word of God, and the word was explained to them. When they listened and understood, they wept aloud because they knew they had sinned against God. They knew that the situation they were in was because of their unfaithfulness to Him. They had to be comforted, and so they said, "This is the day that we should rejoice because of the mercy of God." They read God's word, kept the feast of tabernacles, and renewed their covenant with God. They covenanted with Him once again, and were so determined to serve Him that they placed upon themselves even more than the Lord required. They not only brought their firstfruits to God, they also put upon themselves that each would pay a third of a shekel for the service of the house of God. They also offered wood offerings voluntarily so that the fire would continue to burn in the house of God. In other words, there was a revival of first love towards God (see Revelation 2:4).

IMPORTANCE OF THE WORD OF GOD

If our heart is on the building of the wall, if our heart is to see that there is separation, unity and testimony, then the word of God will work upon our hearts. Every recovery which we know about in the history of God's people is related to His word. Recently, I was reading a huge book on the Reformation; it is probably the best volume on it: not only the Reformation in Germany but in Switzerland, France and England. Again and again in this book the author noted that the Reformation in each of these lands had come about because of the word of God and not anything else. It was God's word which prepared the way. It was His word which was the foundation of the Reformation. We know, of course, that this is a true statement, for the open Bible was the cry of the Reformation.

How important today the word of God is! Oh, how we need to read His word, listen to it and have it explained to us—yet, not only by man but by the Holy Spirit! As we are touched by God's word, then our first love will be renewed.

Have we left our first love? We may go on as usual outwardly like the church had done in Ephesus—with their labor, their work, their understanding, even their discipline still very much intact—yet they had left their first love. So the Lord had declared: "I am against you" (see Revelation 2:1-4). What the Lord is still looking for today is first love towards Him. We need a reviving of first love, and that first love comes by the word of God. Oh, His word is His power unto salvation to all those who believe (see Romans 1:16). So may the word of God become such a power in our midst that our first love may continually be stirred up! So it was that because of God's word His people at Jerusalem made a new covenant with God to love Him fervently and never forsake His house.

CITY LIFE STRENGTHENED

Next, from chapters 11-13 we learn that Jerusalem was large but that very few people lived there. All the leaders, of course, stayed in the city, but most of the people lived outside its wall. So these people, by groups of ten, now cast lots, with one out of every ten moving into the city to stay. Anyone who volunteered to come into the city and live there would be blessed. In other words, the city life had to be strengthened. How good and how pleasant it is for brethren to dwell together in unity (see Psalm 133:1). Not only was there a wall separating them from the world, which thus became their testimony to the world, but they were now being built up together. They strengthened one another. They watched out for one another. They encouraged one another. They loved one another. They were concerned with one another. They were not living far apart, each tending to his or her own interest; rather, they relocated themselves and lived together as one people under one government—the divine government of God.

RECOVERY OF CORPORATE LIFE

Not only worship and service have to be recovered today, but the corporate life of the church must also be recovered. In America we are so brainwashed that all we want is to be independent. We want to live independently. That is good in one sense; but in another sense, it is a great hindrance. We are individuals, and we shall remain as individuals. Our individuality is the gift of God. He never wants us to be uniform; that would be monotonous. God wants variety. However, our individualism must go. We cannot be independent to the extent that we are not related to our brothers and sisters. We need to be related to one another. We not only need to say to the Lord that without Him we can do nothing, we also need to say to our brethren in Christ—and say so, from our heart—that without them, what can we do? God will say that without us He can do nothing; but are we humble enough to say the same thing to our Christian brethren?

We are so independent, and being so as though we live miles and miles apart from each other. I am not talking here about physical miles; but in our spirit we need to move into the city to strengthen the corporate life of the church. We need to be related to one another. Naturally, there are private matters. We do not mean to say that everything in our lives has to be registered or regimented or governed. No, that is not God's will. Yet there needs to be a spirit of relatedness to such a degree that we may pray for one another, that we may seek the mind of the Lord together, in order to strengthen the life of the city—the life of the church.

In the book of Nehemiah we find the recovery of God's testimony. It includes these three aspects: the building of the wall—symbolizing needful separation and unity, the renewing of first love, and the strengthening of corporate living. When these three facets are recovered, recovery is complete. So may the Lord help us.

Let us pray:

> *Dear heavenly Father, we do thank Thee that Thou art calling Thy people to return to Thy original desire and thought. We do praise and thank Thee that there is a return to worship, a return to service. But Lord, there is also the need for a return to testimony so that Thy people will no more be divided from one another; that Thy people will be separated from the world and yet be one together; that Thy people will really have a corporate life which will glorify Thy name; and that first love will be renewed among Thy people. Lord, we are looking for it, we are praying for it, and we do offer ourselves for it. We pray that by Thy mercy and grace Thou wilt stir our hearts so that we may be used of Thee for such recovery. It is for Thine own glory. It is for Thy great name. In the name of our Lord Jesus. Amen.*

ESTHER

GOD'S PROVIDENTIAL CARE

*Esther 2:5-11—There was in Shushan the fortress a certain
Jew, whose name was Mordecai, the son of Jair, the son
of Shimei, the son of Kish, a Benjaminite, who had been
carried away from Jerusalem with the captives who had
been carried away with Jeconiah king of Judah, whom
Nebuchadnezzar the king of Babylon had carried away. And
he brought up Hadassah, that is, Esther, his uncle's daughter;
for she had neither father nor mother—and the maiden was
fair and beautiful—and when her father and mother were
dead, Mordecai took her for his own daughter. And it came
to pass when the king's commandment and his decree was
heard, and when many maidens were gathered together unto
Shushan the fortress, unto the custody of Hegai, that Esther
also was brought into the king's house, unto the custody of
Hegai, keeper of the women. And the maiden pleased him,
and obtained favour before him; and he speedily gave her
her things for purification, and her portions, and the seven
maidens selected to be given her, out of the king's house; and
he removed her and her maids to the best place of the house
of the women. Esther had not made known her people nor
her birth; for Mordecai had charged her that she should not
make it known. And Mordecai walked every day before the
court of the women's house, to know how Esther did, and
what should become of her.*

*Esther 4:13-17—And Mordecai bade to answer Esther:
Imagine not in thy heart that thou shalt escape in the
king's house, more than all the Jews. For if thou altogether*

holdest thy peace at this time, then shall there arise relief and deliverance to the Jews from another place; but thou and thy father's house shall perish. And who knows whether thou art not come to the kingdom for such a time as this? And Esther bade to answer Mordecai: Go, gather together all the Jews that are found in Shushan, and fast for me, and neither eat nor drink three days, night or day: I also and my maidens will fast likewise, and so will I go in unto the king, which is not according to the law; and if I perish, I perish. And Mordecai went his way, and did according to all that Esther had commanded him.

Esther 9:20-22—And Mordecai wrote these things, and sent letters to all the Jews near and far that were in all the provinces of king Ahasuerus, to establish this among them, that they should keep the fourteenth day of the month Adar, and the fifteenth day of the same, yearly, as the days on which the Jews rested from their enemies, and the month that was turned to them from sorrow to joy, and from mourning into a good day; that they should make them days of feasting and joy, and of sending portions one to another, and gifts to the poor.

Let us pray:

Dear heavenly Father, as we continue in Thy presence, we do thank Thee for Thy precious word. We ask Thee, Lord, that Thou wilt give us understanding and wisdom that we may know what Thou art saying to us. We do praise and thank Thee that Thy word is living and operative and is eternal. So we do open ourselves to Thy word to let Thee speak to us. We ask in the name of our Lord Jesus. Amen.

In the Bible Esther is placed after the book Nehemiah; but chronologically speaking, the history in Esther actually occurred before Nehemiah. What happened in the book of Esther occurred during the time of Ahasuerus, who was known as Xerxes in secular history. We know that the events recorded in the book of Nehemiah, and even those in part of Ezra, happened during the time of Artaxerxes Longimanus, who was the son of Xerxes. So historically speaking, what happened during the time of the book of Esther actually stands, time-wise, between the sixth and seventh chapters of Ezra. This was after the return of the Jewish remnant to Jerusalem under Zerubbabel and before the return of the Jews under Ezra.

This book of Esther is unquestionably a historical record, but it is written so vividly and dramatically that it reads like a fascinating short story or novel. We do not know who wrote this book; the only thing we know is that he must have been a Jew in the dispersion because he seemed to know the Persian customs very well. The Jewish Talmud claims that this book was written by the scribes belonging to a great synagogue. Most likely, however, these scribes did not compose the book but merely validated its authoritativeness and performed final editorial supervision.

There are only two books in the Old Testament which bear the name of women: one is Ruth, the other is Esther. Ruth was a Moabitess, a Gentile woman; but she was joined to a Jew because she made the Jewish God her God. Her ultimate union with Boaz resulted in King David and also most importantly in the One who is greater than David—even the Lord Jesus Christ. On the other hand, Esther was a Jewish woman married to a Gentile king, and yet God used her for the deliverance of His people.

Everyone who ever reads this book will not fail to notice one interesting feature—that the name of God is not mentioned anywhere in it. It is definitely a canonical book in the Bible, and yet the name of God or Jehovah is never mentioned. Even in the Song of Solomon, there is at least one place where the name of God is mentioned: 8:6, which is a description of love or jealousy being like the flames of Jah: that is, of Jehovah. Of all the books in the Old Testament this book of Esther is the only one wherein neither the name of God nor the name of Jehovah is ever mentioned. Yet we do find God everywhere in its narrative. Though His name is never mentioned, His hand is nonetheless very evident; for we see how God moved behind the scenes in a hidden way throughout the book's story. What can explain this hidden activity? It is because this book records the history of those Jewish people who did not respond to the call of God to return to Jerusalem to rebuild the temple. These were the ones who remained in the land of captivity, and this book of Esther is concerned with their history.

Furthermore, during this same period God was no longer being referred to as the God of the heavens and of the earth. He now was only addressed or referred to as the God of the heavens because there was no longer any earthly place to put His name. He had indeed put His name in Jerusalem in the temple there; but the temple had been destroyed, Jerusalem was in ruin, and her people had been carried off into captivity. Hence, the name of God was no longer present on earth; it was as though He had completely withdrawn himself into heaven.

But, then, there came the opportunity for the Jewish people to return to Jerusalem to rebuild the temple and let the name of God be upon the earth once again. They were supposed to respond to God's call to return, to rebuild, to live for God and live for His name. Unfortunately, there was only a small remnant of God's people who returned. Most of the Jewish people preferred to remain in the land of captivity because during those seventy captive years they had built up their businesses and their houses and had enjoyed a very good life despite their captivity. Furthermore, as we learned in our discussion of Ezra, they had not been deprived of their religious freedom. They were able to worship God in their synagogues—a very ingenious and convenient human invention. So most of the Jewish people simply remained behind in the land of captivity, not bothering to return. In other words, they lived for themselves and not for God. They preferred their own well-being rather than the well-being of God. And because they stayed behind, the name of God was not even mentioned by the composer of their history. Because of their continued rebellion and disobedience, they remained under the sentence of God, who had said of them: *Lo-ammi*—"not My people" (see Hosea 1:9-10; 2:23). Officially, He had disowned them; but thank God, He did not forget them. God would still take care of them, yet no longer in a public but in a hidden way.

GOD'S CALLING

We know that the study of God's word is to be undertaken for our admonition. Is there any analogy to be noted between this book's events and our historical situation today? Or to phrase it another way, is this book relevant to our own day? Moreover, what are the lessons which God wants to teach us? We know we are living in the last days. And so, it is a time of the recovery of the testimony of God because our Lord is coming soon, and the call has gone forth for His people to come out of Babylon—that is, out of religious confusion—and to return to Jerusalem, the city of peace and harmony. In short, God is calling His people to return to the *simplicity* and the *sincerity* that are in Christ Jesus (see II Corinthians 1:12; 11:3). We have to return, stand on the ground of that simplicity of Christ, and then be built up together as the house of God so that His name may once again be known in this fallen world.

This is God's calling; and yet, how many of His people have heard that call? How many have responded to it? How many really love God and live for Him and for His testimony? How many of God's people simply love themselves too much and are so comfortable that they do not care about His name? Yes, they are religious, and yet religious for their own comfort, not for the testimony of God and for His name. Even today, most of God's people still remain in Babylonian captivity: there is no separation between the church and the world, and God's people are living in great religious confusion. Accordingly, if we are not where we should be or are not what we ought to be, then in a sense we have failed God. You recall our Lord Jesus saying that unless we deny ourselves, take up our cross and follow Him, we are not His disciples. Are we His disciples? Do we truly deny ourselves? Do we really take up our cross and follow the Lord? Wherever the Lamb is, are we there? If not, then we are not His disciples. Even though God has not disowned us as His children, so far as our life is concerned, there is no testimony to His name coming forth.

FAILURE TO RESPOND TO GOD'S CALLING

When the Jewish people did not return to Jerusalem and instead remained in the land of captivity, what happened? Let us please note that had they all returned to Jerusalem, the book of Esther would not have been written. There would have been no necessity for such history. The reason we have this history recorded in Esther is because of the failure of God's people to respond to His call. They remained behind in the land of captivity because they thought they could live a comfortable and peaceful life. But lo and behold, they soon found themselves in the grip of the enemy. If we are not where we ought to be or if we are not what we should be in Christ Jesus, we shall be exposed to all the power and all the oppression of the enemy. Indeed, because God's people back in the days of Esther had decided to remain in the land of captivity, that race was in danger of being completely annihilated. Not only those who lived in captivity would have been annihilated, but we learn from this book of Esther that even those who had obeyed God's command to return to Jerusalem would also have been destroyed. Think of that!

Do let us realize that if we do not obey God and live for Him, we shall be exposed to the enemy's attack and shall come under his power. Furthermore, instead of encouraging those of our brethren who are faithful to the Lord, we shall discourage them and even bring danger to them. This is a very serious situation.

Let us look at Christianity today. Is it not a picture like the Jews in the land of captivity during the time of Esther? The

Jews born then did not even dare to make known their ethnic identity. Mordecai commanded Esther not to tell anybody of her Jewish birth or kindred. They and their Jewish brethren tried to hide their identity because they were hated and despised by the world of that day. Similarly, Christianity today has fallen so deeply in this regard. Yet this should not surprise us since the Bible has predicted that there will be a general falling away before the coming back to earth of the Lord. In fact, apostasy has already begun in Christianity. We find in some quarters of Christian theology the notion that God is dead. Furthermore, Christianity has become so humanized that in some places God is completely out of the picture. We are so ashamed of being called Christians that we try to hide our identity, thinking that by doing so we shall be protected, that we will be preserved; but we are deceived.

Back in the days of Esther the Jewish people entered upon a very dark chapter in their history. They nearly came into total annihilation, and it was all because they were not where they should have been and were not what they ought to have been. Is there something here which speaks to us for our day? How important it is that we, as God's people, truly put Him first instead of putting ourselves first! How important it is that we be faithful to God's call, that we be concerned with His name and with His testimony instead of being occupied with our own things! How important it is that we be where God wants us to be! If not, we will suffer and even bring our brethren into suffering.

GOD'S PROVIDENTIAL CARE

Another feature we can notice in this book of Esther is evidence of the presence of divine Providence throughout the entire narrative. The *name* of God is not mentioned, that is true, but His *hand* can be seen everywhere. At this time God was not referred to or addressed as the God of the earth because the world dominion had passed into the hands of the Gentiles.

Although He was not recognized as such, nevertheless, the heavens still ruled over the affairs of men (see Daniel 4:25). In every little thing and big thing, God's hand was there. Even in the sleepless night of a king, even in the divorce of a queen, or even in the bringing up of a queen—in every instance, God was working behind the scenes. He was not seen, and yet He was working. His providential care was over His rebellious people.

This ought to give us great encouragement. We may sometimes feel that the world is so wicked and the power of darkness so prevailing that we often wonder and are perplexed. But let us remember one important fact: God is still on the throne, and the heavens still rule in the affairs of men. God is for us no matter how rebellious we are; and who then, can be against us? His providential hand is moving all over the world in our individual concerns, in corporate matters, and in national and international affairs. God's hand is continually active and He moves in a mysterious way His countless wonders to perform; and this ought to give us great courage and confidence.

BACKGROUND HISTORY

Esther, chapter one, gives us the background to the narrative we find in this book, and there the reign of Ahasuerus is mentioned. Actually, Ahasuerus is not the name of this king; rather, it is a title like majesty, emperor, king. This Ahasuerus was the one who ruled over one hundred and twenty-seven provinces all the way from the eastern Mediteranean to India to Ethiopia. In other words, it was this Ahasuerus who had the rule over such a vast amount of the earth; and in secular history, we know that this particular Ahasuerus was named Xerxes. And in his third year Xerxes gathered all the princes and nobles from these one hundred and twenty-seven provinces to Shushan, the capital. There they feasted together and he showed forth his wealth and his grandeur to them for one hundred and eighty days. Secular history tells us the reason why Xerxes had

gathered all his servants together for such a long period and why
he showed forth his grandeur: it all was done in preparation for
this Persian emperor's attack on Greece. Xerxes had wanted to
invade Greece because at that time Greece was emerging as a
new major power. So he gathered his servants to Shushan and
tried to prepare them for his invasion of Greece.

After these one hundred and eighty days Xerxes held a
feast of seven days for all those officials and civil servants
who were present in Shushan. During these feast days, of
course, there was much drinking and carousing which went on
in the Persian court. It was not until the last day when, most
likely because he and his nobles and court officials were in a
drunken state, Xerxes summoned his queen, Vashti, to appear
before this gathering and show forth her beauty. *Vashti*, in the
Persian language, means "beautiful." But Vashti had enough
decency not to expose herself before this drunken assemblage;
so she refused to come. Because she refused, Xerxes naturally
became very angry. From history we know that this king was
a person who easily gave himself up to great wrath and did
many angry things. In this instance he became so angry that
he called his counselors together and asked them what should
be done. According to the patriarchal tradition of those days,
a man was king over his house and family. So the counselors
declared to Xerxes that this was not a matter affecting just one
person. They observed that if all the nobles' wives should hear
about this situation and begin to despise their husbands, what
would be the consequences for the empire? They suggested
that Queen Vashti must be deposed; and so it was done. Now
that is the background to all which was about to unfold.

Though this is secular history, God's hand lay behind it; and
so in the second chapter we will observe God's hidden hand
of activity. After Xerxes' wrath subsided, he began to think
fondly of his wife. Yet he obviously could not bring her back
since he had already deposed her. So his servants suggested,
"Why not gather beautiful women from all over the empire,

let them be prepared for you, and then you can choose a queen from among them?" So it was done.

We come to the seventh year of the reign of this Ahasuerus. From the third to the seventh year Xerxes was absent on military expedition fighting against Greece. Unfortunately for him he met defeat on land at Thermopylae, followed by defeat by sea at the battle of Salamis. Now completely vanquished, Xerxes returned to Shushan and naturally began to seek for comfort and solace elsewhere. And that is why it was in the seventh year of his reign that the story involving Esther herself began to move forward.

ESTHER'S CROWNING AS QUEEN

During this time all these women from around the empire had been gathered and were being prepared. For a period of twelve months they had to be purified and beautified with perfume and other cosmetics. It so happened that Esther was numbered among these many women. The Hebrew name for Esther is *Hadassah*, which means "myrtle"; and we learn that myrtle grows in lowland areas. It is thus symbolic of humility and lowliness. But her Persian name was Esther; and in the Persian language, *Esther* means "star," symbolic of exaltation. She was an orphan, her father and mother having died early; therefore, her cousin Mordecai, who must have been much older than she, took her in and raised her up as his daughter. *Mordecai*, in the Persian language, means "little man." We shall find that these meanings figure quite significantly towards the end of the narrative of Esther.

Why did Mordecai and Esther remain in the land of captivity? Why did they not return to Jerusalem? Probably it was not their fault, because if one computes the pertinent years, Esther had not been born when Zerubbabel returned to Jerusalem and Mordecai was himself just a lad. Hence, it was not the fault of Mordecai or Esther, but most likely the fault of their respective parents in not obeying God. Their parents had lived so comfortably in the land of captivity that they refused to return with others to Jerusalem to build the house of God, and that is why Mordecai and Esther had been among those who remained in the land of captivity. And though these two were not at fault, they nonetheless were not where they should have been. And because they were in the wrong place, Esther was numbered among the other chosen women of the empire. Humanly speaking, it was a great honor to be taken for the king, even to be a concubine; not to say, later on, to be chosen the queen. But from God's viewpoint it was a great degradation because His command had been that His people should not be intermarried with Gentiles but were to keep the race pure for the coming of the Messiah. This was another facet to the disobedience of God's people to His command. So far as man was concerned, Esther's selection was a great honor; so far as God was concerned, it was a great shame.

Mordecai was at this time so ashamed of being a Jew that he made every effort to hide his identity. He told Esther not to tell anybody who she was, and Esther obeyed. Meanwhile, she had been taken and soon found favor with everyone. On the day that she was first summoned to come into the king's presence, the latter was so pleased with her that he had a crown placed upon her head and made her queen. There was a great feast for her that was called Esther's Feast. Of course, Esther would not have become queen had Vashti not been deposed. We can therefore discern God's hand behind all things. This is the content of chapter 2.

HAMAN

In chapter 3 Xerxes is seen raising up Haman, an Agagite, to be the prime minister of his empire. It is most interesting that Haman was identified as an Agagite because Agag had been the king of the Amalekites. And we may remember that after God's people had come out of Egypt the first battle they fought was against the Amalekites in the wilderness. When the Israelites were weary from their journey, the Amalekites took advantage and came and attacked them at their rear (see Deuteronomy 25:17-18). So Moses went up a hill to intercede, and whenever his hands were uplifted, Joshua, who was down below on the plain, won the advantage. But whenever Moses grew tired and his hands fell down, the enemy gained the advantage. Hence, Moses' hands had to be supported by Hur and Aaron until the victory was totally won (see Exodus 17). It was recorded at the end of that chapter that God declared He would wage an eternal war against the Amalekites until their name was totally blotted out from the earth because the hand of the Amalekites had been against the throne of Jehovah (see Exodus 17:16 margin). In other words, the Amalekites were enemies of God. Their hand was upon the throne of God to dethrone Him. God would therefore make eternal war against them until they would be completely destroyed.

Later history has shown that the Amalekites gave the children of God many problems. For instance, during the time of Samuel God had commanded King Saul to wipe out the Amalekites to the last man, but Saul did not obey. He kept the finest of their flocks and herds and preserved the life of Agag, the king of the Amalekites. And even though Samuel ended up killing Agag, evidently Saul had allowed some of the royal family to escape. And because of that, many years later this same enemy of God had continued to flourish. And how ironic that because Saul had not entirely wiped out the Amalekites, his descendant Mordecai, a fellow Benjaminite, had to confront Haman, the descendant of Agag! How true it is that when the fathers fail, the children suffer the consequences. Had Saul fully obeyed God, there would have been no Haman. How important it is that we obey God.

THE CONFLICT OF FLESH AND SPIRIT

The Amalekite in Scripture represents the flesh because Amalek was the descendant of Esau, and we know that Esau represents the flesh. The flesh always strives against the spirit. It always tries to usurp the throne of God and God has therefore declared an eternal war against the flesh. And we find that the flesh and the world always work together, for we learn how Xerxes raised up Haman and in turn Haman served Xerxes. The flesh always serves the world, and the world is always in alliance with the flesh. But where should the flesh go? It needs to be hanged! That is where the flesh should go. In short, it has to be crucified (see Galatians 5:24).

The most wonderful thing here is that before Xerxes had raised up Haman, God had already arranged events which placed Esther in the palace. God will always be one step ahead: before the enemy came on the scene in the story of Esther, God had already provided. Nobody else knew about it, but He knew. And such is the providence of God.

NO COMPROMISE

We learn from chapters 4 and 5 that the conflict grows. Haman was raised up by the king to have second place in the empire except for the throne itself, and the king even gave orders that all his servants and officials should bow down before Haman. On the one hand, there was Haman; on the other, there was Mordecai. At that time Mordecai habitually sat at the gate of the palace because he had been made a petty officer—a small official. And whenever Haman passed through the palace gates, all those who were there would rise up and bow; but Mordecai refused to do so. We have already noted that Mordecai was not where he should have been. Had he not been there, there would have been no problem; but unfortunately, he was there. Yet thank God, he had not fallen so far as to make compromise with God's enemy. Moreover, this personal crisis stirred Mordecai up, and consequently, he increased higher and higher spiritually.

Why did Mordecai not bow down to Haman? He had apparently remembered God's word—how God had declared eternal war upon the Amalekites. How, then, could he bow down to God's enemy? He could not do that, for that would be denying God. And because Mordecai refused to bow to Haman, he got into trouble; yet, not only for himself but also for the whole Jewish race. Was it worth it? What would you have done? Would you have compromised?

THE DECREE

Haman became so angry that the thought of simply wiping out the life of Mordecai was too small an issue for him. He was determined to wipe out the entire Jewish race. He explained to the king: "There is a people among your subjects throughout the empire who have a different law, who do not obey your law, and are a trouble in the land. Why not annihilate them, and I will give you ten thousand talents of silver to enrich your treasury?" And the king replied: "All right; you have the money; and I allow you to take this action to destroy, kill, and annihilate." So a royal decree went forth throughout the whole empire to the effect that on a certain day, the thirteenth day of Adar (and Adar on our calendar today is February or March), all over the empire, the enemies of the Jews have permission to rise up and kill them and take their spoils.

When the news went forth, there arose great sorrow, weeping, and fasting among all the Jews. Mordecai, of course, put on sackcloth and wept. Esther was in the palace. She did not know anything of what was going on, but she was told that Mordecai was in sackcloth. So she asked her servant to bring garments to Mordecai that he could change. She thought it was merely an outward thing, but Mordecai refused. Then Mordecai asked those close to the queen to inform Esther what had happened and to tell her, "You must go in before the king and plead for your people." But Esther said, "I cannot do that because there is a law of the Persian court that unless the king calls for you, you cannot enter the inner court. If you enter without being called, you will be killed. And as it happened, I myself have not been called for the past thirty days." Mordecai responded, however, by declaring to his daughter: "Do not think because you are in the palace your life will be spared. If you do not do this, relief and deliverance will come forth from elsewhere; and you and your fathers will perish." Mordecai believed that God was able, and so he told Esther, "Perhaps you are in the palace at such a time as this for this very purpose."

GOD'S PERMISSIVE WILL

We know that Esther's being in the palace was not the direct will of God but His permissive will; for were she living in the direct will of God, she would be in Jerusalem. But God allowed this development; and we can see that He can even use human failure to serve His purpose. He can even use His permissive will as His direct will to accomplish His purpose. Is that not wonderful?

Esther rose to the occasion. She sent a message to Mordecai: "All right, you call all the Jews together in Shushan and pray and fast for three days and three nights, and I will do the same. Then I will go against the law. And if I perish, I perish." In other words, she would rather perish in the will of God than go against His will. In this particular situation, which was highly abnormal because God's people were not where they should have been and because the crisis created would either crush them or strengthen them, we see Mordecai and Esther rising up in their spirits to respond most positively to God. How wonderful!

THE TABLES ARE TURNED

From chapters 5 to 9 the tables are turned. It is quite fascinating to read. Without having been summoned to appear, Esther went into the king's presence to ask for something, and at once the king stretched out his golden scepter. For the king to do this meant that the person entering was accepted and permitted to approach the king. King Xerxes said, "Queen Esther, what do you want, even up to the half of my kingdom?" And Esther replied, "I want you and Haman to come to my feast today." The king accepted and told Haman, "Make haste." Haman was so happy over this because only he, of all people, had been invited to the queen's table with the king. But when he came out of the palace and saw Mordecai sitting there still unmoved at his approach, he grew exceedingly angry. Haman went home and told his wife and all his friends about all the honor and greatness that had been heaped upon him, and then added—"But that Mordecai!" So his wife and friends suggested, "Why not make a gallows fifty cubits high and go to the king and ask to have Mordecai hanged there?" So they made the gallows—in essence, a cross.

At this moment everything seemed to be going against God's people, but God was working. That night Xerxes could not sleep. (Brethren, let us not complain if we cannot sleep; God may have a reason for it; instead, let us thank Him for our sleepless nights.) Because Xerxes could not sleep, he asked his court officials to read to him the chronicles of the empire. This is one of the funniest aspects to this entire episode, because if a person cannot sleep, he should read something that will put him to sleep. The imperial chronicles would probably have been the most tedious kind of literature to have asked to be read; nevertheless, this is what the king requested be read to him! And as these chronicles were being read to him, these officials came to the account of what had happened years before when one day, two of the king's chamberlains who guarded his door had sought to murder him. But Mordecai had learned of it and told Queen Esther who in turn informed the king. The matter was investigated and found to be true, and the two chamberlains were hanged. This incident had then been recorded in the imperial chronicles.

Now when the king heard this chronicle account, he

immediately inquired: "What honor and what reward has been given to Mordecai for this?" And they said, "Nothing." Is that not strange—something this important done and yet no reward bestowed? Once again we can see God behind this oversight. Perhaps Mordecai may have mused within himself: "I performed such a good service for the king, and yet he has forgotten me." He may even have murmured against it; yet, as we shall learn, God had a reason for this delay in honor having been shown Mordecai.

Let us understand that when we do something good and nobody seems to appreciate it or reward us for it, God has a reason for it. Let us not feel bad or complain about it. The reward will come at the right time, for if the reward comes too early, it will not be that good.

So Xerxes said to his court officials: "Mordecai should be rewarded. But who is in the outer court?" It was early in the morning, and at this very moment Haman had arrived for the purpose of asking the king to hang Mordecai. Before Haman could do so, however, the king said to him: "What do you think should be done to a person whom the king wishes to honor?" Haman immediately thought to himself, "He must be thinking of me!" So Haman came up with the best scenario he could think of. "Oh," he replied, "let the one whom the king wishes to honor be clothed with the king's robe. Let that man sit on the king's horse with the crown on his head. Let one of the most noble princes in the kingdom go before him and cry out, 'This is the way the king wishes to honor that one.'" And the king said, "Go, hasten, and do all this to Mordecai the Jew."

How did the king know that Mordecai was a Jew? And why did he say to Haman, "Make haste"? I wonder if King Xerxes had begun to suspect that Haman had overstepped the proper bounds. After Haman had been placed in such a high position, second only to the king, gradually, he had grown ambitious within himself, as is reflected by his very suggestion made to Xerxes to have the king's robe and crown and the royal horse.

So the king said, "Very well; but make haste to do it to the Jew." Stunned by this, Haman nonetheless had to carry out the king's order. But after he had done so, he went home and covered his head in shame.

FEAST OF PURIM

Shortly afterwards some of the king's chamberlains came to collect Haman and said, "Come to the queen's feast." When the king, queen and Haman were together at Esther's banquet, Xerxes again asked Esther what she wanted. She pleaded for her life and for the life of her people. She explained as follows: "Someone in your kingdom has sold us, I and my people, to be destroyed, killed, and annihilated. If we had been merely sold as bondmen and bondwomen, I would not have said a word; for our affliction cannot be compared with the loss to the king." So the king said, "Who is that person, and where is he? Who is he who dares to have such evil thoughts?" And Esther said, "A foe and enemy is this wicked Haman!"

The king in his wrath left the banquet hall and went out to the palace garden; and Haman knew there was trouble. So he remained behind and tried to beg the queen. In doing so he fell on the couch where Esther was reclining, begging for his life. At that moment the king came back inside and said, "He is even trying to force my queen!" Immediately, the court officials present covered Haman's face. That was the sign that he was to be killed. Hence, again we discern the providence of God. One of the chamberlains present reported to the king: "Haman has made a gallows at his home on which to hang Mordecai." So the king said, "Hang Haman on it." Is not that the judgment of God: that the flesh should be hanged? We can see here how the tables had definitely been turned, and there was inaugurated the Feast of Purim which the Jews have continually observed even to this day.

THE OVERCOMERS

We have just reviewed the history of Esther's day. But what is the lesson for us to take away from this review? I believe there is a very good lesson here for us. And it centers upon the fact that there are overcomers in every situation, no matter what the condition. When we look at the broad picture here, the Jewish remnant who had returned to Jerusalem to rebuild the house of God can represent the overcomers of the church. These overcomers are not to be viewed as super-Christians, they are simply normal believers. And then there are Christians who are not where they should be and are not what they ought to be; nevertheless, by the grace of God, there is always a remnant—those who respond to God's call and His grace. And such are the overcomers of the church, whereas those who remain in captivity are the defeated. And yet, even among those who remain behind, there will still be a Mordecai and an Esther. Even in the place where God's people ought not to be, by the grace and mercy of God, there will still be people who are able to stand up for Him. There will be overcomers even in places where we would least expect them.

On the other hand, in those places where we would expect there to be overcomers, there will be those who are overcome. The spiritual condition is not automatically right just because the position is right. Among those who returned to Jerusalem there were some people who could not stand the opposition and privation, and they therefore returned to the land of captivity. Even among those who remained in Jerusalem, some of the Jewish nobles there oppressed the people. Moreover, in the building of the wall, some of these nobles would not put their shoulders to the work (see Nehemiah 3:5). So let us not think that because we are in the right place, we automatically are right spiritually. That is the reason why, even in the church at Philadelphia, there is the call to overcome; for someone even there may lose his crown (see Revelation 3:7a, 11-12a).

Thank God, even in Laodicea, Thyatira and Sardis there is the call to overcome. There will be overcomers even in the wrong places. Though people may be in this or that wrong place, they may be right with God, and He notices them. Obviously, we should be in the right place, for it is far more conducive for us to be there in developing the right attitude and the right condition, but that does not mean people who are in the wrong place cannot be right with God. Now I believe that this is what God wants to teach His people from this book of Esther.

Chapter 10 is the conclusion to the story of Esther, and the conclusion is centered around the greatness of Mordecai. Though as we learned earlier he was a little man in both physical stature and position, this little man nonetheless became great by the grace of God because he had the honor of God and the welfare of God's people in his heart. We, too, are little people; but God can make us great if we put His honor first and if we are concerned with the well-being of His people. So this is the book of Esther. May the Lord help us.

Let us pray:

Dear heavenly Father, we do praise and thank Thee that even though we may be unfaithful, Thou art always faithful because Thou canst not deny Thyself. Oh, how we do pray that we may be faithful. How we do thank and praise Thee because Thy providential care is everywhere. We do experience Thy providential care even in the days of our rebellion. Oh, how gracious, how merciful Thou art. And we do ask Thee, Lord, that Thou wilt strengthen our faith and encourage us so that we may press on to be where we ought to be and to be what we ought to be in order that Thou mayest be glorified. In the name of our Lord Jesus. Amen.

JOB

THE BENEVOLENT GOVERNMENT OF GOD
AND SUFFERING

Job 1:1-12—There was a man in the land of Uz whose name was Job; and this man was perfect and upright, and one that feared God and abstained from evil. And there were born to him seven sons and three daughters. And his substance was seven thousand sheep, and three thousand camels, and five hundred yoke of oxen, and five hundred she-asses, and very many servants; and this man was greater than all the children of the east.

And his sons went and made a feast in the house of each one on his day; and they sent and invited their three sisters to eat and to drink with them. And it was so, when the days of the feasting were gone about, that Job sent and hallowed them; and he rose up early in the morning, and offered up burnt-offerings according to the number of them all; for Job said, It may be that my children have sinned, and cursed God in their hearts. Thus did Job continually.

And there was a day when the sons of God came to present themselves before Jehovah; and Satan came also among them. And Jehovah said to Satan, Whence comest thou? And Satan answered Jehovah and said, From going to and fro in the earth, and from walking up and down in it. And Jehovah said to Satan, Hast thou considered my servant Job, that there is none like him on the earth, a perfect and an upright man, one that feareth God and abstaineth from evil? And Satan answered Jehovah and said, Doth Job fear God for nought? Hast not thou made a hedge about him, and about his house, and about all that he hath on every side? Thou hast blessed the work of his hands, and his substance is spread abroad in the land. But put forth thy hand now and touch all that he hath, and see if he will not curse thee to thy face! And Jehovah said to Satan, Behold, all that he hath is in thy hand; only upon himself put not forth thy hand. So Satan went forth from the presence of Jehovah.

Job 42:1-6—And Job answered Jehovah and said, I know that thou canst do everything, and that thou canst be hindered in no thought of thine. Who is he that obscureth counsel without knowledge? therefore have I uttered what I did not understand; things too wonderful for me, which I knew not. Hear, I beseech thee, and I will speak: I will demand of thee, and inform me. I had heard of thee by the hearing of the ear, but now mine eye seeth thee: wherefore I abhor myself, and repent in dust and ashes.

Let us pray:

Dear heavenly Father, as we wait upon Thy presence, we do ask that the light of Thy countenance will shine upon us. We pray that Thy word will come forth and reach our hearts that we may really bow down and worship Thee because Thou art truly our God, our Lord. We ask in Thy precious name. Amen.

It is commonly acknowledged that Job is the most ancient book in the whole Bible. Its events happened in the time of the patriarchs, probably after Abraham and certainly before Moses; and it was written before Moses wrote his Pentateuch.

We do not know who wrote this book. It could have been Job himself. According to the Jewish Talmud, it was Moses. But most probably Moses did not compose it, although he introduced it into the sacred Hebrew canon. When he fled from Egypt and sojourned in the land of Midian, probably it was there that he heard the story of Job. So he introduced it to the children of Israel and it was passed on to the later generations.

If this be the case, then I think it is very instructive; this is because this first book of the Bible does not deal with the nation of Israel but deals with a man who actually lived before the nation of Israel was formed, and hence he was certainly outside the pale of Israel. That shows us God's interest is in all of mankind and not just in one nation. Even though Israel was later blessed by the Lord, we learn in the book of Job that God's interest is concerned with mankind as a whole. Furthermore, if it was Moses who introduced this book to the children of Israel, then Moses was not as narrow-minded and biased as later generations have made the lawgiver out to be.

This book of Job is classified among the wisdom books of the Bible. These wisdom books are Job, Proverbs and Ecclesiastes, all three of which deal with the practical life of man. They approach this matter from three different perspectives, and yet all three reach the same conclusion—the fear of the Lord:

"The fear of Jehovah is the beginning of wisdom" (Proverbs 9:10).

"The fear of the Lord, that is wisdom" (Job 28:28).

"Fear God, and keep his commandments; for this is the whole [duty] of man" (Ecclesiastes 12:13).

Proverbs is concerned with daily life; Ecclesiastes deals with the matter of prosperity; and Job is focused on the issue of adversity. But whether life is in prosperity or in adversity, it is equally true in both these life situations that the fear of the Lord is the beginning of wisdom.

Job is also listed among the poetic books of the Bible, of which there are five in the Old Testament. Aside from chapters 1 and 2 of Job, and apart from chapter 42:7-17 and a few other fragments that are in prose form, all the rest from chapter 3 to 42:6 is written in poetic verse. That is the reason Job is also classified among the poetic books. All such books deal with the problems of human life throughout all ages. Job deals with the problem of suffering; Psalms, with the problem of worship; Proverbs, with the problem of conduct in daily life; Ecclesiastes, with the problem of the chief goal of life; and Song of Songs, with the problem of love. But whatever problems there may be in life, the solution is only found in the Lord.

JOB WAS A REAL PERSON

The very name Job, in Hebrew, means "the afflicted, persecuted one." In Arabic, it means "he who turns around, repents, and returns to God." Job was a real person who lived in the land of Uz. He was not an imaginary figure. The story of his life here is not fiction but is historical fact. We know that he was a real person because his name is mentioned in other places of Scripture. For instance, Ezekiel 14:14, 20 mentions Job as being among the three righteous men on earth: Noah, Daniel and Job. Now we know Noah was a real person and Daniel was also a real person; so we can justifiably assume that Job was a real person as well. In the New Testament, in James 5:11, we find the endurance and patience of Job is mentioned. So Job must have been a real person.

Job lived in the land of Uz, which means "a soft, sandy soil." Oftentimes in the olden days, a place or area was named after a prominent person who had lived there. If this be true, then we can try to discover if there is any man called Uz in the Old Testament, and we can find three: in Genesis 10:23, the Uz mentioned there was the grandson of Shem, who was one of Noah's three sons; in Genesis 22:21, the Uz named there was the firstborn of Nahor, the brother of Abraham; and in Genesis 36:28, the Uz told of was a descendant of Esau.

Who, then, was the person after whom the land of Uz was named? I can only tell how I feel personally, and others can draw their own conclusion. Probably, the Uz under discussion here was the firstborn of Nahor, Abraham's brother. Now why do I think so? This is because later on in Job we shall learn of a young man who comes upon the scene and plays a significant role in the story of Job; his name was Elihu and he was a Buzite from Buz. Now we learn from Genesis 22:21 that Nahor had another son, who was named Buz. And hence, Elihu was probably related to Job. This, of course, is only my supposition, but others may think differently. Nevertheless, this man Job lived in the land of Uz.

At that time Uz was probably an area in the northern part of the Arabian Desert. So Job lived in that part of the land outside of Palestine which extended up to the river Euphrates. He lived in the days of the patriarchs. He was a man who was perfect and upright—yet not sinless perfect but was perfect in the sense that his heart was perfect towards God. He was a righteous man, one who feared God, and abstained from evil. "Fear God" was the secret of his being perfect; "abstain from evil" was the result of his uprightness. He was a good man. As a matter of fact, there was none at that time as perfect and upright as Job. He was also a wealthy man. He had many sheep, camels, asses, and many servants. Most likely he was a sheik, a prince or even a desert king. Moreover, Job was one of the wise men of the east, but he was greater than these men of the east. The "men of the east" is a term which refers to those who lived in the region extending from Egypt up to the Euphrates, and they were noted for their wisdom. So, most likely Job in his day was numbered among the wise men of the east, and we are further told that he was greater than all those men of the east (see Job 1:3b AV). Furthermore, he was a person who served God because He had repeatedly referred to him as "My servant Job."

In the patriarchal age the head of the family was also the priest of the family. In his function as the family priest he would offer sacrifices for his children in order to make atonement for them. He had a very happy family of seven sons and three daughters, and all were good. These brothers and sisters loved one another. They were all truly one family together and were a happy family. So that we could legitimately say that Job's was the best specimen of everything wholesome and good which anyone could expect of a person on earth.

THE BENEVOLENT GOVERNMENT OF GOD

The book of Job is most valuable. There are so many important and practical lessons we could learn from this book; but to me, the central teaching of Job revolves around the sovereignty and government of God. Our God is the Creator; He is the Sovereign of the universe; therefore government belongs to Him. In the book of Esther we see, in a much more hidden way, God's providential care for His rebellious people. That, too, is part of God's government. But in Job we see the moral or benevolent government of God upon a beloved one of His.

The government of God is a tremendous issue in this universe. It is something we all need to see. He is God; therefore, government is in His hand. He rules and overrules all things. His government is both legal and benevolent. It is legal in the sense that He has the right to govern and rule. He has the right to do anything He likes, and nobody is to question Him. That is legal. At the same time, though, His government is also benevolent; it is for our good.

We read in the Scriptures, this: "I know the thoughts that I think toward you, saith the Lord, thoughts of peace, and not of evil, to give you in your latter end a hope" (Jeremiah 29:11).

Also, David proclaimed: "How precious are thy thoughts unto me, O God! how great is the sum of them!" (Psalm 139:17)

So we know that God's thoughts towards us are benevolent and good. His government towards us is for peace and not for evil. Yet, because His thoughts are higher than our thoughts and His ways are higher than our ways, oftentimes, we do not understand. We question His government; we question His dealings. We insist on asking, "Why?" We may even demand that God give us an explanation. In one sense it can be said that whatever we cannot explain, we will not accept; and oftentimes, we will even rebel. Now that is human. But we must understand that God does not need to explain everything to us. He has a reason for something He has done but He does not need to explain; and even if He should explain, it still may not solve our problem. The solution to our problem concerning the government of God lies not in why but in Who. If we see Him, if we know Him as to who He truly is, then everything is solved. Unfortunately, this is a very difficult matter for us to come to terms with.

SUFFERING

In this book of Job the government of God is especially related to the problem of suffering. Now suffering has been a problem throughout all ages. Why is there suffering? Does God want us to suffer? Who is to suffer? What are the consequences of suffering? Let us be clear: God does not want us to suffer. His thoughts towards us are for peace and not for evil. Then why are there sufferings upon this earth? Of course, if we trace back to the origin of suffering, we must acknowledge that it is the result of sin. When sin entered this world, immediately, the earth was cursed, and suffering began: for instance, henceforth man must sweat to make a living, and woman must suffer pain in childbirth. Therefore, generally speaking, we can say that suffering is the result of sin. Because of sin, suffering is the norm of life upon the earth.

Nevertheless, thank God, He can turn suffering into good. Suffering can be educational today for God's children. In other words, He uses suffering and adversity to mature His children in order that they may reach sonship (see Proverbs 3:11-12; Hebrews 12:5-11; Romans 8:18-19). Only God can do that, and He is doing that with His beloved ones. Regrettably, we oftentimes do not understand and think we do not deserve to suffer. Why is it that God does not prosper us? Sometimes we may even think He is not doing according to what He has promised. We feel that if we fear God, surely we shall be blessed by Him. If we follow Him and do His will, there shall be no suffering come upon us; but because just the opposite has occurred we are offended by the Lord.

The offense of the Lord is a very essential lesson we have to learn. As a matter of fact, to be offended by the Lord is not an experience for a novice or a babe in Christ. If you are a babe in Christ you will never be offended by the Lord because all that you suffer can be explained by your sin, your flesh, and so forth. So it is not the Lord that is offending you. We oftentimes think it is the Lord that offends us. No; it is your own sin, your own flesh, the world, and not the Lord. But for those who truly love God and are one hundred per cent for Him, sometimes He does not act according to His promise. These committed ones have every right to expect God to do certain things, but He does not; and it is at that point that the offense of the Lord becomes a great problem.

John the Baptist came close to being offended by the Lord. He was one who knew the Lord, who was His forerunner, who gave good testimony concerning the Lord, and who fully expected Him to take a certain action. John had every right to expect that of Him. Yet the Lord was doing things for other people but not for John the Baptist who was the closest to Him. The Lord sent word to John: "Yes, I am doing all these things: I heal the sick, I open the eyes of the blind, I cause the lame to walk, and I raise up the dead; but I am not doing all this for you. If you are not offended, you are blessed" (see Matthew 11:2-6).

This man Job had every right to expect God to bless him and not to be afflicted. But he was afflicted, and he was offended by the Lord. However, later on, we learn how this man was immensely blessed because he was no longer offended at the end.

These are the general observations to be made about this book; and now we wish to go into it in greater detail.

GOD CHALLENGES SATAN WITH JOB

The first two chapters of Job form a segment cast totally in prose. There was a man whose name was Job, and he lived in the land of Uz. We have already mentioned that he was a great man—probably a sheik, a prince, or a king and one who knew and feared God, and who lived uprightly; and God had blessed him greatly. Then the scene suddenly shifts from earth to somewhere above the earth. There are days when God sets up His court, but most likely it is not situated in the third heaven where the throne of God is permanently set because Satan has been cast out from there (see Ezekiel 28:16).

So there in the heavenly places (as is said in Ephesians where it mentions the heavenlies), on "the day" God set up His court, all His angels—who are ministering spirits—came and reported to Him. Now this is a description of the government of God; and all these terms are used in a way we human beings can understand.

In spite of the fact that Satan had rebelled against God, he was still God's servant. He was still a ministering spirit. He was among those angels who came to report to God, and it was within this context that God challenged him with Job. God inquired, "Where do you come from?" Satan replied: "Oh, from going to and fro, walking up and down throughout the whole earth." Now that was what Satan was doing—yet not as a traveler but as an accuser and a devourer (see Revelation 12:9-10; I Peter 5:8). He was going through the whole land trying to devour and to kill. That was Satan's unending thought and he did not miss anyone. And God knew this, and so He challenged him by saying: "Have you noticed my servant Job? There is no one like him: so perfect and upright, who fears God and abstains from evil."

Let me ask, Will God take pride in you and me before Satan? I for one am not qualified. God cannot challenge Satan with me because there are too many holes there. But what a man Job must have been that God could use him to challenge Satan! Of all men in the world, Job was definitely the target of Satan's observation. He was the one person above all others whom Satan wanted to devour. So God gave him an opportunity and said to His enemy: "See if you can devour him."

Satan, in reply, was so subtle. He said: "Yes, Job is perfect, he is upright, he does fear God; but does he not fear You for a reason? You have placed a hedge around him; You protect him and bless him. He loves You—yet not because of You. He fears You because of the benefits he receives. But if You take away the hedge from around him and let me attack him, he will curse You to the face." How subtle Satan is and how observing, too! God said, "All right, go ahead and try."

SOVEREIGNTY OF GOD

This that has just been narrated touches upon a very important matter which we should understand. Why is it that we cannot explain many things on earth today? It is because these things are not purely earthly matters. This is because there is also a heavenly element involved in these so-called earthly matters, yet all we see of them is their earthly aspect. And because that is all we see, we cannot discern the invisible and we cannot explain. There is no way for us to explain everything happening on earth with only an earthly vision. We have to explain things with not only an earthly vision but also a heavenly one, because heaven is involved with these matters on earth. And these "heavenly" events recorded in Job are an example of this.

Another thing we need to recall here is the government of God discussed earlier. Even though Satan is called the ruler of this world (see John 16:11), he cannot do anything without

God's permission. When God put a hedge around Job, Satan had no way to slip in. If God did not allow him, then he was not able to touch even a sheep or an ass which Job had. The government of God is so benevolent; we should therefore love His government. Yet sometimes when we mention the government of God, we are afraid; but actually it is a most blessed thing. If it were not for His government, where would we be? Even our very hairs are being numbered by God; and even when an odd bird that is worth nothing falls to the ground, God is with him (see Matthew 10:29-30). Think of that!

You remember the incident of the Lord Jesus saying to Peter, "Satan asked for permission to sift you." God had given the permission for Satan to do that, but the Lord also said to Peter, "I have prayed for you that your faith would not fail." Oh, do let us see that the government of God is a tremendous thing! We are living daily under His governmental care. Nothing can happen to us without His permission. But He sometimes does indeed permit things to happen—and all for a very good reason: to perfect us, to mature us, to bring us into sonship (see again Hebrews 12:5-11, Proverbs 3:11-12).

JOB'S FAITHFULNESS

God gave Satan permission to attack Job, and oh how fierce, how cruel, Satan was. He showed no pity, no compassion. In one single day, everything Job possessed disappeared. Not only the cattle, the camels, the sheep, the servants, but even his children were gone in one day. Bad news came to Job one after another. And upon hearing it all, he shaved his head, bowed down, and worshiped God.   Said Job: "Naked came I out of my mother's womb, and naked shall I return thither: the Lord gave, and the Lord hath taken away; blessed be the name of the Lord" (1:21). In all of this Job did not sin against God.

On another day God again held His court, and Satan appeared among the angels. Again God challenged Satan: "I have given you permission and you have done it. What did you see? Did he curse Me to My face?" Oh, how subtle Satan is, for he declared to God: "Skin for skin. A man is willing to give up everything for his life. But you touch his body and then You will see." We cannot expect any mercy from Satan. So God next said to his enemy: "You can do that, but don't touch his life. Let him live. You can do anything you want but do not take away his life." God was confident of His servant. So Satan immediately went forward and attacked Job with boils. Some scholars think it was a kind of leprosy called elephantiasis, in which the skin takes on the appearance of an elephant's hide with enlargement and hardening of tissues. And because of that, he became an outcast. He even could no longer live in his house but had in great suffering to live outside at a heaped-up place where people burned their refuse. Everybody left him; and even his wife said: "Curse God and die, there is no hope for you." In response, however, Job said this: "You foolish woman! What? Shall we receive good from God and not also evil?" In all this Job again did not sin with his lips (see Job 2:10).

Thank God, here was a man with whom God could challenge Satan, and Satan was silenced. This man Job did not sin. On the contrary, he feared God; He worshiped God; and though he received not only good but also evil from He, he would not curse Him or sin against Him.

So this is the beginning, the prologue, but it is far from the end of the story.

JOB'S FRIENDS

Three of Job's friends heard about his horrible plight and came to comfort him. These friends came from that area outside of Palestine that extends from Egypt all the way north and northeastward to the river Euphrates. They must have been some of the wise men of the east mentioned earlier, and they were also friends of Job. Today, whenever we mention these friends of Job we as it were look down upon them and spit on them; but let us pause a moment and consider the situation Job was currently in: he was an outcast, a leper. Nobody therefore dared to draw near to him; he was completely isolated. However, the friendship of these three friends was so strong that they were willing to come from a great distance to comfort Job; and hence, even though their comfort was not good, they were nonetheless good friends. When they saw Job, they did not recognize him because his features had so radically changed. Their reaction to this scene was that they wept with him; moreover, they sat there without speaking a word for seven days and seven nights, which at that time was the eastern custom of mourning for the dead. In other words, they were mourning for Job as one already dead. Most interestingly, it was the sympathy of his three friends that broke Job down. The fierce attack of Satan could not break his integrity, but the tender sympathy of his friends broke him down and he began to open up his heart. And that will always be the case.

JOB'S FEAR OF GOD

Job began to curse his birth before his friends. Whereas he dared not curse God, Job did curse his birth. And Job also disclosed the following personal information, which was most revealing: "For I feared a fear, and it hath come upon me, and that which I dreaded hath come to me. I was not in safety, neither had I quietness, neither was I at rest, and trouble came" (Job 3:25-26).

Through the tender sympathies of his friends, Job began to open himself up, and we begin to see what was really inside him. Yes, he feared God; but he feared Him with the fear of a servant, not that of a son. He was afraid to sin against God, and was in fact able not to sin against Him. Job was able to do everything right before God; nevertheless, inside him there was always a fear, and that fear was: "Suppose I slip, then what will happen to me? I will not be safe; I will not be in quietness; I will not be at rest."

Let us realize that here is a great difference between the fear of God as a servant and such fear as a son. When you fear God as a servant, you fear Him with fear and trembling: you are never safe; you are never at rest; you are afraid lest you do something wrong, and so, punishment will come upon you. That is the fear of a servant. But the fear of a son is different. Yes, a son fears the father, but he also trusts the father. No matter what happens, he knows the father still loves him. That is the difference. If anything should happen to a servant, immediately he doubts his master's heart as to whether the master's heart is towards him or against him. But if one fears as a son, and no matter what happens, he knows the father loves him. He is safe, at peace, and he has quietness.

Even though Job was perfect and upright, feared God, and abstained from evil, he nonetheless had not arrived at sonship. He was still serving God as a servant. That is why, when things happened which were the opposite of what was his expectation of God, Job was greatly puzzled, dismayed, even lost. On the one hand, he knew he was righteous, that he had not sinned— even though he did acknowledge that no man was sinless perfect. On the other hand, because he was righteous before God, Job did not understand why God did not come forth to defend him. It was as though God was against him. He could not understand. He was lost.

DIFFERENT VIEWS OF SUFFERING

In chapters 3—31 is to be found the lengthy discussion between Job and his three friends. These chapters are cast in beautiful poetic form and divided up into three cycles of discussion. As wise men of the east, they would sit down and discuss philosophical problems; and here they discussed the perennial problem of suffering, and did so from different approaches. Indeed, they had most likely discussed the matter among themselves even before they had arrived; and they had come to a definite conclusion. Evidently, Eliphaz was their spokesman since he spoke first.

Eliphaz approached this problem of suffering from a *mystic* point of view. He said to Job: "I heard a whisper, a spirit; I saw a form, a man speaking to me: Can man be more just than God? Therefore, despise not the chastening of the Almighty." A mystic is one who sees things according to his emotional feeling. He feels that no man is more just than God; and that is true.

The second person, Bildad, approached this matter of suffering from an appreciation of the *traditions* of the fathers. He said this to Job: "Inquire into past history; consider; attend to the researches and findings of the fathers. What conclusion have they come to with respect to this matter of suffering? It is as follows: God will never allow a righteous person to suffer, nor will he join hands with the wicked." That is Bildad's conclusion.

Job's third friend Zophar brought into the discussion a third approach. He was a very *dogmatic* man. He declared to Job: "The eyes of those who are evil will fail." These three therefore concluded that Job suffered because he must be evil. The golden rule of those days (and many today are still holding to that rule) was that God blesses and prospers the righteous but He will curse and punish the wicked. That is the moral law in the universe. Philosophically, whether one approaches the problem of Job's suffering mystically, traditionally, or dogmatically, he comes to the same conclusion: the golden rule of all human life, which is, that God will bless the righteous but He will punish the wicked. "Now therefore, Job, you must have sinned secretly. Outwardly, you may appear righteous, but there must be something wrong inside you, and that is the reason you are suffering. Repent, therefore, and God will be merciful to you." That was the united conclusion of Job's three friends.

SOWING AND REAPING

In one sense, sowing and reaping is a universal law. A person sows, and he reaps what he has sown. God is not mocked: if you sow according to the flesh, you shall reap according to the flesh: its end, corruption. If you sow according to the spirit, you shall reap according to the spirit: and its end is eternal life (see Galatians 6:7-8). That is true; and in his argument, Job likewise agreed to that. For that is what he firmly believed; and because of that, he could not understand; he was left puzzled and bewildered.

We need to understand that the consequences of this golden rule of sowing and reaping will only be realized fully in the future, not at present. For if we look at life today, we do in fact find, as Job has said, that sometimes the wicked live prosperously whereas the righteous suffer greatly. Even though in some instances God punishes the wicked and blesses the righteous, we must acknowledge that this golden rule may not be equally applied to everybody and to every situation today. However, when God shall finally judge all things, this rule will be the absolutely true standard—whether at the judgment seat of Christ having to do with His people or at the great white throne having to do with the world.

SUFFERING IS EDUCATIONAL

Another point needs to be emphasized here, as was alluded to and discussed briefly earlier. Job and his three friends did not see that suffering is not necessarily punitive in every instance. It can oftentimes be educational in nature or have as its purpose child-training. If suffering is only punitive, then we must admit that today the only rule in operation is that God punishes the wicked and blesses the righteous. But Scripture tells us that there is another purpose to suffering today than it being only punitive; in many instances it is educational in nature. God is using suffering to educate His people to bring forth that manchild spoken of in Revelation 12 that is to bring us into sonship (see Proverbs 3:11-12, cf. Hebrews 5:8 and 12:5-6, 7-10); and that is a truth which these friends of Job did not fully discern at that time. Their words reflected the fact of having caught a little glimpse into this aspect of suffering, but for them it was a very dim ray of light. What they chiefly saw was: that God punishes the wicked and blesses the righteous. So, they had concluded, "Job, you must have sinned."

Job, of course, tried to defend himself and said: "No, I haven't. You don't understand and, I too, don't understand." But in defending himself, he unconsciously crossed the line. In short, Job tried to justify himself and in the process condemned God. Even so, we do see that there were flashes of light in his response to his friends. For instance, in chapter 9 he said, "Oh, that there may be an umpire, a mediator, an arbitrator." He was looking for a mediator. And in chapter 13 he asserted this: "Even though he [God] slay me, yet will I trust in him." In chapter 19 he confidently declared: "I know my Redeemer liveth. If I do not see him in the flesh, I will see Him afterwards." And in chapter 23 he perceptively acknowledged: "God knows what will happen to me after he has tested me: I will come forth as gold." In other words, there were a few profound glimpses of light, but Job nonetheless continued to be greatly puzzled as before.

JOB IS EXPOSED

When all four men were arguing back and forth, it eventually drew out from Job one hidden facet to his character, and that was his self-righteousness: Job was righteous in his own eyes; and because he was so righteous, he thought he *was* righteous; indeed, He thought he could stand before God and reason with Him, and to such an extent that he confidently assumed he would come out being right. In Job's mind God could be wrong, but he himself could not be wrong. In other words, he was self-righteous. What is self-righteousness? Self-righteousness is self; good self, but it is self, nonetheless.

As we come to the conclusion of Job's arguments, we discover the element of self-pity in him: "I was blessed of God; I was so great at one time, and now look at me. Everybody looks down on me." He began to pity himself. Let us be clear here that it is the self which God wants to deal with in this righteous man, and the reason God allowed Satan to attack Job was to bring this element of self out. Satan could not bring out this element, so God arranged to let Job's friends do the job. Is it not true—especially for someone who truly loves the Lord, who is really all-out and, as it were, absolute for the Lord—that the greatest problem with that kind of person is his self-righteousness? And that self stands in the way of sonship because it is still "I" and not Christ (see Galatians 2:20a). So God allowed all this to happen in order to deal with what was at the very core of Job's life, his self-righteousness. He had to be humiliated and humbled.

ELIHU'S VIEW

Job was so strong. His friends were silenced; they could not defeat him. But, then, a young man spoke up who had waited until the older folks had ceased talking, which was the custom in the East. The young men were not supposed to say anything while the elderly men were speaking. When they concluded their words, Elihu began his (chapters 32-37). Elihu, whose name means, "whose God is He," served more or less as an interpreter of what was happening. His interpretation came down to this: that this which had befallen Job was the chastening of the Lord. The Lord was engaged in child-training and in disciplining Job in order to bring forth in him something better. However, when his interpretation was not accepted, Elihu himself became angry; and consequently his self, too, came out! Later on, Elihu realized that he had crossed the line, so he drew back. At about that same time, there arose a tremendous thunderstorm; and after the storm, there appeared in the northern sky the light's golden ray; and Elihu ended up describing the majesty of God: it was incredibly beautiful and full of splendor.

JOB SEES GOD

After these five people have had their say, then God began to speak (chapters 38—42:6). Strangely, we find that what God said here was not anything new. Almost all which God said we can find in their earlier discussions. Moreover, God never explained to Job why he suffered. All He did was ask him many questions, and in their essence all of them came down to these few points for Job to consider: What do you know? What can you do? Who are you? God inquired of Job: "When I set the foundations of the earth, where were *you*? Do *you* know where the gate of the spring is? Can *you* control a hippopotamus or a crocodile? If you do not know in perfection, if you cannot control the proud, why do you argue? Why do you try to defend yourself? Why do you condemn Me? Who are *you*?" God showed Job who *He* is. When Job heard all of this and had *seen* God as He truly is, he humbly said: "I have nothing more to say. I am nothing; I am less than nothing. I abhor myself; I hate myself. I repent in dust and ashes." In other words, he gave up his self-righteousness.

We must realize that life's problems are not solved by why, they are resolved by Who; not by what we hear, but by Who we see. We may hear all these arguments, but that does not solve our particular problem. But when we truly *see* God, as Job finally did (see Job 42:5-6), everything is solved. He is the sovereign God. Does He not have a right to do whatever He likes with us? And can we not trust Him and acknowledge that He knows what He is doing and doing it for our best?

After Job learned his lesson, God immediately turned Job's

captivity to himself (see Job 42:10). In James it speaks of "the endurance of Job." Job endured all these sufferings; and finally we see the end—the purpose—of the Lord, that He is full of compassion and is merciful (see 5:11b). If God is for us, who can be against us? God loves us so much that as a son we can trust Him, no matter what He does. In sum, God's government is benevolent.*

Let us pray:

> *Dear heavenly Father, do open our eyes to see Thy benevolent government. Do open our eyes, Lord, to see Thy pierced hand. And our Father, when Thy hand is put upon us, let us see that it is for our eternal good. Give us faith, give us love, give us trust. Oh, how we praise and thank Thee that we are in Thy hands and nothing can touch us, but only Thy hand can mature and complete us. We ask in the name of our Lord Jesus. Amen.*

*For a much fuller treatment of the book of Job by the author, the reader can consult Stephen Kaung, *The Splendor of His Ways: Seeing the Lord's End in Job* (New York: Christian Fellowship Publishers, 1974), 172 pages.

PSALMS

PRAISE AND WORSHIP

Psalm 1:1-6—Blessed is the man that walketh not in the counsel of the wicked, and standeth not in the way of sinners, and sitteth not in the seat of scorners; but his delight is in Jehovah's law, and in his law doth he meditate day and night. And he is as a tree planted by brooks of water, which giveth its fruit in its season, and whose leaf fadeth not; and all that he doeth prospereth. The wicked are not so; but are as the chaff which the wind driveth away. Therefore the wicked shall not stand in the judgment, nor sinners in the assembly of the righteous. For Jehovah knoweth the way of the righteous, but the way of the wicked shall perish.

Psalm 150:1-6—Hallelujah! Praise God in his sanctuary; Praise him in the firmament of his power. Praise him in his mighty acts; praise him according to the abundance of his greatness. Praise him with the sound of the trumpet; praise him with lute and harp; praise him with the tambour and dance; praise him with stringed instruments and the pipe; praise him with loud cymbals; praise him with high sounding cymbals. Let everything that hath breath praise Jah. Hallelujah!

The title of this book of Psalms in Hebrew is Tehillim which means "praises." It comes from the root word which has the meaning, "to shine" or "to make bright." Therefore, when it is applied to God, it means "the manifestation, the shining forth, the display of the majesty, the glory and goodness of

God." The English rendering from the Greek translation has the title: The Psalms or The Psalter. It comes from the root word *psalter* which means, "to play an instrument." It is therefore very fitting that these psalms are praises accompanied with instrumental music.

The composition of this collection of psalms occurred during the time of David and Solomon, continued at the time of King Hezekiah and Josiah, and concluded at the time of Ezra and Nehemiah. Accordingly, this entire collection spans a period of about 600 years.

The book of Psalms is divided into five books corresponding in content with the five books of Moses. In the Pentateuch we have God's Law, and here in this book of Psalms we have the response to that Law. It is a collection of 150 songs or psalms. Of these songs, 100 or so of them have been attributed to different authors who are mentioned by name in their titles: 73 to David, eleven or twelve to the sons of Korah, twelve to the school of Asaph, two to Solomon, one to Ethan, one to Heman, and one to Moses. The authors of 50 of them have been deemed anonymous. But in examining them more closely we can greatly reduce the number of these anonymous psalms. For instance, in Acts 24:25 we learn that the Holy Spirit attributes Psalm 2 to David and Psalm 1 was most likely written by David also. Then there are a number of psalms which are closely coupled together. For example, Psalms 9 and 10 are actually one song; Psalms 42 and 43 are likewise evidently joined together; and it is believed that Psalms 90 and 91 must have been written by the same author, Moses. Hence, we can see that the number of these anonymous psalms can be considerably reduced.

This collection of 150 psalms stands in the middle of the Bible. There are altogether 283 direct quotations from the Old Testament which can be found in the New Testament, and 116 of them are from this book of Psalms alone.

The first of five books in Psalms corresponds in content to Genesis. Genesis tells us of the will of God, and Psalms

1—42 sing of His will. It is Davidic in content, that is, they were mostly written by David. The second book comprises Psalms 42—72, and its content corresponds to the book of Exodus. Hence, like Exodus, it tells us of the work of God; it sings of His redemption. Some of its psalms were composed by the Korahites. The third book contains Psalms 73—89, and it corresponds in content to the book of Leviticus, which speaks of the way of God—centering, as it does, upon the sanctuary, the house, and temple of God. These songs were set down by the school of Asaph, the Asaphites. The fourth book consists of Psalms 90—106, and thus it corresponds in content to the book of Numbers, which tells of the walk of God in the time of the Israelite wilderness journey. It is mostly anonymous. And the fifth and final book has Psalms 107—150, and corresponds in content to Deuteronomy—the Mosaic book in the Pentateuch which contains the Law or word of God; and it, too, is anonymous for many of its psalms.

These various psalms are most valuable because they are the inspired responses of God's people to His revelation and dealings. These psalmists called upon God in prayer, petitions and praises. They communed with God in deep humility and love. They celebrated the works of God in nature and in history, and they recognized or came to see that the solution to life's perplexing problems was in relation to the moral government of God. These songs are the heartbeat of the saints in response to the heartbeat of God. And oftentimes we can find in the heartbeat of these psalmists-saints the heartbeat of our Lord Jesus. Indeed, the hearts of these song writers are like a harp upon which the divine hand has produced the noblest music.

John Calvin observed that this book of Psalms is "an anatomy of all the parts of the soul; for no one will find in himself a single feeling of which the image is not reflected in [these psalms as] in [a] mirror." And that is the reason the book of Psalms is so much read and loved.

THE VALUE OF THE PSALMS

The value of these psalms is great. First of all, we know that they are the word of God. Even though they are written in poetic form, their value is just as great as the prose books of the Bible. God's word teaches, corrects, convicts and instructs the man of God that he may be made perfect, fully equipped for every good work which God has called him to do.

The book of Psalms also has great devotional value. In fact, it was the devotional book of the ancient people of Israel. As the saints of old went through all the various aspects of life and experienced all kinds of situations, they found in God their foundation and their resources. And certain of them, by means of these psalms, poured forth to God their deep love towards Him and their great faith in Him. That is why when we read these psalms, we can identify with the psalmists. And in reading them we are drawn closer to God.

Yet the book not only has great devotional value, it also has moral value. God has set in the universe not only physical but also moral laws by which to govern the universe; and these moral laws never change. They may come to us in the form of law, such as the Ten Commandments, or they may come to us as songs; and very often, we learn more through songs than through statements. However, we have to remember that the people who wrote these various psalms were mostly under the dispensation of Law. That is why we sometimes find some expressions in their songs which seem to be offensive to our ears because we live in the dispensation of grace. Nevertheless, if we can approach these psalms as reflecting the ultimate of God's moral government in the universe, then I think we will not be offended. On the contrary, we will learn some very precious lessons on discipline.

The Psalms not only have moral value, they likewise have prophetic value because David and the other poetic writers were seers and prophets as well as singers. Oftentimes, when they sang they prophesied. There are a number of Messianic psalms that are very evident as being such in this collection of psalms. But even besides these very definite Messianic psalms, there are many other prophecies in the collection as well.

Furthermore, the book of Psalms has historical value; this is because even though in the historical books of the Old Testament we do have the pertinent events recorded, it is only in Psalms that we find the inner spiritual history that lies behind these historical records. For instance, in the two books of Samuel we certainly see what David went through, but the relevant psalms reveal to us his inward feelings as he went through all those different circumstances. They give us a fuller picture of the history of God's children and of the saints of old.

Of all the books of the Bible, Psalms is probably the most read. Its value is beyond description. On the other hand, this collection of 150 psalms is not all the psalms, spiritual songs or hymns of praise found in the Bible. For instance, in Exodus 15 we find Moses' song of victory; in Deuteronomy 32 there is the "swan song" of Moses; Judges 5 has the song of Deborah and Barak; I Samuel 2, Hannah's song; II Samuel 1, David's song over the death of Jonathan and Saul; Isaiah 38, the song of Hezekiah; all the lamentations of Jeremiah; the many poems contained in Job; the entire Song of Songs; and Solomon's 1005 songs. So besides this collection of 150 psalms there are many other psalms and songs to be found elsewhere in the Bible. But these 150 were collected together with a very definite purpose in mind. They are not arranged chronologically but according to a different and definite plan.

THE FIVE BOOKS OF PSALMS

As mentioned earlier, the five books of psalms into which the book of Psalms has been divided correspond to the five books of Moses. They are divided very clearly by the doxology to be found at the end of each book. Such a doxology evidences the fact that the psalms comprising each of these five books are praises to God. And we shall find that the first psalm of each book is the key to all the other psalms which follow in that book, and ending up with a doxology or praise to God. We shall now consider the first psalm of each book in order to get a feel for the 150 psalms. But please note that in some cases we may have to read the first two psalms together because the second one may be very closely related to the first.

FIRST BOOK

The first book consists of Psalms 1—41. They are nearly all Davidic in character even though there are four psalms here which lack the name of the author. But if we read very carefully, we can surmise that most likely Psalm 1 belongs to David since Psalm 2 definitely belongs to him. And Psalm 10 is actually a continuation of Psalm 9, and Psalm 33 definitely follows 32. So we can almost say that all of these 41 Psalms belong to David. And their content corresponds to the book of Genesis.

Genesis tells us of the will of God, and it is centered on man. God desires to have man as His dwelling place. That is the reason why, in the beginning, God created man according to His image. After He created man He put him before the tree of life. Hopefully, by eating the tree of life man would be united with God in life and become the companion, even the helpmate, of His beloved Son.

So Psalm 1 begins with the man whom God desires and blesses: "Blessed is the man who walketh not in the counsel of the wicked, and standeth not in the way of sinners, and sitteth not in the seat of the scorners"—that is negative. "But his delight is in Jehovah's law, and in his law doth he meditate day and night"—that is positive. According to God's will, the man whom God is after is a man who does not walk in the counsel of the wicked, who does not stand in the way of sinners, nor sits in the seat of scorners; rather, he is one who meditates on the word of God day and night. And this man is like a tree planted by the river. Here, we find a tree, as in Genesis. We know, of course, that man, unfortunately, disobeyed God and ate of the tree of the knowledge of good and evil. Man became wicked. Therefore, there is a contrast here between the man whom God desired and blessed, and another man. Or, to put it another way, we find that the same man becomes another man: a wicked man whom God rejects and punishes. The first man, Adam, fell, but the second Man, Christ, came forth to be the Man whom God is really after. With Christ we find the new man—those who are joined to Christ. And this new man is the will of God.

As was indicated earlier, Psalm 2 is closely related to Psalm 1. There we learn that because of the sin of man, there is a conflict. The whole world is under the enemy. How the world has rebelled against the Man of God, the Anointed of God! Nevertheless, God has set His Man on the throne and has given the whole earth to Him as His inheritance.

So we find a continual conflict occurring in this world, and because of that conflict, there will be suffering. But eventually, the Man of God will overcome and will inherit. And this thought can be found throughout the Psalms' first book of five. The most beloved psalm in this first book is Psalm 23. We all love that Psalm.

And then this first book ends with a doxology: "Blessed be Jehovah, the God of Israel, from eternity to eternity! Amen, and Amen."

SECOND BOOK

The second book contains Psalms 42—72, and its content corresponds to the book of Exodus. Twelve of them state in their titles that they are written by the Korahites, but the character and nature of the others is of the sons of Korah. We learn from Numbers 16 that Korah, a son of Levi, along with Dathan and Abiram, had rebelled against God. Because of this rebellion, Korah perished, but Numbers 26:11 tells us that the children of Korah did not die. In other words, when Korah rebelled against God, his sons did not join in the rebellion. Yet even though they did not join in, they witnessed the tragedy which befell their father. Because of this, a very deep sense of repentance developed within the sons of Korah as well as a great longing for the living God. Later on, they became singers and door keepers of the house of God (see I Chronicles 6:33-37 and 9:19).

Within this second book's songs we can discern deep emotional feelings and sentiments being expressed. Psalm 42 itself begins with these words: "As the hart panteth after the water-brooks, so panteth my soul after thee, O God." Here is a man who finds himself so far removed from the outward ordinances and worship of God that he cries out and longs for God's house. It is the cry of a man sunk in depression who—through his doubts and fears— is crying out for a renewal of the presence of God. And finally, he is able to stand his ground by faith. But, then, we learn from Psalm 43 that he asks God to send out His light and truth so as to lead him to the altar that he might offer praises to God. In this second book we also have Psalm 51, David's psalm of repentance. But we also have Psalm 72, a song of victory.

The book ends with a doxology, and it is a little different from the first book's concluding doxology. It declares: "Blessed be Jehovah Elohim, the God of Israel, who alone doeth wondrous things! And blessed be his glorious name for ever! and let the whole earth be filled with his glory! Amen, and Amen." This corresponds to the book of Exodus, for the psalmist sings here of the wondrous works of God and looks forward to the day when the whole earth shall be filled with God's glory. How fitting this doxology is!

THIRD BOOK

The third book of five, consisting of Psalms 73—89, is related to Leviticus and are the songs composed by those of the school of Asaph. Asaph was not only a singer, he was also a seer or a prophet. Most central to this book is the sanctuary or house of God. Its psalms emphasize very strongly the holiness of God—how the holiness of God deals with His people in disciplining them, and how His holiness judges the world in terms of their destruction.

Psalms 73 and 37 address the same concern. The psalmist wrestled over this matter of the moral government of God because, to him, it was in conflict with his personal observation. He had observed that the wicked prosper and the righteous suffer. So if God is just, how can this possibly happen? The psalmist struggled over this matter. In fact, he nearly slipped because this problem can never be solved intellectually. It can only be solved when one enters the sanctuary of God. The change comes in Psalm 73:17, for there we are told that he went into the sanctuary of God. It was then that he understood the wicked's end.

We know that the moral government of God exists and is operating, but based on much human observation it may have the appearance that it does not. Let us never try to solve this perplexing problem with our minds; we never will. The only way we can solve this problem is to enter the presence of God, and there we can see the end.

It is oftentimes true that the righteous suffer, but such is for a purpose. God is chastening His sons and daughters in order that they may be matured unto perfection. It is also sometimes true that the wicked do prosper, but without God's discipline they are heading towards their eternal destruction. And when the psalmist sees the end, there arises within him a stronger desire for God. That is why we read in Psalm 73:25: "Whom have I in the heavens? and there is none upon earth I desire beside[s] thee."

This third book of five ends with Psalm 89, a song of Ethan. It sings of the covenant of God and of His faithfulness. Even though in outward appearance we may not be able to see the moral government of God at work, it is nonetheless there because God is faithful; and He is faithful to His covenant with His people.

FOURTH BOOK

The fourth book is comprised of Psalms 90—106, and in content this book is related to Numbers. Therefore, in this collection of songs we see described many scenes from the wilderness journey of the children of Israel. And hence, this fourth book of psalms speaks of the walk of God. The book begins with a prayer of Moses, the man of God. Evidently, Moses wrote this psalm at the end of the 40 years' journey in the wilderness; he looked back over that entire period. And as a consequence, he is seen describing the brevity of life and the tragedy of life because men are sinful. Moses prayed that God would give wisdom that His people would know how to number their days and that they would not waste them in wandering through the wilderness of life. It is a mournful psalm, but it is followed immediately by Psalm 91—a joyful song because the protection of God is brought into view. When plagues occur and death is happening all around, God protects His own. The picture presented here is one of the wilderness where the children of Israel found themselves wandering and wandering for 38 years because of their rebellion against God and because of their continual unbelief. And during all those wandering years, they fell, one after another, with thousands of people dying every day; indeed, tombs marked their whole journey. But thank God that there were two men—Joshua and Caleb—who were kept by God because they loved Him. They were able to enter the Promised Land. So in Psalm 90 we see the sovereignty of God, and in Psalm 91, the protection of God.

This entire fourth book ends with Psalm 106 which sings of the lovingkindness of God. If it were not for His lovingkindness, we would all be consumed. But thank God, He is love; and because of that there is mercy. It is only in His lovingkindness that we are able to enter into our eternal inheritance.

FIFTH BOOK

The fifth and final book consists of Psalms 107—150, and it is related to the Pentateuch book of Deuteronomy which contains the Law or word of God. Here in the opening song (Psalm 107) the psalmist reviewed the lovingkindness of God: how He led His people through their wanderings into the city of habitation, how He set the prisoners free, how He sent His word and healed the sick and delivered them, how He delivered people who were in the sea. In other words, the psalmist revealed all the acts of the lovingkindness of God, and, because of this, he calls the people of God to sing praises to Him. The most notable psalm in this section, of course, is Psalm 119, God's word written again in action and emotion. The saints of old loved Psalm 119. I think we can all recite Psalm 23, but I wonder who can recite the entire Psalm 119 from memory. It has been said of William Wilberforce, a great saint and nineteenth-century political leader in England, that after a heated debate in the British Parliament, he went to a nearby park to relax by reciting Psalm 119. It is a beautiful psalm.

As with the previous four books of the Psalms this book also ends with a doxology, but does so not simply with one verse but with an entire psalm, Psalm 150. It is not only the proper conclusion for this fifth book, it is the proper conclusion for the entire collection of all 150 psalms:

"Hallelujah! Praise God in his sanctuary; praise him in the firmament of his power." Where do we praise him? We praise him in the sanctuary, we praise him in the firmament of His power. For what are we to praise Him? "Praise him in his mighty acts; praise him according to the abundance of his greatness. Praise him with the sound of the trumpet; praise him with lute and harp; praise him with the tambour and dance; praise him with stringed instruments and the pipe; praise him with loud cymbals; praise him with high sounding cymbals." How do we praise Him? We praise Him with everything that we have. And who will be praising God? "Let everything that hath breath praise Jah [Jehovah]. Hallelujah!" Such is the book of Psalms.

Let us pray:

Dear heavenly Father, we do thank Thee for giving us this book of Psalms to help us to praise Thee, to worship Thee, and to adore Thee. We do pray that Thou wilt create within us that worshiping spirit, that heart of praise, so that we may truly praise Thee seven times a day as we pray to Thee three times a day. Thou art our God, the only God; the God who loves us and sent His beloved Son to die for us. We worship Thee. In the name of our Lord Jesus. Amen.

PROVERBS

CONDUCT AND DAILY LIFE

Proverbs 1:1-7—Proverbs of Solomon, son of David, king of Israel: to know wisdom and instruction; to discern the words of understanding; to receive the instruction of wisdom, righteousness and judgment, and equity; to give prudence to the simple, to the young man knowledge and discretion. He that is wise will hear, and will increase learning; and the intelligent will gain wise counsels: to understand a proverb and an allegory, the words of the wise and their enigmas [riddles]. The fear of Jehovah is the beginning of knowledge: fools despise wisdom and instruction.

The book of Proverbs follows the collection of Psalms. C. H. Spurgeon calls the Psalms, "The Treasury of David." We know that not all of the 150 psalms were written by David. He composed most of them, and all the rest were written in the spirit of David.

This book before us today is called the Proverbs of Solomon. Like David with the Psalms, we learn that probably Solomon spoke most of the proverbs in this book, but there are some which are the words of other people; yet all the recorded proverbs here closely mirror the thought of Solomon.

The Psalms are centered on worship; Proverbs are centered on conduct. The Psalms aspire heavenward; Proverbs reach down to earth. Thus we find that the word of God is perfect and well balanced. Sometimes, we look very highly on spirituality and overlook practicality. There are even people who think that to be spiritual is to be impractical: if people are too practical, they cannot be spiritual. There are even those who think that pure spirituality is above morals, yet in God's word it is not so: true spirituality is deeply practical. Though we are not under law but under grace, even so, grace demands much more than law.

On the other hand, there are others who emphasize conduct or morals so much that they neglect spiritual life. There are people who try to live a moral life, and yet it is all the effort of the old man. They are trying to improve their flesh by putting cosmetics on the old man. Though they may appear good to the world, they are totally unacceptable to God, because He looks upon the heart whereas man looks on the outward appearance. God knows how crooked, corrupted and wicked the heart is.

We need spiritual life to live a spiritual life, which is to say that we need the life of Christ so that we may live a Christian life. These two things must go together. On the one hand, there must be a new life; and on the other hand, by means of this new life, we must express a new manner of living. Solomon is a son of David whose psalms reflect a focus on worship. Therefore, we can conclude that good conduct as seen in Solomon is the result of worship. These two things can never be separated. They go hand in hand.

The title of the book of Proverbs is taken from the very first word which appears in this book: proverbs. This word in Hebrew is *mashal*, which means "a ruling, saying, proverb, similitude or likeness." Proverbs are short pithy sayings, in frequent and widespread use, and expressing some well-known fact or truth. Proverbs are common to all civilizations and in every country, race or culture. They are the accumulation of agelong observations and reflections. Many proverbs are moral and religious in character, but there are others which are purely philosophical or witty sayings. In examining all the proverbs of the world which are moral or religious, we discover that they seem to have a common resemblance because they all appear to reflect the fact that God has put moral laws in the universe just as He has placed physical laws in the universe. Even though these proverbs may vary with different shades of meaning from one culture or country to the other, nevertheless, they basically represent the moral laws which God has set in the universe. We cannot trace a particular proverb to any one person or persons because each and all of them are usually accumulated down through the ages. They are the treasure of the people as a whole; indeed, they mold the character of the people.

CHRISTIAN ETHICS

When we come to the book of Proverbs found in the Old Testament, we find it is very, very different; with some people thinking the book represents the ethics of the chosen people of God in the olden days. In one sense this is true; and yet, the book is more than that. What is ethics? Ethics is the philosophy concerned with the moral rules and laws governing our conduct. They collectively provide us the moral philosophy and standard of value by which we judge our actions; for example, am I doing the right thing? That is ethics. But when we come to the word of God, there is something more to it. We may choose to call it Christian ethics, and Christian ethics is quite different from ethics as we commonly know and understand the term. For the latter is concerned with rules or laws which govern our conduct, but Christian ethics is not a set of rules or laws; it is a Person. Christian ethics is not based upon certain observations, reflections or moral standards; it is based upon a Person, even God himself. Christian ethics is not the result of human improvement or reform; it is the result of the operation of the Holy Spirit in our lives. And this gives us the right approach to the book of Proverbs.

We do not approach this book as though it were a collection of external rules or laws that regulate our moral conduct. On the contrary, we approach it as that which teaches us that if we live by the life of Christ, we will know what kind of conduct, what kind of life, we will live. In other words, this collection of sayings or rulings which we call the book of Proverbs is not something before us that we try in ourselves to do; the book is instead the overflowing expression of the life of Christ within us; that is to say, the statements and sayings in Proverbs are the expressions or outworkings in us of that life.

In approaching the book of Proverbs we must do so in the same way we approach the so-called Sermon on the Mount. People sometimes approach the Sermon on the Mount as though it were a set of moral standards. They then place these standards before themselves and try to imitate or implement them in their lives. I believe we all realize that if we do that, we will be a failure. The more we try in ourselves to implement this Sermon in our lives the more we will fail, because such is humanly impossible. Rather, we shall approach the Sermon on the Mount with the life of Christ in us. This is His life, and if we abide in Him and He abides in us, the fruit will be produced naturally, spontaneously and gloriously.

In God's word we find many parts or portions which seem to govern in the area of conduct or works. Proverbs is one such part. Other such portions are the Sermon on the Mount, Colossians, and the latter part of Ephesians. These tell us how to be a husband, a wife; how to be parents, children; how to be servants, masters; how to live together in the church and in society. Likewise, in II Peter we learn that we need to add one character upon another so that we may enter the kingdom abundantly. All of these sections in God's word— including Proverbs—fall into the area of Christian ethics. But let us remember this: we do not approach them in the way we approach the Law. Instead, we look upon them as being the potential expressions of the life of Christ within us. And what we therefore need to do is to live by His life; and if we do this, we shall find these expressions are the evidences or proofs of His life in us.

WISDOM OF SOLOMON

These proverbs are called the Proverbs of Solomon. Now we have just said that we cannot trace the many proverbs in the world to any man or to a certain group of people because these are the accumulation of the observations and reflections of man down through the ages. Yet here we note that the content of the book of Proverbs is termed as the Proverbs of Solomon. Or, as in some of the old manuscripts, this collection of proverbs is called the Wisdom of Solomon. So it does seem that we can nonetheless trace these particular proverbs to a man.

Now Solomon in his day was the wisest of men. The reason for this was because he had sought wisdom. He knew he was not that wise; therefore, he realized he needed wisdom. So, when God asked Solomon what he wanted, that was the one thing he asked God for. From I Kings 4:29 we learn that God gave Solomon wisdom, great understanding, and largeness of heart, as extensive as the uncountable sand on the seashore.

We are also told that Solomon's wisdom excelled that of all the men of the East as well as surpassed all the wisdom of Egypt. The wisdom of the East was basically philosophical, speculative, and mystical; whereas the wisdom of Egypt was scientific and technological in nature because Egypt had built those great pyramids and other great and massive objects. Yet, Solomon's wisdom excelled that of both the East and Egypt; which meant that it was not just philosophical or speculative nor was it only scientific and technological; it was both. Furthermore, his wisdom was even wiser than that of Ethan, Heman, Calcol and Darda: these people were prophets and singers, and they prophesied with songs and music. And thus we find here yet another kind of wisdom Solomon excelled in which was divine, spiritual, and prophetic, and which touched the purpose and mind of God. And hence, Solomon's wisdom, which was of this kind, was not earthly but heavenly, divine and not human.

In James we learn there are two different kinds of wisdom. One is called the wisdom that is from above; and it is first pure, then peaceful, gentle, yielding, full of mercy and good fruits, unquestioning and unfeigned (see James 3:17). The other kind of wisdom is termed the wisdom which is from beneath; and it is earthly, carnal, and devilish. Solomon's wisdom is of the heavenly kind; it is therefore divine wisdom. And it is out of that kind of wisdom that the book of Proverbs was produced.

We are also told in I Kings 4 that Solomon spoke 3,000 proverbs. He spoke of the trees, the cedars of Lebanon, the hyssop which springs up out of the wall, the cattle, creeping things, the fowl and the fish—all these things in nature. But out of these 3,000 proverbs there are some which are moral and spiritual in character, and these probably found their way into the book of Proverbs. As a matter of fact, in the main part of Proverbs, from chapters 10—24, there are only 375 proverbs. So the content of the main part of Proverbs constitutes only a small portion of these 3,000, but they are nonetheless moral in character.

Of these many proverbs spoken by Solomon he may have adapted some from other sources and put them in his own words; others most likely were the result of his own observation as he was given the wisdom of God. After Solomon had spoken these proverbs, someone else, Bible researchers believe, selected certain ones from the 3,000 and put them into the book of Proverbs. Most probably, the larger part of the book— chapters 1—24—was put together during the time of King Jehoshaphat. He lived about 70 years after the death of Solomon; and if we compare the introduction of Proverbs, chapters 1—9, with II Chronicles chapters 17 and 19, we will see the similarity. In the Proverbs introduction, wisdom is portrayed as crying in the open spaces, at the gates, and in the streets. And we are told in II Chronicles that during the reign of King Jehoshaphat there was a revival, the king having sent out princes, priests and Levites to all the cities with God's Law in their hands to teach the people (see 17:7-9). Later on, Jehoshaphat himself went out from Beersheba to Mount Ephraim calling people back to God (see 19:4ff.). So it was most probably during that time that the larger part of Proverbs was collected and placed into a record.

We are told that the second and smaller part of Proverbs, running from chapters 25—31, was transcribed by King Hezekiah. It so happened that some 300 years after Jehoshaphat's reign there occurred another revival—this one under Hezekiah. And evidently there were some wise men in his court who transcribed this portion of the Proverbs of Solomon. Such, then, is the way the book of Proverbs in its entirety has reached our hands.

Martin Luther once said: "This book may rightly be called a book of good works, for he [Solomon] teaches there the nature of a godly and useful life, so that every man aiming at godliness should make it [this book] his daily handbook, a book of devotions." And J.N. Darby has observed this: "This book of Proverbs is the application of that wisdom that created the heavens and the earth to the details of life in a world of corruption and evil. This book of Proverbs treats of the world and of God's government according to what man reaps of that which he has sown. This book is so important that everyone, especially young people, should make it their handbook."

The book of Proverbs can roughly be divided into three parts: Chapters 1—9 Wisdom Calls; Chapters 10—24 Wisdom Builds; Chapters 25—31 Wisdom Beautifies or Strengthens.

THE PURPOSE OF THIS BOOK

The first six verses tell us the purpose of this book: why we have Proverbs in the word of God. Verse 2 says in part, "To know wisdom and instruction." These proverbs help us to know wisdom and instruction. The wisdom spoken of here has a root meaning in the Hebrew language of being "skillful, practical." Hence, this wisdom is experiential and practical; it is knowledge applied. On the other hand, the word instruction here in the original means "discipline, correction, warning." So we can discern immediately that these proverbs are not speculative or philosophical in character; on the contrary, these proverbs are highly practical, instructional, and concern discipline. They help us to know practical wisdom and discipline; and how much we need to know and experience these things.

Verse 2 also says, "To discern the words of understanding." Understanding comes from keen observation and deep reflection. We are to discern, to know the difference, to discern the words of understanding. Discernment is very important in life. Our problem is we do not know the difference between things. If we do not know the difference, then we do not know how to walk. In Paul's prayer for the Philippian church he prayed: "And this I pray, that your love may abound yet more and more in full knowledge and all intelligence, that ye may judge of and approve the things that are more excellent, in order that ye may be pure and without offence for Christ's day" (Philippians 1:9-10). Some versions of the first part of verse 10 here read: "that ye may distinguish the things that differ." We need to be able to distinguish or know the things that differ. If we are unable to know the difference between right and wrong, good and evil, life or death, then we are lost. We need discernment, and the content of Proverbs can give us this kind of spiritual discernment in our daily life.

Then Proverbs 1:3 says: "To receive the instruction of wisdom, righteousness and judgment, and equity." To put it another way: To receive the discipline of wisdom. The word wisdom translated here is another word in the original. It means "intelligence," which is to say: "to receive the discipline of intelligence, righteousness and judgment, and equity." From all this we can detect advancement in thought here. First, it is to know; then knowing advances to discerning, and discerning has advanced to receiving. You not only can know, you not only can discern, you also can receive the discipline. And this is the discipline which can enable us to live intelligently, rightly, justly and fairly. Now is that not the way we should walk on this earth? And these "enablings" we may receive from these proverbs.

Verse 4 advances the matter further: "To give prudence to the simple, to the young man knowledge and discretion." After we receive, those who are simple are then given prudence. What is prudence? Prudence in the original means "smoothness"; it means "the capacity to escape the viles of evil." That is why the Lord Jesus in Matthew 10:16 said: "Be prudent as serpents and guileless as doves." We are as sheep in the midst of wolves; therefore, we need prudence.

"To give prudence to the simple." Simple here means "open"; in other words, prudence is given to people who are open, readily available to all external impressions. They receive whatever comes from outside. That is a being simple here. And these proverbs can give prudence to the simple so that they may escape all the snares which may come to them; and thus, they may live fairly, justly, rightly and intelligently before God, and be guileless as doves.

"To the young man knowledge and discretion." Discretion here means "thoughtfulness, careful thinking." The problem with young men is that they do things impulsively. They are quite rash, quick, doing things without thinking. These proverbs can therefore give men knowledge and discretion. A young man is able to act according to careful thinking based upon true knowledge, and not rushing into something or saying something without thinking. Such are the purposes of these proverbs.

Yet did Solomon mean to convey the notion that the wise do not need these proverbs? Not at all, for he went on to say: "He that is wise will hear, and will increase learning; and the intelligent will gain wise counsels: to understand a proverb and an allegory, the words of the wise and their enigmas [riddles or dark sayings]" (vv.5-6). In other words, these proverbs are not only for the immature and the simple, they are also for those who are wise and intelligent because they will make them even wiser in the Lord. Hence, this book of Proverbs is for everybody.

So is there anyone who does not need this book of Proverbs? I think probably the reason we are so immature or foolish or sometimes wicked is because we do not read this book. I do hope we will all read it and even do as Luther suggested: make it our handbook and a book of devotion. Then, probably, we will live more to the glory of God.

THE FEAR OF THE LORD

"The fear of Jehovah is the beginning of knowledge: fools despise wisdom and instruction," [that is, they despise understanding and discipline] (Proverbs 1:7). This is *the* proverb of the entire book of Proverbs. It is the foundation to all the proverbs which follow.

This verse actually gives us a picture of the two trees which God had set in the Garden of Eden as mentioned back in Genesis. In the Garden there were the tree of life and the tree of the knowledge of good and evil. If man ate of the tree of life, he would live; if he ate of the tree of the knowledge of good and evil, he would die. The way of the wise is the tree of life; the way of the fool is the tree of the knowledge of good and evil. So there are these two ways before us: we can either live the way of the wise or the way of the fool. It depends upon from which tree we eat. And hence, in this opening of Proverbs we have pictured before us these two trees: the fear of the Lord is the tree of life. Despising wisdom and discipline is the tree of the knowledge of good and evil.

"The fear of Jehovah is the beginning of knowledge." The word beginning here in the Hebrew language means "the principle part." The fear of the Lord is the principle part of knowledge. It is not only the beginning of it, it is the main part, the essence, the substance of real knowledge. We will recall how the Lord Jesus, in His high priestly prayer found in John 17, said: "To know God and to know the One whom He has sent—that is eternal life."

"The fear of the Lord ..." The word fear has many shades of meaning. The particular shade in any discussion will depend upon circumstance and relationship. For example, if you do not know God, if you live a sinful life, you will have a fear of God because, intuitively, you know that one day there will be judgment and that torment is awaiting you. Therefore, in the world we find people who do not like to hear the word of God or even to hear the name of God mentioned. So the fool says in his heart: "There is no God"—yet not because the fool does not know intuitively that God exists but because he knows he cannot bear to see God out of fear that His judgment will be accompanied with torment. That is the reason why, when people who do not know God die, they are usually afraid: they know that after death there is judgment. Now that is one kind of fear of the Lord.

There is another kind of fear of the Lord which is expressed by those who are under the Law, just as were the children of Israel. God gave the Israelites the Ten Commandments, and they had to keep them with fear and trembling. Such fear is that of a servant or of a slave. They were afraid they could not keep the Law, and consequently they would be punished. That is another kind of fear.

Thank God that we today are the children of God, and as such, the kind of fear which has connected with it torment or punishment is not present for us. That is why we read in I John 4:18: "Perfect love casts out [the] fear" which has torment in it. We do not have that kind of fear—which is the fear of a sinner, of a slave, or of a servant. Thank God, we are forgiven, even as God's word tells us: "There is forgiveness with thee, that thou mayest be feared" (Psalm 130:4).

It is because we are children of God who have been forgiven that we do indeed have one particular kind of fear, but that fear is a filial, affectionate reverence towards our heavenly Father and towards His will: we are afraid we may not please Him. Such is our particular fear, which stems from our love for the Father and His will. Yes, love does in fact have an element of fear in it, in that if you love a person very deeply, you are afraid you may do something to displease that person; you want to please that person in everything. Now it is that kind of fear which must be in the children of God. If it is not there, then we become careless and irreverent. As God's children we do have a fear, but it is a filial, affectionate reverence towards our heavenly Father. We want to please Him in all things.

It is most interesting that when we read these three books of wisdom—Job, Ecclesiastes and Proverbs—all three come to the same conclusion. In Job 28:28 it says: "Lo, the fear of the Lord, that is wisdom; and to depart from evil is understanding." Ecclesiastes 12:13 reads: "Fear God, and keep his commandments; for this is the whole [duty] of man." And Proverbs 9:10 declares: "The fear of the Lord is the beginning of wisdom; and the knowledge of the Holy [one] is understanding."

All these books of wisdom come to the same conclusion— "The fear of the Lord." Strangely, however, the Hebrew name for God or the Lord in this phrase is different in Proverbs from the Hebrew name invoked in Job. In the latter wisdom book the name is Elohim—Creator.

In Proverbs, though, it is "The fear of *Jehovah*," which is the memorial name of God. It means "I AM that I AM." It is God's covenantal name with His people. Recall the incident recorded in Exodus 34 of God appearing in glory to Moses: "And Jehovah passed by before his face, and proclaimed, Jehovah, Jehovah God merciful and gracious, slow to anger, and abundant in goodness and truth, keeping mercy unto thousands, forgiving iniquity and transgression and sin, but by no means clearing the guilty; visiting the iniquity of the fathers upon the children, and upon the children's children, upon the third and upon the fourth generation" (vv. 34:6-7).

Knowing that our God is merciful and gracious, slow to anger, keeping mercies to the thousands, and forgiving our sin, transgression and iniquity, there is therefore a fear of God the Father within us. We fear Him because we love Him. We fear Him because we want to please Him. We fear Him because we want Him to be happy and satisfied with us. And it is this kind of fear that constitutes the chief part of knowledge.

In Proverbs 9:10 it says: "The fear of the Lord is the beginning of wisdom." The word beginning there in Hebrew is another word. It means "the principle"; that is to say, the fear of the Lord is the principle of wisdom. The very principle of wisdom is the fear of the Lord. So, if we fear the Lord, we have knowledge and wisdom, but if we do not fear the Lord, and no matter how much knowledge we accumulate in the world and no matter how wise we may appear to people, in the sight of God we are fools. A person may not have much knowledge of this world and he may not be wise in the eyes of the people, but if he fears God, he has wisdom and knowledge. And this is the knowledge and the wisdom which we who are believers must seek.

Who are the fools? They are those who despise practical wisdom and discipline. We live in a world which is wicked and undisciplined. How we need to respect the practical wisdom and discipline which comes from above. And such is the essence of this book of Proverbs.

WISDOM CALLS

The first nine chapters of Proverbs form this book's introduction. Wisdom is going about calling out on the streets, at the gates, and along the broadways. She is calling for the "simple ones" to come to her to seek wisdom. The beginning of wisdom is to seek wisdom, and not only to seek after it, but also to treasure it. If we deeply value wisdom, we will have intelligence, understanding, and prudence—all of these. Wisdom is our treasure.

This wisdom is represented by a woman. Woman in Scripture always represents subjective truth. Wisdom is not just objective teaching, it is also subjective truth that can be experienced. Wisdom is something we need to experience, and we *can* experience it. She is the *good* woman and she provides a feast for us to come and really enjoy. But then, in contrast to her, there is the *bad* woman. If the good woman represents the wisdom from above, the bad woman represents the wisdom underneath. It is earthly, sensual, and devilish.

In chapter 8 of Proverbs we see it even more clearly. Wisdom there is personified; it is a Person; indeed, wisdom is Christ. Christ is the wisdom of God. Solomon is a man *of* wisdom, but the Son of Solomon is wisdom itself. We need to hear the wisdom of Solomon. Even more so, we need to hear the One who is greater than Solomon. God has made Christ our wisdom, and righteousness, and holiness, and redemption (see I Corinthians 1:30). God is calling us to Christ. And if we come to Christ, treasure Him, seek Him, and find and possess Him, then there is wisdom, there is knowledge.

WISDOM BUILDS

The second segment of Proverbs is found in chapters 10—24. This is the main part of the book with 375 proverbs therein, and in chapter 9 we are told that wisdom builds the house and that she hews out seven pillars (see v. 1). Now by taking that as a kind of hint or clue, we can group all these proverbs into seven categories—the seven pillars. As a matter of fact, we will discover these proverbs to be sayings for character building. What is character building? Well, we have the life of Christ in us and this life that is in us has a new nature. But this new nature needs to be exercised and developed into new character; that is to say, Christian character. Christian character is not the improvement of the old nature; it is not trying to put cosmetics on the old man. That is pretense. Christian character is the developing, cultivating, growing, and exercising of the new life of Christ in us according to the new nature. And when we follow that new nature long enough, it becomes character. In other words, we are being characterized by that which is Christ. And that is what Christian character is. It is not a given; on the contrary, it has to be built up in us. Yes, Christian *life* is given, but Christian *character* has to be developed and built up. How much character have we built with this new life?

Furthermore, let us realize that these Christian characteristics are what will build the house of God. They are the essential pillars of the house. The reason the house of God is so dilapidated, and why so much of it is in ruin today, is because of the lack of Christian character. The building up of Christian character builds the house of God. I will simply mention and briefly comment on these seven pillars or characteristics, but they can be found all through this main part of the book of Proverbs:

(1) Righteous versus Wicked
(2) Diligence versus Slothfulness
(3) Love versus Hate
(4) Lowly versus Proud
(5) Gracious versus Cruel
(6) Discipline versus Foolish
(7) Truthfulness versus Lying or Faithfulness versus Hypocrisy

Please note that all of these constitute the character of Christ. Christ is the righteous One, and that righteousness of His is not a matter of position; it is a matter of condition. Christ lived a righteous life. We who are the Lord's are exhorted in I John to practice righteousness. We not only are positionally righteous, we also need to live righteously. In other words, in order to be right in the sight of God and before man we must live a right life. Then, too, our Lord Jesus is most diligent. In the Gospel of Mark we discover that the way of the Lord in this regard is described as "straightway"; that is, everything is immediate with Him. He is so diligent. By contrast, we are naturally lazy. Some people may be less lazy than others, but when we come to the things of God we are all the same, we are all lazy. We may be diligent in other things, but in addressing the things of God we are lazy. By contrast, our Lord Jesus is most diligent. He is diligent in hearing God and in doing the will of God. How we need to develop that diligence.

Then, of course, we need love in order to be gracious, kind, gentle and generous rather than being cruel or stingy. We are not to be loose but we need, if necessary, to be disciplined. And, oh, how we need to be faithful, truthful and real instead of being those who lie and are hypocritical.

All these character traits must be developed within us. Paul's exhortation to Timothy was that physical exercise is profitable for a little but exercise towards godliness is profitable for everything, since the latter holds out the promise of life both for this present age and the age to come (see I Timothy 4:7b-8). Such is godliness; which simply means to be like God. Hence, exercising ourselves towards godliness is something that we all need very much.

WISDOM STRENGTHENS AND BEAUTIFIES

Proverbs chapters 25—31 bring into focus how wisdom strengthens, beautifies or overflows. Chapters 25—29 are the proverbs of Solomon transcribed by the wise men of King Hezekiah (see 25:1). They are almost the same in content as that in the main part of Proverbs. They are more pictorial, even quite picturesque, but they are more or less the same as those proverbs in the book's chief passage.

However, in chapters 30—31 we find something very different. These two chapters are not the proverbs of Solomon but are the prophecies or words of Agur the son of Jakeh, of Massa (30:1 ASV mgn) and of King Lemuel (31:1). According to the original, Proverbs 30:1 can be translated even more fully as follows: "The words of Agur, the son of the princess or the queen, or she whose dominion is Massa." In the word of God, Massa was a place outside of Palestine. It was located in northern Arabia on the southeasterly border of Palestine. These prophecies therefore belong to a people outside of Israel and who belonged to the Ishmaelitish kingdom (cf. Genesis 25:1-16). It is very interesting to note that when Solomon was on the throne, the queen of Sheba came from the south to test Solomon's wisdom, to ask questions, to solve all of her enigmas or riddles. The queen of Sheba was very wise herself, but she came to the wisest person of that day, Solomon, to receive further wisdom. In a symbolic sense, we can say that Solomon represents our Lord; He is the personification of Wisdom itself—that is to say, He is Wisdom. Outwardly, these prophecies were the words of Agur and Lemuel, but they were actually the words of their mother. And most likely, the queen referred in 30:1 was the mother of Agur and Lemuel; and hence, these were the *mother's* prophecies. She was like the queen of Sheba coming to Solomon seeking wisdom. And so this chapter 30 serves as a response from this queen of Massa.

Typologically speaking, this queen may represent the church. Here we find Christ being wisdom, and we become the sons of wisdom. We are Gentiles and yet we come into contact with Christ, "the Greater than Solomon." And having thus become the sons of wisdom, we belong to the church. And so we read here in chapter 30 the words of wisdom coming forth from that mother through the sons.

I only want to mention one portion from that chapter: "Two things do I ask of thee; deny me them not before I die: Remove far from me vanity and lies; give me neither poverty nor riches;

feed me with the bread of my daily need: lest I be full and deny thee, and say, Who is Jehovah? or lest I be poor and steal, and outrage the name of my God" (vv. 7-9).

How much we need that prayer. We need to pray that God will deliver us from vanity and lies. In fact, this is what the whole world is: vanity and lies. And we need to pray that God will deliver us from seeking or participating in such vanities and lies. We also need to pray that God will neither give us poverty nor riches, because if we become too rich we may forget Him, and if we are too poor we may disgrace Him. I think that this portion of chapter 30 is a most beautiful prayer. We truly need to pray that we may live in a godly way.

Finally, chapter 31 presents a beautiful picture of a man and of a woman. The man is a king and the woman is a queen. Typologically speaking, it betokens Christ and the church. The man is to be just, sober, sympathetic; the woman is to be virtuous, diligent, gentle, kind. And all this concludes with verse 30: "Gracefulness is deceitful and beauty is vain; [but] a woman that feareth Jehovah, she shall be praised." In other words, mere outward appearance is deceitful and vain, but the fear of the Lord is praiseworthy.

So may the Lord help us, and create within us a real desire to study this book of Proverbs.

Let us pray:

Dear heavenly Father, we do praise and thank Thee for giving us this book of Proverbs. Thou dost not want us to be immature or foolish but Thou desirest that we be wise. We do praise and thank Thee that Thou hast given us Thy life. And now Lord, we do pray that we may, by Thy grace, exercise godliness in the fear of the Lord, that our life on earth may really glorify Thee, and that Thy church may be built. In the name of our Lord Jesus. Amen.

ECCLESIASTES

FEAR GOD, KEEP HIS COMMANDMENTS

Ecclesiastes 1:1-11—The words of the Preacher, the son of David, king in Jerusalem. Vanity of vanities, saith the Preacher, vanity of vanities! all is vanity. What profit hath man of all his labor wherewith he laboreth under the sun? One generation passeth away, and another generation cometh, but the earth standeth forever. The sun also riseth, and the sun goeth down, and hasteth to its place where it ariseth. The wind goeth towards the south, and turneth about towards the north: it turneth about continually, and the wind returneth again to its circuits. All the rivers run into the sea, yet the sea is not full: unto the place whither the rivers go, thither they go again. All things are full of toil; none can express it. The eye is not satisfied with seeing, nor the ear filled with hearing. That which hath been is that which shall be; and that which hath been done is that which will be done: and there is nothing new under the sun. Is there a thing whereof it may be said, See, this is new? It hath been already in the ages which were before us. There is no remembrance of former things; neither shall there be remembrance of things that are to come with those who shall live afterwards.

Ecclesiastes 12:13-14—Let us hear the end of the whole matter: Fear God, and keep his commandments; for this is the whole [duty] of man. For God shall bring every work into judgment, with every secret thing, whether it be good or whether it be evil.

Let us pray:

> *Dear heavenly Father, we do praise and thank Thee that through Thy Son, our Lord Jesus Christ, we are brought into Thy very presence. How we praise and thank Thee that in Thy presence there is light and there is life. So we do desire, Lord, that Thou wilt shine upon us and open Thy word to our hearts, that we may really take Thy word into our hearts and patiently bear fruit unto Thee. Lord, we do desire that Thou wilt be glorified in the midst of Thy people. We ask in the name of our Lord Jesus. Amen.*

There are three wisdom books in the Old Testament —Job, Proverbs and Ecclesiastes. This book of Ecclesiastes is not only the most difficult to understand of all the wisdom books, it is probably the most difficult to understand in the whole Bible; and because of this it is the most misunderstood. One dear saint of God said: "We should expect some difficulties in a revelation coming from such a Being like God to such a creature like man." Actually, we should rejoice in these difficulties because they are the occasions of growth in grace. They exercise our humility. They remind us of our weakness and ignorance and of the power and wisdom of Christ. They drive us to Him and to His gospel.

However, in spite of difficulties we do find in this book of Ecclesiastes valuable lessons which we must learn; yet we are too slow to learn them. It is important for us to see and to have that deep conviction of all the vanities under the sun in order that we may appreciate and come to enjoy the true happiness and fulfillment which is in Christ Jesus.

The title Ecclesiastes is a transliteration of the name which the Greek translators gave as an equivalent to the Hebrew title Qoheleth. It means "to assemble as a congregation." In other words, the people were called to assemble together for the purpose of having someone address them, and that is the reason we find in our English versions the subtitle, The Preacher.

This book of Ecclesiastes gives us the words of the Preacher. In chapter 1:1 it says: "The words of the Preacher, the son of David, king in Jerusalem." Of all the sons of David, we know there was only one son who sat on the throne in Jerusalem— King Solomon. So from the information we have here, it is evident that the Preacher is none other than King Solomon, the man of wisdom. We may recall that after he completed the temple he called the people together as a congregation, and there he prayed for them, blessed them, and exhorted them to be faithful to God. This we can find in I Kings 8. So, indeed, we can rightly believe that Solomon is the Qoheleth, the Preacher.

We do not know exactly when Solomon composed Ecclesiastes, but it is assumed that he did so in his old age as he looked back over his past life. He had enjoyed the wealth, the pleasure, the honor, and all the other things of this world as nobody else had ever before experienced. He had also fallen into great sin—even that of idolatry—but he had repented. Therefore, as he looked back over his past and reviewed it with his keen observation of all things around him, he gave his conclusion, which became the text of this book of Ecclesiastes which he wrote.

It is said that Solomon wrote The Song of Songs in his youth, Proverbs in his middle age, and Ecclesiastes in his old age. In his youth, there was the vigor of love; in his middle age, the accumulation of wisdom; and in his old age, the maturity of perception. Even though we do not have a clear, direct statement or record in the Bible that he had repented from his fall in his old age, indirectly I think we can rightly infer that he did return to God after his fall. For instance, I Kings 11:41 tells the rest of his life in a single sentence, and that, of course, has reference to his old age; for it states that the acts and the works that he did, and his wisdom are recorded in the book of the acts of Solomon. So from this statement we can deduce that even in his last days his wisdom had not forsaken him. In other words, he still had wisdom in his old age.

In another passage, II Chronicles 11:13-17, we learn that after Solomon died, his son Rehoboam came to the throne and the nation was divided into ten tribes and two tribes. But Jeroboam, the king of the northern kingdom of Israel, began to make golden cows in an attempt to keep the people from going to Jerusalem to worship Jehovah God. Because he did that, those who were faithful to God—the Levites and many people in the different tribes—still went up to Jerusalem to worship God in the temple there. This strengthened the hand of Rehoboam and the southern kingdom, and it is said that for three years they continued in the way of David and of Solomon (see v. 17). Accordingly, if they continued in the way of David and Solomon, we can assume that Solomon must have repented in his old age because that was the way just like that of his father David.

Ecclesiastes can be compared with the book of Proverbs. In one sense, they seem to be contrary to each other; yet both come to the same conclusion: in Proverbs Solomon declares that "the fear of the Lord is the beginning of wisdom" (9:10), and in Ecclesiastes he says: "Fear God and keep his commandments; for this is the whole [duty] of man" (12:13). However, their approaches are the opposite: in Proverbs we are told how to walk on this earth intelligently, righteously, justly and fairly; whereas in Ecclesiastes we are told of the vanities of all things under the sun. Nevertheless, they are not contradictory; in fact, they are complementary. This is because, on the one hand, we need to walk on this earth righteously and intelligently; but on the other hand, we need to discern the facade of this world so that our hearts will not be engrossed in the things here below. In Proverbs we read that life *begins* with the fear of the Lord and in Ecclesiastes we read that life *ends* with the fear of the Lord. The fear of the Lord not only regulates our walk on earth, it also directs our hearts heavenward.

VANITY OF VANITIES

Beginning with the second verse of Ecclesiastes chapter 1 Solomon says this: "Vanity of vanities, saith the Preacher, vanity of vanities! all is vanity." This seems to be the overall theme of Ecclesiastes. Now this is a statement made by the Preacher, yet not just any preacher. This is a statement made by the Preacher who was king in Jerusalem and who happened to be the wisest man in the world. He not only had possession of much riches, honor and wealth of this world, he also had the capacity for experiencing and enjoying all of them. So this statement is not a casual one, nor can it be construed as being an expression of sour grapes, but it is the statement of one who had had so much experience and so many possessions; and after he had possessed all and experienced all, he came to a most wise conclusion: "Vanity of vanities, all is vanity"; that is to say, there is nothing permanent but all things are temporary, transient, fleeting, unsatisfying, unfulfilling, and with there being nothing eternal and real about them; in sum, everything is vanity.

Let us ask ourselves, Do we dare to face reality? If we dare to do so, we will also come to the same conclusion as did Solomon, that under the sun all is vanity, empty, meaningless. But does God make this world to be such? Is it God's will that our life should be vain and without meaning? Is it God's will that we should not enjoy what He has created? In short, is it true that the world is basically tragic? If we go back to the beginning told of in the very first verse of the Bible, back to when God had created the heavens and the earth, we learn further from Scripture that the morning stars sang for joy and the angels praised God for his creation (see Job 38:7). God created this world to be a place of joy and rejoicing, that it was to be something to enjoy, something for which to praise God. There was absolutely nothing tragic about it. Yet, when we go on to read the very second verse of the Bible, Genesis

1:2, we are told this: "The earth was waste and empty." The creation that God had created in the beginning was very pleasant, very enjoyable, most satisfying, most fulfilling; but something disastrous happened to it—the earth became waste and empty; it lost its meaning and purpose, having become aimless, drifting, even having become a wasteland.

Now from Isaiah 14 and Ezekiel 28 we learn that it was because one of the archangels whom God had created, Lucifer, sinned against God. He had wanted to lift himself up to be equal with God, and because of this, punishment came upon him, upon those who followed him, and upon the particular realm under his dominion. And hence, the earth became waste and empty; and Lucifer became Satan, the adversary, as we know today. But thank God, we learn from Genesis 1:3 that the Spirit of God brooded over the face of the deep. The love of God came upon this ruin and restored the earth in six days so as to be inhabitable, which was then followed by God creating man and declaring that all was: "very good." Now if God says that something is very good, it certainly had to be very good—not only that the man he created was very good but that the earth he had restored was likewise very good.

Then we are told that God put man in the Garden of Eden. Eden means "pleasure, the garden of pleasure." All the trees growing there were good for food, and in the midst of the Garden, was the tree of life. God had restored the earth and created man, and there was thus the possibility of the fulfillment of God's purpose in creation. The wasteland could be turned into fruitfulness and the emptiness could be turned into purpose. Unfortunately, however, man sinned and rebelled against God, and because of that, not only was man cursed, the earth was also cursed. Indeed, this is the reason all creation came under vanity, as we are told in Romans 8:20-22: that all creatures have entered into vanity and into the bondage of corruption, and that man subjected all things into that bondage, and even from that day way back then until now all creation groans and travails together with us in pain, hoping for that release and for that restoration and for the manifestation of the coming of the children of God.

How very true it is that everything under the sun today is vanity. All things are vain, empty, fleeting, unsatisfying. Nothing on the earth is fulfilling or purposeful or real. Today we live in a world of vanity. Our times on the earth are times of vanity. Life itself is vain and all things in this world are too. "Vanity of vanities, all is vanity." That was the conclusion given by Solomon the Preacher who had experienced and enjoyed all things in this world. And from the mouth of that same Preacher we hear the Spirit of God speaking. It is more than merely a preacher who is preaching; it is the Spirit of God who is speaking through that particular preacher. And what is the voice of the Spirit of God saying to us today? "Vanity of vanities, vanity of vanities, all is vanity." If this in fact is all that we are seeking, searching, laboring, toiling and working for, then the end is truly vanity.

SEEK AFTER THE KINGDOM OF GOD

Why does the Preacher speak like that to us? Does God want to deprive us of the little pleasure which we can enjoy in this world? Is it true that He does not want us to live a happy life? Does He want to make us miserable? On the contrary, God knows we live under a big lie and under deep deception. If we are not awakened, then one day the bubble will burst and there shall be nothing left; and worse, there shall be judgment. This is the reason the Spirit of God, through the mouth of the Preacher, is trying to wake us up so that we may not be totally occupied with the things of this world. If all things are a vanity, then the striving for these things is like pursuing after the wind. Even so, the purpose of this book is not negative but positive in nature. Yes, in the beginning the Preacher did indeed say, "Vanity of vanities, all is vanity," as though all is very negative.

And this caused the Preacher to add: "I hate life; it is better not to be born. It is better to be stillborn than to see the world and, having experienced all these things, to come to nothing." Nevertheless, he concluded the book by saying: "Fear God and keep his commandments; for this is the whole [duty] of man." And that is most positive.

Do let us clearly understand that it is not God's will that we should live a miserable life even though life in this present world is in truth miserable. It is not God's will that we should not enjoy what He has created. He did create all things for our enjoyment; but if that is all we look for, then it is vanity. This world and all that it is and has is vanity; and yet, we must live in this world of vanity. So the question to be considered here is this: How can we live in this world of vanity but not be engulfed in its vanity? How can we live in this world of vanity and yet enjoy what God has created without our being judged along with the world? We need to have a right understanding and a right attitude. We need to understand clearly that this world is vanity. We need to face up to reality and not try to deceive ourselves. By our seeing that this world is vain and purposeless we will develop a right attitude towards it. In other words, we will acknowledge that the purpose of life lies not in this world nor in the things of this world, because the world and the things of the world are passing away (see I John 2:15-17).

On the other hand, if you make this world and the things of this world your life, then you are in deep deception and you will not know how to live in this world of vanity. In fact, this world of vanity will turn you into vanity also. But if you truly see that this world is vanity, then you will realize that you need to seek first the kingdom of God and His righteousness and all these things shall be added to you (see Matthew 6:33).

Why is it that so many people, even God's people, are seeking after the things that are passing away? We cannot blame the worldly people, people who do not know Christ, for doing this, because that is all they know and that is all they have.

But why are we who know the Lord Jesus, who are redeemed by His precious blood, seeking after the things of the world—and doing so with just as much enthusiasm as the people of the world? Should we not know better? Should we not turn our hearts to the things above which are eternal rather than to the things below that are transient? Let us not put the world before God. Let us not put our body before our soul. Let us not put time before eternity. Let us seek first the kingdom of God and His righteousness and all these things shall be added to us. In other words, if we fear God, then we can enjoy whatever He has given us with a heart of thankfulness and thus we will not be judged afterwards. Otherwise, the things of this world which we have sought after in our life and the things which we have enjoyed today will one day rise up to condemn us. But if we fear God and keep His commandments, then we will use all the things God has created and given us in a way that will be pleasing to Him, and so we will not be judged. That is the purpose of this book of Ecclesiastes.

Oswald Chambers said: "Job tells us how to suffer; Psalms tells us how to pray; Proverbs tells us how to act; Ecclesiastes tells us how to enjoy; and Song of Songs tells us how to love." Is that not a wonderful summary of these Bible books? And in particular, Ecclesiastes tells us how to enjoy.

John Wesley once wrote (and here I am paraphrasing): As I began to expound the book of Ecclesiastes, never had I realized the meaning and the beauty there. I could not imagine that all the several parts of it came together in such an exquisite manner and that tell us but one thing: that there is no happiness outside of God.

And Martin Luther noted that the book of Ecclesiastes is actually a book of consolation. Now if you can find consolation in this book, you have touched the spirit of the book.

The first eleven verses of Ecclesiastes present us with the preamble or theme of this book: "Vanity of vanities, all is vanity." And the last six verses of the book, chapter 12:9-

14, serves as the epilogue. It gives us a comprehensive view of the entire book and makes a recommendation to us to fear God and keep his commandments; for such is the whole of life. In between stand chapters 1:12—7 whose subject is vanity illustrated; that is the negative side. Chapters 8:1—12:8 have as their subject vanity mastered; and that is the positive side.

PREAMBLE

"Vanity of vanities, saith the Preacher, vanity of vanities! All is vanity." This word vanity in Hebrew means "worthless, unsatisfied, transient, vanishes quickly like a vapor or a bubble." When Adam's first son was born, he and Eve called him Cain which means "acquisition." They thought God's promise of the seed of the woman (see Genesis 3:14-15) had now come. But this first descendant was such a failure. So when the second son was born, they called him Abel, and Abel in Hebrew means "vanity" or "breath" or "transitoriness." That is the very word. Nothing in this world satisfies or fulfills; it is like a breath. When one breathes in the winter time, the vapor comes forth, condenses, and then quickly disappears. Now that is a picture of what the world is. It seems to give you a little contentment, but just when you try to enjoy it, it is gone. There is nothing real there. How tragic if that is all you have! Everything is vanity. So whether you look at each thing of this world separately or you put all such things together, it all ends up being nothing but a great heap of vanities. It leaves you with an aching void, a blank that can never be filled. "Vanity of vanities."

In verse 2 of his preamble the Preacher makes a statement; yet it is more than a statement, it is actually a summary pronouncement. He pronounces his judgment over all things by declaring: "Vanity." Whatever thing one can think of—whether of honor, wealth, position, power or whatever—he pronounces his summation over it all: "All is vanity."

But in verse 3 he poses a question and in doing so he throws down a challenge: "What profit hath man of all his labor wherewith he laboureth under the sun?" What profit? The word profit here in Hebrew means "that which is left over after a transaction is executed" or, "the surplus." You have put so much labor into an undertaking, activity or desired goal; yet what is the result of the effort? What is left over? Perhaps, in the process of putting all labor and effort into the endeavor, you did experience some pleasure or some enjoyment, but after the transaction has been completed, what is left over? What profit?

The word vanity appears many, many times in Ecclesiastes. I tried to count them but each time I had a different total! The phrase, under the sun, is also mentioned many times in this book. In fact, this entire book only deals with the things *under* the sun; it does not touch at all upon the things *above* the sun. Above the sun there is glory and eternity, there is life and fulfillment, there is pleasure and happiness. Yet this book is concerned exclusively with all things under the sun.

Whatever endeavor is under the sun, we labor at it; and man is supposed to labor: it is due to his fall; for after man fell, God cursed the earth, and thus man has had to toil and labor and sweat in order to make a living. Even woman has had to travail in labor. In other words, toiling and laboring is humanity's lot in life. We who live on this earth are required to labor and toil, but what is the profit? What is left over? If you labor your whole life, what at the end do you gain or have? The Preacher's answer: "What profit does man have of all his labor wherewith he labors under the sun?—All his strivings," adds the Preacher, "are vexation of spirit and a vain pursuit after the wind." Let anyone try to grasp hold of the wind and he shall find that it is futile. Do you believe otherwise? Solomon the Preacher will prove to you the truth of all this later on.

Then Solomon made a further observation. He noted that one generation comes and goes, followed by another generation that does the same thing. This cycle repeats itself generation after generation. He then noted the following phenomena of nature: the sun rises, labors, goes down, and comes back up again; the wind blows towards the south, then turns towards the north and goes around in its circuit; the water from the river empties into the sea, yet the sea is not full, for the water evaporates, becomes rain, falls on the mountains, becomes the river again, and empties once more into the sea. Moreover, the eyes can never be satisfied, and the ears are never filled with hearing enough. And though there is constant changing, things never change. In truth, the world is not a merry-go-round but a sorrow-go-round. Yes, things under the sun appear to be new, but this is because we have forgotten; and, therefore, we think they are new. Oh, what a weariness! Yet this is the world that man loves; this is what it really is.

VANITY ILLUSTRATED

Now in case there are those who would challenge the Preacher's question—What profit?—he proceeds in those chapters of Ecclesiastes from 1:12 through 7 to illustrate to such challengers the vanity of all things. He explains in part as follows:

"I, the Preacher, was king over Israel in Jerusalem. And I applied my heart to seek and to search out by wisdom concerning all that is done under the heavens: this grievous occupation hath God given to the children of men to weary themselves therewith. I have seen all the works that are done under the sun, and behold, all is vanity and pursuit of the wind" (1:12-14).

Solomon, the son of wisdom and the king in Jerusalem, searched his heart, using his wisdom in trying to discover the meaning of life under the sun; that is to say, what is the meaning of all things under the sun? And after doing that, he concluded that all is vanity and a pursuit or striving after the wind. Furthermore, Solomon sought to discern the difference between wisdom and the foolishness and folly of men (see

1:17). He went on to say this: "I perceived that this [wisdom concerning the things of this world] also was a striving after wind, for in much wisdom is much vexation, and he that increaseth knowledge increaseth sorrow" (1:18).

If we seek wisdom regarding the things of this world, what will we have? The Preacher's reply was that the more wisdom one has, the more vexation that one has. If we increase our knowledge, we increase our sorrow. On the other hand, in speaking of folly he declared that "folly is madness" (see again 1:17).

Let us acknowledge that this book is full of contradictions. Indeed, if a person does not know the Lord, he will think that this is a book which contradicts itself all the time. It is true, life is full of contradictions. On the one hand, wisdom is better than folly, just as light is better than darkness. On the other hand, the more wisdom you have, the more vexation you will have. But if you are foolish, you are just mad. Nevertheless, whether you are wise or foolish, you both will end up going to the same place: the place of death.

Now because Solomon could not discover the meaning of life by means of the mental arena, he tried to do so by immersing himself in the physical realm: he would now give free rein to those material and sensual objects and activities which could provide him with every delight, pleasure, or imaginable joy. So he set his heart upon the things of this earth which he could enjoy and find pleasure in, and here he had at his disposal every conceivable resource by which to do that. He built houses, palaces, gardens, and planted parks, forests and vineyards; he had numerous menservants and maidservants; he possessed great herds and flocks; he had many wives and concubines; he collected huge quantities of gold and silver as well as the treasures of kings and of the provinces; he acquired men-singers and women-singers; and indulged in all the delights of men—including wine, musical instruments of every sort, and pleasure of every kind. In fact, said Solomon, he withheld from his eyes nothing which they desired after nor denied to his heart whatever gave it joy. He went on to say that as he was experiencing and/or laboring on all these things, it seemed to give him some kind of comfort and joy, but when he looked back on all his works and on all his labors, he had to conclude that "all was vanity and a striving after wind and that there was no profit under the sun." In other words, a person may work hard day and night, but for what? Then Solomon said: "I saw someone who had nobody else; yet he worked day and night and lost his sleep, and for what? I, being wise, do all these things, and when I die I leave the results of all my labors to one who has not done anything. I do not know whether he is wise or foolish." That is a vexation of spirit.

Solomon went on to say that man does not control time. There is a time to weep and there is a time to laugh, etc., etc., but we cannot control our time. We may think we control everything, but the world is not under our control. God controls all. On the one hand, we have to labor and we have to do our best; on the other hand, there is time and chance. It is not always that in life the best or the fastest wins. On the contrary, life is a paradox. How can anyone explain life? It is not logical. Therefore, the only way to live one's life is by faith. If a person has faith, he can live—no matter what; but if a person does not have faith, he is finished.

Solomon not only experienced all things himself, he also keenly observed all things in life. Nothing escaped his observation. He recognized that God had created man perfect, but man himself invented many devices. Let us not think that those who oppress others are happy. The oppressed, of course, are in a pitiful situation, but the oppressors are equally pitiful; they have no comfort. Who is he who thinks that man is better than the beast? Do they not all—both man and beast—die? What *is* life? Do we know love and hate? We do not. We are not in control of our circumstances; our circumstances control us. And the result: "Vanity of vanities, all is vanity."

VANITY MASTERED

Chapters 8:1—12:8 reveal how vanity is to be mastered. This is a world of vanities, and yet God has put us in this world; and, therefore, we must engage in a life of vanities as we live in this world of vanities. How, though, are we going to master these vanities? There is a way, and that way is to fear God and keep his commandments. The word fear here conveys the idea of filial reverence. If there is that affectionate, filial reverence towards God, that is to say, if there is the desire in us that we want to please God in all things, then we will be able to live on this earth—as Scripture has told us—as strangers and pilgrims (see Hebrews 11:13). We will be able to use the things of the world as though we are not using them. We will not allow the things of the world to occupy our hearts and master us; rather, we will master all the things which come to us and use them for the glory of God. It is not God's will that we should live a miserable life. It is not His will that we should be either an Epicurean or a Stoic or an ascetic. God wants us to love Him and enjoy what He has given us for His glory.

In this second part of Ecclesiastes Solomon the Preacher addresses especially the young people. As is well recognized, young people are full of life; everything is new to them. They are curious about all things, and they want to try out and taste of everything. So Solomon offered up this advice: "Young man, enjoy your life; do what you want to do; go where you want to go; but remember one thing: God will judge what you do. Therefore, remember your Creator in the days of your youth before the evil days shall come." God does not want young people to live like miserable old misers. God wants young people to enjoy their life, but they are not to forget their Creator. He created you young people with a purpose so that you may glorify Him and enjoy Him. In glorifying and enjoying Him, you can take pleasure in the things which He has prepared for you, and when the evil days come, you will not be judged (see 12:1, 14).

OLD AGE

Then Solomon painted a most vivid picture of old age; the evil day comes when the vigor of youth is abated. It is a fascinating picture. We know that the Bible sometimes likens the human body to a house; for example II Corinthians refers to our body as a temporary tabernacle (5:1, 4) as does II Peter (1:13-14); so Solomon employed a similar comparison between a house and our body in describing old age:

"In the day when the keepers of the house tremble"—these are our hands and arms. "The strong men bow themselves"—these are our legs and thighs; in other words, we bend. "And the grinders cease because they are few"—most of the teeth have fallen out, so the grinders are few now. "And those that look out of the windows are darkened"—our eyesight grows dim. "And the doors are shut toward the street"—our ears cannot hear very well now; they are well-nigh shut. "When the sound of the grinding is subdued"—our speech becomes very low. "And they rise up at the voice of the bird"—the aged among us cannot sleep at night for too long. "And all the daughters of song are brought low"—we do not enjoy life as we did before. "They are also afraid of what is high [afraid of heights], and [afraid of] terrors that are in the way"—we become fearful of heights and are afraid to go out into the streets. "And the almond [tree blossoms]"—our hair turns white. "And the grasshopper is a burden [drags itself along]"—our strength is gone. "And the caper-berry is without effect"—our desire is gone. "The silver cord be loosed"—our spinal cord is broken or severed. "The golden bowl be broken"—our brain has degenerated. "The pitcher be shattered at the fountain"—our heart is broken. "And the wheel be broken at the cistern"—our lungs give out (see Ecclesiastes 12:3-6). This is a description of old age, and the time of death and mourning has come (see v. 8). This, then, is life on earth, from youth to old age. Yet, if this is all that life is, what is the meaning of it? Is it not true that under the sun all is vanity—all is meaningless?

Are we awakened by what this book has to say to us? Should we not seek those things which are above? We know and acknowledge that our life, our fulfillment, and our satisfaction are all in God. That is where we can find all of it. Not here on earth; for we are just passing through. Therefore, we should not allow these things under the sun to occupy our hearts. Let us live in this world loosely and unattached, as it were, from the things of this world, and let us seek the things that are above; for the things of this world are transient, but the things that are above are eternal (cf. II Corinthians 4:18b).

EPILOGUE

In the epilogue (12:9-14), the Preacher asserted that these words of his are words of truth; and further, that they are like goads. Now goads are sharp instruments; so these words are sharper than a two-edged sword: they penetrate; they divide the soul and the spirit (see Hebrews 4:12). These words are also like firmly embedded nails. In other words, they enter deeply into our very conscience. And these words, he added, come from the one shepherd—that is, from the Lord, who is our Shepherd. They do not just come from Solomon the Preacher, but they come from wisdom itself—that is, from God himself. And what does he say is the end of the whole matter? "Fear God and keep his commandments; for this is the whole [duty] of man." The Lord Jesus said: "If you love Me, keep My commandments" (see John 15:10). I John tells us: "If we love Him, we keep His commandments" (see 5:3). Everything will be judged, even secret things whether they be good or evil. But if we fear God and keep His commandments, then we can see His face without shame.

In closing, I would like to quote the words of two men whose comments about this book of Ecclesiastes are worthy of our consideration. One is Charles Simeon (1759-1836)—

longtime influential preacher and pastor of Trinity Church in Cambridge, England—who remarked: "There are only two lessons a Christian should learn. One is to enjoy God in all things; and the other is to enjoy all things in God."

The other comment is from that godly man and would-be missionary in India, Henry Martyn (1781-1812) a protégé of Simeon, who said: "O what vanity has God written upon all things under the sun. Adored be the never failing mercy of God. He has made my happiness to depend not in the uncertain connection of this life, but upon His own most blessed self, a portion that never faileth."

Let us pray:

> *Dear heavenly Father, we do trust Thy Holy Spirit to bring these words of Thine into our hearts that they may be like goads, like well-driven nails. We pray that Thy word may be registered in our hearts and that they will deliver us from the vanity amid which we live and that we may be able to master such vanity and turn it all to Your glory and to our rightful enjoyment. We ask in the name of our Lord Jesus. Amen.*

THE SONG OF SONGS

THE LOVE OF GOD IN CHRIST JESUS

The Song of Songs 1:1—The song of songs, which is Solomon's.

The Song of Songs 2:16a—My beloved is mine, and I am his.

The Song of Songs 6:3a—I am my beloved's, and my beloved is mine.

The Song of Songs 7:10a—I am my beloved's, and his desire is toward me.

The Song of Songs 8:6-7—Set me as a seal upon thy heart, as a seal upon thine arm: for love is strong as death; jealousy is cruel as Sheol: the flashes thereof are flashes of fire, flames of Jah [Jehovah]. Many waters cannot quench love, neither do the floods drown it: even if a man gave all the substance of his house for love, it would utterly be contemned [despised].

Philippians 3:10-11—To know him, and the power of his resurrection, and the fellowship of his sufferings, being conformed to his death, if any way I arrive at the [out] resurrection from among the dead.

Let us pray:

Dear heavenly Father, how we do praise and thank Thee. It is because of Thy great love towards us, manifested in Christ Jesus, that we are able to gather together unto Thy name. We do praise and thank Thee knowing that Thou art here with us. We have read Thy word and now we trust Thy Holy Spirit to quicken it to our hearts and draw us that we may enter into the reality of Thy word, to the praise of Thy glory. We ask in the name of our Lord Jesus. Amen.

Of the thirty-nine books in the Old Testament, three are attributed to Solomon: Proverbs, Ecclesiastes and The Song of Songs. Proverbs speaks of wisdom, Ecclesiastes tells us of vanity and Song of Songs shows us love. Chronologically speaking, it may very well be that Solomon wrote Song of Songs in the vigor of his youth, Proverbs in the accumulated wisdom of his middle age, and Ecclesiastes in the maturity of perception in his advanced years. But according to the sequential order followed in the Scriptures, it is Proverbs, Ecclesiastes and The Song of Songs. I believe these three books have been placed in that order because, spiritually speaking, Proverbs must come first. There needs to be wisdom in our Christian walk first; and the beginning of wisdom is the fear of the Lord. Then out of that wisdom and the fear of the Lord there will come the understanding that under the sun all is vanity. But that is not all; such understanding will move us into the heavenly realm where we can realize the love of God in Christ Jesus. Whereas Ecclesiastes delivers us from the subtlety of this world, Song of Songs ushers us into the reality of love.

We have been told that Solomon wrote 3,000 proverbs and 1,005 songs. He spoke of the cedar trees of Lebanon and the hyssop which springs out of the wall. He talked about cattle, creeping things, fowl, and fish. Of all the many songs he wrote there is no trace of 1,004 of them. The only one which is known today is this Song of Songs, which is a song of love. This can betoken to our hearts the fact that though everything else may fail and fade away, love never does.

Now we can interpret The Song of Songs in several different ways. Many Jewish writers view the book as God's way of making known the sacredness of married love. They believe this song sings of the blessedness of wedded life. But some of the more spiritual among the Jewish writers have looked deeper into this song and have concluded that it speaks of the love relationship between Jehovah and the nation of Israel, because in the Old Testament God was sometimes looked upon as the Husband of the nation of Israel and the latter was deemed to be His wife. So they considered this song to be a book of communion.

However, in the Christian era people have looked at this song from two different viewpoints. One view is that The Song of Songs typifies the sacred love relationship between Christ and His church. There we see the conquering love of Christ and the response from the church. The other viewpoint is that it speaks of the personal love relationship between Christ and the individual saint. Hence, we can approach this book in four different ways: literally, it speaks of the blessedness of wedded life; dispensationally, it speaks of the divine relationship between God and Israel; typically, it speaks of the love relationship between Christ and the church; and, personally, it speaks of that loving relationship between Christ and the individual soul.

No one is certain of the correct background to the story we find in The Song of Songs. There are many theories, and one is the so-called shepherd hypothesis. It is advocated by Godet, Scroggie and other Biblical scholars. They contend that there are three main characters in this song and that Solomon is the villain among them. There is a love relationship between an unnamed shepherd and a maiden-shepherdess. According to this hypothesis, Solomon attempted to come between these two and entice the maiden away from the shepherd, but he failed. And that this therefore shows the purity of married love.

Another theory put forward is that there are two main figures in the song: Solomon and a young Shulammite lass. It typifies the love between Christ and the saint. And H. A. Ironside has constructed the following narrative for it, based as it is on information and inferences gleaned from the song's text itself. Solomon had a vineyard in the north country in the district of Ephraim and he rented out the vineyard to keepers, a family of Ephraimites. Evidently, the father and husband of this family had died, so the mother was left with at least two brothers and two sisters. And the elder of these two sisters was the Shulammite; indeed, she is the "Cinderella" of the story. Her brothers did not treat her well, they forcing her to tend the vineyards—that is, trim and prune the vines, set the traps for the intrusive foxes, and even commanding her to shepherd the flocks and the kids out in the wilderness.

One day, while this shepherdess was watching her flock, she lifted up her head and, to her embarrassment, she found a tall, handsome shepherd looking intently at her. So she cried out, "Don't look at me; I am black. I am burned by the sun." But the shepherd responded by saying: "I see nothing in you but what is fair. You are spotless." Gradually, their friendship developed into affection, and to a certain degree the shepherd had won the love of the shepherdess. Then he told the maiden that he was going away, but he would come back and claim her as his bride. So he left.

A long time went by with no news of the shepherd's whereabouts, but the maiden continued to believe in him. She was probably the only one who so believed. Sometimes she dreamed of him as though she were hearing his voice, but it was only a dream. Finally, one day, there was a commotion in the village. The royal caravan had made its way into the village and a messenger was dispatched to the maiden saying that the king demanded her presence. In obedience she went forth and, to her great surprise, she found that this king was none other than the shepherd. She cried out and said, "I am my beloved's and his desire is towards me."

Now we do not know whether this is the real background to the song's story or not, but it is actually of no significance. What is important is that this Song of Songs is one of the books in the sacred writings. It is divinely inspired. It is the word of

God. We believe that among its various purposes the song does speak of the blessedness of married life, but we need to go beyond this particular interpretation of the book and see in it as well a picture of that binding love between Christ and each one of His own; and ultimately, of course, to see it further as the loving relationship between Christ and His church.

As we have noted, this Song of Songs is a song of love. Now we must acknowledge here that the entire relationship between Christ and ourselves is one of love. As we contemplate the love of Christ, we come to realize how steady, steadfast, faithful, unchanging, long-suffering, and perfect His love is towards us. But when we consider our love towards Him, how easy it is for us to lose our first love (see Revelation 2:4). We must admit that our love often falters and fails, but thank God, *His* love will never let us go. The love of Christ is always there beckoning us, calling us, stirring us, disciplining us, and encouraging us until His love shall be so wrought in us that we ultimately arrive at mature love and deep union with Him in eternity.

THE STAGES OF LOVE

There are many ways to divide this Song, but here we would like to use the three recorded acclamations of the virgin as a way to divide this song. As a matter of fact, however, love is something which we cannot compartmentalize. There is no way to divide love up into different things, but for the sake of convenience we may note that in this song we shall find recorded three acclamations of the virgin which can represent, so to speak, the development or the stages of love.

The first stage is represented by the acclamation of the virgin to be found in chapter 2, verse 16: "My beloved is mine, and I am his." This we would identify as the initial stage of love. The second acclamation is found in chapter 6, verse 3: "I am my beloved's, and my beloved is mine." This stage is one of growing love. And the third acclamation is in chapter 7, verse 10: "I am my beloved's, and his desire is toward me." This is the stage of matured love. Or we may even describe these three stages as, respectively: courtship, engagement, and marriage.

COURTSHIP

INITIAL LOVE

This song does not begin with initial salvation. In other words, it does not tell us how a soul comes into salvation—into the knowledge of the Lord Jesus as his or her Savior. It is assumed that this maiden is a virgin. And we know that in the Scriptures a virgin always speaks of a saved one, because if we are not saved we are still wedded to the world and, in the sight of God, we are adulterers and adulteresses. But thank God, because of the blood of the Lamb, our sins are cleansed. Thank God that because Christ died on the cross for us we receive new life, even eternal life; therefore, we become virgins in the sight of God. So this maiden has already experienced the forgiveness of her sins. She has already experienced the gift of eternal life. Her stiff neck has already been kissed by the heavenly Father and has been softened. So, spiritually speaking, this song tells of a saved one, a believer.

Now we who know the love of God in Christ Jesus, we who have tasted the love of Christ in His atoning death and His suffering for our sins, we who have experienced the blessedness of the gift of eternal life, there must invariably be in us a desire and a longing for more of His love. To put it another way, we should want to know more of Him. Who is rescued and has no desire to know the one who rescues him? Of course we want to know Christ more. His love has so constrained us that we do want to love Him, we do want to know Him more, we do want to know more of His love. That is something natural, even supernaturally natural. So if this does not happen to a person who is supposed to be saved, then there is doubt concerning his salvation. If one has tasted the love of Christ as demonstrated in the atoning death of our Lord Jesus on Calvary's cross, and if one has tasted the freshness and livingness of eternal life, then surely it stirs within that one a longing for Christ and a longing to know more of His love. So here we read at the very outset of King Solomon's Song these words: "Let him kiss me with the kisses of his mouth." There is no need to mention the name of her beloved because, to the maiden, there is only one. So she simply uttered the words: "Let him kiss me with the kisses of his mouth." In other words, she longed for a more intimate relationship with the beloved.

Is this not true with every one of us, that we do long for a more intimate relationship with our Beloved—even Christ? We are satisfied, in one sense, that our sins are forgiven, that we have received eternal life, that we are now God's children; yet there is always that holy discontent. We want to know Him more; we want to experience more of His love; we want to draw closer to Him in a more intimate way. And why? Because like the virgin in this song, we have experienced and have known that His love is better than wine (1:2b).

Wine speaks of what the world can give—joy, pleasure and comfort—but we have found that the love of our Lord Jesus is far better than wine, is better than all that the world can ever give to us. Christ is altogether fragrant; indeed, His name is an ointment poured forth because it betokens to us what He is. It is quite natural for the virgins to love Him (see 1:3). We remember what the apostle Paul declared in II Corinthians 11:2, that he has espoused us as chaste virgins to Christ; and if we are virgins, surely we love the One to whom we belong.

So speaking in Christian terms, we shall find that in this initial stage of love there is the longing for Christ the Beloved, a longing to know Him and know more of His love. In this stage of love it is probably more a matter of affection and emotional love. And because of this affection and this longing for her beloved, the maiden is rewarded by being brought into the king's chambers (1:4a). These rooms in the palace can speak to us of the different provisions of God. If we really have a longing for Christ, we will be rewarded by knowing the many provisions of God in Christ Jesus. He has provided for us not only physically, mentally, spiritually and environmentally but also, in every area of life we shall experience the bountiful supply of our Savior-King. He will not allow us to be in lack; He knows all which we need, and He will add all things to us. It will be just like being led into a king's chambers and seeing all the provisions which are there.

In addition, God sets us at His table, the King's table (1:12a). This speaks of the riches of Christ. There we begin to experience some of the unsearchable riches of our Lord Jesus Christ. Not only that, God allows us to lie down in green pastures. That bed is green (1:16b) and it speaks of the rest which is to be found in Christ Jesus—how we find in Him our rest. More than that, He leads us to the house of wine— the banqueting house— and the banner over us there is love (2:4). In other words, if there is a longing and a desire and an affection towards Christ, we will be rewarded by His amazing and great love towards us.

At the same time, this virgin realizes that though she does have a heart for her beloved, she senses there is nonetheless a dullness in her. It seems as if she is drawing back. It seems as if she is not able to move forward as she should. She therefore cries out, "Draw me and we will run after thee" (see 1:4a).

In our initial stage of love as Christian believers, we do find that we need the drawing of our Lord Jesus. If He does not draw us we will either stay put or even fall back. How easy it is for us to lose our first love towards Him. We frequently have to cry out: "Draw me, draw me." And when He draws one of us, all the others will run after Him as well.

The maiden also realizes that though she does have a heart

for the Lord, she knows she is black; she has been burned by the sun (1:5a, 6). And such is true even with us today, that the more we try to draw near to Him, the more we realize how black we are. It is people who are in darkness who think themselves fair, because they cannot see. The more we draw towards the Sun of Righteousness (see Malachi 4:2; cf. Isaiah 60:1-2), the more the light shines upon us, and we discover our nakedness and blindness and poverty (see Revelation 3:17).

Then there is another side. Whenever there is a soul who begins to show a love and a longing for Christ, immediately, that one's siblings and other family members will put that one to work. Whenever there is any indication that you love the Lord, people closely related to you will say, "All right, go to the vineyards." They will try to place all kinds of works upon you until they just suffocate you; and thus, you neglect your own vineyard; that is to say, your spiritual life suffers because of the many activities which you are being asked to do (see 1:6b). Is that not true with us today? Because of this, the maiden as it were cried out, "I am suffering; my spiritual life is suffering. I do not have the time to be with my beloved. I miss that communion with him. I seem to have even missed his presence." Though the work may prosper in her hand, her personal life suffers greatly, and because of this she cries out to the beloved: "Where do you tend your sheep and where do you make your flock to rest at noon? Why should I be as a veiled one beside the flocks of thy companions?" (see 1:7)

Because of her cry, the beloved one answered her in this way: "If you do not know where I am, follow the footsteps of the flock" (see 1:8a). We know that God has only one flock. In John 10:16 the Lord Jesus is recorded as speaking of "one flock, one shepherd." There may be many folds, yet there is but one flock; and we know that the one Shepherd is Christ and that the one flock is the church. If we do not know where the Lord is, let us follow the footsteps of the church. Throughout these twenty centuries the footsteps of the church—the real church, the church that God has ordained, the church that our Lord Jesus is building—are there, and if we follow these footsteps we will find the Shepherd.

It is true that during this period it seems as though this virgin's progress is faster than that of the rest of the daughters of Jerusalem. The daughters of Jerusalem represent all the believers, but this virgin seems to run faster than any of them; indeed, she is likened to a steed among Pharaoh's chariots (1:9). However, her energy is mainly natural; even her seeking after her beloved is out of her natural energy. We read in the song these words: "We will make thee bead-rows of gold with studs of silver" (1:11). Gold in the Scriptures represents the nature of God and silver the redemption of Christ.

Let us note that sometimes our running or the speed of our running after Christ does not necessarily mean it is done out of the divine energy in us; sometimes it is our natural energy at work. Formerly, we could use our natural energy to do things *against* God. Now we employ our natural energy to *serve* God, and this needs to be redeemed and transformed.

If we can employ Christian terminology here, we would say that in this initial stage of love, the virgin has experienced something of the cross. She has experienced the cross in being misunderstood and mistreated by her own family. She suffered because of the many duties her brothers had placed upon her. She has thus experienced misunderstanding and persecution. Through the cross she has begun to see what the world truly is and has begun to be delivered from pursuing after it. She may even have had to be delivered from the religious world. She is being delivered somewhat from tradition, from activities, and from works. She has come to know something of the cross working in her life, delivering her from sins, the power of sin, the world, and some of the activities of the flesh. While seated at the king's table, she was moved to say this: "A bundle of myrrh is my beloved unto me; he shall pass the night between my breasts" (1:13). In other words, she has come to know something of the cross in her life and this she now loves. Hence, this is the first stage of love, and it can be summed up in her confession and acclamation: "My beloved is mine, and I am his" (2:16). In her spiritual pursuit, though, she is still the center: "My beloved is mine"—that is, I first, and then: I am my beloved's; still more of her and less of her beloved. In other words, she is still self-centered instead of being Christ-centered. She is still I-centered, instead of being He-centered. Christ does have a place in her life, but it is for herself, even though she is for Him. We can therefore say that this is an accurate picture of the first stage of our spiritual life in Christ.

How important it is to know the cross. The cross delivers us from sin and from its power. The cross delivers us from the world just as Galatians 6 says—that there is a cross standing between me and the world (v. 14). We need to know the working of the cross in our life in its cutting off the works of the flesh. This is important, but we need to be forewarned that when the cross begins to work in our life and we begin to have some experience of the cross, there is the following danger. In the beginning we despise the cross and try to flee from it; we do not want the cross. Yet once we allow the cross to begin its work in our lives, we discover how good it is and how it delivers us. But then we go to the other extreme and say we love the cross; in fact, we love it so much that we want to stay eternally in the cleft of the rock (cf. 2:14a) and even hide ourself from Christ. Among Christians today there are very few who know the cross, and that is why our Christianity is so shallow. But when there are people who begin to know the meaning of the cross and experience it in some way, they develop an inordinate love for the cross, and somehow, they become engrossed with the cross instead of with Christ. The result is that such people become negative, passive and unsocial in the spiritual sense. That is, they simply want to keep to themselves. And the result is that we can easily behold the cross written all over their faces: death, death, death—and more death.

ENGAGEMENT

GROWING LOVE

Eventually the beloved comes to stir the virgin up, and this action commences the second stage of love. This stage of love lasts a long period. In spiritual terms it can be said that this period begins with a calling to experience the power of Christ's resurrection unto ascension life and into the fellowship of His sufferings, being conformed to His death (see Philippians 3:10-11). This maiden is so satisfied with the first stage of love that she has remained in bed in an inactive state. She is staying put; for she just wants to stay there forever with a wall built around her. Indeed, she thinks in terms of it being "our" wall—she and her beloved, she not realizing, however, that the beloved one is *outside* the wall and not there with her (2:9a). Now we need to realize that this Song of Songs is a song of experience. Therefore, so far as spiritual truth is concerned, our beloved Christ never leaves us nor forsakes us, but so far as our experience or our feeling is concerned, we sometimes feel He has left us behind.

So here we read of a new calling, a new stirring: "The voice of my beloved! Behold, he cometh leaping upon the mountains, skipping upon the hills" (2:8). Her beloved is full of life, but he is outside the wall. Fortunately, there are still windows; so the beloved glanced through the lattice and began to speak: "The winter is past and now it is spring. Everything is full of life; arise and go with me" (see 2:9b-13). But she did not respond. Spiritually speaking, she was so satisfied with her present state in the shadow of the cross of Christ that she had no desire to rise up and enter into the power of His resurrection life. In the Song the maiden had tried to find her beloved in her room on her bed over many nights (3:1). So her response was very slow because she was too satisfied with her current state.

How often it is true that when we experience something

of the Lord, we are so satisfied and so contented that we do not want to move on. Yet our Lord is always moving on. So in the Song of Songs, we read that after many nights lying in bed attempting unsuccessfully to conjure up the presence of her beloved, the love of her beloved within her constrains her, and she finally rises up. She goes out to the city and meets the watchmen (3:2-3a). In other words, for the longest time you, like this maiden, may simply keep to yourself. There is no fellowship with your Christian brethren. You believe that the Lord and you are everything you need; but when you discover that the Lord has gone on and you are left behind, then you begin to seek fellowship among God's people (the watchmen). You begin to ask help from those whom God has put in leadership: "Where is my Lord?" The strangest thing is, that at the very moment of her asking, she turned around and there she found her beloved (3:3b-4a).

By this turn of events, this virgin now entered upon a new phase in the life of love. We may say that, in spiritual terms, she entered upon the experience of the power of the resurrection life of our Lord Jesus. Only then did the beauty of the new creation begin to be manifested in her life (see II Corinthians 5:17). Only at this point was she addressed as "my spouse, my sister" (see 4:8-12; 5:1-2).

As we move onto resurrection ground, we move into the resurrection life of our Lord Jesus. Then the characteristics of this new life begin to characterize us. We begin to be transformed, and Christ's character begins to be manifested in us. So it is not only knowing the power of His resurrection, but there is that *further* and higher calling into ascension life: "Come with me from Lebanon, my spouse" (4:8a). We are not only raised together with Christ, we are also being seated together with Him in the heavenlies. Formerly, we looked up, but now we can look down from above. In other words, we begin to experience the ascension power of our Lord Jesus. There is no fear of our enemies because we are on higher ground. We can look from the mountains of the leopards and from the lions' dens (4:8b-c). We are in the victory of our ascended Lord. We have experienced the power of His resurrection victory and the power of His ascension that is above all principalities and authorities and every name that is named, because we are united with Him in the heavenlies.

It is during this period that a transformation came upon this virgin. As was noted earlier, she was now being addressed as "my spouse, my sister." We will recall that our Lord Jesus once said: "Who are my brethren? Those who do the will of my Father are my brother, sister and mother" (see Matthew 12:47-50; Mark 3:32-35). So this maiden is growing in love, yet not just emotionally, she also is growing into more union with her beloved; and during this period she is like a garden enclosed (4:12a). She is for her beloved, and he begins to enjoy her (4:9-15). But this is not the end.

"I slept, but my heart was awake. The voice of my beloved! he knocketh: Open to me, my sister, my love, my dove, mine undefiled; for my head is filled with dew, my locks with the drops of the night" (5:2). This is a picture of our Lord Jesus during the agony He endured in the Garden of Gethsemane. In spiritual terms we can say that when this maiden began to experience the resurrection and ascension life of our Lord Jesus, she was being called into the fellowship of His sufferings, being conformed to His death. We may think that by knowing the power of His resurrection and having ascension experience we are in the heavenlies. It is such a glorious experience that it must be the peak of spiritual life. But let us understand that such experience is not only for us to enjoy; it is also for the purpose of preparing us to give our life away.

So here we see that the virgin is once more in bed. She is again resting, staying put, not desirous of moving on; for even though she discovers that her beloved is again outside knocking at her door, she temporizes by putting forth excuses for not arising and responding to his call. She excuses herself by saying that she has removed her dress and "how, then, can I put it back on again?"—and that, further, she had washed her feet for the night, so "how can I dirty them again?" (5:3) Fortunately, however, there is an opening, a hole, in the door; and soon the beloved one extended his hand through the opening. Her reaction was immediate and profound: that pierced hand of her beloved melted the heart of the virgin. In fact, the literal Hebrew reads that her "bowels" were moved and aroused for him (see 5:4).

This is a picture of an even deeper experience of the cross. We may know something of the working of the cross in our lives delivering us from the power of sin, delivering us from the enticement of the world, and delivering us from the works of our flesh. But we need to know a deeper work of the cross in order to deliver us from our self, even from this self that has already known the cross and its sufferings somewhat, even from this self of ours that, like this virgin's attitude, is considered by us to be holy: "I have washed myself; therefore, I must not defile myself again" (see again 5:4). In other words, we wish to maintain our holiness, our integrity, our wholeness; but let us bear in mind that it is still I, it is still that self-life in us. We who know the Lord Jesus are expected by our God to give away our life. That is the reason people who love the Lord and have been drawn into a deeper depth discover that God is calling them to lay down even their grace and their gifts with which He has beautified them. God is going to strip them in order that they may be able to give up themselves for the Lord completely in the fellowship of His sufferings.

There is one part of Christ's sufferings, however, which we can never participate in, and that is the suffering of our Lord Jesus in atoning for mankind on the cross. He had to tread that winepress alone for us. We only receive the good of that suffering. But there is another side of His sufferings with which He calls us to have fellowship. As the apostle Paul wrote: "I rejoice in my sufferings for your sake, and fill up on my part that which is lacking of the afflictions [sufferings] of Christ in my flesh for his body's sake, which is the church" (Colossians 1:24 ASV).

In II Corinthians chapter 4 Paul declared that this earthen vessel of ours has to be broken so that the radiance of the light within may be manifested (vv. 6-7). There has to be the dying of Jesus in our body that the life of Jesus may be upon others (see v. 10). We are thus called into the fellowship of His sufferings. Now this is love. This is not merely affection or emotion. Emotion alone cannot accomplish this. Love is practical; love is giving; love is the forgetting of ourselves; love is the laying down of ourselves for others. The Lord said, "If you love me, lay down your lives for your brethren" (see I John 3:16).

Now this virgin cannot immediately respond to her beloved's entreaty to open to him; and yet her response—when it does finally come—is much quicker than previously. It was not, as before, over many nights; on the contrary, the moment she saw the pierced hand she was deeply moved in her heart. She got up, went into the streets of the city, and tried to find her beloved who had left before she opened the door (5:4-6). But do we know what then happened to her? The watchmen who went about the city found her and beat her. It was not as before. This time the watchmen beat her and wounded her (5:7a). Moreover, these keepers of the wall took away her veil (5:7b). Nobody understood her. They thought she had morally fallen; but that created in her such a love for her beloved that she cried out for help. Yet from whom does she cry out for help?—from the daughters of Jerusalem (5:8a).

Spiritually speaking, we can say that these daughters of Jerusalem are merely simple believers, so how can they help her? For the virgin had advanced far ahead of these other daughters of Jerusalem in their relationship with the Lord, but in her desperation she had now been stripped of everything—stripped of her grace and her gifts; she as it were was left naked, and so she cried out for help, even from these less advanced believers. She said to them, "Just tell him that I am sick of love" (5:8b). That word stirs the hearts of these daughters of Jerusalem, who replied: "What is your beloved more than anybody else that you tell us so?" (see 5:9b) Here she begins to pour out her heart concerning her beloved: "He is the fairest and most outstanding among ten thousand" (see 5:10b). That stirs the hearts of these other believers who say: "Now where is he? We will go and find him with you" (see 6:1). And because of her testimony she found her beloved immediately. She knew where he was; and, hence, she came forth with a second acclamation: "I am my beloved's, and my beloved is mine" (6:3). In this we see that he is now first, she herself second— that is, more of Christ, less of self. And that is a summation of the second stage of love, a love that has grown considerably.

MARRIAGE

MATURE LOVE

The last stage is that of mature love. Employing Christian terminology once again, we may say that as this virgin has advanced spiritually through the knowledge and experience of the resurrection and ascension life of the Lord Jesus and has entered into the fellowship of His sufferings, she continually being conformed to His death, there is now a deeper union with her beloved Lord. She has grown in spiritual stature; indeed, it is not unlike what we read in Ephesians 4: "Until we all arrive at the unity of the faith and of the knowledge of the Son of God, at the full-grown man, at the measure of the stature of the fulness of the Christ" (v. 13).

There is today a spiritual stature in her. She is matured and is now able to enter into a marriage relationship with her beloved. She is now one with him, and for the first time in this song she is called a Shulammite (6:13). The term *Shulammite* in Hebrew is the feminine form of the masculine name for Solomon, meaning "the beloved." So here we observe that in Christian terms we can say that the character of Christ has completely characterized her. She is now one with Him, yet not only one in life but also in character and likewise in purpose. Let us realize that our union with Christ begins in life, but that union with Him will eventually arrive at God's purpose. And here we can discern that the Lord's purpose has become her purpose.

The Song's virgin now thinks of her younger sister, she desiring that her sister may also grow up into maturity. She is no longer thinking of herself anymore. Moreover, this maiden has a vineyard, but King Solomon can have anything and everything of hers. She wants nothing for herself (see 8:8ff.). When a person arrives at mature love, there is a spirit of rapture in that one. For this maiden comes out of the wilderness (8:5a), and, like Enoch who walked with God for three hundred years, she walks and walks and is then gone. In other words, like the apostle John, she is ready to be raptured. Her whole desire is, "Haste, return, come back, Lord Jesus" (see 8:14a; cf. Revelation 22:20).

Now this is love which has matured, indeed. For this virgin's cry to her beloved is: "Set me as a seal upon thy heart, a seal upon thine arm"—the pledge of love. Love is permanent, like "a seal set upon the heart." Love is powerful, like "a seal set upon the arm." Love is strong: "strong as death." Love is possessive: "Jealousy is cruel as Sheol." Love is warm, and purifies like fire: "[Love's] flashes are flashes of fire, flames of Jah [Jehovah]." Love perseveres and endures: "Many waters cannot quench love, neither do the floods drown it" (see 8:6-7a).

Finally, "even if a man gave all the substance of his house for love, it would utterly be contemned" (8:7b). In other words, if a person would attempt to buy love, that one would be despised and treated with utter contempt. So love is beyond price: one cannot exchange anything for it. Such is the love of God in Christ Jesus. And this is the love which has to be wrought into the very life of each one of us so that we may love

Him as He has loved us.

This, then, is The Song of Songs of King Solomon.

Let us pray:

> *Dear heavenly Father, we have tasted Thy love in Christ Jesus and we do long for more. We do praise and thank Thee because Thy love is so fervent, always steadfast, faithful, unchanging, enduring, perfect; but our love always falters and fails. And yet, Lord, we do praise and thank Thee that Thou dost never give us up. Thou art calling us, stirring us, encouraging us, disciplining us so that we may be perfected in love. Oh that we may love Thee as Thou hast loved us. We ask in Thy precious name. Amen.*

OTHER TITLES AVAILABLE
From Christian Fellowship Publishers

By Watchman Nee

The Basic Lesson Series

Volume 1 - A Living Sacrifice
Volume 2 - The Good Confession
Volume 3 - Assembling Together
Volume 4 - Not I, But Christ
Volume 5 - Do All to the Glory of God
Volume 6 - Love One Another

CD Rom—The Complete Works of Watchman Nee as Published by CFP

Aids to "Revelation"
Back to the Cross
A Balanced Christian Life
The Better Covenant
The Body of Christ: A Reality
The Character of God's Workman
Christ the Sum of All Spiritual Things
The Church and the Work – 3 Vols
"Come, Lord Jesus"
The Communion of the Holy Spirit
The Finest of the Wheat - Volume 1
The Finest of the Wheat - Volume 2
From Faith to Faith
From Glory to Glory
Full of Grace and Truth - Volume 1
Full of Grace and Truth - Volume 2
Gleanings in the Fields of Boaz
The Glory of His Life
God's Plan and the Overcomers
God's Work
Gospel Dialogue
Grace for Grace
Interpreting Matthew
Journeying towards the Spiritual
The King and the Kingdom of Heaven
The Latent Power of the Soul
Let Us Pray
The Life That Wins

The Lord My Portion
The Messenger of the Cross
The Ministry of God's Word
The Mystery of Creation
Powerful According to God
Practical Issues of This Life
The Prayer Ministry of the Church
The Release of the Spirit
Revive Thy Work
The Salvation of the Soul
The Secret of Christian Living
Serve in Spirit
The Spirit of Judgment
The Spirit of the Gospel
The Spirit of Wisdom and Revelation
Spiritual Authority
Spiritual Exercise
Spiritual Discernment
Spiritual Knowledge
The Spiritual Man
Spiritual Reality or Obsession
Take Heed
The Testimony of God
Whom Shall I Send?
The Word of the Cross
Worship God
Ye Search the Scriptures

By Stephen Kaung

Discipled to Christ
The Songs of Degrees - Meditations on Fifteen Psalms
The Splendor of His Ways - Seeing the Lord's End in Job
God Has Spoken – Vol. I: Seeing Christ in the Old Testament, Part One
God Has Spoken – Vol. II: Seeing Christ in the New Testament

Order From: 11515 Allecingie Pkwy Richmond, VA 23235

www.c-f-p.com